# SINAI

## TREASURES OF THE MONASTERY
## OF SAINT CATHERINE

# SINAI

## TREASURES OF THE MONASTERY OF SAINT CATHERINE

GENERAL EDITOR

KONSTANTINOS A. MANAFIS
Professor of Byzantine Literature, Athens University

EKDOTIKE ATHENON

PUBLISHERS
George A. Christopoulos, John C. Bastias

MANAGING EDITOR
Ioanna Boucouvala-Diamantourou

ART DIRECTOR
Angela Simou

PHOTOGRAPHY
Nikos and Kostas Kontos

PROOF READING
Angela Pantou

GLOSSARY - INDEX
Dora Comini - Dialeti

TRANSLATIONS
Geoffrey Cox (Church Gold Embroideries,
Church Metalwork)
Sharon Gerstel, Doula Mouriki, Frances Flint
(Middle and Post-Byzantine Icons)
David Turner (Prefaces, Introductions, Wall Paintings)
Louise Turner (Architecture, Library and Archive)

PRODUCTION DIRECTOR
Emil C. Bastias

COMPOSITION
F. Panagopoulos &Co.

COLOUR SEPARATIONS
Colour Unit, Ltd.

STRIPPING
A. Aloskophis

PRINTED BY
St. Karydakis, Graphic Arts, S.A.

JACKET AND SLIPCASE
E. Daniel & Co., S.A.

BOUND BY
E. & J. Zervinis

ISBN 960-213-158-6
Copyright © 1990
by Ekdotike Athenon S.A.
1, Vissarionos St., 106 72 Athens
Printed and bound in Greece

# LIST OF AUTHORS

NIKOLAOS B. TOMADAKIS
  Professor Emeritus of Byzantine Literature,
  University of Athens

KONSTANTINOS A. MANAFIS
  Professor of Byzantine Literature, University
  of Athens

PETER GROSSMANN, Dr. Ing.
  Specialist Advisor for the History of
  Architecture, German Archaeological Institute
  of Cairo

KURT WEITZMANN
  Professor Emeritus of Art and Archaeology,
  Princeton University

ATHANASIOS D. PALIOURAS
  Professor of Byzantine Archaeology,
  University of Ioannina

GEORGE GALAVARIS, F.R.S.C.
  Professor of Art History, McGill University,
  Canada

DOULA MOURIKI
  Professor of Art History, National Technical
  University of Athens

NIKOLAOS B. DRANDAKIS
  Professor Emeritus of Byzantine Archaeology,
  University of Athens

MANOLIS L. BORBOUDAKIS
  Ephor of Byzantine Antiquities

MARIA THEOCHARIS
  Byzantinologist-Archaeologist

YOTA IKONOMAKI-PAPADOPOULOS
  Art Historian

PANAYOTIS NICOLOPOULOS
  Associate Professor of Byzantine Literature,
  University of Athens

NIKOLAOS LIVADARAS
  Professor of Classical Literature, University
  of Athens

HERMANN HARRAUER
  Assistant Professor, Director of the Papyrus
  Collection, National Library of Vienna

YIANNIS E. MEIMARIS, Ph. D.
  Research Fellow of the Centre of Greek and
  Roman Antiquity (N.H.R.F.)

SEBASTIAN P. BROCK, F.B.A.
  Reader in Syriac Studies, University of Oxford

IOANNIS C. TARNANIDIS
  Professor of Theology, University of
  Thessalonica

Hieromonk DEMETRIOS DIGBASSANIS
  f. Librarian of St. Catherine's Monastery
  at Sinai

ANGELIKI NICOLOPOULOU, Ph. D.
  Philologist

# CONTENTS

*View of Mount Sinai and the Monastery of Saint Catherine (41 × 47.5 cm.), by Domenikos Theotokopoulos (El Greco). Oil and tempera on wood. Private Collection. c. 1570. This work by the great Cretan painter is his second and most well-known painting of the Monastery of Saint Catherine in the Sinai landscape. The three rocky summits with the Monastery of Saint Catherine at the base of the Mountain of Moses, the 'kathismata' (dependencies) of the Monastery and the human figures in the foreground are enveloped in an apocalyptic light that corresponds to the personal vision of the great genius. As in his unique variants of the Toledo landscape, in the extraterrestrial Sinai landscape the painter gives us a symbolic dimension.*

# PROLOGUE

*The Holy Monastery of St. Catherine on the God-Trodden Mount Sinai has long desired that the Monastery's ecclesiastical treasures and its collection of Byzantine icon painting should be presented in an appropriate and correct manner. The icons represent a living tradition that has been miraculously preserved from the 6th century up to our times, and exemplify the stylistic trends of the great centres of icon painting in the Byzantine empire, including those which developed after the Fall of Constantinople.*

*Scholars agree that the icons of the Byzantine period preserved at Sinai are more in number than the total of those in the rest of the world, and that their artistic value is beyond estimation.*

*Bearing in mind that the complete presentation of the Monastery's works of art and holy treasures according to categories is an ambitious task, the completion of which demands a great deal of preparation and time, the Holy Chapter of the fathers conceived the idea of a selective presentation drawn from all the categories of art works that for centuries have been held by the Monastery and its Metochia in the world. Included here are the ancient buildings of the Holy Monastery, and the world-famous Sinai Library whose many codices, illuminated or not, are superb products of the calligraphic scriptorium at Sinai.*

*In order to bring this idea to fruition, the Holy Monastery came into contact with Mr. G. Christopoulos, president of the publishing company 'Ekdotike Athenon', famous world-wide for the high quality of its work. Mr. Christopoulos immediately adopted the Monastery's proposal and, after a series of consultations, willingly undertook to publish an ambitious and lavish tome on the treasures of Sinai. The present volume, the result of long experience and painstaking care, completely fulfills the Monastery's expectations and constitutes an endeavour of the first rank from a scholarly, publishing and artistic viewpoint. Our warmest thanks thus go out to Mr. Christopoulos who spared neither effort nor expense in the execution of this project.*

*Deepest thanks are due to the fathers of the Monastery who for months generously strove to assist all those who cooperated in the volume's publication. Warm and sincere thanks are given to the distinguished Professor of Byzantine Literature at the University of Athens, Mr. K. Manafis, who undertook general editorial surpervision, as well as to the specialist scholars who contributed to the work. We pray that God, ever just and good, will bestow them with great rewards in their intellectual pursuits.*

*Should the reader by studying this exquisite volume come to know the Greek Orthodox tradition of the Monastery and appreciate Byzantine Art, and thus be led from that material host of colours and created light that soothes the eye, to the heavenly colours and indescribable divine beauty that calms the soul, our joy and that of the fathers of Sinai will be great, the objectives of this work will have been realized, and the labours of all who strove to this end may enjoy their just rewards.*

*DAMIANOS, ARCHBISHOP of SINAI*

# PREFACE

The Holy Monastery of St. Catherine on Mount Sinai has been characterized by scholars as the most celebrated of the world's monasteries, while in the conscience of the Orthodox peoples it was and remains the most revered and longed-for focus of pilgrimage after the Holy Places.

In the course of the Monastery's 15 centuries of uninterrupted life, and despite the great difficulties faced in the midst of alien peoples, not only has St. Catherine's managed to maintain the Orthodox faith intact and provide the Church and the Ecumenical Patriarchate with pre-eminent figures of Asceticism, but it also secured special privileges from the Prophet Mohammed and, at a later date, from popes of Rome and leaders of both the East and West. The Monastery thus proved itself a great spiritual hearth of Hellenism, rendering the most distinguished service to monasticism, Orthodoxy, the Church and the Greek people.

At the same time, the Monastery acquired international fame as a unique centre of Byzantine icon painting. Here the specialist may study the uninterrupted development of this art from the 6th century up till the present day. Furthermore, the Monastery also developed its own Sinaitic school of icon painting with its own stylistic techniques and 'Sinaitic' subject matter. Examples of this school's work are encountered not only in icons but also in illuminated manuscripts of the calligraphic and chrysographic workshop of the Monastery's world-famous Library.

The Monastery of Sinai, moreover, surrounded as it is by the fortification walls built by its founder, the Emperor Justinian, and isolated in the inhospitable desert, was through the centuries a secure haven for invaluable works of art sent from all corners of the Earth as devout offerings of the faithful. Byzantine, Post-Byzantine and Modern Greek works representing all types of ecclesiastical art make up the artistic treasures of the Monastery.

The Monastery's treasures, which the Sinai fathers — a veritable vanguard of Greek Orthodox tradition — keep with constant care and devotion, were entrusted to me by the Holy Monastery to present for the first time in this lavish tome, published in Greek, English, German and French. I consequently feel especially honoured; but also a great sense of responsibility.

This work, 'Sinai – Treasures of the Monastery', proudly presented here to the public by 'Ekdotike Athenon', contains the following chapters, each fully developed and accompanied by a wealth of illustrative material: Architecture, Mosaics and Wall Paintings, Icons, Church Gold Embroideries, Church Metalwork, Illuminated Manuscripts, and the Library and the Archive.

The preparation of this tome was undertaken by university professors and other scholars, and specialists involved in the artistic preparation who all worked with devotion, zeal and respect with the aim of presenting these treasures in the most authoritative manner. As publisher, I am, together with all those who strove for the realization of this undertaking, greatly honoured to have participated in the promotion of those treasures of Byzantine art that have been sheltered for centuries in that radiant ark of Orthodoxy and Hellenism, the Monastery of St. Catherine at Sinai.

*The Publisher*
*GEORGE A. CHRISTOPOULOS*

# HISTORICAL OUTLINE

The Holy Monastery of Saint Catherine on Mount Sinai, crouched between the granite mountains and the inhospitable desert of the Sinai peninsular, is the world's most important and intriguing Monastery. Here one can witness the miraculous presence of a centuries-old religious, spiritual, intellectual and philanthropic tradition. For Hellenism, furthermore, St. Catherine's represents a miraculous survival that surpasses human measure. The Monastery, indeed, delineates another Greek Orthodox miracle for it was here on Sinai that Greek Orthodox monks made and continue to make history.

The Sinai peninsular, and more particularly its southern extent, constituted a junction for people and goods moving from Egypt or the Ethiopian coast to Palestine, the Promised Land. Early on, the entire peninsular came to be known as Petraian Arabia from its main city, Petra, located on the Mediterranean.

After the persecution of the Christians by the official Roman state ceased at the beginning of the 4th century A.D., the desire for perfection and the inspiration of new ideals led many to seek places in the desert in order to devote themselves to things higher than the mundane; to the search for the divine and the cleansing of the soul. Early on, areas such as the deserts of Egypt and Syria had attracted anchorites. But the Holy Places of Palestine, where Jesus Christ, the Apostles and the first Christians had lived, were more challenging areas. Sinai, of course, with its miraculous history of God's revelation during the Pre-Christian period as well as its deserted and arid expanses was an ideal place for the exercise of an eremitical life.

At an early date, the area became inundated with anchorites exercising in caves or tents. We also hear at this time of the slaughter of monks, such as the murders of the Holy Fathers at Sinai and Raithou by Arabs under Diocletian (284 - 305), or the annihilation of the monks of Raithou during an invasion of the Blemmyes from Africa. The memory of both these incidents is celebrated on the 14th of January. These martyrdoms were recorded by the monk Ammonios and the ascetic Neil, but also by the monk Anastasios of Sinai during the 7th century. However, it seems that those narrations attributed to Ammonios and Neil are works from a later period. Nevertheless, during the first centuries of ascetic life on Sinai the monks must have suffered from attacks by the peninsula's inhabitants, the Arab Bedouins, as well as by invasions from without, such as in the case of the Blemmyes.

In about A.D. 400 when an aristocratic lady from Galatia, St. Sylvia (or Aetheria) visited the Holy Places and Sinai, the area was at peace. In her account of the pilgrimage, she mentions that there was a small church on the summit of Mt. Sinai, another further down at Choreb and yet another next to the Bush with a beautiful garden next to it. The church by the Bush should be identified with that founded by St. Helen according to tradition. Unfortunately, our information for the early stages of the life of the Sinai Monastery is very limited. We do know that the most important centre on the peninsula was to be found not at the Monastery but at Pharan, the residence of the bishop of Sinai where remains of a magnificent basilica and other buildings can still be seen.

The names of two bishops of Pharan are known: Makarios to whom the Emperor Marcian addressed a letter (A.D. 450), and Theonas *(by the grace of God presbyter and legate of the Holy Mountain of Sinai and the desert of Raithou and the holy church at Sinai)* who wrote in A.D. 536 to the Patriarch of Constantinople, Menas.

The main history of the Sinai Monastery, however, began with the foundation of the imposing church and the building of strong fortification walls by Justinian. The Emperor, submitting to the appeals of the monks on Sinai, *raised a church dedicated to the Theotokos... not on the mountain's heights, but much further below... At the mountain's foot, the emperor also built a most strong fortification, a noteworthy garrison for soldiers to deter the barbarian Saracens who, since the land was desert, passed thither to invade Palestine by stealth* (Procopios).

Justinian's policy was thus two-pronged. He wished firstly to protect the monks who felt unsafe amongst the barbarian tribes of the desert, and secondly to secure communication between Egypt and Palestine from incursions and to deter any attack on Palestine. Thus a military reason also existed for the walls around the church on Sinai.

Both church and fortifications must have been built between 548, the date of death of Justinian's wife, Theodora, and Justinian's own death in 565. This conclusion is based on inscriptions on the beams of the church roof which record: *For the salvation of our pious sovereign Justinian. For the memory and rest of our empress Theodora.*

For the building of the church and the walls, as well as of the other adjacent buildings, Justinian employed a Greek architect named Stephanos from the nearby city of Aila (present-day Eilat, Akamban). Inscriptions on the ceiling beams state: *Lord God, He who was beheld in this place, save and have mercy on your servant Stephanos of Aila, builder and craftsman [who has raised] this shrine, and on Nonas, and make rest in peace the souls of his children, George, Sergios and Theodora.* For the construction of both church and walls, Stephanos used the hard red granite found in the area.

Justinian's foundation of the church and the garrison complex effectively mark the beginning of the Monastery's history. As Procopios remarked, the monks of Sinai could now securely devote themselves to the contemplation of death, given that apart from the church and the secure walls, a company of two hundred men with their families (transferred by Justinian from Thrace and Egypt) guaranted the military security of the monks as well as that of the Egypt - Palestine corridor.

Justinian's erection of the church and the fortification walls for the Monastery, which was initially dedicated to the Theotokos whose symbol was the Burning Bush, established its reputation far and wide; testaments about it begin to become more frequent. Antonios from Placentia who visited the Monastery in around 570 wrote of many monks, three abbots, the Holy Summit, Choreb and the Monastery. Men of distinction became *hegoumenoi* such as Longinus, contemporary with the building of the Monastery, Anastasios, later Patriarch of Antioch, the famous writer John Climacus, George, and another Anastasios, the writer of the *Odegos*. Pope Gregory the Great (590 - 604), to whom the Holy Liturgy of the Presanctified is attributed, supported the Monastery with many gifts and vestments, building a hospital there, the famous *xenodocheion*.

Unfortunately, however, life at the Monastery of Sinai remained under Byzantine administration for only a short time. At an early date, the expansion of Islam encroached into Petraian Arabia and the Monastery was subjugated. Not only the Arabs of the peninsula but also the Christians converted to Islam and were assimilated into its culture. Only the Monastery and its monks remained as a strong bastion of Christianity in the midst of alien creeds and races.

Generally speaking the Moslems respected the Monastery and the conquest was accompanied by only small scale plundering rather than total destruction. This tolerance is attributed to the famous *Achtiname*, the 'Testament' of the Prophet Mohammed who protected the monks from many dangers and exempted them from heavy taxation. While some doubt that the Achtiname is genuine, the fact that it was always respected by Moslem leaders, the Arabs to begin with, and later by the Turks, indicates that the Moslems did consider it the will of the Prophet.

The spiritual life of the Sinai Monastery continued under the Arabs. Apart from the Achtiname this was due to the philanthropy of the monks, mainly through their distribution of food to poor inhabitants of the peninsular. Very little information is available for this period. The name of one bishop, the Monothelite Theodore, is encountered at the Sixth General Council (680 - 681) where he was condemned. It seems that early on in the 8th century, the Monastery of Sinai was raised to a bishopric and then to an archbishopric after the decline of Christianity in the peninsular and the abolition of the bishopric of Pharan. The raising of the Monastery to episcopal and then archiepiscopal rank was necessary since the *hegumenos*, isolated as he was in the desert and under Moslem control, was obliged to ordain deacons and priests for the spiritual needs of the Monastery and its *metochia* in the Sinai peninsula and elsewhere. The first bishop of Sinai we encounter is a certain Constantine who participated in the anti-Photian Synod of 869. Another bishop of Sinai mentioned is Solomon, probably active during the 10th century. Unfortunately, the Episcopal List is incomplete.

Sinai and its Monastery became widely known after the discovery of the relics of St. Catherine, the Alexandrian martyr. St. Catherine was known to Symeon Metaphrastes already by the 10th century. Consequently, the tradition concering the translation of her relics to the mount of St. Catherine and thence to the Monastery of Sinai must have developed during the 8th and 9th centuries. Moreover, at the beginning of the 11th century, the Sicilian monk from Sinai, Symeon the 'Five-Tongued' brought relics of St. Catherine to the West, especially to Rouen and Trèves. Thus the fame and veneration of St. Catherine in the West became even more widespread while the Monastery of Sinai came to be held in even greater esteem. Symeon's initiative saw the start of votive offerings being made to the Monastery by Western rulers, while the Monastery acquired its first *metochia* in Normandy.

At this time the Monastery of Sinai finally changed its name in honour of St. Catherine, while the Theotokos was especially honoured with the side-chapel of the Holy Bush. (We are reminded of the original dedication of this church made by Justinian to the Transfiguration by the mosaic therein). Thenceforth the Monastery is known in history as the Monastery of St. Catherine.

Life with the Moslems was not always easy despite the existence of the Achtiname, especially during the persecution of the Christians by the Fatimid Caliph Hakim (996-1020). During the period 1101-1106 it would seem that necessity dictated the conversion of an old christian building, the refectory, into a mosque. In this way, any threat of menace, especially under the Mamelouks, was dispelled and new, and sometimes favourable terms for Sinai were secured up to 1517 when Egypt and Sinai passed into the possession of the Ottoman empire.

Meanwhile, the activities of Symeon the 'Five-Tongued' which had helped spread Sinai's fame in the West began to bear fruit. The Pope of Rome took an interest in Sinai and, despite the fact that the schism had divided the Churches, Sinai does not seem to have been greatly effected. Pope Honorius III, with a bull in 1217 to the bishop of Sinai Symeon, took all the landed property of Sinai under his protection including estates in the East (Egypt, the Sinai Peninsula, Palestine, Syria, Crete, Cyprus, Constantinople). Honorius'

*The Monastery at Sinai painted on the back of the Archiepiscopal Throne in the central aisle of the katholikon. A work of the painter Ioannis Kornaros. Tempera. 18th century.*

example was followed by other Popes such as Gregory X (1271 - 1276) and John XXII (1316 - 1334) who endowed Sinai with benefices and offerings.

One of Sinai's greatest benefactions, however, proved to be the Monastery's metochia in Crete for which the Venetians secured privileges and protection. Not only were the monks of Sinai exempted from taxes, forced labour, and other obligations, but they also were allowed to have their own ship together with the possibility of exporting goods without taxes being levied. In manuscript no. 2246 in the Sinai Monastery, copies have been preserved of documents dating from the beginning to the end of the Venetian period in Crete (namely 1212 to 1669). Here one can observe the interest which the Venetians had for the metochion of St. Catherine at Chandax (Heraklion) in Crete.

Despite the fact that Sinai was from early on outside the boundaries of the Byzantine empire, the ties with Byzantium were imperishable. These consisted not only with links between the Monastery and the first throne of the Orthodox Church, the Patriarchate of Constantinople, but also with the Byzantine political administration even though these were often discreet and indirect, so that the Moslems would not be aroused. Monks from the Sinai were used by the Byzantine state as intermediators for the settlement of certain questions, such as George of Sinai who was sent by Manuel Comnenos (1143-1180) as ambassador to Baldwin III, King of Jerusalem. It has been proved that the Emperor John Vatatzes (1222-1254) assisted Sinai while it seems that Michael VIII Palaeologos (1261-1282) did likewise. Later on, the Patriarch George Scholarios of Constantinople (1454 - 1465) dealt with matters relative to Sinai.

With the conquest of Sinai by the Turks, a worthy Greek named Tsernotabey assisted in the renewal of the Monastery's privileges. Tsernotabey had some influence with the Sultan Selim and in 1517, while the latter was in Cairo, he arranged a meeting of Sinai monks with the Sultan in order that they should show him the Achtiname and thus secure more privileges. Selim, however, took possession of the original document and took it to Constantinople where it must still exist in the archives. Furthermore, with the completion of the Ottoman conquest of the Eastern Mediterranean and the subsequent unification of the area, Sinai found itself once more part of a unified Orthodox community and consequently had immediate access to Constantinople and the other Patriarchates of the East. During this period the activities of the Archbishops of Sinai increased greatly, although the greater part of their time was now spent at the metochion of Tzouvania in Cairo in order to be in immediate contact with the authorities. Not infrequently they travelled in the East and even to the Principalities of Wallachia and Moldavia (modern Rumania) and to Orthodox Russia. Monks from Sinai, many of them of Cretan origin, appear in the sources, as Archbishops of the Monastery, especially during the 18th century: for example Nikephoros Marthalis Glykys (1728-1747), Constantios (1748-1759) and Cyril of Crete (1759-1790).

During this period special relations were developed with the princes of Wallachia and Moldavia. Sinai came into possession of important metochia in present day Rumania, while substantial help for the Monastery was provided by the princes Basil Loupos, John Constantine Basharaba, Michael Cantacouzenos and others.

During Napoleon I's campaign in Egypt, Sinai benefitted greatly. Napoleon not only assisted in the rebuilding of the Monastery's north wall which had collapsed after long and heavy rain in December, 1798, but he also issued a special decree on 8 December, 1798 by which the privileges of Sinai were confirmed and, furthermore, he allowed the monks free communication and exempted them from various financial obligations.

During the 19th century and towards the end of Ottoman domination over Sinai, the Monastery was shaken by internal divisions mostly due to external interference rather than to the Monastery itself. It was at this time that the famous Sinai Codex (*Codex Sinaiticus*) was stolen by K. Tischendorf with the collusion of the Russian panslavist ambassador to

Constantinople N. Ignatief. Under Anglo-Egyptian rule the Monastery managed to survive thanks to the activities of the great Archbishops Porphyrios I, II and III, although its metochia in Rumania and Russia ceased to function due to the international situation.

Under these multifarious conditions, the Monastery of Sinai was obliged to adopt a flexible administrative framework. Of course, it is based on the *typikon*, or charter, of the Monastery of St. Sabbas in Palestine although the regulations have been adapted to meet the special demands of desert. The head of administration, the *hegumenos* of the Monastery must hold the office of (arch)bishop so as to meet the need for priestly ordinations. He is, however, bound by the Holy Consistory which shall gather on serious matters of faith and canonical order. At the same time the office of *Oikonomos* developed greatly, as did the position of the *Oikonomoi* of the various metochia who took care to utilise them well for the economic support of the Monastery.

The *Dikaios* substitutes for the Archbishop while the latter is absent and in general regulates the spiritual training of the monks. The *Skevophylax* is in charge of the Monastery's treasures, the decorum of the church and, assisted by the *bibliothekarios* (librarian), of the rich library of manuscripts. The consecration of the Archbishop is undertaken by the Patriarch of Jerusalem whose name is mentioned in the Liturgy during commemoration. The Holy Monastery of Sinai is, however, autonomous and independent, having only a spiritual tie with Jerusalem. At the same time, the metochion in Cairo regulates any matters which might arise in relations with the Egyptian state. With this flexible administrative system, the Monastery is able to overcome the various problems created by the see's distant position in the desert, but also regulate its relations with other national or religious administrations.

Another factor quite apart from the administative structure has helped the Monastery to survive, namely the philanthropy and spirituality of the monks of Sinai. With unceasing activity they care to provide bread, flour, rice, other food stuffs and medical help to the Arab Bedouins. This interest for the inhabitants of the Sinai, who are of the Moslem faith, this philanthropy unaccompanied by any wish to proselytize or interfere in the Bedouins' religious devotions contributes to the respect in which the Moslem inhabitants of Sinai hold the Monastery.

Philanthropy alone, however, is not the only factor conductive to the deference which the Monastery enjoys. The spirituality of the Sinai monks raised their Monastery to a spiritual centre of ascetic life for all the Orthodox Churches. Great figures of monastic life rose to prominence in the desert and Monastery of Sinai: men such as John Climacus, Anastasios of Sinai, Gregory of Sinai, Philotheos Kokkinos, who became Patriarch of Constantinople, and others. This spirituality combined with philanthropy, and adaptability and flexibility in the light of new situations, have all contributed to help the holy Monastery of St. Catherine of the 'God-trodden' Mount Sinai to continue the tradition of Justinian's great monastic centre. At the same time the Monastery is a bastion of Hellenism and Orthodoxy in the midst of different races and creeds in an inhospitable and arid land which, however, the monks of Sinai have transformed into a beloved House of God.

# INTRODUCTION

T
here where the heavens touch the earth and God appeared to man, where absolute solitude and an imposing landscape of granite masses towers above an expanse of sand dunes changing shape at the whim of the wind, where the well of Moses still quenches men's thirst and the bush unconsumed by fire still thrives, there at the foot of Mt. Choreb in the southern extent of the Sinai peninsular, where God delivered the Tablets of the Law, ascetics began to congregate from the first Christian centuries to devote themselves to a life in Christ and spiritual perfection. The solitary communion with God enjoyed by these first Sinaitic ascetics was often disturbed by incursions of the local nomads. A short-term solution to these ills was provided by St. Helen who, according to tradition, built a chapel to the Theotokos (the so-called 'Kyriakon') at the Holy Bush, and close by erected a tower for the ascetics to take refuge in when the many and varied enemies from the desert or passing nomads chose to attack.

When this small group of ascetics became in time organized into a monastic community and expanded in number, their needs and the dangers that faced them likewise increased. The Emperor Justinian, however, came to their aid by answering supplications made by the Sinai monks for a building complex for a new monastery which would include the older installations. Justinian fortified the new monastery with high and sturdy walls thus protecting the fathers from attack; at the same time a safe route from Egypt to Palestine was secured. He also built a new and magnificent church for liturgical needs which was dedicated to the Metamorphosis (the Transfiguration) of the Lord, but most of all provided the Orthodox faith with the most important centre of monastic life in the desert. This centre, with the passage of time, proved to be an unshakable bastion of Greek monasticism in general. It is perhaps not a coincidence that the other two great monastic centres of the Greek Orthodox world were likewise founded with imperial patronage and support, the Monastery of the Megiste Laura (Great Lavra) on Mt. Athos founded by St. Athanasios with the help of the Emperor Nikephoros Phokas some four centuries after Sinai, and the Monastery of St. John on Patmos founded by Christodoulos with a chrysobull of the Emperor Alexios I Comnenos in 1089. The geographical axis Athos - Patmos - Sinai literally passes through the centre of Hellenism, the Aegean, and the presence and work of these monastic centres with their continuous existence from the day of their foundation highlights the important contribution they have made to the Greek people and the Orthodox Church in general.

The life and struggles of the monks both within the walls of the Sinai Monastery (which cover some 6,500 square metres), and without in the 'metochia', 'kathismata' and 'sketes' is a neverending battle for perfection in which the monk is clad with the spiritual armour of those ascetic rules and preachings laid down by the great anchorites of the desert and the Fathers of the Church. The Sinai monks developed their own 'type' of spiritual exercise which during the 7th century was brilliantly formulated by the Monastery's Abbot St. John

Climacus, who wrote: *A monk partakes in the incorporeal life within a material and corruptible body, and constitutes a category and specific entity of that life. Only the monk expresses the wishes and words of God at all times, in all places and in all things. A monk constantly rises above his natural state and is a complete prison of the senses. A monk is a purified body, a pure mouth and an enlightened mind. A monk is a dolorous soul in perpetual thought of death; ever calm yet wakeful.* These are only few of the traits which should distinguish the monks in their spiritual exercise. However, the ascetic tradition of the desert is not always only that 'trial of the conscience' which marks every day of a monk's life on Sinai, but can also require a 'trial of blood'. The 40 Monks of Sinai and the 40 of the Monastery of Raithou, slaughtered by the Blemmyes and the Saracens at the end of the 4th century as well as the host of named and anonymous fathers who lived a life of spiritual exercise to be martyred in the Sinai desert, represent that 'trial of blood' which was never rejected by Sinaitic monks wherever they were found: the Sinaitic neo-martyrs of Cyprus, Crete, Chios and elsewhere. Other monks from Sinai are honoured as Saints in the Church calendar: Galaktion and Episteme, Julian, the 'Holy Fathers martyred in Sinai and Raithou', Neil, John Climacus and the Anastasioi.

Organized monastic life in Sinai is an uninterrupted struggle for the cares of everyday life under hard and sometimes inhuman conditions; a struggle for survival and to meet the basic material needs of the community; a struggle to maintain the Monastery buildings, and to preserve the independent operation of the Monastery without let or hinderance; but especially a struggle for its freedom.

Within this context, which is after all more or less shared by all monastic communities, the Sinai Monastery stands out having achieved in her 15 centuries of life an illustrious monastic tradition and — more importantly — a truly distinguished spiritual life, as well as having pioneered certain traits which now mark monastic life in general.

The preserved writings of the Sinai fathers constitute a font of knowledge for the history of the area. The ideas expressed therein acted as models for the monastic and ascetic life, as well as making a theological contribution towards the confounding of various heresies.

Already by the 6th century we encounter the blessed Neil, probably the author of the narration on the Martyrs of Sinai. Cosmas Indicopleustes wrote at the beginning of the 6th century while the 7th saw the famous John Climacus, Abbot of the Monastery and, amongst other things, one of the most distinguished theoreticians of 'spiritual renewal' after Maximos the Confessor. His *Ladder to Paradise* or *Spiritual Tablets* (on the analogy of the Tablets of the Law) constitutes a fundamental work of ascetic literature. In the work's thirty Homilies (as many as years in Christ's life prior to His baptism and in the rungs of the ladder Jacob saw in the Sinai desert) John began from the *repudiation of life* to terminate at the thirtieth step, *the heart that is wakeful for the multitude of love*. Thus, by means of the 'Ladder', monasticism is raised to a work of love, and not just a spiritual exercise. In the same century, the writings of Hesychios prepared the transitional stage from Sinaitic Mysticism to Hesychasm; while Anastasios wrote his *Guidelines*, a learned handbook against heresy. Under the name Anastasios of Sinai a work has been preserved entitled *Various Narrations on the Holy Fathers of Mt. Sinai*, but the possible identification of this Anastasios with the writer of the 'Guidelines' is disputed by some scholars. The period of Arab rule and the consequent difficulty in communications with Constantinople did not interrupt the spiritual development of the Sinai Monastery. The Synod held in Constantinople in 869 against the Patriarch Photios was attended by the Abbot and representative of the Monastery, a certain bishop Constantine. The monk Philotheos must have lived in the 10th century; his *Neptika Kephalaia* place him amongst the more ardent Hesychast thinkers. Many Sinaitic monks of the 12th century and after are known to have

1. *View of the Holy Monastery of Sinai at sunset from the northeast. The pronounced chiaroscuro created by the masses of red granite at the foot of Mt. Choreb have been softened while the fissures between the rocks are more sharply outlined.*

2. *The Bedouins, depicted here in front of the Monastery walls, are descendants of the two hundred Christian families settled in Sinai by the Emperor Justinian to serve and protect the Monastery, to which they continue to offer their services. The camel, ideal beast of burden for the desert, remains for the Bedouin the main means of transport.*

been active in Constantinople and were employed by virtue of their education in diplomatic missions or were famous as painters and spiritual fathers. For example, the 14th-century monk Gregory is considered the forerunner of the Hesychast movement on Athos and taught distinguished ecclesiastical figures such as the Patriarch Callistos of Constantinople and the Patriarch of Bulgaria, Euthymios. In more recent centuries, Sinai had not lost its spiritual importance if one judges from the preface to the famous decree concerning the Monastery issued by Napoleon Bonaparte in 1798 where it is stated: 'The Monastery of Mt. Sinai is inhabited by educated and civilized men in the middle of the barbarians of the desert which they inhabit'.

This spiritual tradition, faithfully continued unabated till today under distinguished archbishop-abbots and brothers of the Monastery, together with those relations fostered over the centuries with the entire world, has elevated Sinai into a cultural and spiritual centre of international significance.

As mentioned above, however, the Monastery at Sinai has certain distinguishing features which render it unique:

— The Monastery on Sinai is the oldest in the Orthodox world. It is indeed moving to attend the Liturgy there today and hear the supplication sung *... on behalf of the founders of this Holy Monastery, our pious emperor Justinian and empress Theodora of blessed memory,* a supplication repeated without interruption from the 6th century. Notwithstanding many adverse circumstances, the Monastery managed to preserve its Greek character intact even after the Arab conquest of 633, when a new Moslem overlordship was imposed. Thereafter the monks were to live under foreign rule and an alien religion. The preservation of the Monastery's Greekness was due to its own resources, and especially to the position taken by the monks who managed to gain the respect and protection of the Arabs, the Turks and the Egyptians by means of the famous Charter or *Achtiname* given by the founder of the Islamic Faith, the Prophet Mohammed himself in order to preserve the Monastery's rights. Diplomacy also gained the respect of the co-religionist Popes of the Western Church even after the schism between the Orthodox and Roman Churches in the 11th century when the monks on Sinai refused to betray their own faith or make any concession to the West by silently refusing to sign the confession of the Roman Catholic faith when asked to do so.

— The Monastery of Sinai, built at the cross-roads of three religions (Judaism - Christianity - Islam), always sustained the influences of each and was never averse to holding dialogue with them. The monks established good relations and co-operation with the Moslems, and the Crusaders who established themselves there were well received; foreign monks were welcomed into the brotherhood. Sinai, however, remained a crucible for that unique synthesis: the Greek Orthodox tradition.

— Sinai is the only Monastery-Archbishopric. Although scholars today doubt the originality of Justinian's *Novella* according to which from the Monastery's foundation its abbot had to be an archbishop *(Our Royal authority honours the abbot of most exalted rank who shall henceforth preside at Sinai ... that he may also garb himself in the vestments of an archbishop),* it is certain that during the 8th century Sinai became a bishopric and later an archbishopric. It thus constitutes the smallest autocephalous archbishopric and the largest monastery in the Orthodox communion.

— The Monastery's reputation was and remains great throughout the world. Apart from the close ecclesiastical and ethnic ties which linked it to Constantinople and the Ecumenical Patriarchate even after the Arab conquest, history testifies to the respect shown to Sinai by the princes of Europe whether Western or Orthodox, as well as the ready help offered in times of need and even when religious differences and splits between East and West led to acts of fanaticism and destruction. The main reason for this state of affairs was the cult of St. Catherine. Byzantine monks were responsible for the cult's introduction into Western Europe in the 9th century and by the 11th century it had spread considerably, due to the substantial contribution of, amongst others, the Sinai monk Symeon the 'Five-Tongued'. In the later Crusader period, the cult of the Saint dominated the West where numerous churches were built in her honour. A Knightly Order was founded named after her in the 12th century aimed at protecting her tomb and pilgrims thereto. In France, the Brotherhood of St. Catherine was founded to care for the sick, while the Philosophical Schools proclaimed her their Patron Saint, thus making her the patron of Philosophical studies and students in the West. In the medieval Mystery Plays, St. Catherine was always represented as a paradigm of virginity and wisdom. Her name was included amongst those of the Fourteen Supporting Saints who were especially popular in Germany, Hungary and Sweden. Distinguished painters depicted the Saint and her martyrdom.

The spread of the cult of St. Catherine helps explain why Venice protected the Monastery's interests in Crete and elsewhere, and why Portugal, Spain, France, Germany and other countries were always ready to offer it moral and material help. The ships which raised the Monastery's flag of an icon and monogram of the Saint on a white ground sailed unmolested in the Mediterranean. The leaders of the Orthodox communions in Russia, Georgia, Moldavia and Serbia sent rich gifts to the Monastery, sometimes in response to requests by the monks and at others out of respect for the Saint. The Monastery was endowed with chrysobulls and other charters as well as with wealthy monasteries, churches and estates which constituted (together with those already on Greek soil) the Monastery's famous metochia scattered throughout the East and West. Thus the Monastery's spiritual presence was pronounced and its fame grew. (A list of the Monastery's metochia is provided on p. 380. This list does not include landed wealth, nor should it be considered definitive. It is certain that continued study of the Monastery's archives will make it considerably larger).

— The Monastery preserves the oldest functioning monastic library in Christendom, and one of the richest in foreign-language manuscripts. Perhaps it is not possible to speak of the existence of an organized library housed in a specific area immediately after the Monastery's foundation. However, the first manuscripts from Constantinople which Justinian most probably donated to the new Monastery to cover its liturgical and spiritual needs must have been kept somewhere. In a liturgical 'typikon' of the 13th century we read: *The Sexton shall set out three loaves of bread, of which the brothers shall partake from the basket above the library.* The 'Library' here is no doubt the Psalter's lectern, an ideal space for the placement of books. Certain scholars maintain that some of the extant manuscripts were written and illuminated in the Monastery already by the 8th and 9th centuries. This fact bears witness to the existence of a scriptorium which must therefore indicate that a library also existed from at least this time or a little afterwards, in the 10th century, when we know that an illuminated manuscript workshop existed in the Monastery.

The many foreign-language manuscripts throw some light on the monks of various nationalities who at times served in the Monastery. Some of these manuscripts are works of Greek authors which are unknown in the original. The illuminated manuscripts have made a great contribution to the study of iconography; the literary hands to paleography. The manuscripts' contents tell us much about the interests of the monks at Sinai, while the valuable papyri preserve material which help unravel the history of the first years of the Monastery's life. The Monastery's archive can also be said to be unique, a claim justified by the time-span it covers and the variety of languages employed in the numerous documents. The systematic classification and study of the archive will enrich our knowledge of the Monastery's history, but also that of the areas from which the documents originated. The Monastery's manuscript codices provided spiritual sustenance for the monks throughout the centuries while the rich library of printed books assisted many young monks to study during absences in Crete or in Patmos and elsewhere since they were permitted by the community to take some works from this collection with them.

— All scholars agree that the portable icons which adorn the Monastery's katholikon, chapels or other special areas constitute a unique collection not only due to the time-span covered, the quantity and artistic value, but also the stylistic variety expressed therein. Nearly all schools of icon painting are represented from the 6th to the 18th centuries. This is the only collection where the specialist can study the development of Byzantine icon technique, iconography and related subjects from the 6th century until today. If the importance of the Sinai icons is unique for the scholar, it is no less significant for the faithful who may commune with the divine without taking into consideration the theological subtleties formulated with certain classical perceptions by distinguished theologians such as St. Basil the Great, St. John of Damascus, or St. Neil Scholasticus. Objects of veneration and education for the faithful as well as works of art, the icons constitute an imposing presence in the Monastery. In addition to icons given as offerings to the Monastery from other artistic centres, the Monastery also had its own icon workshop with its own individual stylistic traits, yet another indication of the inspiration, and also of the synthetic and assimilative abilities of the Sinai monks, who thus created an iconic oasis in the aniconic desert of the Moslem religion.

— Sinai is the only Greek Monastery whose fortification walls and the structures therein have not been totally destroyed from the 6th century till today, and is thus a unique object for archaeological and architectural research. Most importantly, the Monastery's katholikon has remained intact and unchanged. Apart from the rare architectural members which distinguish it (masonry - roof - columns - floor - revetments - wooden doors etc.) an unsurpassed mosaic adorns the bema apse, a fine example of mosaic work and of the artistic genius of its anonymous creator.

The historical outline given elsewhere in this volume together with the few pages of this Introduction aim at presenting a picture, however brief, of the historical and spiritual development of the Monastery of St. Catherine over the many centuries of its life, as well as all the factors which make it unique. It is hoped that the reader will thereby be prepared for the other, spiritual treasures of the following pages.

Even though in every true piece of art there must necessarily exist an identification of the creator with each of his creations, in Byzantine religious art this was difficult to realize since here faith alone together with artistic gifts are the paragons of a work's success. The artistic treasures preserved today in the Monastery and in its various metochia are creations of faith and religious piety; they should never be considered as simply museum pieces, although they certainly betray the artistic taste and knowledge of the monastic community. The Icons, the Illuminated Gospel Books and the other theological and liturgical manuscript codices, the Mosaics, the Wall Paintings, the Church gold-embroideries (holy vestments, epitaphioi, chalice covers etc.), objects of Church metalwork (mitres, crosses, pastoral staffs, censers, candle-holders, chalices and liturgical plates etc.), the architectural programmes: all were used and are used still as usable or liturgical objects. Devotional offerings, most of them made by pious pilgrims, powerful emperors, kings and princes, distinguished patriarchs or humble monks and priests are specimens of the artistic sensibilities of their donors and express the art of their time. The monks at Sinai accepted these offerings as gifts of the faithful; the individual object was never appraised on artistic merit or material value. Instead, the more lavish objects were used during great Church Feasts and on grand occasions, and consequently were safely stored. On the other hand, the monks were sometimes forced during periods of dire depravation to sell or melt down valuable treasures in order to meet pressing needs.

The volume in hand constitutes an attempt to present an accurate picture and appraisal of the importance of the art-works in the Monastery of St. Catherine on Sinai, a veritable repository of the heritage of the Orthodox Church and more specifically of the Greek people. This undertaking was by no means easy. The amount and variety of the objects in each category is so great that specific volumes could be written on individual categories; something indeed which has already been done elsewhere for some. This challenge led to the assignment of certain chapters to more than one specialist, the chapter on Portable Icons and that on the Library for example. The authors sometimes encountered immense difficulties in their selection of objects to be studied and published. The problems involved here for the specialist in each field can be imagined, especially when text and illustrations are not intended for fellow-scholars but for a broader non-specialized public. Furthermore, the difference in artistic value between objects to be selected was often so small or non-existent as to make choice more of a dilemma. Finally, the demands on both space and style for a book of this character also had to be taken into consideration. The art works of Sinai, however, pose yet another problem in that in many individual cases a full and specialized bibliography is absent, due to the fact that many of the objects have never been studied; on the other hand, some works more well-known to scholars and the public have not yet been investigated in detail. Thus the collaborators on this venture often had to undertake original study of their own. Each scholar visited the Monastery and worked where the treasures are carefully kept and are still used, marvelling them from close quarters, many of which are described here for the first time. The objects were studied in detail and, where possible, associated with other similar objects in the Monastery's collection. From the introductions at the beginning of each section the reader may find a short but full and authoritative scholarly assessment of the material under study. Bibliographical testimonies, some detailed, others more general are based on the requirements of the texts, while the illustration subtitles help complement and explain them.

This opportunity should be taken to offer deepest thanks to all those colleagues who contributed to this volume for their exceptional cooperation in its realization.

Finally, all concerned with the production of this volume express their most profound thanks to the Archbishop of Sinai and Hegumen Damianos and to the fathers of the Monastery for the sincere affection shown to all during our various stays in the Monastery as well as for the willingness with which they afforded every assistance to this work, so that the priceless treasures of the Monastery could be presented as best as possible.

# ARCHITECTURE

# ARCHITECTURE

The Monastery of Saint Catherine belongs to the very few Early Christian building complexes which have never been destroyed or fallen into enemy hands. We have detailed references to the Monastery almost from the date of its foundation, and the abundance of manuscripts and a multitude of icons provoked the solicitude of scholars early on. In contrast, archaeological investigation has progressed only slowly.

The oldest plan of the Monastery, accompanied by the earliest scholarly description, was produced by R. Pococke in 1743.[1] A new plan was made by the Alexandria-Michigan-Princeton expedition between 1958 and 1965, more in keeping with the standards of modern scholarship.[2]

## THE ORIGINAL HERMIT SETTLEMENT

As is known the Monastery in southern Sinai (figs. 1, 2) built under Justinian and named since the 9th century after St. Catherine had its origins in an Early Christian anchorite colony[3] on the foothills of Mount Moses. The existence of this monk settlement is testified by travellers as early as the 4th century. Even today numerous small cells are to be found near the Monastery. But no special study has yet been made of their original plan and we are not certain of the date of their construction.[4] Various finds of late antique pottery in the area allow us to conclude that some of them already existed in the Early Christian period.

Nothing, however, survives of the small church which the same 4th - century travellers tell us stood in the Valley of the Burning Bush.[5] Justinian's church may well have been built on its site, just as elsewhere it is known that newer work obliterated older structures. The original building possibly no longer served the needs of the monastic community which was steadily increasing in size. Only remains of a small tower survive, its purpose the protection of the inhabitants from marauding bands. The first reference to it is made between 373 and 381 by the Egyptian anchorite, Ammonios.[6] Its remains lay today within the Monastery enclosure, close to the Burning Bush as his description confirms.

The tower's visible walling consists of courses of large, unworked, granite blocks. The joints between the courses are filled with small, flat stones. The same kind of masonry is to be seen in the buildings of the neighbouring town and episcopal see of Pharan, modern Fayran, dating to the 4th and 5th century, which to some degree represents the local building style.[7] Therefore without doubt the erection of the tower can be ascribed to a date before the reign of Justinian. The relations are confirmed also by the Chalcedonian Patriarch of Alexandria, Eutychios, around 935,[8] who mentions a tower of the 4th century standing in the enclosure of Justinian's Monastery.[9]

The thickness of the tower walls varies from 100 cm. to 110 cm., the thickest to be found in the present day Monastery, and exceeded only by the Justinian outer walls. Its base is roughly square. If the later additions are ignored, its internal plan is made up of two areas, of unequal dimensions. The larger, the northern, has a door in its northern side, serving as the entrance. In the dividing wall, another door connected the two rooms. The other wall openings are later in date. The ground level placing of the outer door is unusual, and might be explained by the fact that at one time the ground sloped differently at this point, because the base of the cliff outside the door appears to fall suddenly a few metres further north. Even so, the positioning of the entrance does not seem to correspond to the measures taken for the safety of other Early Christian monastic settlements.[10] Such towers usually had a stair within a turret which led to the upper floor of the main tower by means of a movable bridge. We do not know whether a turret of this kind existed in this case: it seems improbable. However, one should bear in mind that the model for towers of this sort did not come from Egypt, but from the fortified-dwellings of Syria and Palestine where the entrances were usually positioned at the ground floor.[11]

The internal communication between floors is likely to have been by movable ladders, possibly resting against an opening in the vault of the ceiling. In the event of attack these ladders could easily be drawn up inside the building.[12] We do not know the original height of the tower; the walling makes three storeys possible. The upper part of the tower may be envisaged as a flat roof circled by a simple parapet.


## THE JUSTINIAN MONASTERY

### THE ENCLOSURE WALL

According to the testimony of the Byzantine historian Procopios and of the Chalcedonian Patriarch Eutychios[13] the walled Monastery (drawing 1) was built by the Emperor Justinian, who heeded the petition of a delegation of hermits living on Mount Moses and immediately put the work in hand. The architect-engineer in charge was probably a Byzantine army officer, since a large number of soldiers were drafted into the work force, a fact which left the informant of Procopios under the impression that the operation was the construction not of a monastery, but of a military castrum.[14]

There was in fact little difference. The Monastery closely resembles a fortress, the likeness strongest in the solutions adopted at the Monastery of St. Catherine to produce an amalgam of the characteristics of both types of building in order to produce the greatest possible area of living space. Dissimilarities only emerge when the two types of building are compared from the point of view of their respective defensive capabilities. The four towers were built as simple re-inforcements of the four corners of the Monastery enclosure wall. The slightly bigger tower at the northwest corner (fig. 6) must have been used as a watch tower.[15] The only protection provided for the main, west gate, and the entrance to the Monastery is consists of a *meurtrière* placed above it. Down its chutes and from within its protection it was possible to throw pitch or pour boiling oil on any who attacked the entrance. Other than this, no further means of defending the walls were provided to repel sustained attack; given that a bellicose way of life accorded ill with the monastic ideal, further measures were perhaps thought unnecessary. Nevertheless, the walls were made stout enough to allow the monks to feel safe, particularly bearing in mind that their attackers then would have been nomadic Arabs who certainly stood no chance of success against such sturdy thickness.

*Drawing 1*
*General plan of the Justinian Monastery.*
*1. Defence tower (keep).*
*2. The Church of the Transfiguration of the Saviour.*
*3. Main entrance, now walled up.*
*4. Postern door.*
*5. Granary.*
*6. Remains of a stair.*
*7. Two-aisled hall.*
*8. Napoleonic repairs to the enclosure wall.*
*9. Medieval oven.*
*10. Latrine tower.*

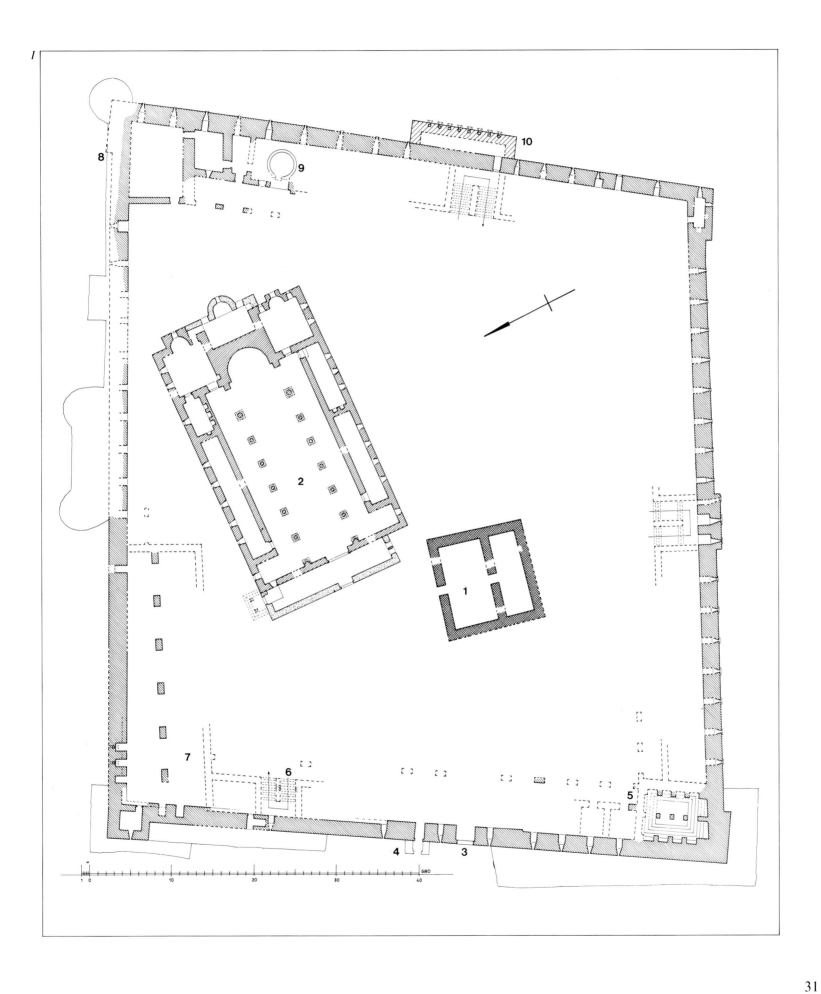

The main facade of the Monastery looks down the valley which stretches westward, the Wādi ad-Dayr. Almost exactly in the centre of the west wall is a small postern with a modern porch in front of it, still in use today as an entrance to the Monastery. A few yards further south stands the large, main entrance which, for security reasons, has long been walled up. In earlier times it was only opened on special occasions, although camels loaded with supplies for the Monastery could pass through it.

There are numerous loopholes in the outer face of the wall which, on the inner face, widen into small niches of two stone courses high and roughly 60 cm. wide. They are found on two floors, one above the other, and served as windows for the monks' cells constructed originally against the inner faces of the walls. Neither the original sizes of these cells, nor the thickness of the internal dividing walls, is known, because no traces have been left of the abutments. It is possible that the partition walls were built in another material, possibly of crude bricks. A solid portion of wall still standing at the southern end of this area gives us the original depth. In front of this space was a row of pillars which supported a narrow gallery, providing access to the cells in the upper floor. At some points traces of other pillars of this colonnade are still visible.

At the southwest corner of the wall stand the remains of a grain store (fig. 5). This seems to have remained unfinished and was never used. It is a quadrangular structure, with series of steps on all sides. To add another storey a row of double arches was built. They rest on rather long buttresses at the sides and square pillars in the centre. Without exception, every arch demonstrates an excellent bond with wedge-shaped stones characteristic of Justinian masonry.

Roughly in the middle between the narrow inner passage and the northwest corner of the Monastery a wide semi-circular arch was built against the wall. It has to be considered as the load-bearing structure which supported a stair leading in the direction of the wall. Although later building work has covered other traces there is no reason to doubt that the stairs themselves were built according to the customary way, with regular bonding into the inner wall. There were probably two flights.

Immediately next to the stair, which certainly has to be considered as one of the main approaches to the upper floor, is, inside the fortification wall, a small corridor with an odd twist, the final direction of which is unknown. Possibly it is connected to a window.

Finally, at the northwest corner of the walls, the internal layout alters. Almost parallel with the northern enclosure wall, though very clearly diverging from it, run two rows of super-imposed arches, in turn standing on rectangular pillars of granite.[16] They formed the inner support of a larger, possibly two-aisled, hall. Whether they have in the same time separated two floors, is possible but this has not been proved. The level of the ground floor room is significantly lower than the actual level outside the wall. It was probably so from the beginning because the window openings of this floor still to be found in the north and west walls are not at the same height on the outer face of the wall, but rather higher.[17] Communication between the outside of these openings and the inner windows is by means of a narrow passage, like a chimney. The purpose of these windows was ventilation, not light.[18]

It is not possible to ascertain how far east along the north wall this two-aisled hall extended. It cannot, however, have been much beyond the last visible pillars, because otherwise it would get in conflict with the position of the church wall. Furthermore, regular fenestration re-appears in the outside wall to the east of the building.

Remains of other internal structures are preserved in the northeast corner of the Monastery. In the corner itself a larger, two-storey structure housed an old mill. In its eastern wall are two windows. At ground level its northern wall is covered by walls of a later period. On the upper floor, however, the whole length of the original wall is to be seen. Because there are no traces of windows in its upper section we should accept that there were none at the lower level either. We may therefore conclude that the walls in this corner, where today rises a round tower of Napoleonic date (fig. 3), were also once strengthened by some kind of square tower, similar to those at each end of the southern side of the enclosure wall.

The rooms stretching southwards from the corner room along the eastern wall differ all in plan. Their arrangement is, however, the same as on the western side. In the third room the remains of an old oven are preserved.

Further south still, on the outer side of the east wall, is a flat tower which has, at its base, a row of similar-shaped drainage openings, spaced fairly closely together. The tower may have been the Latrine Tower (fig. 4), though its internal arrangement is not yet known. Probably the two doors of the two floors of the east wall, placed one above the other, are connected with the latrines of the tower. Obvious reasons of hygiene dictated the need for provision of such amenities; the care and attention paid to them, found in many Early Christian hermit colonies as well as in the buildings of monastic communities in Egypt, makes it clear that this was a matter which did not go neglected.[19] Thus it is surprising that there is no bonding between this tower and the walls of the Monastery. Also the difference in building material, the noticeably smaller size of the granite blocks from that found elsewhere in the Monastery, shows that the tower was certainly constructed at a later date. Probably originally a more simple structure was chosen which proved a failure and was in time replaced by the actual tower.

At the remaining points on the walls only loopholes and other openings (figs. 11, 12, 13) have survived from the once adjacent inner rooms. As in the western walls, the windows are arranged in two continuous rows; the inner buildings must therefore have been two-storey. Inevitably, if the upper floor was to be reached, we must assume that there were galleries supported on a colonnade, running its whole length.

While at the south side of the enclosure the completion of such an arrangement is very easy, the repetition of a similar set of inside rooms with an extended colonnade and balconies up above ran into considerable difficulties because, as we have said, the katholikon lies too close to the wall to leave enough space for a similar series of rooms between the western two-aisled hall and the mill in the northeast corner of the enclosure. Even so, the repeating rows of windows are to be seen. We may thus conclude that instead of the room arrangements found on the other sides, here there is at least a colonnade with a gallery above running the length of the wall.

The problem about the inter-communication between the floors of the inner buildings by stairs remains unsolved. Only on the western wall, as we have said, are physical remains which would suggest a stair to be seen. It cannot, however, have been the only example; more probably there was one on every side. It may therefore by conjectured that a stair existed on the south side of the wall, where the existing external buttressing, in the form of a tower, may be reckoned to correspond to some alteration of the internal plan. Furthermore, the outside windows at this point are placed almost in the middle of two rows of internal windows. The inner embrasures may have been related to the level of an intermediate stair landing, different from the floor levels in the neighbouring rooms. On the upper floor towards the side of the outer wall, there is a small chapel which still preserves traces of a painted imitation of marble revetments.[20]

We have still less evidence for the position of a stair on the east side of the enclosure.

There is a further difficulty here in that the internal buildings assumed to have existed did not stand at the same height but, as may be inferred from the position of the loopholes which are visible from the outer side, contain slight differences, which were made up by small steps in the area of the inside ground-level colonnade and its overhanging gallery. One indication as to the position of the stair comes from the siting of the Latrine Tower. A modern architect would certainly have linked the entrance to such a space to stairs; it is not impossible that someone in the past had a similar idea.[21]

## THE CHURCH OF THE TRANSFIGURATION OF THE SAVIOUR

The construction of the new church (figs. 7, 10) was started independently of the building of the enclosure wall.[22] The original plan was only for a three-aisled church with an apse turned to the east, without the lateral rows of rooms, in other words, it was a smaller building than the today's church. The choice of site shows that there was no initial intention to enlarge the building in the future. It seems, however, that enlargement was decided upon after the erection of the Monastery walls had advanced to the point where a change of alignment was not viable (drawings 2, 3). Furthermore, the cells on the inside of the north wall of the Monastery, the windows of which were already ready, cannot have existed when the first enlargement was planned, otherwise there would not have been sufficient room for it. It seems that the extension started even before the completion of the original basilica which consisted of lateral rooms, two small towers for stairs on the west side,[23] which, however, were never completed and two pastophoria built on either side of the eastern apse.[24]

The original single entrance, at the western end of the central aisle — today between the narthex and the nave —, lies well south of the central building axis. The uneven slope of the ground is thought to be one of the reasons for this. Each valve of the two-leafed folding door is made up of panels (figs. 15, 16, 18), which are magnificent examples of wood-carving of the Justinian period. They are embellished with panels of relief depictions of plants and animals.[25]

The main nave of the katholikon has two rows of six columns (fig. 24), each with a differently carved capital (figs. 19-21). The last pair of columns to the east are larger in diameter because the space until the buttresses right up to the eastern wall of the nave is wider. The western end of the columns finishes in two half-columns. Arches link the columns; above them is a row of small windows, each over the apex of the arch.

The transverse joists over the ceiling of the nave are preserved; their sides and underneath are encased by thick, decorated boards. The first beam from the west and the two central beams bear legible inscriptions (fig. 14) on their western side, indicating that the church was built in the last years of the reign of the Emperor Justinian, after the death of the Empress Theodora (June 548).[26] We also learn from these inscriptions that the architect of the nave was Stephanos of Aila, a Nabataean. At one time bridges were placed breadthwise between the joists, which explains the uneven spacing between the words of the inscriptions. When, probably in the 19th century, during one of the many restorations of the roof, the coffers were replaced, these were so positioned between the joists that today the inscriptions can no longer be seen from below. Originally the coffers must have been fixed on the upper side of the joists as is demonstrated by the decorated casing boards of the joists which show at their upper edge a frieze of plant leaves.[27]

The roof over the side aisles is flat. The aisles (fig. 22) are lit by a single row of two-light windows. The first pairs of windows of the two sides at the western end of the walls were later closed by the addition of the two towers with stairs, and were finally blocked up.

The Sanctuary apse, slightly deeper in plan than an ordinary semi-circle, at the east end of the central aisle, is today enclosed externally on its outer side by a square and very stout outer casing. The need for this can be explained only by the existence of the two corner chapels which were built during the first enlargement of the Monastery church. Before that it may be supposed that there was a simpler version of this external shell, probably polygonal in plan such as the one which emerges today above the roofs of the side chapels.

The floor of the apse which, like that of the presbytery which extends westwards into the nave until the easternmost pair of columns, rises three steps above the floor level of the nave. These steps did not originally exist. From the screen which formerly enclosed the Sanctuary two panels survive, linked to the buttresses at the eastern end of the colonnade in the central aisle. They are made of Prokonnesian marble, carved with two confronting gazelles standing on either side of a cross.[28] In front of the Sanctuary apse is the altar, to the right of it the later added shrine containing the remains of St. Catherine (fig. 23). Within the apse also stands the *synthronon* with the remnants of the episcopal throne in the centre. The throne was altered at the end of the 18th century using carved marble plaques on a column-supported base. The curve of the apse is clad in marble, the slabs zealously chosen, their grey graining forming a variety of patterns.[29] The revetment continues above the bilobed window right up to the spring of the half-dome which covers the Sanctuary. The half dome is decorated with a mosaic which ranks amongst the most important works of Byzantine mosaic art (see Mosaics, fig. 2). It depicts the Transfiguration of the Saviour, the original dedication of the Church.[30] The mosaic continues over the wall above the vault in which there is another pair of arched windows.

Both pastophoria, the floors of which are a few steps lower than the floor of the church, have their own small apse. They were added during the first enlargement of the church, but before the completion of the original church. The same is true of the lateral rows of rooms which extend the length of the north and south walls of the church, and also of the western towers, for stairs, which were never completely finished. The irregular bonding of the tower walls with those of the original church gives some an idea of the height they had reached when the work of the first extension got under way. The arch stones of the entrance to the south tower are not present; it would thus appear that on the southern side the church wall had already reached the height of the windows. It is therefore probable that the doorway to this tower, located below the first pair of windows in the southern church wall, was opened later. On the other hand, on the north wall, the corresponding entrance to the tower was completed with a bonding of wedge-shaped stones.[31] On that side of the church therefore, the height of the wall must have reached a lower level. All the entrances needed for this first extension were thus made at the time of its construction.

The original purpose of the lateral rows of rooms has not yet become clear. They were probably intended to accommodate worshippers; they are used today as side chapels. For this purpose they have been divided even further, with the result that the symmetrical arrangement of the windows in the outside wall has been disturbed, and it no longer corresponds to the division of the space within. The small niches in the dividing walls are all of later date.[32]

Later still the narthex and the Chapel of the Burning Bush were added (fig. 25). In both, the joints of later building work are clearly to be seen. The narthex does not extend over the whole width of the church,[33] but stops a little short of its southern wall, owing to the difficulties created by the slope of the ground where it was necessary to leave a passage between the old tower (keep), already discussed, and the southwest corner of the church. There were two entrances to the narthex; the western one, built more or less on the axis of the church, is considered to be the main entrance. The carved wooden door leaves date to the time of the Fatimids. The middle panel depicts, on the left, the Transfiguration of the Saviour, on the right the Prophet Zechariah (fig. 17). A second small door exists on the northern, narrow side of the narthex; it originally had an external porch.[34] The considerable slope of the floor of the narthex to the north which imposed the need for steps shows the original awkward nature of the site. This is the explanation why the central door, which leads into the middle aisle, is not aligned on the central axis of the nave, a fact that after the addition of the narthex was not any more visible. The same factor probably also explains why doors were opened into the side aisles only after the addition of the narthex.

Another addition of later date is the Chapel dedicated to the Burning Bush, the Monastery's holiest place, built behind the eastern apse of the nave. Because the Chapel is enclosed by the pastophoria which project well to the east of the Sanctuary apse, their inner side walls also served as the side walls of the Chapel of the Burning Bush. It was therefore only necessary to provide in some way for the construction of the chapel's eastern wall, together with a small apse. This eastern wall, of necessity, joined with the external casing of the small apse of the northern corner chapel and the northeast corner of the southern corner chapel, where, at the junction, one of the windows was slightly obscured. Passages obviously opened during a later date in the lateral walls between the pastophoria and the Chapel of the Burning Bush gave access to the new chapel.[35] A third entrance, which is perhaps the original, was achieved by means of a narrow, right-angled corridor which led from a low niche in the east wall of the northern pastophorium. There must have been series of steps in this entrance passage, because the new chapel's original floor level was lower than it now is, which is still several steps below the floors of the two pastophoria. Above the entrance in the north wall of the chapel is a niche; there was probably another in the corresponding position in the south wall. The altar stands on a socle in the small apse on the eastern wall. The walls are clad in Damascus tiles and decorated with portable icons.

It has not been established when the Chapel of the Burning Bush was built. G. Forsyth considers that it was built in mediaeval time.[36] This view, however, is contradicted by the nature of the masonry which is exactly similar to the building style of the 6th century as seen in the walls of the church and the outer, enclosure wall, both of which were built in Justinian's reign. The chapel must therefore have been constructed when craftsmen trained in these techniques were still available; this presupposes that, at the time of its construction, the Sinai region was under Byzantine sovereignty. It should therefore be dated before the attacks of the Sassanian Persians in 614 (Fall of Jerusalem).[37]

## THE CHURCH AT MOUNT MOSES

The Monastery of St. Catherine has close links with Mount Moses (Mt. Horeb). Julian of Saba had already built a small chapel there on the occasion of his pilgrimage to the mountain.[38] Its dimensions, 6 × 6 roman feet (approx. 180 cm. per side), are known to us from information supplied by the Anonymous of Placentia.[39] It was a very small chapel, which must have had a proportionately small apse, or perhaps only a small niche in the eastern wall.

In the course of the building of Justinian's Monastery in the Valley of the Burning Bush this mountain-top chapel was also renovated.[40] The work can only have progressed slowly,

*Drawing 2*
*The building phases of the Justinian Church.*
*1. The original, unfinished building.*
*2. The structure of the original Church.*
*3. The first additions to the original Church, the Narthex and the Chapel of the Burning Bush.*

*Drawing 3*
*Plan of the Church of the Transfiguration of the Saviour (the katholikon).*
*1. The nave.*
*2. Left pastophorion, the Chapel of St. James the Less.*
*3. Right pastophorion, the Chapel of the Holy Fathers from Sinai and Raithou.*
*4. Sacristy.*
*5. Chapel of St. Antypas.*
*6. Chapel of Sts. Constantine and Helen.*
*7. Skevophylakeion (Treasury).*
*8. Chapel of Ioakeim and Anne.*
*9. Chapel of St. Symeon Stylites.*
*10. Chapel of St. Marina (north tower).*
*11. Chapel of Sts. Cosmas and Damian (south tower).*
*12. Narthex.*
*13. Chapel of the Burning Bush.*

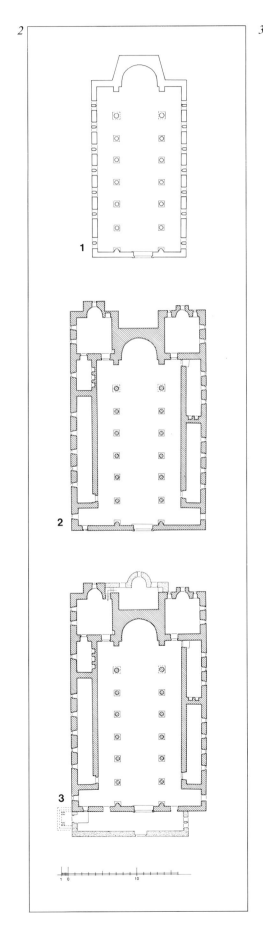

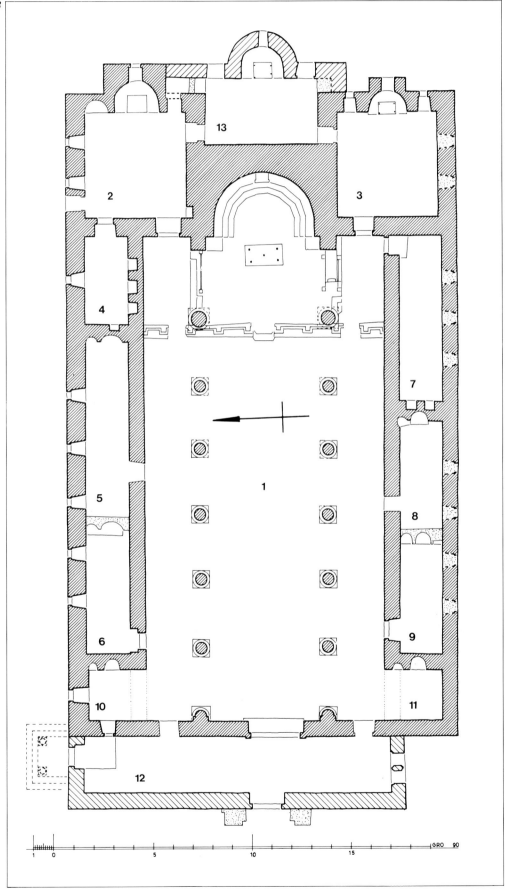

since the Anonymous of Placentia, whose visit has to be placed around 560, still saw Julian's original structure. Equally, Procopios omits any mention of a new building, possibly because his informant had not yet managed to visit it.

The Justinian church no longer survives[41] (drawing 4). A new building, re-using some of the older material, was erected over it in 1934, which encloses roughly half the central aisle of the Justinian church.[42] It does, however, embrace part of the impressively thick masonry of the Justinian apse.[43] The apse has a polygonal external casing; inside it is rounded. The bilobed window at the centre of the curve is of a later date. In the right hand part of the apse the original junction with the east wall of the southern side aisle has also been preserved. There cannot therefore have been pastophoria.

Further traces are still to be seen today only at the western end of the Justinian church. It is possible to trace the western entrance wall for most of its length. Above a foundation of huge, unworked granite blocks, varying in size and colour, which are scattered all over the slopes of the summit, follows the wall proper which consists in its remaining part of a row of squared smaller granite blocks, built up on their narrow sides. All these stones were cut from the same vein and are all of the same beautiful red colour, a fact which explains their uniformity in size. They must have been transported here from a great distance, for use above the irregular stones which were not supposed to be shown in the visible part of the wall. In the south wall these equally squared blocks of granite are preserved over a considerable distance even in two lines. The thickness of the wall can therefore be estimated.

The foundations of two rows of large, amorphous granite blocks, interpreted as the stylobate of an inner colonnade, can be traced from the inner face of the west wall. The distance which separates them is small in relation to the whole width of the church, so that the central aisle cannot have been much wider than the side aisles.

Clear remains of the walls of the narthex which, as also in the Monastery church, is a later addition, are preserved. The entrance was in the short, south side where also the path which climbs Mount Moses ends. This, the southern wall of the narthex, is the only one still to stand to any significant height until the lintel of the door. The opening of the door is now walled up to its full height. Because the wall served as terracing for the construction of a small mosque from the beginning of the 12th century,[44] it was never pulled down, hence its good state of preservation.

## LATER BUILDINGS OF THE MONASTERY

No particular interest attaches to the later buildings. The old Refectory dates from the middle Byzantine period, and was constructed above the terrace west of the church. It is a three-aisled hall with cross-shaped pillars. In contrast to the older buildings, all of which are constructed from squared granite blocks, the Refectory is built entirely of limestone.[45] The entrance is in the north wall. The key stones of the forward-most arches bear chiselled crosses. Much of the outer walls are built of brick. The building was converted into a mosque at the beginning of the 12th century.

A room, whose purpose is not known, roofed with Gothic pointed vaulting, dates to the end of the 12th or to the 13th century. Its narrow, eastern side is decorated with a painting of the Judgement Day, executed in 1573. Pilgrims from Western countries were housed here in the 15th century, many of whom scratched their names or Latin inscriptions on the walls. The room was later used as the monks' Refectory.[46] In it stands a wooden table, decorated for its entire length by 18th - century carving.

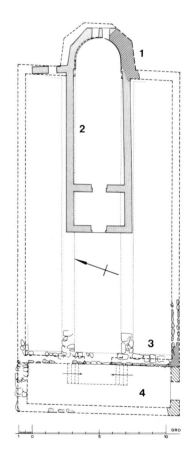

*Drawing 4*
*Plan of the Justinian Church on Mount Moses.*
*1. Remains of the Justinian Apse.*
*2. Modern Chapel, built in 1934.*
*3. Remains of the original west and south wall.*
*4. Justinian Narthex.*

ARCHITECTURE

The many small chapels within the enclosure are all based on the same plan and are of recent date (fig. 9). Each is a small, single-aisled room, the eastern end embellished with an apse. The iconostases are often made up of disparate and sometimes quite old elements. The Chapels of St. John Prodromos (the Baptist) and of St. Stephen, in the southern part of the Monastery, are both barrel-vaulted. The former has a facade painted in the stylized manner of the 18th century and remains of the entrance hall. The lintels of the many openings (door, windows, niches) were decorated with wooden planks taken from older ceilings (fig. 26).

The Chapel of the Five Holy Martyrs of the East has a flat ceiling constructed of wooden beams. The Chapel of St. John the Theologian, on the first floor of the northwest corner of the Monastery, seems to have been built only in the 19th century.

1. *View of St. Catherine's Monastery in the valley of the Wādī ad-Dayr.*

2. *General view of the Monastery of St. Catherine's from the northeast.*→

3. *The northeast corner of the Monastery walls with the round*
*tower of Napoleonic date.*

4. The Latrine Tower in the east wall.

5. The south wall of the Monastery, seen from the southwest.

6. The northern termination of the west wall of the Monastery with the remains of the old corner tower.

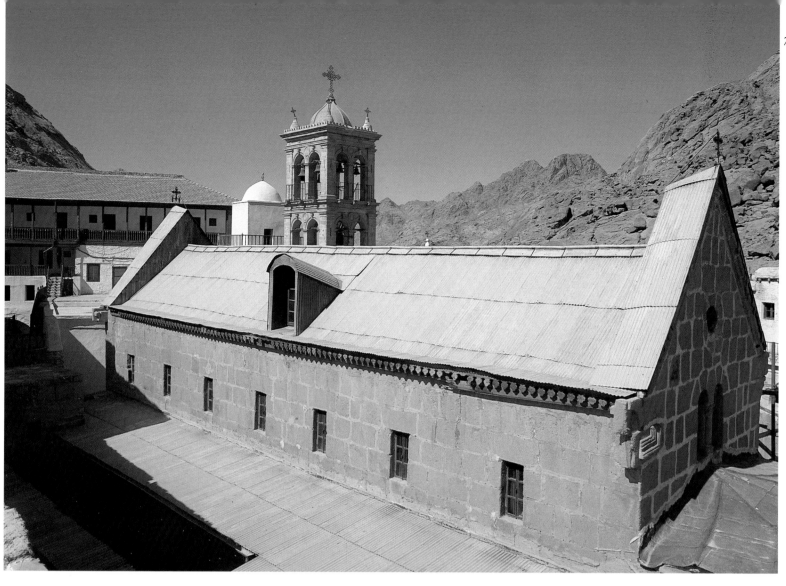

9. Buildings in the southwest part of the enclosure of the
Monastery with the dome of the Chapel of St. James.

7. The south side of the central aisle of the Church of the
Transfiguration of the Saviour, the katholikon.

8. Buildings within the Monastery enclosure. View to the
living quarters and the guesthouse, 'archontariki', on the
western side of the enclosure.

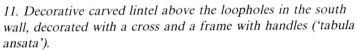

11. Decorative carved lintel above the loopholes in the south wall, decorated with a cross and a frame with handles ('tabula ansata').

12. Decorative carved lintel above a loophole on the southern side of the wall with a cross inside a circle; on the upper part is a cross and a frame with handles underneath an arch, supported on two small columns.

13. Decorative carved lintel on the southern wall with a cross between two rams and a frame with handles ('tabula ansata').

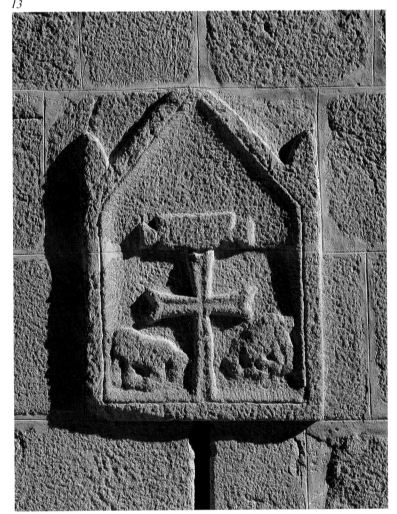

10. The upper part of the western wall of the Church, i.e. the facade of the katholikon.

49

14. Section of the ceiling beam from the katholikon, bearing the inscription 'ΒΑΣΙΛΕΩΣ ΙΟΥΣΤΙΝΙΑΝΟΥ.'

17. Wood-carved panel – made up of many wooden sections joined together – from the narthex door of the Fatimid period. The main depiction in the centre shows the Prophet Jechariah.

15-16. Wooden panels from the Justinian door to the central aisle of the katholikon carved with a goat (fig. 15) and birds with plants (fig. 16). Details of fig. 18.

18. The Justinian door and jambs to the central aisle of the katholikon.

*19. Two-zone column capital with rams' heads and the schematized decoration in the shape of a basket, in the katholikon.*

*20. Two-zone column capital with rams' heads and spirals above crosses and palms, in the katholikon.*

*21. Column capital of a half-column in the katholikon, with stylized acanthus, bulls and cows.*

*22. The northern aisle of the katholikon.*

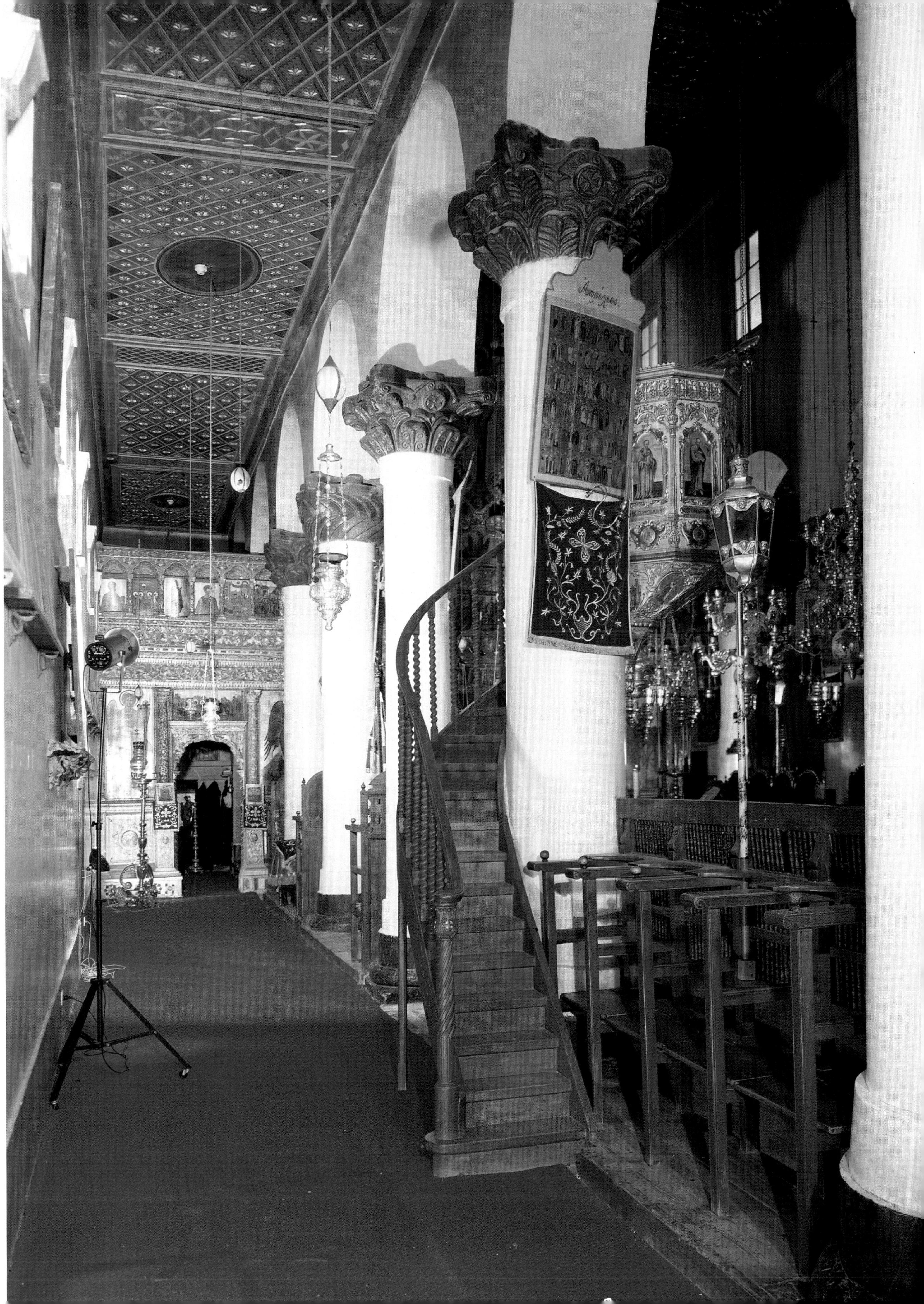

*23. The shrine of St. Catherine in the Sanctuary of the katholikon.*

*24. The central aisle of the katholikon.*

54

25. *The Chapel of the Burning Bush in the katholikon.*

*26. The Chapel of the Five Holy Martyrs in the Monastery.*

# MOSAICS AND
# WALL PAINTINGS

# MOSAICS AND WALL PAINTINGS

T he focal point, not only of a Christian church, but of any cult building — pagan as well as Jewish — is the apse, to which everyone entering the building will be drawn. In a Christian church there is usually depicted a figure of Christ or the Virgin or the title saint, but rarely — as at Sinai — a scenic composition: the Metamorphosis. However, when one enters the church today, the view into the apse is hidden by a 17th-century carved wooden iconostasis which is surmounted by an enormous Crucifixion group that reaches to the ceiling. The original iconostasis, surely in marble, was certainly so low that whoever entered the church was immediately attracted by the apse mosaic.

## MOSAICS

### THE APSE MOSAIC

This mosaic is one of the greatest masterpieces of Early Byzantine art and there is every indication that it was made when the basilica was constructed — as the inscriptions on the roofbeams prove — at a time after the death of the Empress Theodora (548) and before the death of the Emperor Justinian (565). That it entered the art historical discussions rather late is due to the relative inaccessibility — until very recently — of the Monastery and the difficulty of producing satisfactory reproductions of the mosaic.[1] The first and, so far, only satisfactory, publication in colour and considerable detail[2] was achieved by the Alexandria-Michigan-Princeton Expedition to Mount Sinai between the years 1958 and 1965. But before the photographs could be made, two actions had to be taken first:

1) A close inspection, after a scaffold had been erected, showed that the centre of the mosaic, especially the figure of Christ, was detached from the wall and in danger of collapsing. After removing the disfiguring iron beams of an earlier restoration attempt, the American expedition succeeded in fastening the mosaic with copper clamps to the granite ground and filling the holes.[3]

2) Over the centuries, the mosaic had become covered by heavy layers of dirt, varnish and a kind of glue which had contributed, not only to the darkening, but also in many spots to a discolouring of the surface. All these layers were removed with painstaking care and underneath, the colours of the cubes reappeared in their original freshness.

But most surprising and gratifying was the fact that the mosaic had never been restored — contrary to those in the churches of Ravenna which, since the 18th century, had repeatedly been restored — and that all cubes were still in their original positions at varying angles so as to catch and break the light falling on them. Looking at the Metamorphosis (fig. 2), the beholder will immediately be absorbed by the figure of Christ (fig. 1) standing on the axis within an aureola whose intense blue colour isolates Him effectively from the gold ground and heightens the illuminescent colour of His garment (*and his raiment was white and glistening*, Luke 9:29). Christ is flanked by Moses at the right (fig. 4) and Elijah at the left (fig. 3), each raising his hand in a gesture of speech (*and, behold, there talked with him two men which were Moses and Elias*, Luke 9:30). Both stand on a strip of ground and there is no indication of a mountainous landscape, i.e., Mount Tabor. This means that not the historical setting is stressed, but the idea of an epiphany. Their firm stance contrasts effectively with the kneeling positions of John (fig. 5) and James (fig. 6) which correspond with each other, and Peter (fig. 7) who has been lying asleep on the ground and, under the impact of the vision, is just awakening (*But Peter and they that were with him, were heavy with sleep*, Luke 9:32). These six figures are depicted in varying degrees of physical reality. Christ has the most dematerialized body which, though showing such details as the free leg and the veiled left hand, is comparatively two dimensional. Moses and Elijah have heavier and more solid bodies and their vivid gestures of speech and facial expressions suggest perception of the surrounding world. They are rendered in what one might call a second degree of physical reality. A third degree is used for the disciples. An element of 'contraposto' in the kneeling poses of John and James leads to a marked emphasis of the upper legs as three dimensional masses jutting out of the picture plane; and the pose of Peter with his right knee drawn up and his left leg extended, suggests stretching at the first moment of awakening. This introduces a remarkably naturalistic element, justified by the textual source.[4]

The artist is equally subtle in the characterization of the heads. Christ's is the most abstract, being contrasted to those of Moses and Elijah who look at Christ out of the corner of their eyes with human awareness. Moses looks with inner calm, Elijah with an expression of great pathos. The same distinction is made between John and James, but in reverse. John, at the left, wears an expression of utter calm and James, at the right, one of anxiety. By such chiasm the artist achieves a balance of compositional expressions that match the compositional harmony.

The Metamorphosis is framed above by a row of medallions (figs. 12-19), with portrait busts of the Twelve Apostles. They are closely integrated thematically with the Metamorphosis in that the three disciples of the Tabor scene, i.e., Peter, John and James, are not repeated in the medallions, but are replaced by the two Evangelists, Luke and Mark and by Matthias. Moreover, the witnesses of the New Dispensation are supplemented below by those of the Old, i.e., the major and minor prophets. In these portraits the artist displays the ability to depict faces full of character. Some are square, bald and energetic like Jonah; others, like Jeremiah (fig. 12) have thick black hair and the piercing eyes of a religious fanatic. Yet they are standard types and can by found very similarly in 10th - century manuscripts of the Macedonian Renaissance that hark back to Early Christian models.[5]

There are four more medallions. The one above the head of Christ, marking the axis, shows a simple golden cross, and the one below, in the midst of the 16 prophets, the bust of David (fig. 19). The golden cross is set against the tripartite blue circles, i.e., heaven, corresponding with the aureola behind the figure of Christ. David is depicted wearing a purple *chlamys* and a crown like a Byzantine emperor[6] and must be understood as an allusion to the genealogy of Christ (*Born of the tree of David according to the flesh*, Romans 1:73). The two juxtaposed medallions of the cross and David must be understood as a pictorialization of the Two Nature doctrine. At the same time the figure of David resembles very much the portrait of Justinian as he is represented in the mosaic of San Vitale in Ravenna, and the idea of the artist was obviously to make in this manner an allusion to the founder of the Monastery which at the time of the foundation was dedicated to the Virgin. This is by no means a unique case where a biblical or legendary figure is depicted in the guise of a Byzantine emperor. I need only to point at a Sinai icon in which King Abgarus (see Icons, fig. 13), is depicted in the guise of the Emperor Constantine VII Porphyrogenitos.[7] There is an old tradition, defended by the monks of the Monastery, that Justinian and Theodora were represented in the apse mosaic, namely in the two medallions of the triumphal arch. While this identification, as we shall see, cannot be maintained, there may be a grain of truth in the tradition, that at least Justinian, though in the guise of David, is in this form commemorated as the founder of the Monastery.

In the corner medallions are depicted the portraits of two monks who must be identified as the donors of the mosaic, both with a square nimbus, indicating that at the time the mosaic was made they were still among the living. At the right we see Longinus (fig. 15), whom the dedicatory inscription at the bottom of the Metamorphosis names as the abbot in whose reign the mosaic was executed[8] and at the left the Deacon John. Unfortunately, the dates of both are unknown. These two portraits show another aspect of the artist's range of expression. Here he is portraying not character faces as in the case of the apostles and prophets, but individual features with a sense of sharp psychological observation: the sensitive intellectual face of the Deacon John whom some scholars have proposed identifying with John Climacus, the author of the *Scala Paradisi (The Heavenly Ladder)* — an identification not likely since John Climacus (c. 570-649) lived later than the execution of the mosaic in Justinian's time — is effectively contrasted with the energetic face of Longinus with high cheekbones, apparently a man of action.

Moving up from the apse into the triumphal arch[9] one sees on the same axis as Christ and the cross medallion of the apse conch yet another, but smaller cross in a medallion against which is set the Lamb of God in three-quarter view. His head is turned so as to fit perfectly into the shape of the disc. Two angels (figs. 9, 11) with peacock wings, filling the spandrels, are flying toward the centre to offer the sceptre and orb to Christ in quite the same manner as flying Victories in the spandrels of an imperial triumphal arch offer the very same attributes. Small crosses as terminals of the sceptres and on the surface of the globes are the only changes by which an image of imperial iconography is adapted by the Christian artist to Christian imagery, particularly suitable in a church which is an imperial foundation.

The lower parts of the spandrels with two medallions which, as mentioned before, the tradition of the Monastery wrongly identifies with Justinian and Theodora but which, no doubt, represent John the Baptist and the Virgin, are set against a silver background.[10] For the depiction of the strictly frontal head of the Virgin the same abstract means are used as in the Christ of the Metamorphosis: strong symmetry, clear geometric lines in the staring eyes and the arched eyebrows. In the strongest possible contrast John the Baptist is turned in three-quarter view and the expression of great pathos shows even a higher degree of emotion than the comparable head of Elijah in the Metamorphosis. The eyebrows are even steeper and the impression of pathos more pronounced. The eyes are more deeply set in the sockets and the mass of somewhat dishevelled hair falls upon his shoulders. Essentially these are the same elements on which the emotional impact of the tragic mask is based. A marble mask from a fountain in Pompeii[11] has a very similar design with the deep contracted eyebrows and the high *onkos* with the flowing hair. It seems to us more than likely that the mosaicist not only used a tragic mask as his model, but did so with the realization that this was the most effective way to express in pictorial form the tragic genius of John the Baptist. In juxtaposing the type of John with the abstract Virgin the artist once more succeeds by pictorial means to express the difference between the divine and the human.

The uppermost zone of the eastern wall contains two scenes from the life of Moses to the left and right of a double window which is encased in a rich ornamental border and divided by a column, base, capital and ornamented shaft, all executed in mosaic, that pictorially imitates these architectural members. At the left Moses is seen loosening his sandals before the Burning Bush and looking up to the commanding hand of God issuing from a segment of heaven (fig. 8). The high rock behind Moses' back suggests that the artist was, indeed, influenced by the actual landscape, i.e., the granite mountain of Sinai. This is even more true of the right scene in which Moses, receiving the Tablets of the Law in the form of a parchment scroll, is shown standing within a deep mountain gorge (fig. 10). There is one significant detail in which the scene of Moses receiving the Law deviates from the Bible text. He receives out of the hand of God not, as usual, a pair of tablets of stone, but a closed scroll, surely meant to be of parchment. According to some Jewish sources Moses received not only the Ten Commandments at Sinai but the whole Pentateuch written in tiny script on a stone that 'can be rolled up in a scroll'.[12] The Sinai mosaic is not a unique case of this peculiar iconography. It appears in a miniature of the 11th - century *Christian Topography* of Cosmas Indicopleustes.[13] This copy of the Cosmas manuscript was, as we believe, written at Sinai and thus it seems that the legend of the law being written on a scroll was particularly well known at Sinai.

The rather large surface area covered with mosaic required the team work of a whole group of mosaicists, and a close look reveals that the quality differs. To make a sharp distinction among the segments, however, is quite impossible because the principles of medieval workshop traditions were not such that individual artists were commissioned to execute certain parts of the surface area independently. The varying levels of skill were apparently used more economically in such a way that the master craftsman of the atelier concentrated on the heads which are usually executed with smaller cubes while the assistants made the garments and the least trained just the background. It can be observed that the best hands concentrated on the Metamorphosis. The medallion of John the Baptish stands out also as a work of exceptional quality while the two flying angels in the same triumphal arch are the work of a comparatively weaker hand. Yet there is a uniformity in the technique which leaves no doubt that the whole mosaic surface was executed within an apparently rather short period.

The wealth of the artistic forms and expressions has its counterpart in the complexity of the content. On this the artists were advised by a learned cleric as was customary in Early Christian and Medieval art. He advised the artist on the accuracy of the iconography. There are several layers of meaning involved which only an intensive study can unravel.

The first iconographical aspect which the Sinai mosaic shares with the one other contemporary mosaic apse, namely San Apollinare in Classe in Ravenna, though here it is rendered in a much more abstract form,[14] is the eschatological outlook. A portrayal of Christ in the apse, the spherical shape of which suggests heaven, is quite often and in various forms associated with the Second Coming. In Sinai this association is suggested by the surprising absence of any indication of Mount Tabor, a feature so essential to the narrative and never omitted from later depictions of this scene. There is a passage in John Chrysostom's Homily on the Metamorphosis in which he equates the vision on Mount Tabor with the Second Coming of Christ: *Thereafter he shall appear in the glory of the Father, not only with Moses and Elijah, but with an unlimited host of angels not with a cloud over his head, but surrounded by heaven.* This is precisely the impression which the Sinai mosaic conveys.

Most basic is the question of why the subject of the Metamorphosis was chosen at all. In the Orthodox church the Metamorphosis is one of the twelve Great Feasts of the ecclesiastical year, and the reason for its inclusion in the cycle is dogmatic. One dogma in particular had the greatest impact on Byzantine art in general: the dogma of the two natures of Christ as formulated in the Fourth Ecumenical Council of Chalcedon in 451. What better visualization of this dogma could there be than Christ's transfiguration from the human to the divine nature and from the divine to the human before the eyes of the apostles who had accompanied Him to Mount Tabor?

The dogma of the two natures, one of the main concerns of whoever laid out the program of the mosaic is, as mentioned before, also apparent in the two medallions on the axis with the Christ figure. These two medallions are juxtaposed in such a way that the golden cross, set against three concentric strips, symbolizing the Trinity, alludes to the divine nature of Christ, while the bust of David alludes to the genealogy and thus to the human nature.

The idea of the two natures spills over into the triumphal arch where the sacrificial lamb in the central medallion emphasizes the human nature of Christ and the gold cross, set once more, against the three concentric strips, the divine. However, there is still another reason for the depiction of the lamb in the centre of the triumphal arch: namely his relation to the two flying angels and the medallions of the Virgin and John the Baptist. This very grouping of Christ, the Virgin, John the Baptist and the Archangels is known in Byzantine art as the *Deesis*, i.e., the Supplication, in which the Virgin and John the Baptist represent the intercession for mankind, the one for the New and the other for the Old Dispensation. The Sinai mosaic is a forerunner of the classical representation of the Deesis as it becomes familiar in the Middle Byzantine period, in which Christ had to be represented in human form because after the Quinisext Council of 692 the symbolic rendition of Christ as a lamb was forbidden. In the Middle Byzantine period the Deesis is moved from the triumphal arch to the centre of the iconostasis beam in the midst of the 12 liturgical feasts and thus becomes an element of the liturgical worship.

Furthermore, there are the two Moses scenes above the triumphal arch. Who, looking at Moses loosening his sandals would not be aware that right behind this wall there is the Chapel of the Burning Bush, the *locus sanctus* of the Monastery? And who, seeing Moses receiving the Tablets of the Law, would not be reminded of the fact that through the clerestory windows one sees the high mountain of Ras Satsafa beyond which rises, though invisible from the Monastery, the Gebel Musa, whereon, according to tradition, Moses received the Tablets? In the mosaic, Moses is shown standing in a gorge which suggests that the artist was inspired by the serrated peaks of the actual locality. At the same time the topographical aspect is stressed not only by the presence of the various Moses figures but also by the Elijah figure in the Metamorphosis. Halfway up the Moses mountain one passes by the Chapel of Elijah in which the *locus sanctus* is the cave of Horeb where he had been hiding (III Reg. 19:8).

Yet this topographical connection, self-evident as it may be, was not the primary reason for the choice of these scenes in this place. Of even greater importance is the typological reason. Moses must be understood as the forerunner of Christ the Messiah; and just as Moses had given the old Law so had Christ given the new Law. The choice of the two Moses scenes for the decoration of the sanctuary is, thus, not confined to the Sinai church, but occurs, about the same time, in the choir of San Vitale in Ravenna. It is not even an invention of Christian art to relate these two Moses scenes to the focal point of the place of worship, because already in the 3rd-century Synagogue of Dura-Europus[15] they flank the central panel above the Torah shrine where the Messianic King David takes the same place which in Christian art will be taken by Christ enthroned. The appearance of God to Moses is an epiphany just as is the Metamorphosis, and in this sense the Moses scenes foreshadow typologically an event in the life of Christ. Yet whereas in the Old Dispensation neither Moses nor Elijah was permitted to look upon the Lord but only to hear His voice (Ex. 3:4; Ex. 33:20ff.; III Reg. 19:13) the basic difference is that on Mount Tabor the two Prophets did see the Lord in the manifestation of Christ and thus the Metamorphosis includes also an allusion to the dogma of the Incarnation. Obviously both, the topographical and the typological meaning, are implied in the two Moses scenes.

With its six layers of meaning — eschatological, dogmatic, liturgical, topographic, typological and imperial — which, as discussed above, are involved in the representation of King David in the disguise of the Emperor Justinian, we may not even have exhausted every facet of the rich and complex content of the Sinai mosaic, but we hope to have touched upon the most obvious and the most important. It is one of the great achievements of the artist in charge of the execution of this mosaic that he was able to find for such a complexity of content a clear and balanced composition which the beholder would be able to grasp immediately in its essentials.

Where did the artist or the artists come from? Who executed this mosaic? We have no records and are dependent only on inferences since no parallel is known today in the same style which might give a hint to a possible workshop connection. We pointed out that the chief master had an extraordinary facility for differentiating between various degrees of physical reality in the case of divine figures avoiding human emotion altogether, and for the human figures rendering various modes of behaviour from self-assured calm to exalted pathos. This power of expression is matched by the refinement of execution. Each garment gives the effect of an almost monochrome colouring when seen from a distance, but at close range shows a considerable variety of subtle shades. What appears as black hair or the black borderline of a garment is in reality deep purple, lightened at intervals by individual deep sea-green cubes (ordinary green cubes turned over) and amber cubes (gold ones reversed). Moreover, it will be noted that in the upper zone the gold cubes are slightly tilted so that light reflects on them when one looks up from the floor of the church. Thus, a diffusion of sparkling light is calculated to be experienced by looking at the mosaic from a certain angle. It also should be observed that the Moses figures in the top zone are much taller than the figures of the Metamorphosis, a differentiation which has led some scholars, like Kondakov, to believe that the former must be dated later. Yet when one stands in front of the altar and looks up, one sees the two Moses scenes at a very steep angle and the correcting eye reduces the tall proportions to normal size. These and other refinements undoubtedly point to a workshop which had developed them in a long tradition, established and continued by a highly trained team of craftsmen. We believe that in the time of Justinian only Constantinople could have supplied such highly trained craftsmen and, moreover, what could be more natural than that the emperor's personal patronage was responsible for sending these most skilled artists to the Monastery of which he was the founder?

After the mosaic decoration of the apse, the triumphal arch and wall above was finished, there is only one other spot in the church where this technique was applied. In the Chapel of the Burning Bush behind the apse of the basilica its little apse was decorated with a mosaic whose only decoration is a geometric pattern in a circle.[16] At the bottom of the mosaic runs an inscription which states that it was finished in the days of archbishop Solomon, but the year following his name is, apparently purposely, eradicated,[17] and since we do not know the years of the reign of this archbishop and since the decoration of the mosaic is too simple, there is no way to date this mosaic with any precision. The fact that a mere geometric pattern was preferred as decoration could be explained in a twofold way: that the mosaic was made during the Iconoclasm or at the time when Sinai was already occupied by the Moslems and the monks were concerned not to provoke the new masters of the land. After all, the Chapel of the Burning Bush is to the present day a place of worship by the Moslems of Moses as well as of Aaron, i.e., Harun. Some later sources mention a mosaic with the Virgin to be seen at the west wall over the entrance door. Our expedition investigated this part carefully but found no trace of a mosaic under the whitewash.

## THE TWO ENCAUSTIC PANELS IN THE SANCTUARY OF THE KATHOLIKON

Not long after the completion of the decoration of the bema with the precious materials of marble revetment and mosaic, the idea of expanding the programme must have arisen. Since no space was available for additional representation in mosaic, the artist resorted to a very unusual and perhaps unique solution, namely that of painting two further scenes directly on the marble revetment in encaustic technique. The two panels are to be found on the pilasters left and right of the apse, so that the beholder can immediately relate them to the mosaic decoration and perceive them as part of an all-inclusive iconographic programme for the Sanctuary.

The panel on the pilaster to the left depicts the Sacrifice of Isaac,[18] skilfully fitted into the narrow format. The altar is a tall structure, composed of three cubes in order to provide a platform for the kneeling Isaac and bring him within reach of Abraham who grasps him by the hair and holds the dagger-like knife menacingly close. The patriarch's head is averted as if to avoid witnessing the intended slaughter with his own eyes. The Sacrifice of Isaac, alrealy a favourite subject in Jewish art as substantiated by several floor mosaics and by the fresco above the Torah shrine in the Synagogue of Dura, was also frequently depicted in Christian churches and especially in the altar room, where it is intended to prefigure Christ's sacrifice. The mosaic in the choir of San Vitale in Ravenna may be cited as a parallel of similar typological significance.

The pilaster at the right of the apse was covered by an icon of St. Catherine in a heavy marble frame of the 18th century, because in front of it stands the tomb of St. Catherine. I reasoned that in all probability there would be another encaustic painting underneath the icon, i.e., a comparison piece to the Sacrifice of Isaac. In 1960 the icon was temporarily removed and under it the lower part of a human figure became visible, executed in the same encaustic technique as the Abraham panel. It depicted a soldier drawing a sword. The obvious implication was that this soldier should be another witness from the Old Testament and that the scene should be a further prefiguration of the death of Christ.

In 1963 the archbishop gave his gracious permission to have the rococo marble frame removed, a task performed with the greatest care by E. Hawkins. The total figure emerged with an inscription that left no doubt as to the subject matter of the scene, which came as a great surprise.[19] The soldier is Jephthah, who, before joining battle, had made the vow that, if victorious, he would sacrifice whatever would come out of the door of his house (Jud. 11:30ff.), and thus he felt obliged to sacrifice his only child. The encaustic panel actually depicts the gruesome slaughter of the little girl by her own father. She is kneeling on an altar constructed of three cubes like that of Isaac, while Jephthah, dressed as a Roman soldier, holds her by the hair and, bending back her head, cuts her throat with his sword. The panel is surely by the same hand as the Abraham and Isaac panel and composed, as a counterpart, the actions of both being oriented towards the centre, i.e., toward the altar that stands between them. Without doubt, then, Jephthah's Sacrifice must also be understood typologically as a prefiguration of Christ's sacrificial death.

Artistically, these panels are not only somewhat weaker than the Metamorphosis mosaic as far as the treatment of the organic structure of the human body is concerned, but also more ornamentalized in that Abraham is covered with a more geometrical system of highlights and Isaac's tunic with an all-over pattern of circles. Apparently somewhat later than the mosaic and most likely belonging to the 7th century, these panels nevertheless are surely Pre-Iconoclastic and in all probability Pre-Islamic.

There is no indication that the basilica contained in the Justinianic period or in the time shortly thereafter any further wall decoration, either in mosaic or encaustic or fresco painting or that any further decoration was even planned. Yet it seems very unlikely that its walls, especially the north and south walls of the aisles, were meant to be left bare. Apparently they were used as background for icons, either to be placed on pedestals or hung up. Some of the stately early encaustic icons, like that of the Pantocrator bust, the Virgin enthroned between Sts. George and Theodore Stratelates,[20] the bust of St. Peter (see Icons, figs. 1, 2, 4, 5) and others must surely have been set against the wall so that they could be worshipped, but unfortunately, we cannot be sure about their precise location. It is not before the Middle Byzantine period, especially the 12th and 13th centuries, that an all-over programme for the distribution of icons in various parts of the church emerges.[21] This programme reflects the liturgical needs and it is manifested in the following:

1) When the marble iconostasis of the Early Christian church with curtains in the intercolumnar spaces was replaced by a wooden one, it was crowned by a painted epistyle whose chief subject was the cycle of the 12 great liturgical Feasts, the Dodekaorton, and the intercolumnar spaces filled with larger icons of the Deesis and additional saints.

2) Title saint icons made for the chapels dedicated to them: there is only one such title saint icon still *in situ*, that of St. Stephen in St. Stephen's Chapel.

3) The set of calendar icons which are hung up on the columns supporting the nave of the basilica. A candle is lighted in the nave of the basilica and another one in front of the one icon which contains the saint whose day is commemorated.

4) The collection of icons on the north and south walls of the aisles are arranged according to the calendar of the year, and on the feast day it is taken from the book and placed on the *proskynetarion* for special worship.

This clear programme is today somewhat obscured by the fact that the walls are filled in the manner of a picture gallery with icons which were not meant for the present display, like diptychs and triptychs which were destined for private worship and not in the church. Even so, the main purpose of the icon collection on the walls of the church is still maintained, to serve devotional purposes.

## WALL PAINTINGS

In comparison with the astounding number of portable icons, only a few murals are preserved in the Monastery of St. Catherine on Mount Sinai. These are scattered in various places in the katholikon and the chapels of the labyrinthine building complex, and extend in date from the 6th to the 16th centuries.

The techniques and genre apparent in the wall paintings vary from one unity to another, constituting in each case an expression of art at the time. Another observation can be made as to the paintings' style and quality which naturally varies according to the artist's abilities and the importance of the area location of the work itself, namely the katholikon, chapel, refectory or the small niches found in the inner side of the fortification walls. Both specialist and interested visitor would agree, however, on it being quite clear that at no time were large-scale painting programmes organized for the katholikon or other places of worship. The explanation is simple: the iconographical demands of religious worship were abundantly provided for by the large number of portable icons, many of which were executed in the Monastery by the monk-painters themselves.

The choice of the murals' subject matter is self-evident. Here we find Sinaitic themes such as the depiction of the Theotokos as the Burning Bush, of Moses receiving the Ten Commandments from the Hand of God, of St. Catherine or of the medallion with St. John Climacus. On studying the wall paintings, one is imbued with the sensation of the uniquely mystical and profoundly religious character of the iconographical subjects developed here in the desert, in that desert which from the depths of time has been so intimately linked with the presence and the voice of God: the Sacrifice of Abraham and of Jephthah are painted next to the Sanctuary of the katholikon, while the Theotokos arising out of the *fiery and unquenchable bush*[1] is depicted only a few metres away from the famous Bush of Moses.

Those who inspired the formulation of these themes, as well as the artists who depicted them, lived without doubt in this holy place, interpreting iconographically the deepest meaning of those moving moments of the presence of God to which the desert at Sinai bore witness. Thus no part of the Monastery is fully decorated with wall paintings. Today we can literally only refer to 'fragments' of wall paintings and to decorated niches. Moreover, a few wall paintings remain unknown even to the specialists.[2]

## THE CHAPEL OF JUSTINIAN

Situated in the south wall of the monastic complex, at the landing of the wide stairway leading from the first to the second floor of cells and the gallery, is a small elongated barrel-vaulted chamber measuring 330 cm. long, 92 cm. wide and 240 cm. high. On the narrow east side is a small conch while the west side terminates in a smaller blind apse. The only access to the chamber is from the stairway door.

This Chapel is dated to the time of Justinian (6th century), a fact confirmed by the decorative motifs which are still in a relatively good state of preservation.[3] No figural iconographic wall paintings exist, however.

The entire vault is covered with a linear painted green cross-hatch pattern, the squares being decorated with a group of green birds and brownish-red rosettes. The decoration is completed by green circles and brownish-red zig-zag motifs. In this way, the vaulting seems to imitate ancient Greek coffers with their geometric design and pronounced colour combinations. The side walls are decorated in another manner: an attempt has been made to copy marble revetments in paint. Brownish-green antae with bases and column capitals frame square plaques, so that one has the impression of marbles placed in harmonious colour relation on the wall. This original decorative device aimed at highlighting the apse where, below the apse conch decorated with a shell in the centre of which appears Mt. Sinai (?) surmounted by a cross, appears a large Greek cross adorned with precious red stones and green, square and oval gems. The ends of the horizontal arms of the cross are linked to its top by gold chains.

The Chapel's programme successfully reproduces the motifs employed in Early Christian decorative schemes such as those known from mosaic floors of Christian basilicas in the eastern Mediterranean. These aniconic motifs were no doubt imposed on the painter by the limited space and small wall surfaces that he had at his disposal.

## WALL PAINTINGS REMOVED FROM THE OLD REFECTORY

In 1977, murals from the Monastery's old refectory were removed at the Chapels of St. John the Baptist and St. Anthony. Despite the time that has lapsed, the works have not yet been studied since they still await restoration. Moreover, they are unpublished and their contents unknown.

Mention may be made here of the only example which it was possible to photograph, part of the figure of a saint, perhaps the Prophet Elijah. This wall painting alone is enough for us to recognize here the product of an important painting workshop operating in the Sinai during the 13th century, to which this depiction must surely be dated. The plastic rendering of the figure of the Prophet Elijah (?), the free play of brushstrokes used in the wavy whitish-grey hair, the cherry-red colour of the cheeks, the thick lines with a strong coal black highlight of the eyes, the yellowish gold halo: in general all these stylistic characteristics are common to monumental painting of the 12th - 13th century, especially of the 13th.[4]

## THE CHAPEL OF ST. JAMES, THE BROTHER OF CHRIST

The Chapel of St. James, the brother of Christ, is located at the northeast corner of the katholikon of St. Catherine and, together with the Chapel of the Holy Fathers which takes up the southeast corner of the same church, flanks and communicates with the Chapel of the Bush immediately behind the Sanctuary. In the apse of this chapel we find an iconographical subject purely Sinaitic in its inspiration.

The composition extends over the entire surface of the apse semi-cylinder, its lowest part terminating at a black band (still discernable towards the north section) 157 cm. above the green floor. Investigations of the stucco show that the lower part of the apse probably remained undecorated or, had it ever been painted in an earlier phase, the composition was subsequently destroyed.

Iconographically speaking, we find ourselves before an unusual composition, which, however, is directly related to the Sanctuary area and is admeasured amongst the so-called Sinaitic themes. In the wide semi-circular zone, portraits of saints are rendered in groups of two: John Climacus and St. John Chrysostom to the north and St. Basil and Moses to the south. Between both these groups we see the Theotokos as the Burning Bush. The three Fathers wear *phelonia* and *omophoria* decorated with crosses, and hold scrolls with their respective liturgies. Moses (fig. 23), wearing a *chiton* and a *himation* with many pleats, is depicted at a youthful age and holds the Tablet with the Law of God. The Theotokos is shown full-length in the centre with her arms raised up in supplication in the Platytera pose. She wears a red *maphorion*. Delicate, supple branches in deep red with small pointed greenish leaves surround the body of the Theotokos up to the shoulders; at the middle of her body they blend with the maphorion, thus representing the flames of the *fiery and unquenchable bush.*[5] In the conch of the apse at a vertical axis above the Theotokos appears a bust of Christ (fig. 21). He wears a gold-orange chiton and a white himation with highlighted pleats bordered by a gold-red clavus. Christ's crossed-halo is outlined with a gold-red arc surrounding two semi-circular bands of different coloured tones. He spreads His arms offering James a codex of the Saint's liturgy, and to Moses the Tablet with the Commandments.

We have before us an original composition in which the usual motif of the apostles or saints, which decorates the lower walls of the Sanctuary apse from the 11th century onwards, is dominated by the Theotokos as the Burning Bush and Christ as Lawgiver, the latter a common motif since Early Christian times.

As an integral entity, this compositional arrangement is not encountered in any other monument from any period, although specific motifs or components of it can be found employed individually. The attention of the viewer is always centred on Christ who, anachronistically, presents the Commandments to Moses and the Liturgy of the Presanctified to James, the Chapel's titular-saint. Concurrently, the bush is symbolic of the impeccable virginity of the Theotokos-the Unconsumed Bush, according to the teachings of the Church Fathers, in particular by the hymnographer, St. John of Damascus.[6]

Such an iconographical composition, which remained unknown until 1963 when it was cleaned and restored,[7] leads us to inquire as to the painter or the team of painters who may, indeed, have been monks of the Monastery and therefore may also have painted murals elsewhere in the Monastery, not to mention, as we shall see, portable icons. This argument is supported by the close association of technique and style between the figures in the apse wall paintings and a group of older portable icons from the 12th and 13th centuries in the Monastery's collection,[8] which constituted the wall painting's iconographical model. The moulding of the facial features in the chapel paintings bears little relation to the strong faces of the original icon models. Likewise, the somewhat naive and lifeless look of the first group is nothing like the vigorous expressions one sees in the second.

The figures in the apse do seem to come from a period later than their possible models. They are reminiscent of the Giving of the Commandments at the 15th - century Eleousa church at Ano Myrtia in Aetolia,[9] of Cypriot wall paintings, and especially of murals in the Chapel of the Archangel Michael at Pedoula (1474)[10] or even those of Symeon Auxenti at Galata in Cyprus executed shortly afterwards (1511 and 1513).[11]

Consequently, the most likely date of execution for the apse composition in the Chapel of St. James should rest in the middle or the second half of the 15th century and, moreover, the work was carried out by a Sinaitic workshop.

## THE CHAPEL OF THE PROPHETS AND SAINTS

This small Chapel is literally 'perched' on the inner side of the fortification walls at the north of the Monastery and at a small distance from the Bush. Its most interesting element is the conch at the narrow east side (60 cm. high, 65 cm. at the base and 35 cm. deep) adorned with an icon of the Panagia Hodegetria, and the semi-circular intrados arch decorated with medallion busts of prophets and saints associated with Sinai.

A red $X$ (the greek initial letter of 'Christ') appears on the arch's keystone. To the north in successive medallions appear the Archangel Michael, Moses, Elijah, John Climacus; to the south, the Archangel Gabriel, Aaron (figs. 24, 25), Elisha and St. Catherine, namely the Sinaitic Prophets and Saints.

Stylistic elements lead to comparative parallels with the wall painting of the apse of the St. James Chapel. Thus, these also should be dated to the mid or late 15th century. At some point in the middle of this century, the monk and painter Pachomios decorated the small area with aniconic designs, thus creating an 'extravagant colourful atmosphere' anything but harmonious with the mien of the conch.

## THE MOSES CHAPEL

A small set-back in the southeast corner of the Library serves as the tiny vaulted Chapel dedicated to Moses. The small apse therein is adorned by an exquisite wood-carved surround for the Sanctuary doors which may possibly have been brought here from another chapel. The Panagia Platytera (fig. 22) with her arms stretched out in supplication against a deep red ground decorates the small apse. In the conch above we see a bust of Christ. He holds a closed Gospel-Book and gives a benediction. In the tympana to left and right, and under depictions of stylized architectural forms, we see full-length portraits of Moses and Aaron with their distinguishing dress and symbols: Moses with his rod, and Aaron with his censer. Two large candelabra flank the Old Testament symbols below the conch of the Platytera: the Urn, the Lamp and the Ark. Between the Theotokos and the symbols appears the inscription *Holy of Holies*. Cherubim and crosses complete the composition. The expressive countenance of the Theotokos, the brown-red maphorion with its gold strokes, and the warm ochre of the halo, and (least of all) the face of Christ are the only elements which remain untouched by the re-painting undertaken on the whole composition. More specifically, the prophets have been redrawn according to their original outline, but no new colour was added. It is almost certain that this 'restoration' was the work of Pachomios during the present century.

The features of the Theotokos' face, with its broad colour surfaces and the delicate 'sweetening' of the tones with a greenish-red colour, not to mention the entire technique through which the stance of the figures is achieved, makes this a work of the same Sinaitic workshop which decorated the Chapel of St. James and that of the Prophets and Saints in the mid or late 15th century.

## THE WALL PAINTINGS OF THE OLD REFECTORY

Painted below the ogee arch on the east side of the Monastery's old refectory, and covering almost the entire height and width of the wall, is a representation of the Second Coming of Christ (250 cm. high and 450 cm. wide at the lowest point, namely 230 cm. from the ground). The wall painting covers the upper part of the arch and is preserved complete today, which indicates that any decoration of the lower zone would have depicted a different subject. At the centre of this large arch at a height of 98 cm. from the ground there is a conch (230 cm. high and 230 cm. at the cylindrical axis) within which appears a mural of the Hospitality of Abraham.

These two themes are immediately associated with the sublime goals of Christian teaching, and are especially relevant to the monastic life. The Second Coming on the walls of a monastic refectory acts as a constant reminder of the eschatological goal to which the monk strives, and that all his thoughts, actions, and testimonies shall be 'submitted' as evidence at the Hour of Judgement. The Hospitality of Abraham, on the other hand, unveils to the world of the vain and to its soul the revelation of the Triune God while simultaneously calling the monks, who partake together of their 'daily bread' in their refectory, to join with the angels and the patriarchs at the spiritual table of God.

The association of the food of the spirit with the Last Day, quite apart from its adroit manifestation in the two depictions, is also rendered in a masterly fashion, thus revealing the great abilities of the anonymous artist who painted both works in the eighth decade of the 16th century. He dated the works (Last Judgement: 1573; Hospitality of Abraham: 1577), but did not deign to sign them.[12]

*1. Christ. Mosaic. Detail of fig. 2.*

*2. The Transfiguration. Christ with His disciples John, James and Peter is flanked by the Prophets Elijah and Moses. In the frame of the apse, medallions with portrait busts of the Apostles, the Evangelists Luke and Mark, Matthias, prophets, the Abbot Longinus, John the Deacon and King David. Mosaic in the apse of the Sanctuary of the katholikon. Middle of the 6th century.* →

73

3. *The Prophet Elijah. Mosaic. Detail of fig. 2.*

+ΜΩΥCΗC

ΚW

*4. The Prophet Moses. Mosaic. Detail of fig. 2.*

*5. The Apostle John. Mosaic. Detail of fig. 2.*

*6. The Apostle James. Mosaic. Detail of fig. 2.*

*7. The Apostle Peter. Mosaic. Detail of fig. 2.*

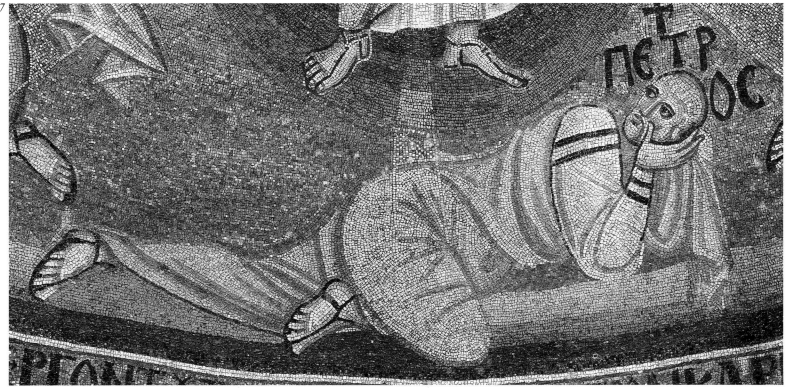

8. *Moses loosening his sandal before the Burning Bush. Mosaic. Upper part of the eastern wall, above the triumphal arch, in the Sanctuary of the katholikon. Middle of the 6th century.*

9. *Flying angel. Mosaic. Spandrel of the triumphal arch in the Sanctuary of the katholikon. Middle of the 6th century.*

10. Moses receiving the Tablets of the Law.
Mosaic. Upper part of the eastern wall,
above the triumphal arch in the Sanctuary
of the katholikon. Middle of the
6th century.

11. Flying angel. Mosaic. Spandrel of the
triumphal arch in the Sanctuary of the
katholikon. Middle of the 6th century.

12. *The Prophet Jeremiah. Mosaic. Detail of fig. 2.*

13. *The Prophet Malachi. Mosaic. Detail of fig. 2.*

14. *The Prophet Daniel. Mosaic. Detail of fig. 2.*

15. *The Presbyter Longinus, Abbot of Sinai at the time of the creation of the mosaic. Mosaic. Detail of fig. 2.*

16. *The Apostle Andrew. Mosaic. Detail of fig. 2.*

17. *The Apostle Paul. Mosaic. Detail of fig. 2.*

18. *The Apostle Bartholomew. Mosaic. Detail of fig. 2.*

19. *King David. Mosaic. Detail of fig. 2.*

20. *The Theotokos as the 'Burning Bush'. Chapel of St. James the Brother of Christ. Detail of the Bema apse. Mid or second half of the 15th century.*

21. *Bust of Christ. Chapel of St. James the Brother of Christ. Detail of the Bema apse.
Mid or second half of the 15th century.*

22. *The Theotokos 'Platytera'. Chapel of Moses. Detail of the conch.
Mid or second half of the 15th century.*

ΒΑ Ο
CΙ ΡΟ
ΛΕΙ ΦΗ
Ο ΗΙ
C C

ΜΟΥCΗC

23

23. The Prophet Moses.
Chapel of St. James the
Brother of Christ.
Detail of the Bema apse.
Mid or second half of the
15th century.

24. Bust of the Archangel Gabriel. Chapel of the Prophets and Saints. Medallion in the conch of the apse. Middle or second half of the 15th century.

25. Bust of the Prophet Aaron. Chapel of the Prophets and Saints. Medallion in the conch of the apse. Middle or second half of the 15th century.

ICONS

# ICONS

Pious pilgrims who journeyed to Sinai from East and West, in the accounts of their visits, single out the wonders of the Holy Monastery, among which a special place is given to the icons. Some pilgrims speak of miracle - working icons set in the *iconostasis* or on the *proskynetarion* or on the walls of the basilica and in the various chapels that mark the way to the summit. Others are impressed by the icon-menologia that hang on the columns of the nave of the *katholikon*, placed over the relics of saints which are set in the columns. Many of these pilgrims carried with them an icon, made in a distant land, as a gift to the Monastery; it was presented as offering seeking a favour from the Saint, or as a thanksgiving for a favour already received. In other cases, icons were presented as a sign of the supplicant's perpetual presence on holy ground. Of course, not every icon was the gift of a pilgrim. For, in the days of Justinian, when the Monastery was founded, icons must have been sent from Constantinople for the liturgical needs of the monks. Icons must have also been produced in the Monastery for the same reasons. But the growth of Sinai's fame brought about an increase in the number of icons collected in the Monastery. For the monks, donors, and pilgrims all these icons were neither works to be displayed for their aesthetic values nor documents of patronage. They were objects of cult which reflected God's beauty and splendour. Above all it was the liturgical function of the icon that was stressed by the monks. For, while the apse of the katholikon was decorated with splendid mosaics (see Mosaics, fig. 2), the walls were left blanc in order to receive not mosaics nor frescoes but icons. Indeed the north and south walls of the basilica are covered with icons. Among them the large icons were not to be removed from the walls but the smaller ones, arranged in rows, could be taken down as the need arose, and be placed on the proskynetarion. The monks and the faithful could meditate on the icons on the walls and at the same time could venerate the icon of the day.

## EARLY ICONS AT SINAI (FROM THE 6th TO THE 11th CENTURY)

### THE IMPORTANCE OF EARLY ICONS

The veneration of the icons, closely related to the cult of martyrs, had already begun in the Early Church despite theological conflicts, for it took some time for the Church to finally accept the image as an essential component of the new faith. By the 6th century the icons were established and, above all, icons 'not made by human hands' had been accepted. Soon thereafter, religious and political reasons and conflicts of nationalities brought about the well-known iconoclastic controversy which opened in 726 and lasted nearly 120 years.

Sinai, however, being in Islamic territory since about 640, was not touched by the iconoclastic decrees of the Byzantine emperors. During this period, when in Byzantium the icons were destroyed and their worshippers severely punished, icons continued to be produced in Sinai and in surrounding territories, especially in Palestine. Here a school of icon painting existed, the centre of which must have been Jerusalem. After all it was here in the Monastery of Saint Sabbas that Saint John of Damascus declared his war against the Iconoclasts and wrote his famous treatise on the defence of the icons.

There is no other icon collection outside Sinai that enables us to study in an uninterrupted way the icons from the 6th century to the present. The earliest icons, dating from before Iconoclasm, are from Sinai. They are executed in the *encaustic* technique, i.e. the technique of hot wax paint. White wax — mixed with coloured powder — was made up into cakes which, when about to be applied, were melted on heated metal palettes. The coloured wax was laid on with a brush, but when it grew cold it set quickly and it was re-touched with moderately hot irons, which fused the tints. The technique enjoyed great favour in the Hellenistic world, and it was beautifully applied on the mummy portraits. These icons make a most important contribution to the study of icon painting and to the history of the veneration of the icons.

Paradoxically the triumph of Orthodoxy in 843 which restored the cult of icons and had enormous ramifications for the development of Byzantine civilization — Constantinople became the most important city in the world — did not have a great impact on Sinai. Icons from the 9th and 10th centuries are not numerous. The 11th century, however, is marked by a large number of calendar icons, menologia. They contain minute scenes or figures and are coupled with inscriptions which prove that these icons are closely related to manuscript illumination. They are splendid examples of the interrelationship of the media and of the importance illustrated manuscripts had for the transmission of themes and styles. Later periods, dealt with elsewhere in this book, reflect artistic and historical changes that occurred in Byzantium in general and in Sinai in particular.

For a long time the scholarly world knew only four encaustic icons, which were taken from Sinai —they are now in Kiev — by the Russian archimandrite Porphyrius Uspenskij in mid-19th century, along with leaves from manuscripts and complete codices. The first, however, who drew proper attention to the large number of icons in Sinai and who published many of their inscriptions was the Greek scholar Constantinos Amantos. He was followed by two other great scholars, George and Maria Soteriou who were invited by the Monastery in 1938 to study the icon treasures. The result of their labour was a two-volume work published in Athens in 1956 and 1958. It was this book that attracted the American scholar Kurt Weitzmann who prompted the Universities of Michigan, Princeton and Alexandria to undertake a series of campaigns for the study of Sinaitic monuments with the participation of Greek scholars, including Dr. Manolis Chatzidakis. Kurt Weitzmann has already published one volume on the early icons, and a second volume is to appear soon.

## THE HOLY PORTRAITS

It seems that the first icons created were portraits of holy persons honoured, however, not as common portraits representing a person in the corruptible state of his flesh, but images showing man partaking of divine life. They represent Christ, His Mother, Apostles and saints — all manifestations of the mystery of the Incarnation and its great meaning for man.

In an encaustic panel, from the first half of the 6th century, we have a bust-portrait of Christ Pantocrator (figs. 1, 2). Christ is represented holding a jewel-studded Gospel book, and blessing. The artist has set the bust against a niche which creates the impression of atmospheric space. The type depicted here is characterized by full, parted hair falling on the left shoulder, and a rounded beard. According to tradition, the features of Christ on icons go back to miraculously formed images such as the cloth of Kamouliani in Cappadocia. The type, however, in our icon seems to be associated with the emperor, for it was used on imperial works and on the coinage of the 6th and 7th centuries. It may well reflect a famous icon of Christ of the Chalke Gate as Chatzidakis, who first studied this icon properly, has proposed.

The icon, a Constantinopolitan product, is the work of a great artist. Christ's eyes are not fixed on a particular point and He appears to be removed from ordinary reality into a realm of timelessness, a way by which Christ's divine nature is expressed. But naturalistic details, such as the raised eyebrows, make clear reference to the human nature of Christ. These characteristics are found in later representations of this type.

Christ is shown as the God-Man, according to the doctrine of Chalcedon, the Almighty who holds everything in His hand. Although the inscription $\varphi\iota\lambda\acute{a}\nu\theta\rho\omega\pi\sigma\varsigma$ 'the lover of man' is a later addition (the original may have not been inscribed), the artist has conveyed the meaning of this epithet in his rendering.

The type and its imperial connection may strengthen the view that this icon may well be a gift of Justinian or of his court to the Monastery. Remarkable for its artistic quality, the icon invites the faithful to *walk with Him for ever in the glory of His face* (cf. Triodion, p. 77).

But early enough Sinai began receiving pious gifts from devoted Christians from areas other than Constantinople and the imperial court. In another encaustic icon, from the early part of the 7th century, we see another iconographic type of Christ (fig. 3). He is represented enthroned, seated on an arc of heaven, a brightly coloured rainbow, resting His feet on a globe according to Isaiah (66:1, *the heaven is my throne, and the earth is my footstool*), and within a mandorla which is carried by the four cherubim of the Prophet Ezekiel (10:12) of which only one, on the upper left, has been preserved. The inscription indicates the type as *Christ E[mma]nouel*, that is the incarnate Word of God. But in Early Christian and Byzantine art this type is represented as a young, beardless, beautiful Greek hero.

The apparent change here conveys rich dogmatic ideas. In fact the image presents not one but three manifestations of Christ; the white hair is that of the Ancient of Days, the pose is that of Christ Pantocrator, the inscription refers to the eternally young Christ, the Incarnate Logos. The dogmatic idea of the homoousian nature of the Father and the Son is also suggested. The glory, carried by the cherubim, relates to the visions of the Prophets Isaiah and Ezekiel which entered the iconographic programmes of Christian art in the form of a *Majestas Domini*, an apocalyptic theme which came to be related to the Eucharistic Liturgy and found a place in the apses of Early Christian churches. These three manifestations of Christ are represented separately in illustrated Byzantine Gospels.

The body is imposing, the folds are deep and wide. The effect is hieratic. The style suggests, perhaps, an Egyptian origin. The icon was presented as a gift by an unknown, pious pilgrim, who cited his prayer on the frame of the icon: *for the salvation and remission of sins of Thy servant and Christ loving...* The name is lost.

The Saviour of the World was born of a Virgin. Her image holding the infant Child became the most common subject on icons. In a well-known, repeatedly published encaustic icon, Mary, holding the infant Christ in her lap, is represented enthroned between two military saints who may be identified, according to their types: the one without a beard as Saint George, and the other as Saint Theodore Stratelates (fig. 4). Behind the throne two angels holding sceptres turn their head upwards to the hand of God from which issue rays of light on Mary's head. There is a rich architectural background and a small segment of blue sky above it.

In this hieratic composition we see a Constantinopolitan work, most likely of the 6th century, and possibly another imperial gift to the Monastery. Compositions with Mary flanked by saints and angels already existed by the 6th century. But here the unknown artist has moved the angels to the background. Mary's eyes turn away from the beholder. She is thus removed from everyday reality, while her movement contrasts to the frontality of the military saints. At the same time the infant Christ, placed at the very centre of the icon, presents a contrast between the childlike body and the mature head, a way by which the doctrine of the two natures of Christ is represented. Furthermore, Mary's body is dematerialized suggesting her divinity. But the angels in their white, shimmering garments, are rendered as ethereal beings, directly based on classical antique models, thus revealing the strong continuity of the Hellenistic tradition, enhanced by the imperial splendour seen in the sumptuous garments.

One of the earliest representations of Peter is found in an encaustic icon on Sinai (fig. 5). He is shown in bust form, holding the keys and a cross-staff, placed before a niche in a very dark olive colour serving as a background for his garments. On the upper zone there are three medallions with Christ in the centre, Mary to the right, and a youthful Saint, probably John the Evangelist, to the left. These three medallions may allude to the Crucifixion, an idea suggested by the huge cross around the head of Christ. The cross-staff in Peter's hands may refer to his own death on the cross. George and Maria Soteriou have pointed out the relationship of this composition to the 6th-century consular diptychs, Christ taking the place of the emperor. It has also been suggested that the artist, following the hierarchical arrangement of the diptychs, has stressed the position of Peter who is placed after Mary and John the Evangelist. The familiarity of the people with consular diptychs and imperial iconography would have made the meaning of the icon clear.

The various brush techniques, the effect of flickering surfaces, and the smooth transition in the varieties of red in the flesh tones, draw the beholder to the face which is calm but at the same time it reveals an inner tension. The icon must have been produced in Constantinople in the latter part of the 6th or at latest the first half of the 7th century.

Peter's compatriot was Philip — both were from Bethesaida — who also became an Apostle. It was his request at the Last Supper that elicited Christ's declaration: *He that hath seen me hath seen the Father... I am in the Father and the Father in me...* (John 14: 8-9). The portrait of Saint Philip is to be seen in an icon from the second half of the 10th century (fig. 14). Standing frontally, he blesses with his right hand and holds a scroll in his left. He is blessed by Christ shown in the upper corner. It is the side glance of Philip that relates the two figures. The striking characteristic of the icon, however, is the rendering of the nimbi by an incised double line against the gold background and by rough surfaces which catch the light. If one moves around the icon, the nimbi seem to rotate. Perhaps this is the earliest example of this technique which, for several centuries to come, was extensively applied on icons. The rendering of the body of the Saint shows a great deal of plasticity and the treatment of the folds with a carving effect reminds one of 10th-century ivories produced in Constantinople where the icon was probably made.

## THE HISTORIES

It was natural for the great events of the Church — the Histories — whether the life of Christ or of His saints, which had already adorned religious buildings and pages of holy books, to find a place in icons. Histories from the Old Testament were the earliest to enter Christian art because their iconography had already been established before the Christians began shaping the iconography of the New Testament. Themes from the Old Testament were seen as prefigurations of the New but they also served to emphasize certain aspects of the Holy — as stated in the liturgical texts repeatedly.

In a 7th-century icon, assigned to Palestine, we see the Three Hebrews in the Fiery Furnace standing in a sea of red flames (fig. 8). The icon is remarkable for its expressive style, most noticeable being the application of white highlights which help the modelling of the body in the Classical manner. The theme, the earliest examples of which are found in the Roman catacombs, is one of the most popular subjects in Early Christian art. Stressing the soteriological aspect of this art, it served as an example of a sign of divine deliverance from the furnace and from the hand of the wicked King. Later, another meaning was given to the theme: according to liturgical texts, the three Hebrews prefigured the Trinity and the Incarnation of Christ.

In the Sinai icon, however, a special place is taken by the angel at the side holding a long staff terminating in a cross which shows that the Three Children were saved by the power of the cross. This particular motif is found in Coptic frescoes in the Saqqara monasteries from the 6th and 7th centuries, and in the famous frescoes from the Faras cathedral in Nubia, now in Khartoum, in which the angel is identified as Michael. The theme has been dealt with by Dr. Karel C. Innemée in an excellent study (*Drie Jongelingen in Khartoum*, University of Leiden, 1981).

The icon, therefore, has preserved a form of iconography that was formed very early in the Christian East and which is very distinct from that found in monuments in the West. Kurt Weitzmann has pointed out a peculiarity in the costume of the Three Children: the vertical, broad, red band, fastened around the neck is not part of the traditional Persian costume worn by the Three Hebrews, but it recalls a monk's megaloschema. This betrays the influence of asceticism which was flourishing in the 7th century.

Sinai has a number of early icons of importance with histories of the New Testament. In a Nativity from the 8th or 9th century, we see the scene of the birth of Christ conflated with the Adoration of the Shepherds on the upper left, and the Bathing of the Child on the left foreground (fig. 6). In a fragmentary inscription Mary is referred to as Η ΑΓΙΑ ΜΑΡΙΑ (Holy Mary), found also in other early icons. The panel has retained several features of Early Christian tradition of which most important is the altar-like manger with a niche reminiscent of the cave sanctuary in Bethlehem where the original altar stood. From there representations of this iconography passed into other objects of which most famous is the painted lid of the reliquary from the Sancta Sanctorum, now in the Vatican, a pilgrim's souvenir from Jerusalem assigned to the 7th century. It is also found in Nubian frescoes, an area in which the Early Christian tradition survived strongly and which had close relations with Jerusalem and Palestine. The Sinai icon belongs to the same area and reflects the same tradition. It is remarkable for the absence of space and the ornamental tapestry-like arrangement of its compositional components. This and other significant subjects from the New Testament underwent liturgical changes (figs. 7, 12) when, for liturgical reasons, a selected repertory of Great Feasts, the *Dodekaorton*, was created. These changes are outlined below.

Another icon with the Crucifixion (fig. 9) depicts Christ wearing a colobium (the red-brown colour is a substitute for purple) between the two thieves, in much smaller scale, named as ΓΕCΤΑC and ΔΗΜΑC. Before the discovery of this icon, these names were known only from later Cappadocian frescoes. Mary, inscribed in a monogram as Η ΑΓΙΑ ΜΑΡΙΑ, does not express a particular grief. The composition includes the narrative episode of the soldiers, depicted in still smaller scale, casting lots for the seamless robe of Christ. This icon has the earliest representation of Christ dead on the cross, and it is the first known example depicting Christ with a crown of thorns. For the first time we have here an image of the suffering Christ Whose blood is also stressed — with eucharistic implications — as it gushes with water from His side and flows on a rock behind Mary.

Stylistic features, above all the faces with piercing eyes, indicate that the icon was made in Palestine in the 8th century. It is related somewhat to the famous Crucifixion found in the Syriac 6th-century codex known as the 'Rabula Gospels', now in Florence.

An icon of the Ascension from the 9th or 10th century belongs to the same Palestinian school of painting (fig. 10). The rendering follows the iconography known in early Christian monuments which have direct relations to the Holy Land, such as the Syriac Rabula Gospels, the 7th-century lid of the reliquary box from the Sancta Sanctorum, now in the Vatican, and the ampullae from the Holy Land.

The Virgin, and the Apostles on either side of her, are witnessing the Ascension of Christ who is carried into heaven (marked by the sun and the moon) by four angels. The composition, however, contains some unusual features. Christ is depicted seated and yet He is floating because the seat, the usual arc of heaven, is not shown. The mandorla takes the form of a metal frame held by the angels. The billowing mantles of the lower angels form a lyre-shaped pattern pointing to the Virgin Mary, a pictorial device by which her position in the theme is emphasized. In addition, her importance is stressed farther by the pearl-studded footstool on which she stands, not required by the event which takes place in the open. Furthermore the Virgin is framed by a bush of flamy, red blossoms. Although trees in the Ascension are found in a Coptic fresco at Bawit, in Saqqara, here these flowers seem to relate to the Burning Bush of Mount Sinai. They foreshadow renderings found in later Sinai icons. Among other early Christian elements is the completion of the inscription. Next to the normal $\overline{\text{IC}}$ $\overline{\text{XC}}$, the Υ(ιὸς) Θ(εοῦ) has been added, which is common in early icons and other objects.

Stylistically, the icon has all the characteristics of the Palestinian school of painting: the colour scheme, the reds and the browns, the peculiar linear highlights and the ornamental stylization. The last feature is best seen in the hems of the garments of the lower angels, and the transformation of the mountains, normally in the background of the composition, into a series of red scales. The theme which has been studied by Nicholas Giolés (originally it may have been created for a monumental composition) relates to the Liturgy of the Ascension. The icon stresses above all the person of the Virgin Mary.

Other early icons in Sinai contain histories not taken from the accounts of the Gospels but from the lives of the saints and the cult of relics. On the right, upper part of an icon consisting of two pieces framed together (originally a triptych), we see the King Abgarus of Edessa holding the Mandelion with the miraculous imprint of Christ's face (fig. 13). Behind Abgarus and to the left stands the messenger Ananias, who brought the Mandelion to Edessa from Jerusalem. The figure corresponding to Abgarus on the left side (the left wing of the original triptych) is the Apostle Thaddaeus who baptized the Edessenes. The lower parts represent standing ascetics: Paul of Thebes and Saint Anthony, the most famous ascetics of Egypt, and Basil the Great with Ephraim the Syrian, ordained deacon of Edessa by Basil. Kurt Weitzmann has made a case for dating the icon to the middle of the 10th century. The historical associations are compelling.

The veneration of the Mandelion began with its rediscovery in 544 and its cult was popularized after the famous relic was transported to Constantinople by the Emperor Romanos I in 944. A year later, on the anniversary of the event, the Emperor Constantine Porphyrogenitos wrote or inspired someone else to write an encomium. The text passed into the Metaphrastian menologion and was illustrated, as shown by extant Greek and Georgian manuscripts, from the 11th century and later. The head of Abgarus is that of a Byzantine emperor, the portrait of Constantine Porphyrogenitos.

The icon was made with the intention of disseminating the idea that Constantine was a pious emperor whose spiritual concern was the collection of famous relics. It is the earliest representation of the Abgarus legend. Abgarus and Thaddaeus are rendered in the Constantinopolitan style. The broader brushstrokes applied on these two figures reflect strongly the Classical tradition. There is nothing, however, Constantinopolitan about the monastic saints below. These relate to Syro-Palestinian works. The icon, based on a Constantinopolitan model, may have been produced as a gift to an eastern monastery, the monastic saints being added for this purpose. Their choice may be explained by their cult in monastic centres, above all in Sinai which may have been the recipient of the icon.

Among the few early icons in Sinai with stories from the lives of the saints, there is one whose subject and style is of special interest. The icon depicts an episode relating to the legend of the martyr Mercurius (fig. 11). A soldier saint who had excelled himself in the battle-field, Mercurius is described in the Synaxarion as a tall, blond, beautiful young man. The painter of the Sinai icon stressed the military costume of the Saint and the cross as a weapon against evil. The Saint with a large head looking directly at the onlooker, clad in full armour, on horse-back, pierces with a long, red cross-lance an enemy whose bleeding head, partly preserved, is shown below the red boots of the Saint. (The icon, discovered in two pieces, has suffered some restoration along the edge of the lower triangle). The order for the killing comes from an angel on the right-hand side of the icon, who holds a long cross-staff. On the opposite side, the hand of God appearing from the sky offers a crown of martyrdom within rays of light. That the Saint has indeed suffered martyrdom is suggested by the string of pearls which he wears on his head. The scene takes place within a landscape in which genre-like elements have been included such as a barking dog between the horse's forelegs, and another quadruped between the hind legs. Stylized bushes complete the landscape, while white rosettes fill the sky above.

The icon represents an episode from the legend of Saint Mercurius, told by Byzantine chroniclers such as Sozomenos and Malalas according to which Mercurius, ordered by Christ, killed Julian the Apostate. The episode was depicted in a narrative fashion in the Chronicles, as relative miniatures in two manuscripts of the Homilies of Gregory Nazianzenus in Paris (cod. gr. 510) and Athos (cod. Panteleimon 6) show. In the icon, the weapon against the evil personified by Julian is the cross which is emphasized by the Saint and by the Angel who gives the order for the killing. In fact we are reminded of the cross held by Michael in the icon of the Three Children in the Furnace (fig. 8).

The extremely decorative character of the icon does not find any contemporary parallel among the Sinai icons. The love for ornament is shown in the design and the special decorative effects such as the dotted, white rosettes in the background, the bright contrasting colours, and the extension of the feeling for the decorative on the frame. Its popular style and iconography finds best parallels in Coptic manuscripts of the 10th century. Most probably the icon was produced in a Coptic atelier at that time.

## ICONS AND THE LITURGY

From the 6th to the 10th century, portraits and histories showed a gradual increase in the influence of the Liturgy and of ritual in general. Since the 10th century, and especially in the 11th century, this tendency becomes very strong. The idea of grouping portraits in one panel or introducing smaller, additional portraits had already appeared in the early centuries. However, this scheme became increasingly common after Iconoclasm. The supplementary portraits were not directly related to the principal portrait, but were there to express theological ideas or as a result of the ritual. Above all, they were arranged in the liturgical order in the manner of the liturgical programmes developed after the triumph of the icons.

The cult of bishop saints became important after Iconoclasm, probably on account of the role played by Constantinopolitan patriarchs against the iconoclasts. More important, however, was the renewal of the Liturgy after 843, which stressed the cult of bishops and saints in general.

One of the most popular bishop saints in the Byzantine Church is Saint Nicholas whose iconography has been studied by Nancy Ševčenko. Represented in bust form, he fills the central part of a Sinai icon (fig. 15). Dressed in bishop's vestments, he holds a large codex in his left hand, while his right hand is before his breast. His large nimbus has been roughened to create a rotating effect, just as the nimbus of the Apostle Philip whose portrait has been discussed above (fig. 14). Ten medallions with saints are set in the gold frame: at the top is Christ between Peter and Paul. At the sides, there are matching pairs, Saint Demetrios and Saint George and below Saint Theodore and Saint Procopios. At the bottom there are three physician Saints, Cosmas and Damian, and Saint Panteleimon. The two first carry instrument cases and the third a golden pyxis. Christ, the Apostles, the military and the physician Saints are represented in the liturgical order of rank and it is this element which shows the impact of the Liturgy. Perhaps this is the earliest icon known with medallions on the frame.

The icon reflects an early type of Saint Nicholas in which the facial features are not as yet fixed to create the stylized, ascetic type known from later icons. The saint has a vivid expression, mainly the result of the different shape of the eyes and of a certain asymmetry in the hair and the beard. The overall impression is that of hieratic dignity combined with spontaneity. The high quality of the style and the brilliant colours of the medallions which imitate the Byzantine cloisonné enamels attest to a Constantinopolitan atelier at the end of the 10th century.

More drastic were the changes brought about in New Testament episodes. From Christ's life a selection was made of certain great events which were of special liturgical or dogmatic significance and which eventually were to form the Twelve Great Feasts, the *Dodekaorton*. In the process these selected scenes were gradually transformed. The transformation took place while the narrative illustrations of the Gospels were changed into the liturgical ones found in the Lectionary.

Sinai has a fragment, the centre of a triptych, which constitutes a collective panel (fig. 7). In three rows, one sees depicted the Nativity, a fragment of the Presentation in the Temple, the Ascension, and the Pentecost. Dating from the second half of the 9th or early 10th century, this fragment in its formal arrangement relates to the famous lid of the reliquary box from the Sancta Sanctorum, now in the Vatican, of the 7th century.

This icon, one of the earliest examples of a collective icon, shows selections of themes, a choice of important compositional elements, the employment of symmetry and other formal means by which the depicted events acquire a hieratic appearance and splendour. There is also a reduction to essentials that gives special meaning to the themes.

Sinai has many collective icons from the late 11th and later centuries with liturgical feasts, as well as individual panels with feasts which can conveniently be displayed on the proskynetarion on the particular feast day. It is in front of this icon that the priest and deacon bow at the beginning of the Liturgy.

It is generally believed that the formation of the fixed cycle of the Twelve Great Feasts took place in the 10th century. From the first half of this century Sinai has only one panel depicting the Washing of the Feet (fig. 12). It illustrates the lection for Maunday Thursday, a theme that is not always part of the Dodekaorton. Christ, in imperial-purple and blue garments, stretches His hands towards Peter, but does not attempt to wash Peter's feet, who protests strongly. One iconographic peculiarity is the wall in the foreground and the door which is common in representations of the Incredulity of Thomas.

This icon belongs to the rich collection of numerous iconostasis beams in Sinai with the Twelve Great Feasts and a Deesis in the centre. It is the earliest known iconostasis example with the depiction of one of the liturgical feasts. The icon displays the Classical style in the proportions, the strong modelling of the heads and the highlights on the drapery. And yet the linearity of these highlights does not enhance the modelling of the bodies, while the grouping of the Apostles is rather rigid and archaic. The icon betrays the influence of the Macedonian Renaissance movement, so strong in Constantinople in the 10th century, but it was not executed in the capital.

The Church, in addition to the movable feasts has also the feasts of fixed days, beginning September 1. This fixed calendar comprises the *Menologion* which is one of the most important liturgical books. Prior to the 10th century the Menologion contained a selection of the lives of certain saints, which in illuminated manuscripts were illustrated by extensive narrative cycles. Towards the end of the 10th century, Symeon Metaphrastes compiled the Lives of Saints with the intention of having one life for each day of the ecclesiastical year. This meant a reduction of the illustration, usually a portrait at the beginning and the martyrdom at the end. This mode invaded icon painting at the time and Sinai has the largest and oldest collection of calendar icons which reach back almost to the time of their invention at the end of the 10th and the beginnings of the 11th century. In these calendars standing saints and scenes of martyrdom agree in iconography and style with corresponding miniatures in illustrated Menologia and it may well be that the icons copied manuscripts. The idea, however, to collect the saints in one panel may have been realized first in the icons for liturgical reasons. A collective panel enables the faithful to meditate on the lives of the saints of a whole month. Furthermore the expansion of a collective panel to the size of a polyptych — and Sinai has many polyptych icons from the 11th century — probably took place in the 11th century in order to accomodate the increasingly elaborate liturgical programmes.

As an example of these calendars, we reproduce here a menologion from the second half of the 11th century which is made from a set of four icons. It contains the saints for every day of the year, each panel having saints for three months. In the leaf shown here (fig. 16) we see the saints of September, beginning with the portrait of Saint Symeon Stylites (September 1), October and November. Certain feasts are clearly distinguished despite the minuteness of execution. For example, the Miracle of the Archangel Michael at Chonae and the Birth of the Virgin Mary (September 6 and 8, upper row), the Elevation of the Cross (September 14, second row), and the Entrance of the Virgin into the Temple (November 21, last row). The martyrs are decapitated or crucified or put to death through various tortures. Saints and scenes are depicted directly on the gold ground without any essential suggestion of locality or landscape. Iconography, style and minuteness of execution have direct relation to illuminated manuscripts of the 11th century. The colours are bright, the tones are rich as in Constantinopolitan manuscripts of the second half of the 11th century, which apparently have provided models for the icon. This and other icons of the period have inscriptions in Greek and Iberian (i.e. Georgian) giving the date, the name and the type of martyrdom a saint had suffered. These inscriptions speak of the colony of Iberian monks settled in Sinai during the 10th and 11th centuries. From an epigram running on the back of the four leaves, we learn that it was the work of a painter by the name of John.

Another icon in the form of a diptych, from the second half of the 11th century, represents the menologion of the entire year. Astonishing for the minuteness of execution, it combines the saints of the year with an image of Christ and the Virgin Glykophilousa, both within gold discs on the very top, surrounded by the Great Feasts in medallions, declaring the mystery of faith (fig. 17). The saints of each day are represented in groups of three with clarity. The monotony is interrupted by Church feasts, especially those relating to Mary, or by larger groups of martyrs such as the Forty Martyrs of Sebasteia (first row of the right wing). The feasts follow the sequence of the calendar. Some have a special place in the life of the Church and are easily recognizable. Such is the Elevation of the Cross (September 14, first row of the left wing). This composition is dense but the double cross, a symbol of victory, raised by the patriarch in the ambo of the Church of Saint Sophia, is distinctly depicted. The representation of this liturgical ceremony gained popularity from the 10th century and above all in the 11th century as a result of the strong impact of the Liturgy on Byzantine art. Distinguished is also Mary the Egyptian, a great symbol of repentance and asceticism (second row, right wing). The diptych, important for its iconography, execution and its relation to illuminated manuscripts, probably belongs to the area of Constantinopolitan art.

In these and the other numerous Sinai menologia, the iconographic subjects reflect in many ways liturgical programmes in monumental art. These icons, therefore, exemplify the interplay of book illumination, icon painting and monumental art — all stressing the liturgical aspect of Byzantine art. There are other, later icons in Sinai, which present the liturgical order in which holy images of saints and feasts are placed in church decoration, and show the development of liturgical programmes which were systematized in the 11th century, although they were not invented at the time.

The miniature-like style and the liturgical character so strong in these 11th-century menologia are not exclusive features of this century. An early 12th-century icon illustrates the persistence of these trends and brings this chapter to its conclusion. This panel, originally part of a triptych from the Constantinopolitan area, depicts the story of the Birth and Infancy of Christ (fig. 18) and is iconographically most important. The birth is in the very centre of the upper part of the panel, framed by the Annunciation to the Shepherds and the Adoration of the Magi. Above, two choirs of angels headed by two Archangels in imperial costumes — a reflection of the Divine Majesty — stress the liturgical character of the Christmas feast picture. Below, a series of scenes depict the Departure of the Magi, the Dream of Joseph, the Flight into Egypt, which includes on the left three youths carrying the luggage, two of whom may be the sons of Joseph by an earlier marriage mentioned in the apocryphal Gospel of James, the Flight of Elisabeth with the infant John hidden on a mountain, and finally the Massacre of the Innocents. All these episodes pictorialized the lections for December 26 and 29 and parallels are found in illustrated Lectionaries of the

11th century. The manner by which the landscape is formed isolates the episodes and betrays the efforts of an icon painter copying an illuminated manuscript. These episodes derive from the apocryphal Gospels of James and of Pseudo-Matthew which influenced the liturgical texts followed by the icon with clarity and simplicity.

The choirs of angels express the joy which fills the Christmas liturgy: *Rejoice universe, when you hear it heralded: with the angels and the shepherds, glorify Him who chose to be seen as a new-born Babe, while remaining God in all eternity.* Angels and men rejoice because earth and heaven are united on Christmas day. The episode of the Bathing of the Child, below the cave, represented as a genre scene, testifies to Christ being indeed the Son of Man and at the same time the Messiah who at last has come. The Gospels do not mention the cave. On the contrary, the apocryphal Gospels and tradition, that found a place in the liturgical texts, speak of the mysterious depths of the earth and provide a striking interpretation of the icon. The dark opening of the cave is Hades. Mystically the Birth of Christ includes heaven and hell. This is a direct reference to Christ's Descent into Hell and a definition of the plan of God in history. But also the placing of the Infant in the darkness of the cave makes a reference to the prologue of the fourth Gospel: *And the light shineth in darkness, and the darkness comprehended it not* (John 1:5). A complete analysis of the icon cannot be attempted here. I can only suggest that the icon is a form of pictorial theology which became richer in the course of centuries through the continuing impact of the Liturgy upon the piety of the people.

This icon-anthology has not exhausted the treasures of early icons or fully unlocked their secrets. It has been only an attempt to make the reader conscious of their beauty and manifold importance. From the time of Justinian to the end of the 11th century icons were presented to Sinai as gifts, but icons were also produced in the Monastery. These icons have displayed a wide range of expression, reflecting different dates and localities which speak of the cosmopolitan character of Sinai, being the focal point for pilgrims. With the exception of icons going back to the days of the foundation of the Monastery, most other early icons relate to Syro-Palestinian icon painting. Other, Post-Iconoclastic icons seem to have combined the elegance and brilliance of the art of Constantinople with the austere rules of a monastic tradition. These should most probably be recognized as the output of icon painters working in Sinai, who resumed contact with artistic movements in the capital. Regardless their origin and different artistic tastes, all these icons have a common point of contact. They are cult objects created for the glory of God, mirrors of the beauty of God. They tell us the early history of the veneration of the images of Christ and of His saints, in which the Church worships the risen Lord and looks towards His Kingdom which is not of this world. They present to us early compositions which have remained unaltered since a dogmatic truth has been established. We see icons reflecting the liturgical programmes set out on the walls of churches and showing the close interplay of the arts, all of which serve the Liturgy. By the 11th century all these trends have been fully established. Above all, these treasures, going back to the earliest ages of the Church, are testimonies to a life of prayer. Their significance for our century and for centuries to come cannot be fully understood. For in them there is a reality in which one discerns dimly the mysterious form of the Kingdom of God.

# ICONS FROM THE 12th TO THE 15th CENTURY

Icons at St. Catherine's at Sinai bear witness to the long history of the Monastery, as determined by its geographic position in the desert, where, according to tradition, the Law was given to Moses. A centre of asceticism for centuries, this area was noted for the co-mingling of peoples of different religions and homelands. Sinai has the richest collection of icons in a Greek monastery, not only in number and in chronological range, but also in the variety of stylistic expression, proof of the far-reaching influence of this religious centre. The collection of icons at Sinai offers invaluable evidence for the history of the Monastery and Eastern monasticism in general, for the development of Byzantine and Post-Byzantine painting and, more broadly, for artistic activity in the Eastern Mediterranean. It gives us a unique opportunity to examine with new criteria the complex problems which concern the relationships of the peripheral centres to Constantinople and to each other.

The division of the Sinai icons for analysis is not an easy one since the creators of these works, members of the monastic community or secular professionals who came from outside, rarely ignored the older icons housed in the Monastery. In all periods they had the opportunity to examine and receive inspiration from even the Pre-Iconoclastic icons which were preserved in the Monastery as a result of its location and, also, to some extent, due to historical chance. Rarely has an icon remained untouched by the brothers of the Monastery in more recent times, which is not surprising if we take into consideration that a preoccupation with artistic activity was natural within monastic circles. It is significant that the oldest name of an icon painter preserved among the works of the Monastery is that of the monk Ioannis.[1] Of the painters who left traces on the icons of Sinai, perhaps the most unfortunate case is that of the Cretan painter of the 18th century, Ioannis Kornaros, who lived for some time in the Monastery. Kornaros left an original work, but he also devoted himself to the 're-aging' of icons, by painting new representations on older layers, changing the signatures of the painters and severely meddling with the inscriptions.[2] By contrast, the monk Pachomios, who died in 1960, restored a number of damaged icons in a more appropriate manner, often inspired by the related genuine works preserved in the Monastery.[3]

The icons from the 12th through the 15th centuries preserved at Sinai may be attributed to Greek painters who came to the edges of the Sinai desert either from the central cultural region of Byzantium, or from the Orthodox communities of the Near East. A fair number of icons are works of painters of ethnic groups other than Greek, who belonged to the Christian minorities within the broad area dominated by Islam. But a portion of the icons housed in the Monastery, which are datable mainly to the second half of the 13th century, acquires a special character due to osmosis from Western art.[4] It remains problematic whether these works were painted by Western artists, or whether the majority should be attributed to Eastern 'borrowers' from Western art. The latter idea is plausible since a number of centres of icon production had already developed in the Eastern Mediterranean during the period of the Latin Occupation.

The numerous icons with Western elements in the Monastery present several variations. If one hesitates to accept the opinion that these works were painted at Sinai by Westerners, there are still several problems which remain open regarding the identity of the painters and their origins. Due to historical circumstances, the Monastery was forced to entertain dialogue not only with Greek Orthodox Byzantium and its diaspora, but with peoples of various ethnic groups and different religions. The Monastery maintained ties with the

Crusaders of Palestine and, according to one theory, the Orthodox archbishop of Sinai was a suffragan of the Latin bishop of Petra.[5] Relations with the Christian Syrian and Arab communities of the Near East, from which monks had been drawn in certain periods, were much closer. The Monastery of Sinai was in close contact with the great urban centres of Palestine and Syria, where it had important metochia. Thus, one would expect artistic connections mainly with Jerusalem and Damascus.[6] Since the Western presence in Syria and Palestine was long-term and had created a suitable climate for the intermingling of elements from the Byzantine, Islamic, and Western traditions, familiarity with the painting produced in these areas is very useful for the study of the Sinai icon collection, especially from the 13th century. The fact that the Greek Patriarchate of Jerusalem possesses only one icon which may be attributed to the 'Crusader' group (most probably of Sinaitic origin in view of its iconography – Moses before the Burning Bush), does not assist in the study of this problematic material.[7] Until now, only Cyprus has preserved convincing evidence of being a centre of icon production with a special character during this period. Certain Sinai icons suggest very close ties to this island, easily understandable in view of the properties held there by the Monastery.[8] Another centre that may have had organized ateliers of icon production in the 13th century is Crete, which had already emerged as an important centre of artistic activity in this period, as evidenced by its monumental painting, although no icons datable before the 14th century have been identified there. The Sinai Monastery maintained even closer relations with this island than with Cyprus, as seen from the extensive properties which it possessed there.[9]

In order to discover the provenance of these 13th-century icons, the evidence of the language of inscriptions must be taken into consideration as well. From the 12th until the first half of the 15th century, few Sinai icons bear inscriptions in foreign languages. Latin inscriptions are found on only four icons, Latin and Greek on three, Arabic, only as a translation of Greek inscriptions, in rare works, Syriac in one case, Georgian and Greek inscriptions in two instances.[10] Even icons with annotations in a foreign language (this has been noted only with Arabic) are extremely limited.[11] It is important to take into consideration that a large percentage of the icons of the so-called 'Crusader' group do not contain inscriptions on the open ruled scrolls held by the saints. Moreover, in many cases inscriptions seem to have been applied in a later period. One final observation is related to the writing of Greek in the inscriptions, where, unquestionably, the misspellings and poor syntax often surpass the limits of toleration. It would be risky, however, to attribute this phenomenon in all cases to painters or scribes of a different ethnic group. We must not forget in this context that the monks of Sinai were multilingual.[12]

If we take into account the intrinsic characteristics of portable icons from the Byzantine period proper, it is not surprising that only in rare cases do the Sinai icons present evidence concerning their donors. Twice in the 13th century the Archbishop of Sinai can be identified as the donor of an icon.[13] In a number of examples the donor is a monk, undoubtedly a member of the Sinaitic community.[14] In a few instances the donors are laymen.[15] In at least four instances, the donor can be considered a member of a non-Greek ethnic group on grounds of his costume or name.[16] Only once can the commission of the work be safely attributed to a woman.[17] Of special interest are the few icons which name as donors the painters who created them. The oldest example may be attributed to the monk Ioannis. Other examples preserve the names Stephanos[18] or Petros,[19] both laymen.

The 12th, 13th, and 14th centuries constitute exceptionally fertile periods in the history of the Monastery with regard to icon painting. The variety of material in form, scale, and subject matter reveals the role of the Monastery as a great pilgrimage centre of the East. At the same time, it shows the continually rising importance which icons held in the Church in relation to the Liturgy and to various ceremonies and, also, their function in private devotion. Kurt Weitzmann has recently observed that many icons of the Monastery constituted iconographic programmes for specific needs in the main area of the katholikon, in its chapels, as well as in the remaining chapels inside and outside the walls of the Monastery.[20] It should be pointed out that, with the exception of the mosaics in the Bema, very little monumental decoration was employed. Consequently, in many cases portable icons took the place of mosaics and mural painting.

An impressive number of small-scale panels can be considered as works meant for private devotion or as small proskynesis icons to be used within the church. Diptychs, triptychs and polyptychs, which are especially suited to complex iconographic programmes, are also well represented. The liturgical aspect of the iconographic programme of several of these works might indicate that they were not intended for private use but were employed by the monk-priests of Sinai in their frequent visits to the various *kathismata* around the Monastery in order to perform the Liturgy on Sundays and on major feast days.[21]

The production of icons at Sinai increased dramatically in certain periods. Contributing factors to this artistic blossoming were a climate of greater security and economic prosperity, as well as the world-wide interest of Christians in the pilgrimage sites of the Near East following the Crusades. In addition, the creative initiative of certain remarkable bishops of Sinai unquestionably influenced icon production. However, the rise in the international prestige of the Monastery was associated preeminently with the translation of the relics of Saint Catherine to the Sinai Monastery, an event dated in the 10th century. The Monastery of the Virgin, which was dedicated in Her honour by its founder, the Emperor Justinian, broadened its authority in the East and in the West at about the time when it became known as the Monastery of Saint Catherine in the 13th century.[22] Besides Saint Catherine, the Monastery renders special honour to the Virgin and to Moses.

Some representative works at the Monastery of Sinai will be discussed in chronological sequence. It is, however, necessary to take into consideration that the material often presents special problems as far as dating is concerned, due to the conservative character of this artistic medium. Historical circumstances heightened this conservative nature since, during certain periods, as already mentioned, the Monastery was obliged to suspend contacts with the outside world. Thus those who worked there were frequently encouraged to reproduce older models from the rich Sinai collection. None of the large number of icons in the Monastery from before the Fall of Constantinople preserves a date. The few icons with portraits of archbishops of Sinai and their names do not help at present to date the works more precisely, due to the absence of information associated with bishops of certain periods. On the whole, very few icons may be dated on the basis of identifiable historical personalities.[23] The dating of this varied material depends on iconographic and stylistic analysis and, to a small degree, on the paleographic examination of inscriptions, since technical information regarding the recent conservation work applied to a large number of icons is still not available to scholars.

## ICONS OF THE 12th CENTURY

The icons of the 12th century in the Monastery form a considerable group in comparison to those preserved from earlier periods. However, the picture of artistic creation during the first phase of the Comnenian period based on the extant icons remains unclear, even though the group may be enlarged by several icons which have been frequently dated to the second half of the 11th century. With few exceptions, the icons of the 12th century at Sinai follow contemporary developments in Byzantine painting, as introduced by Constantinople. This is explained by the close ties which the Monastery maintained with the capital during the Comnenian period.[24] It is uncertain whether some works were painted at Sinai by artists from Constantinople, or whether they were commissions or gifts from the capital. The first hypothesis is supported by the presence of one detail which is the most characteristic technical feature of Byzantine icons painted at Sinai from the 10th until the 13th century, and which has not thus far been noted on icons from other centres. This technique involved creating a special reflection of light on the gold background by the use of a compass equipped with a small brush. Another interesting technical component is the standardized painted decoration on the reverse side of the icons, usually comprising alternating bands of wavy brushstrokes, red and blue-black, in many works of the 12th and 13th centuries in the Monastery.[25] The choice of iconographic subjects, the unity of style and the need to follow certain dimensions as determined by the function of the icons, support the hypothesis that many of these panels were produced at Sinai. Works painted by members of foreign Christian communities of the Near East, or even by Western artists are not easily identifiable among the 12th-century material in the Monastery.

As for the function of the 12th-century icons, it is evident that a significant number of works played a specific role in direct connection to the performance of the Liturgy and to further church ceremonies. To this period can be dated several of the most important iconostasis beams, with the Deesis, the Dodekaorton and other scenes, including episodes from the lives of the saints. To this period also belong icons of the Menologion and also individual panels with Dodekaorton scenes not belonging to the epistyle of the templon.

The earliest example of a Virgin of the Kykkotissa type (fig. 19)[26] ranks among the most distinguished Comnenian icons in terms of its comprehensive theological content and artistic quality. The Virgin and Child are surrounded by Christ in Glory, John the Theologian, John the Baptist, Paul and Peter, Moses, Jacob, Aaron, Zechariah, Anna, Elisabeth, David, Isaiah, Ezekiel, Daniel, Habakkuk, Solomon, Balaam and Gideon. Joseph, Adam and Eve, and Ioakeim and Anna occupy privileged positions below the Virgin and Child. From an iconographic viewpoint the work is pioneering, since it epitomizes the mystery of the Incarnation with its redemptive power for mankind through the inclusion of Old and New Testament figures that played an important part in its realization. The passages which have been written on their scrolls[27] and the depiction of some of the symbols of the Old Testament (the Burning Bush of Moses, the Ladder of Jacob, the Gate of Ezekiel etc.) clarify the meaning of the composition. The sophisticated iconography of the work suggests a dating to at least the first half of the 12th century. The icon reflects, moreover, contemporary stylistic trends in Constantinople and may be attributed to the sphere of its artistic influence.[28]

The oldest examples of painted iconostasis beams preserved in the Monastery are datable to the 12th century. In the development of the form of the Byzantine templon, iconostasis beams (also known as epistyle icons) painted on wooden boards took the place of analogous works of marble or still richer materials. These panels formed the uppermost register of the architectural screen which divides the Sanctuary from the nave in the Orthodox church. From the 12th century onwards, the typical subject matter of the painted epistyles consisted of scenes from the Twelve Great Feasts of Orthodoxy, the so-called *Dodekaorton* (Annunciation, Nativity, Presentation in the Temple, Baptism, Transfiguration, Raising of Lazarus, Entry into Jerusalem, Crucifixion, Anastasis, Ascension, Pentecost, and the Dormition of the Virgin). The scenes are evenly grouped on the right and left of the Deesis. According to the desired dimensions in each case, the subject matter could be broadened by the addition of more Christological scenes, important scenes from the life of the Virgin, Archangels, the Apostles Peter and Paul, and hagiographic portraits. The Deesis and associated scenes are normally represented under painted arches. It is almost certain that the iconostasis beams which are extant at Sinai were painted at the Monastery. Ten of them, which are datable from the 12th to the 15th centuries, are preserved in their entirety or in sections.

Among the earliest examples of iconostasis beams is a relatively small work in two sections, with the Deesis and eleven scenes, mostly posthumous miracles of Saint Eustratios (figs. 20-22).[29] These scenes include two healing miracles of persons suffering from a prolonged fever, two healings of insane persons, a scene of the expulsion from the church of a money changer who hindered the chanting of the orthros hymns, an episode involving youths striking the bells on the feast day of the Saint, an undecipherable scene with the Saint on horseback, the healing of the daughter of Synglitiki, the healing of a nun, the healing of a woman who was mute and motionless (in this case by the entire group of the Holy Five), as well as the healing of a man who suffered from tetanus. These miracles, for which the corresponding hagiographic text has still not been discovered, are accomplished by the epiphany of the Saint, usually due to the beneficent presence of his relics in the cult centre of the Holy Five of Armenia at Sebasteia in Asia Minor. The cycle of the miracles of this beam attests to the protective role of saints in medieval society, especially that of a healer. Moreover, the scenes provide specialized information on everyday life in Byzantium regarding secular attire and the interior decoration of private dwellings. The beam is of very high quality, especially the left section; the right section is clearly the work of another painter. The colours, with many reds and deep blues, are in keeping with the Comnenian aesthetic. This iconostasis beam, the only surviving one with a saint's life as its only subject matter, may be dated to the second half of the 12th century. In all likelihood, it was made to be used in the Chapel of the Monastery dedicated to the Holy Five of Armenia, among whom Saint Eustratios held the leading position.[30] The measurements of the iconostasis beam match the dimensions of the Chapel of the Holy Five within the walls of the Monastery. Technical details, such as the reflection of light on the gold in the nimbi and in specific areas of the background, as well as the painted decoration on the reverse side, also confirm that this work was painted at Sinai.

The left and central portions of another iconostasis beam, originally in three sections, are preserved in the Monastery (figs. 25-27).[31] The subject matter originally comprised the Deesis, two scenes from the Life of the Virgin (her Birth and Presentation), and the Dodekaorton. As opposed to the Saint Eustratios iconostasis beam, this work was quite large, and was probably used on the main templon of the basilica. This iconostasis beam illustrates one of the leading trends in the painting of Constantinople in the last quarter of the 12th century. An important characteristic of this trend is the gracefulness of the figures, achieved through the balanced combination of drawing and colour. At the same time, a somewhat manneristic feeling is conveyed by the rendering of details of architectural background and landscape, which create an artificial atmosphere.

Another section of an iconostasis beam (figs. 31-33), which in its entirety comprises the Deesis, the Birth of the Virgin, the Presentation of the Virgin, and the Dodekaorton,[32] exhibits a more pioneering style than that of the preceding works. It reveals an unusual handling of colour and light and a marked painterly approach in the brushwork, which has not yet been noticed in any other portable icon of the Middle Byzantine period. Great importance is given to the landscape, while the architectural background is played down. The colours are considerably removed from Comnenian pictorial examples which gave the immediate impression of luxury works, such as enamel. In this work, on the other hand, the orange and brown mountains with their 'snowy' peaks, the light blue of the water and of the garments, and the radiant pink often used for fabrics convey a modern approach. Due to the nervous brushstrokes, the painted surface vibrates with flowing energy. At the same time, the spiritual quality, which is usually conveyed by human faces in Byzantine painting, has given way to a much more mundane psychological expression. It is very likely that this iconostasis beam was painted toward the end of the 12th century, perhaps close to 1200.

Among small icons with a subject matter appropriate for placement on the *proskynetarion* (icon stand) on the day of the corresponding feast, is included a panel with the theme of the Miracle at Chonae (fig. 23).[33] This took place at the most important cult centre of the Archangel Michael at Kolossae or Chonae in Phrygia in Asia Minor, where a church dedicated to him was built next to the holy water of a spring, which had healing properties. The intervention of the Archangel was provoked by the pagans ('Hellenizontes'), who attempted to destroy the church by diverting a river towards it. The scene illustrates the moment when the Archangel appeared and stemmed the flow of the water before the eyes of the astonished monk Archippos, founder of the church. This work, with its slender, ethereal figures, the graceful poses and gestures, and especially the refined harmony of colours, may be counted among the masterpieces of the Late Comnenian period, and epitomizes the aristocratic trend which characterizes Byzantine painting of that time.

The icon of the Heavenly Ladder (fig. 24),[34] belongs to the group of didactic works that derived elements from the monastic literature which blossomed in the Monastery of Sinai from an early period. A major author was John Climacus, the 7th-century Abbot whose name is derived from his well-known treatise for the moral perfection of monks, the *Heavenly Ladder.* In order to reach the goal of heaven, the monks must acquire thirty virtues which are presented in metaphorical form as the equivalent number of rungs of a ladder. The composition on this panel is the earliest extant pictorial example of this metaphor for the code of perfection of monastic life on a portable icon. The struggle of the monks for moral perfection and the resulting heavenly salvation is demonstrated to be difficult and often unattainable. The only certain victors are John Climacus himself at the top of the ladder and the Archbishop Antonios of Sinai behind him.[35] The dematerialization of the figures in the broad expanse of the gold background, which interacts with the brown, olive, and ochre of the monks' garments, is the main stylistic characteristic of the icon. The psychological intensity on the faces and the agitated drapery with the wavering highlights on the robes argue for the dating of the icon to the late 12th century. Moreover, the decoration on the reverse side of the panel is of the same type as that found on the icon of the Annunciation (fig. 29) which can be dated to the late 12th century on more definite stylistic criteria.

The Sinai icon of the Annunciation (fig. 29)[36] has been generally acknowledged as a masterpiece of Late Comnenian art, despite the alteration in colour caused by excessive use of varnish in a much later period, which resulted in the loss of the brilliance of colours and the delicate gradation of tones. A rare iconographic element is the Child, rendered in grisaille within a transparent mandorla at the breast of the Virgin, according to the scheme of prolepsis, since the Annunciation prepared the way for the Incarnation. The waterscape with its impressive variety of animal life remains a striking peculiarity of the iconography of the scene. Nevertheless, the hint of water appears from the 12th century onwards in a few examples which depict a fountain. The inclusion of the stream in the Sinai icon has been attributed mainly to the influence of hymnography, which addresses the Virgin as the 'Source of Life', but also to rhetorical texts that praise the coming of Spring, which coincides with the date of the feast of the Annunciation (March 25).[37] The icon must have been painted by a Constantinopolitan artist at the Monastery, as is suggested by the technical handling of the gold and by the intricate painted design on the reverse, also found on the icon of the Heavenly Ladder (fig. 24), a tetraptych with the Dodekaorton (fig. 28), and another tetraptych including the last Judgement, the Dodekaorton, two scenes from the Life of the Virgin, and saints; all works which must have been painted at Sinai.[38]

Many of the 12th-century icons at the Monastery have the form of diptychs, triptychs and tetraptychs in small dimensions, and consequently do not constitute works that can easily be placed on a wall. Among the exceptions, due to its large dimensions, is a tetraptych with the Dodekaorton and with four half-length images of hierarchs (John Chrysostom, Gregory the Theologian, Nicholas, and Basil) in the spandrels formed by the relief arches of the two central panels (fig. 28).[39] The Dodekaorton has close iconographic and stylistic affinity with certain iconostasis beams at the Monastery. Among its rare iconographic details are the 'hanging' garden behind the Virgin in the Annunciation and the small ladder which leads to it, the gold tunic of the Christ Child in the Presentation in the Temple, the Hebrew, who shows only his back, in the Entry into Jerusalem, as well as the shroud of the Soul of the Virgin in the Dormition, rendered in the same way as that of Lazarus in the homonymous scene. A stylistic characteristic that allows for a more precise dating of this work is the dynamic quality that pervades the figures in their poses, gestures, facial expressions, and in the drapery. The tetraptych has not the well-known Constantinopolitan style, but neither can it be considered provincial. It is more than likely that it copies, within the abilities of a local painter, an ambitious model found in the Monastery. The production of the tetraptych at Sinai is strongly suggested both by the technical handling of the gold and by the type of decoration on the reverse sides of the two central panels.

The works of the Monastery with a specific function in the church include a number of Menologion icons mainly from the 11th and 12th centuries, with saints, or, more rarely, scenes of feasts of the year. When conciseness is considered necessary, all of the saints and feasts of the twelve months can be concentrated on one diptych (fig. 17), triptych, or at the most on a tetraptych (fig. 16). In at least one case, there are twelve icons, one for every month, which can be found today in what are probably their original positions, i.e., on the twelve columns of the nave of the basilica, positions which they have in all likelihood retained from the time they were painted. The icon for March (fig. 30)[40] is representative of this group. The saints are arranged in superimposed registers, individually or in groups, in the order in which they are celebrated in the year. They are insubstantial figures with the distinguishing mark of the nimbus which reflects the light in a different way from that of the background, as a result of the familiar Sinaitic technique. Occasionally, the gallery of portraits is interrupted in order to insert a scene which depicts the corresponding feast, as is the case in March with the episode regarding the Forty Martyrs of Sebaste (Sebasteia) and the Annunciation. In view of the relaxed treatment of the facial features and the painterly brushwork, these icons may be dated close to 1200.

## ICONS OF THE 13th CENTURY

The icons of the 13th century are impressive in number and remarkable in their variety. These works prove that many Constantinopolitan painters spread the artistic ideas of the capital throughout the Eastern Mediterranean as a result of the fall of the Byzantine Empire to the Latins. Through the study of these icons, one can also understand the serious social and cultural upheavals at Sinai and in neighbouring areas a little later due to the retreat of Byzantine authority, the increase of the Western presence, and the domination of Islam.

In the first decades of the century, the Monastery 'produced' high quality icons which followed contemporary trends in the development of Byzantine painting, evidently employing painters of the diaspora. Twenty years later, however, it entered a phase of artistic stagnation, no doubt due to the interruption of the flow of artistic ideas from Constantinople. When the Monastery again began to amass icons, mainly in the last quarter of the 13th century, the material presents an entirely different picture. The works reveal a lack of awareness of new developments connected with the early phase of Palaeologan painting. At the same time, they illustrate various trends which reflect the cultural traditions of different peoples of the Eastern Mediterranean. Palestine, Syria, Egypt, and Cyprus contributed elements to the new artistic idiom of this period. The same can be said for the West, which strengthened its presence in the Near East at this time. To the second half of the 13th century has been assigned the 'Crusader' group of icons of the Monastery, which will be discussed below.

The icons of the Monastery from the 13th century reveal new orientations which constitute revolutionary innovations in the history of icons in general. Evidently, in response to a predetermined programme, a large number of individual panels were produced in various sizes, as well as diptychs or triptychs, and followed Sinaitic iconography in the broadest meaning of the term. Their purpose was to fulfill the liturgical and devotional needs of the Monastery,[41] or to be offered as 'blessed gifts' to prestigious pilgrims.[42] Thus, there was an emphasis on holy figures, such as the Virgin, Moses and Saint Catherine, on whom particular veneration was bestowed at the Monastery. The cult of Saint Catherine rendered the Monastery a centre of worship for a Christian martyr, elevating its prestige chiefly among Western pilgrims. At the same time, special reference was made to the sites which tradition has associated with the Theophany of the Burning Bush and with the Giving of the Law to Moses. The oldest cult centre in the area where the Monastery was built, the Chapel of the Burning Bush, brought together the worlds of the Old and New Testaments due to typological associations with the Virgin. Moreover, large proskynesis icons, some of which depict scenes from the life and martyrdom of a saint around his portrait, played an important role. Likewise, sets of icons of the Deesis in its condensed form ('Trimorphon') or in its expanded form ('Great Deesis') enjoyed great popularity, most likely in connection with the developments in the form of the templon. The production of painted iconostasis beams also continued: two of these, datable to the second half of the century, bear the characteristics of the 'Crusader' group. If we take into consideration that the earliest set of independent Dodekaorton icons for the templon which are extant at the Monastery may also be placed in the 'Crusader' group, the provenance of these works becomes even more enigmatic.

The large icon of the Prophet Elijah (fig. 34),[43] a masterpiece of Byzantine art, is a wonderful introduction to the climate of artistic life in the Monastery around the beginning of the 13th century. The monumental figure of the Prophet belongs to an intermediate type between a portrait of a holy figure and the protagonist of a narrative scene (Kings I 17:6), related to the nourishment brought to Elijah by a raven when he had fled into the desert. The name of the painter and donor, Stephanos, is included in an invocation inscribed both in Greek and in Arabic (with Cufic characters) on the lower border of the panel. The Greek metric inscription reads: ΜΟΡΦΟΥΝΤΙ ΘΕCΒΗΤΑ CE [C]Τ[ΕΦ]ΑΝΩ ΔΙΔΟΥ ΤΟΙC COIC ΙΛΑCΜΟΙC ΠΤΕCΜΑΤΩΝ [Α]ΜΝΗCΤΙΑΝ. Whereas the posture of the Prophet suggests astonishment and expectation in accordance with the contents of the narrative text, his raised arms and the inclusion of the Hand of God in the upper right corner may be related to the supplication of the donor. The monochrome rendering of the face, which is framed by the thick brown hair and beard, illustrates the simplicity with which the remarkable Byzantine painter simultaneously brings forward the psychological and spiritual dimension of the personality of the Prophet. The muted tones of olive, orange, brown, and ochre are enlivened through their interaction with the gold ground. The figure radiates a spirituality and an austere ethos, in accordance with the humanist spirit which appears as a new characteristic of Byzantine painting at the beginning of the 13th century.

The icon of the Prophet Elijah forms a pair with the well-known icon which depicts the Giving of the Law to Moses.[44] According to the inscription, in Greek and in Arabic, Stephanos again was the painter and, most likely, the donor of the work. Aside from the iconography which is clearly Sinaitic, technical details and the Arabic inscriptions suggest that the two panels were painted at Sinai. It is not certain whether they were commissioned for the Chapel of Moses on the peak of Mount Sinai and that of Elijah, a little below,[45] or to be integrated as a pair into the icon programme of the katholikon of the Monastery.

At least from the 12th century we have evidence that the traditional subject for the decoration of the central portal of the Sanctuary (the Beautiful Gate) was the Annunciation on account of its symbolism in relation to the Incarnation. The oldest Sanctuary doors preserved at Sinai, however, depict Moses and Aaron (fig. 35).[46] The two figures are connected to the symbolism of the templon and especially of the Beautiful Gate as indicated by their frequent depictions in Post-Byzantine Sanctuary doors as well (fig. 90).

Moses, a youth wearing a light blue chiton and a himation in a soft pink colour (according to Middle Byzantine tradition), carries in his left hand the marble Tablets of the Law, while he raises his right hand in a gesture of speech. Aaron, with a torrent of white hair and beard, also wears the antique costume, despite the fact that he is a high priest; the only feature indicating this role is the red mitre of the Hebrew high priest.[47] The ethereal figures with their diminished volume and the light garments with wavy hems reveal a link with the Comnenian tradition. However, the rendering of the faces, which show the character of the depicted figures, indicates that the work may be dated around the year 1200. The anxiety emanating from Moses' face is encountered in the faces of figures in further pictorial works dated or datable to this period. Despite the considerable loss of gold, the Sinaitic technique for the reflection of light in the nimbi is seen also in these icons.

The two icons with Moses before the Burning Bush and Moses Receiving the Law (figs. 36 and 37) represent the two most important moments within the scheme of Divine Economy for the salvation of mankind as foretold in the Old Testament. These panels are the only such pair among the icons of the Monastery.

In the first icon (fig. 36)[48] Moses unties his sandal in front of the Burning Bush which has been chosen for the Theophany.[49] In the lower left corner of the border is depicted a minuscule donor in proskynesis. The style of the icon is characteristic of monumental painting from the beginning of the 13th century. The face of Moses emits innocence and vigour, qualities which are stressed by the soft brushwork and the light flesh tones. The plastic quality of the figure and its convincing integration into the landscape point to the new style. The wavy planes of the ground in olive tones, together with the 'granite-like' edges of the rocks give the impression of aerial perspective and endow the landscape with a sensitivity unknown in Middle Byzantine art.

In the second icon (fig. 37),[50] which depicts the Giving of the Law to Moses, the Prophet turns with a rapid step toward the left in order to receive the Tablets of the Law which the Hand of God holds out to him from the upper left corner. This panel represents one of the most popular subjects of Sinaitic iconography. The dynamic feeling created by the almost monochrome appearance of the himation of the adolescent figure, which wraps the body and suggests through its diagonal folds the picture of a stretched bow, forms a sharp contrast to the introspective mood of Moses before the Burning Bush and to the somewhat decorative effect created by the careful combination of a great variety of colours. However, features such as the individualized method of rendering the hair, the agitated drapery (visible in the second icon only in the light blue hem of the chiton), the sensitive treatment of the landscape, and the interaction of the composition with the gold background, reveal that the two panels are the work of the same painter. Perhaps it is not by chance that the donor of the panel of the Burning Bush is depicted wearing an Arab turban, if we take into cosideration that the two large icons of Moses and Elijah (fig. 34) bear inscriptions in Greek and Arabic. Moses was widely venerated, and the Chapel of the Burning Bush was visited even by Moslems, as revealed by the accounts of Western pilgrims to Sinai during the Middle Ages.[51]

Icons with single portraits of female saints are extremely rare in Byzantine art. This holds true even for icons of Saint Catherine at the Monastery, datable before the Fall of Constantinople. To such exceptions belong two icons of small dimensions with portraits of Saint Theodosia and of Saint Phevronia.

The icon of Saint Theodosia (fig. 39)[52] is the earliest example in a substantial group of panels depicting this Saint that are preserved in the Monastery. The special honour enjoyed by the Constantinopolitan nun Theodosia, a Saint from the period of Iconoclasm, is due to her important contribution in the safeguarding of icons. The figure of the Saint emits a strong monumentality. The broad face, which is framed by her monastic veil, radiates a rich inner life. Despite its overpainting, the panel must be attributed to one of the best painters who worked at the Monastery in the early 13th century.

The icon of Saint Phevronia (fig. 38),[53] a nun in Nisibe in Mesopotamia martyred under Diocletian, is the only individual panel of the Saint preserved in the Monastery. Her oval-shaped face with its fleshy cheeks, long nose, and small mouth, possesses a certain naivete which forms a sharp contrast to the aristocratic self-sufficiency of the portrait of Saint Theodosia. The modelling is compact with restricted shading on the contour of the face and around the eyes, as well as with faint pink touches on the cheeks. The general impression of the icon comes closer to wall painting. The panel can be dated to the second half of the 13th century. From technical details, such as the drawing of the figure with incised lines, it can be concluded that the icon came to Sinai from outside.

The panel of the two warrior Saints, Theodore Stratelates and Demetrios (fig. 40),[54] epitomizes the predominant characteristics of a group of transitional works which were painted at the Monastery in the early 13th century. These panels combine the Comnenian features, such as the refined linear faces and the enamel-like colours, and the new spirit of temperance and calm in psychological expression, as seen in works of the beginning of the 13th century. The tall monumental figures are projected entirely against the gold background, without the usual strip of green ground at the bottom. This, as well as the ample use of vivid red and chrysography in the garments and the reflection of light on the nimbi, conveys a sense of luxury. The shield held by Saint Theodore, in its shape, colour and decoration consisting of a gold star surrounded by four crescent moons, is repeated in another Sinai icon depicting Saint George and a Georgian king whom I identify as George

Lacha (1213-1222).[55] Since other iconographic and stylistic details are shared with this icon, they may be considered the work of the same painter.

In the 13th century, many proskynesis icons of large dimensions, especially with the Hodegetria, are gathered at the Monastery. One of these icons is remarkable for its three-panelled form, as well as for its iconographic programme. To my knowledge, this is the earliest Byzantine icon in which the representation of the Virgin and Child is combined with scenes from her life (figs. 54, 55).[56] The icon, which is known in the Monastery by the name 'Bematarissa' (of the Bema), is considered to be miracle working.

The figure of the Virgin has received drastic overpainting (of 'Cretan' style with a Western stamp) in the face and less so in the garments. Western influence on the original layer is confirmed by the Latin inscription addressed to Christ: CONDITOR EST MUNDI QVE[M] VIRGO CONTINET ULNIS (Founder of the world is He whom the Virgin holds in her arms). The most notable iconographic deviation from the miraculous archetype of the Monastery of the Hodegon in Constantinople is the fact that Christ has lost the hieratic stiffness of the model and instead is reclining in the arms of His mother. His bare feet and the red sash wound around His chest are frequent features in 13th-century representations of the Virgin and Child. The twelve scenes from the life of the Virgin on the wings of the triptych do not preserve inscriptions, but their identification can be based on the apocryphal text of the Protoevangelium of James.[57] A number of Comnenian characteristics may be identified in these scenes, such as the agitated drapery and the pathos on the faces with their scowling, wide-open eyes underlined by black, curved shading. However, the dating of this work later, to the early 13th century, is suggested by the broad facial features and the emphasis on the volume of the body, by the importance given to the architecture and by the attempt to emphasize the third dimension through the representation of side views of buildings. The figures of the Virgin and Child must be attributed to a more accomplished artist than the one who painted the angels on the upper spandrels of the central panel and the scenes of the wings. In both cases, the painting lacks the high quality which characterizes other icons of the Monastery from this period. The triptych presents many of the familiar elements of technique which are encountered in Sinaitic works of the 12th and 13th centuries.[58]

Within the group of panels with Sinaitic iconography is a pair depicting the Holy Fathers Massacred at Sinai and Raithou (figs. 43 and 44).[59] In the uppermost zone of the icon of the Sinai Fathers, Christ, enthroned within an aureole, is flanked by the Virgin, Saint Peter, and Saint Paul of Mount Latros to the left, and by John the Baptist, Saint Paul and Saint John Climacus to the right. In the icon of the Fathers of Raithou, the central figure in the uppermost zone is the Virgin Blachernitissa, between two venerating angels. She is flanked by John Climacus to the left and by John of Damascus to the right. The subject matter of the two icons is based on the *Narratio* by the Egyptian monk Ammonios concerning the monks of Mount Sinai and Raithou, who suffered martyrdom during the period of barbarian invasions at the end of the 4th century. Stylistically, both icons, works of the same painter, are characterized by hasty brushwork and an attempt to diminish the monotony of the rows of figures by varying facial types, poses, and garments. These panels were in all likelihood painted at Sinai in the early 13th century.

To the group of works with Sinaitic iconography belongs the panel of the Virgin Blachernitissa between Moses and Euthymios II, Patriarch of Jerusalem (fig. 48).[60] The contents of the composition is elucidated by a large, badly spelt inscription which covers the wide border of the icon. Of special interest is the inscription at the lower section of the panel: ΔΕ(ησις) ΠΕΤΡΟΥ ΖΩΓΡΑΦΟΥ (prayer of the painter Petros), one of the very few from this period which preserves the name of the painter. Stylistic analysis of the icon confirms its dating to the third decade of the 13th century, as attested by the portrait of the Patriarch. Aside from the face of Euthymios, which is rendered with great sensitivity giving the impression of a real portrait, the painting does not show a very high quality. In terms of style and technique, the panel should be placed in a very small group limited to this and three other icons which can all be attributed to the painter Petros.

One of these icons is the Virgin Kyriotissa (fig. 45),[61] labelled *Μή(τη)ρ Θεοῦ ὁ* (sic) *τῆς Βάτου* (Mother of God of the [Burning] Bush), flanked by four monastic figures of Sinai. From left to right are: Georgios Islaelites, Neilos Sinaites, Anastasios Sinaites abbot, and John Climacus, abbot of Sinai. At the bottom of the panel there is again an inscription with the name of the painter *ΔΕ(ησις) ΠΕΤΟΥ* (sic) *ΖΩΓΡΑΦΟΥ*. This work is the only icon that provides evidence about such a group of monastic personalities from the early history of the Monastery.[62] At the same time it is the only icon which records the name of the iconographic type of the Virgin of the Burning Bush which enjoyed special honour in the Monastery — most likely due to the fact that this type was associated with a specific icon located in the Chapel of the Burning Bush.

I attribute the icon of Saint Procopios (fig. 47)[63] also to the painter Petros. At the bottom of the panel, on the left, is an inscription, in part palimpsest, for which the reading *ΔΕ[ΗϹΙϹ ΠΕΤΡΟΥ] Ζ[ΩΓΡΑΦΟΥ]* can be proposed. The selection of the depicted Saint is interesting since, according to Eusebius, he was the first martyr of Palestine. His highly ornamented attire in this panel suggests that the painter was inspired by a miracle-working icon from an earlier shrine of the Saint in Palestine. The hypothesis that the painter Petros escorted Patriarch Euthymios II from Jerusalem may offer an explanation for one technical feature of the group of icons attributed to him, implying its practice in this city. This is the use of a deep brown varnish, usually on top of silver leaf, perhaps intended to give the impression of gold.[64]

The panel of the Protomartyr Stephen (fig. 56),[65] located in the chapel dedicated to the Saint within the walls of the Monastery, belongs to the group of large proskynesis icons. The Saint, dressed in traditional deacon's garb, treads on a strip of cypress-coloured ground which is decorated with skeletal gold plants. This is a bold pictorial conception, as indicated by the large, almost uniform surface of the drapery in an almond green colour with abundant white highlights, as well as by the red material of the liturgical cloth held by the Saint against the gold background. The face is characterized by light flesh tones, with red touches on the cheeks and ample green shading. The head is small in proportion to the body. The symmetry of the facial traits and the indifferent, aloof expression are typical Comnenian characteristics. The smooth modelling of the face, however, radiates inner tranquillity which fits the new conception of the rendering of the human figure in the early 13th century. This icon is evidence that a number of accomplished painters worked on commissions of the Monastery at this period. That the panel was painted at Sinai is suggested by the presence of the familiar device for the reflection of light on the gold ground and by the type of decoration on the reverse side.

Sets of icons at the Monastery with the Deesis in its condensed form, the Trimorphon (with depictions of Christ, the Virgin and John the Baptist), or in its expanded form, the Great Deesis (with the additional figures of the Archangels Michael and Gabriel), have significantly increased in the 13th century.[66] Two icons with the half-length figures of the frontal Christ and the Archangel Michael in a three-quarter view towards the right (figs. 42 and 41) belong to the scheme of the Great Deesis. Preserved also are the panels of the Virgin, Gabriel, and John the Baptist.[67] These icons rank among the masterpieces of the monumental style of the early 13th century as illustrated by works preserved at the Monastery.

In the icon of Christ (fig. 42), the overpainting of the background has only partially been removed. The face of the Saviour with its classical appearance is rendered differently from depictions of the Comnenian period and seems to have been inspired by the magnificent encaustic portrait of Christ from the 6th century (figs. 1, 2). The free painterly technique of combining warm and cool tones enhances the sculptural quality of the face. Further elements which are taken from the encaustic Christ are the shape of the face, the slight asymmetry of its features, especially the eyes, and, above all, the deep humanistic expression.

The representation of the Archangel Michael (fig. 41) also reveals the sensitivity of the painter for his subject. The diminished presence of the body and the refinement of the facial features are in keeping with the Comnenian tradition. However, the restricted role of line and the handling of colour and light, which create a fluid painterly effect, and which enhance the calm introspection of the face, are features of the figure style in the Constantinopolitan painting of the early 13th century.

The exact function of Deesis sets in the concise or the expanded form remains unclear. Even if one considers that the position of these icons was exclusively on the templon, one must ask in each case: in which of its two zones of decoration were they placed? The dimensions of the icons are important for determining this matter, since large icons would be suitable for the intercolumniations of the templon, and small ones for its uppermost register. From the viewpoint of size the Sinai material presents great fluctuations, which makes it difficult to formulate persuasive hypotheses concerning their use in each case. The five icons of the Great Deesis from the beginning of the 13th century are among the earliest examples of this iconographic scheme formed by independent panels.

Three icons of Christ (fig. 50), the Virgin (fig. 49), and John the Baptist[68] illustrate some of the predominant characteristics of Late Comnenian painting, especially the figure of Christ. The gold striations in the light brown chiton and in its purple clavus, the gold letters on the open Gospels with their deep red pages which imitate purple dyed parchment, and the use of the familiar technique for the reflection of light on the gold ground give the impression of a 'precious' work. The closest related examples are icons of approximately the same period from Cyprus.[69] In the faces of figures from both groups we see a preference for light tones for the iris and for the smooth modelling of the flesh, with a sharp contrast between the warm ochre and the abundant red. Impeccable technique is exhibited in the detailed rendering of line and colour with many fine brushstrokes, following older trends. The withdrawn, somewhat introspective expressions also convey an archaizing effect. However, compared to the icons of Cyprus, the panels of the Deesis at Sinai display a more pronounced Classical character, greater monumentality, and less emphasis on linear elements, especially in the faces. Thus, despite the diminished volume of the body, the Sinai icons may be placed at the beginning of the 13th century.

Historiated icons with the representation of a saint in the centre of a panel surrounded by scenes of his life and martyrdom form an especially interesting group of works at Sinai. Six panels from the early 13th century and two others from the second half of the century may be assigned to this group.

The icon of Saint Catherine with scenes of her life and martyrdom (fig. 46)[70] is among the earliest examples of historiated icons and is the oldest panel of large dimensions with the portrait of the Saint which exists at Sinai. Saint Catherine is depicted frontally in imperial garments which emphasize her royal lineage. The majority of the twelve scenes on the border, which do not always follow the sequence of the narrative, are identified by the extant inscriptions.[71] Emphasis is placed on the refusal of the Saint to give up the Christian faith and on aspects of her martyrdom. Stylistically the icon cannot be placed among the masterpieces which were painted at the Monastery in the same period.

In the earliest historiated icon of Saint Nicholas at the Monastery (fig. 51)[72] the half-figure of the hierarch is bordered by sixteen scenes of his birth, his education, his ascent through the ranks of the priesthood, some well-known miracles traditionally associated with the Saint, and, finally, his burial. The style of the icon presents close ties to the Late Comnenian tradition, especially in the rendering of the central figure with his lean face, the intense touches of red on the cheeks, and the stylized facial features. On the other hand, scenes from his biographical cycle, which were painted somewhat hastily and may perhaps be attributed to another painter, show a certain freedom and liveliness, which suggests that the icon may be dated to the beginning of the 13th century. The style of the painting, which is related to other works of the Monastery,[73] and the inclusion of a number of Sinaitic technical details suggest that this work  was painted at Sinai.[74]

The only preserved Byzantine icon with scenes from the life of Saint Panteleimon is an outstanding work of the group of historiated icons (fig. 53).[75] Biographical cycles of the Saint in other media are few and the only other known Byzantine cycle which chronologically precedes the Sinai panel is found in the wall paintings of the homonymous church at Nerezi near Skopje (1164). The young healing Saint, together with Saint Nicholas and Saint Catherine, received great honour both in the East and in the West. The cycle of sixteen scenes from the life of Saint Panteleimon is composed of five units: two introductory scenes of his education, the scene of his baptism, six scenes of his miracles, another six from his martyrdom, and one with his entombment.[76] The arrangement of the scenes presents small inconsistencies in the sequence of the narrative.[77] Stylistically the icon can be placed within the group of transitional works, dependent on the art of the Late Comnenian period and on early examples of the so-called monumental style of the 13th century. The Comnenian tradition is revealed mainly in the detailed rendering of the hair, the strict symmetry of the facial characteristics, and the compact modelling, as well as in the diminished volume of the body. The face, nevertheless, radiates calm and self-sufficiency, characteristics of the figure style of the early 13th century. The refined character of this icon is also evident in the rendering of the narrative scenes of the border, which, in addition, show a feeling of depth created by the placement of the figures in their setting, thus supporting the dating of the panel to the early 13th century.[78] The icon of Saint Panteleimon must have been painted at the Monastery; indeed, close stylistic affinity with the great Deesis (figs. 41 and 42) indicates that the work is by the same painter.

Another historiated icon depicts John the Baptist with fourteen scenes from his life and martyrdom, including his birth, ministry, decapitation, and the discovery of his head (fig. 52).[79] The Baptist wears only his mantle, leaving portions of his body uncovered. With his left hand he holds a cross-staff and an open scroll with the customary inscription. An interesting addition is the portrait of a male figure kneeling at the feet of the Saint, in all likelihood the donor of the icon. The style of this panel also belongs to the transitional phase between the Late Comnenian aesthetic and the free monumental approach of the beginning of the 13th century. The 'painterly' trend is visible as much in the central portrait as in the framing scenes. The figures possess nobility and follow types usually found in works tied directly or indirectly to the artistic trends of Constantinople. Hypotheses concerning the identity of the anonymous donor of the icon, who is bearded, tonsured, and wears a solid white robe, cannot be easily proven. He may be an ecclesiastic of an Eastern ethnic group outside of the Greek sphere. If we take into consideration information provided by Western pilgrims that Georgian ecclesiastics were characterized by a circular tonsure,[80] we are provided with one possible clue for the identification of the figure.

In the small panel representing the head of Saint George (fig. 57)[81] the Saint turns toward the side, thus averting direct communiction with the viewer. The rendering of the head and neck only of the figure is very rare in Byzantine art. Few parallels exist among the icons of the Monastery, none of which may be dated before the 13th century.[82] The turning of the head to the left perhaps indicates that the icon was a section from a Deesis with the Virgin on the other side. The face of Saint George radiates the inner life and self-awareness which characterize figures in early examples of the monumental style of the 13th century. Despite serious overpainting, it is clear that this is a masterly work which approaches the style of the icons of the Great Deesis painter (figs. 41 and 42).

Of the numerous 13th-century icons of the Virgin in the Monastery the majority depict the Hodegetria with the Child on her left (Aristerokratousa) or right arm (Dexiokratousa). The Hodegetria was the most favoured of all icon types of the Virgin throughout the Byzantine period and constituted the starting point for the formation of new variants which expressed the preference for a more tender, intimate relationship between the Virgin and Child. Three of the most remarkable icons of the Monastery with the Virgin and Child, datable to the second half of the 13th century, present elements which have been connected with the Western tradition.

A notable iconographic detail in the icon of the Hodegetria Dexiokratousa (fig. 62)[83] is that the Child is not seated on the forearm of His mother, but is depicted reclining in a pose which is reminiscent of that of Christ in representations of the Anapeson. This pose of the Child, in combination with the immense sorrow on the face of His mother, foreshadows His future Passion, in accordance with hymns and certain homiletic texts. The style of the icon reveals a close tie to the developments in Early Palaeologan painting. Western influence, on the other hand, is suggested by various details, such as the youthful appearance of the Virgin, the very light flesh tones, the red colour of her maphorion, the double punched line which marks the circumference of her nimbus, and the original decoration of the blue nimbus of Christ with rays in ochre. The partially abraded inscription on the border contains an invocation for the remission of sins. The Virgin is named πυρφόρος (fire bearer), a reference to the Burning Bush and evidence that this work was probably painted at the Monastery of Sinai. Its subject and dimensions suggest that it was placed in the main church as a large proskynesis icon.

The icon in the standard type of the Hodegetria Aristerokratousa (fig. 60)[84] has been retouched many times and certain observations need to be confirmed by technical investigation. In its original form the background was gold on top of silver, but later it was covered with an ochre colour. The Latin inscription, [M]A[T]ER DOMINI, and the ligatures, MH(τη)P Θ(εο)Y, are original.[85] The most striking technical feature of the icon is the plaster relief decoration on the nimbi of the Virgin and Christ, as well as on the borders and the ornaments of the maphorion of the Virgin. This type of decoration was most probably an inexpensive substitute for the aesthetic effect created by metal revetments of the icons. It is known mainly from Cyprus, where a large number of related examples from the 13th century and later are preserved, a fact which has led to the hypothesis that the use of plaster relief was applied for the first time in Frankish- occupied Cyprus. A further similarity with Cypriot icons may be noted in the compact linear modelling with very light flesh tones, and the intense red touches on the face that characterize our icon. However, the decoration of the garment around the neck with pearls set in a black line, although not unknown in

Cyprus, is more prevalent in the icons of the Monastery tied to Syrian or Arabic artistic trends. The same applies to the use of black, as in the ribbon around the scroll held by the Child. The shading of Christ's gold tunic with numerous red lines is not a characteristic of Byzantine works. Many of the 'non-Byzantine' elements of the icon can be attributed to osmosis from works of Western art. The presence of a Latin inscription for the name of the Virgin may indicate that the icon was painted on the initiative of a Western donor. Nevertheless, this does not prevent the proposal of Cyprus, at that time in the midst of a great artistic and economic revival, as being the place of origin of the icon or of its painter. Taking into account that many of the current views concerning the 'Crusader' material of Sinai may be revised with the publication of further pictorial material from the Latin-occupied areas of the Near East, the icon may be proposed as a product of Cyprus and can be attributed to the Syrian rather than Western minority of the island.

The Virgin Blachernitissa (fig. 61)[86] is the only large icon of this iconographic type preserved at the Monastery. It is, moreover, one of three Sinai icons with the characteristic technical handling of gold for the reflection of light which can be dated to the second half of the 13th century.[87] Small shining discs do not only cover freely the background of the icon, but also form rows on its border and, in a minute scale, frame the gold nimbus of the Virgin, as well as several of the large discs of the background. A number of iconographic and stylistic elements of this panel hint at connections with the artistic sphere of Cyprus. Noteworthy is the fact that the Archangels Michael and Gabriel, depicted in half-length in the upper corners, hold censers, a Western feature which appears frequently in various compositions and in representations of the Virgin Blachernitissa in monumental painting and in icons in Cyprus from the 13th century onwards. Other striking details are the gold garments and wings of the angels, which are distinguished from the gold background by means of black lines for the contours and the shadow lines. The aesthetic approach is reminiscent of a number of icons of the Monastery from the 13th century which can be connected with the Christian Syrian communities. The pearls which decorate the border of Christ's medallion, as well as His chiton are encountered in many icons of Sinai that have been attributed to the Crusaders. This feature is, however, widely used in the painting of the Eastern Mediterranean in this period. On the other hand, the decoration of the vertical edges of the icon with a rinceau pattern in relief framed by two dotted rows and painted with a deep red colour, has not been noticed in any other icon at Sinai or anywhere else. Stylistically the Blachernitissa icon may be linked to a group of icons of the Monastery which Kurt Weitzmann attributes to a Crusader workshop of artists from Cyprus or Southern Italy. In all of these works, the figures are flat with large heads atop long, cylindrical necks. Their rigidity gives the figures an archaizing appearance. With some hesitation, they could be removed from the group of Crusader works and placed within the artistic activity of the Orthodox population of the Eastern Mediterranean. Cypriot and Syrian elements seem especially strong. The technical handling of the gold, which copies icons of the Monastery from the 12th century, suggests the fact that this panel was painted at Sinai.

The majority of Sinai icons which can be dated to the second half of the 13th century display Western features. Consequently, these works have been assigned to the 'Crusader' group, which numbers around 120 icons. According to Weitzmann, placement in this group is based on three criteria: a) Production within a Crusader state, b) a Western artist, and, c) a Western (Crusader) donor. Aside from isolated examples, these icons may be subdivided into three groups on the basis of style: a) Icons of the French group, which have affinities with miniatures of the manuscripts from the 'School of Acre', b) Icons of the

Venetian group, and c) Icons which have connections with works of Cyprus or of Southern Italy. The Crusader icons blend Byzantine and Western elements, the latter from the Italian and French traditions.[88] The great number of these icons led to the hypothesis that many of them were the work of Western artists established at the Monastery.

To the very few works of this group with Latin inscriptions belongs a large two-sided icon with the Crucifixion (fig. 63) and the Anastasis (fig. 64).[89] The icon is unique within the 'Crusader' group and has been attributed to a Venetian workshop.[90] The Crucifixion scene is distinguished by many Western features. Apart from the Latin inscriptions, JESUS NAZARENUS REX JUDEORUM, MATER D(omi)NI, S(an)C(tu)S JOHANNES, especially noteworthy are the three nails of the Crucified Christ (instead of the four from the Byzantine tradition). The punched decoration of the nimbi and of the gold background corresponds to the purely Western (Italian) technique used from the middle of the 13th century. In the Anastasis, several Western iconographic details are also observed, such as the pink colour of the mandorla of Christ and of the arc of heaven, the golden stars of the blue background, the small jewel-encrusted cross of Christ, and the elderly Eve. The realism in the rendering of the figures and the handling of colour do not conform to the principles of Byzantine painting. Stylistic parallels have been noted among the figures of the mosaics of San Marco in Venice.

The Crucifixion icon (fig. 67)[91] is one of the most beautiful panels of the 'Crusader' group. Notable Western details are: the deep blue loincloth of Christ, the three nails, the swooning of the Virgin, the differentiation of Mary Magdalen from the other Maries in terms of her placement, gestures, and garments (her robe opens perceptibly at the neck, and her maphorion, which is also open in front, is a brilliant red colour), the small size, colour and decoration of the shield of the Centurion, as well as the inclusion of soldiers in the scene. Elements which may be attributed to a Venetian atelier include the chrysography on the loincloth of Christ and on the garments of the Virgin and John. More general characteristics of the 'Crusader' icons are the painted pearls which frame the nimbi and the rows of gold lozenges on the black ground of the border. We may hypothesize that this work, with its brilliant colours and feeling of luxury, could easily have been produced in Italy, in an area under Venetian cultural influence, or, more likely, in an area of the Eastern Mediterranean where Venetian control was strong, such as Cyprus or Crete. These islands had especially close ties to the Sinai Monastery during this period. I consider the work 'Crusader' since it may have been painted by a Western artist in the Latin-occupied East. However, there are no indications that the icon was commissioned by a Crusader.

The impressive diptych representing Saint Procopios in military garb and a variant of the Virgin Kykkotissa (fig. 65)[92] has also been attributed to a Venetian painter, most likely residing in Jerusalem. Saint Procopios is framed by the figures of Christ and of the Archangels Michael and Gabriel in the upper section of the border. On its vertical sides are symmetrical representations of saints: Peter and Paul, John the Theologian and Thomas, Theodore Stratelates and George. On the lower border is depicted Saint Christopher between Saints Cosmas and Damian. On the upper border of the panel of the variant of the Kykkotissa is the Virgin Orans before the Burning Bush, flanked by Ioakeim and Anna. On the vertical sides of the border are depicted the pairs of Moses and John the Baptist, Saints Basil and Nicholas, and Saints John Climacus and Onouphrios. On the lower border Saint Catherine is flanked by Constantine and Helen. This diptych was in all probability a special commission intended for presentation to the Monastery, as evidenced by its monumental size and the sumptuousness in the rendering of the figures. The provenance of the diptych and the origin of its artist remain unclear. The rich appearance of Saint Procopios, and the epithet Περιβολίτης (of the Enclosure), which accompanies his name, must refer to a certain celebrated icon of the Saint.[93] The same applies to the Virgin and Child on the other panel, inspired by the famous icon of the Virgin of Kykkos, one of the three miraculous archetypes in the East which, according to tradition, were painted by Saint Luke. In the diptych, elements which come from various cultural traditions are united. In terms of iconography, a few divergences from the Byzantine tradition in favour of a Western source may be noted. The most important change is that John the Theologian is represented as a youth and is paired with Thomas. This, as well as the chrysography on the garments, the pearls on the borders of the nimbi of many of the figures, and the series of gold lozenges on the black ground of the border have been considered characteristics of 'Crusader' painting. An 'Eastern' element, which suggests a tie to the Islamic tradition, is the garment of the Child, which does not fall freely at the bottom, but closes at the feet with two highly ornamented patches. The fleshy faces with the broad features and also the shape of the eyes of the three central figures, moreover, may be linked to some area in the Eastern Mediterranean where different ethnic groups co-existed. The suggestion by George and Maria Soteriou of a Cypriot provenance for this diptych is supported by recent research concerning the cultural history of Cyprus during the period of the Lusignans. One further feature which strengthens this view is the dedication of several churches in Cyprus to Saint Procopios. In Nicosia, in particular, there still exists a metochion of the Monastery of Kykkos dedicated to the Saint. It is likely that this diptych was made in one of the organized workshops in Nicosia, where the co-mingling of Byzantine, Western, and Eastern elements is explained by historical facts.

The earliest certain Dodekaorton formed by independent panels and intended for a templon in the Monastery can be reconstructed on the basis of two extant icons depicting the Nativity and the Baptism (figs. 68 and 69).[94] Their subject matter and dimensions conform to the requirements of icons with this function. By chance, a section of the central icon of the set depicting the Deesis is also preserved in the Monastery.[95] The Nativity panel has been dated by Weitzmann to shortly after 1250 and placed in the French group of Crusader icons. Western elements, such as the red beam of light in the Baptism, are few, while the wide-open eyes and the pearl decoration on the contours of the nimbi are considered standard characteristics of Crusader painting.

Saints Sergios and Bacchos (fig. 66)[96] are depicted on the reverse side of a large two-sided icon, which has on its main face the Hodegetria Aristerokratousa. It is one of two bilateral procession icons extant in the Monastery.[97] Sergios and Bacchos are depicted on horseback, a rare scheme for these two Saints, also found on a small icon of Sergios preserved in the Monastery. The two panels have been dated to the end of the 13th century and attributed to a Crusader workshop located in Cyprus or, more likely, in Southern Italy.[98] Two iconographic elements foreign to the Byzantine tradition are the Western white banner with the red cross and the quiver which has a Persian appearance.[99] The figures of the martyrs of the two-sided icon are characterized by a flat rendering of the body, and a polished linear modelling in the bare areas, where very light tones predominate. The youthful, delicate faces radiate a haughty, worldly character, which is emphasized by the profusion of ornamental details. These features may relate the two works to Cyprus and, more specifically, to the resident Syrian minority whose presence there was stronger after the middle of the 13th century.[100]

A number of icons that could be considered 'Crusader' display elements consistent with their production by Eastern, probably Syrian, artists. Characteristic examples are the panels of the Hodegetria Dexiokratousa and the Crucifixion (figs. 59 and 58),[101] which have roughly equal dimensions, similar stylistic rendering, and the same red backgrounds. These icons should be considered a pair, since the Hodegetria and the Crucifixion form complementary subjects, commencing with the miraculous two-sided icon of the Monastery of the Hodegon in Constantinople.[102] Specific details in the two icons, such as the knot in the loincloth of Christ and the swooning of the Virgin in the Crucifixion, may be considered Western. There are also iconographic errors, such as the Child who blesses with His left hand, while His right hand rests on a small tablet with the familiar Gospel passage (Luke 4:18). Both icons have relief decoration on the nimbi and the borders, and include a series of painted pearls in black lines as in many Syrian and Arab works. The red background is seen frequently in miniatures of Syrian manuscripts of the 13th century, as well as in wall paintings of Cyprus from the same period. Despite the fact that the folk character of the icons renders an accurate dating difficult, a dating in the first half of the 13th century may be suggested.

The small panel of the Forty Martyrs of Sebaste (Sebasteia) (fig. 70)[103] may be placed among the group of icons in the Monastery painted by Christian Arabs. The iconographic rendering agrees with the established tradition of one of the most popular subjects of Byzantine art. The facial characteristics and the garments of Christ, however, like the facial types of the martyrs, are remote from the Byzantine tradition and recall representations of Christ and other figures in Syrian and Coptic works. A significant role is played by the black line for contours and detail such as the parallel wavy lines of the water, another feature to be found in Syrian and Coptic works. Of further interest is the deep brown colour of the background as in the group of icons of the painter Petros from the early 13th century (figs. 45, 47 and 48). The date of the work may be placed, with some reservation, in the late 13th or early 14th century.

The icon of the Crucifixion and the Nativity (fig. 71)[104] is a unique work. The arrangement of this subject matter in two superimposed zones has no parallel in Byzantine art, but may be observed in some icons of Ethiopian origin. Western elements in the iconograpny of the two scenes are obvious. For example, in the Nativity, while the two figures nearer the manger are identifiable as kings in accordance with the established convention, the third figure, who is black, neither wears a crown not bears gifts. He may be identified as the black attendant of the Magi.[105] This icon is, as far as I know, the only work in the Eastern Mediterranean in which this peculiarity is encountered. The Magi, who wear crowns of a strange shape, are kneeling. The earliest Eastern examples of the kneeling pose of the Magi are probably those in a miniature of the Armenian Gospel of Queen Keran of 1272 and in the Second Gospel of Vasak, datable in the early 1280s. Western elements of the Crucifixion include the three nails, the bright-coloured garments of Mary Magdalen, the coat of arms (a lion rampant) on the shield of the Centurion, the realistic rendering of the skull of Adam, as well as the golden stars in the deep blue background. All these features also appear in Armenian manuscripts of this period, whose miniatures are influenced by Western art. On the basis of such arguments, I attribute this problematic icon to an Armenian artist. Additional features that may support this attribution include the vivid colours, which have a decorative effect, the rendering of the faces with very light unmodelled tones, the restricted green shading, the expressionistic facial traits and the blue background of the icon. This last feature is also found in a few early panels in the Sinai Monastery (i.e., fig. 11) which exhibit a clear Eastern character. Inscriptions with the title of each scene are absent on our icon, while the ligatures for the names of Christ, the Virgin and John in the Crucifixion have been rendered with white letters, in a manner perhaps indicating that the scribe did not know Greek.

## ICONS OF THE 14th CENTURY

The 14th-century icons of the Monastery indicate that communication was established with Constantinople, the cradle of Palaeologan art, after the interruption caused by the Latin occupation. These panels, which can be dated on the basis of stylistic analysis, reflect the new ideas that prevailed at the Monastery concerning the use of icons. In the first place, one is struck by the nearly total absence of large icons with the traditional subject matter (Trimorphon or Great Deesis, representations of Christ and of the Virgin and Child or of important saints). This void cannot be explained by the presumed dependence of the Monastery on the large number of 13th-century icons in its possession. Rather, one might conjecture that the conditions prevailing at the Monastery during this period were no longer favourable for attracting painters to reside there in order to carry out certain serious commissions. Elements of iconography and style which characterized earlier works are difficult to detect in icons of the 14th century. Neither the technical handling of gold for the reflection of light nor the typical decoration on the reverse side found in icons of the 12th and 13th centuries can be observed in these panels.

The icons are small individual panels, usually on thin boards, with subjects that give the impression to have been painted, in many cases, for private devotion. On the other hand, there are small diptychs, triptychs, and polyptychs whose subject matter and arrangement of the representations below relief arches indicate an influence from the iconographic programme and form of the templon. The fact that no icons with this form are preserved outside of Sinai may be accidental. It is not impossible in certain cases that these icons were intended as in earlier times for specific liturgical use in neighbouring chapels dependent on the Monastery.

Some 14th-century icons meet the highest standards of art of Constantinople in this period.[106] Certain of the icons with the arrangement of the representations under relief arches[107] in all likelihood were not painted in the capital. There are indications that a number of these small works arrived at the Monastery as gifts. For example, a high quality tetraptych in the Palaeologan style with Georgian inscriptions was sent to Sinai from Georgia in 1780.[108] The ties of 14th-century Sinai icons with Western art is also suggested in certain cases. The question of the attribution of certain icons from this period to Syrian and Arab Christians remains open until a systematic study of the material is undertaken.

The small hexaptych of the Dodekaorton (fig. 72)[109] is a representative example of one group of icons of this period preserved in the Monastery. Six thin, small boards have been worked so that each one presents two scenes from the Dodekaorton below two superimposed relief arches. The subject matter and the relief arches suggest that a Dodekaorton of a templon was condensed into two zones. Despite the restricted surfaces, the indifference to superfluous narrative details produces a monumental feeling in the representations. A sense of luxury is due to the fine quality of the gold background and to the extensive use of chrysography for the wings of the angels, details of garments, furniture, and vessels. The elegant figures and the manner in which they are situated within their architectural surroundings and landscape are reminiscent of the mosaics of the Monastery of the Chora, Constantinople (c. 1320). The icon can be dated to around the middle of the 14th century. The return to models from the beginning of the century illustrates a conservative tendency which is characteristic of later phases of Palaeologan painting.

The altarpiece with the portrait of Saint Catherine (fig. 73)[110] belongs to the few works among the treasures of the Monastery which were painted in the West. The name of Saint Catherine, S(ancta) CATERINA, is inscribed at the lower left of the strip of ground upon which the Saint is standing. A little lower is an inscription in black letters in old Catalan from which we learn that the donor was the Consul of the Catalans in Damascus, Bernardo Maresa, who commissioned the work in Barcelona in 1387: *Aquest(a) retaula, sia fer.lo honrat, e(n) Be(r)nat M(ar)esa, ciutada de Barch (ino)na. Consol. de. Cathalans. en Domas en l'an M.CCC.LXXXVII.*[111] From the three coats of arms on the panel, that located in the upper left belongs to the kings of Catalonia, the upper right to the Balearic islands, and the lower left to the donor, whom the inscription presents as a nobleman.[112] On the back of the panel the signature of the painter has been preserved: MARTIN(us) D(e) VILANOVA PIN-XIT.[113] In the depiction of the Saint, the crown emphasizes her royal lineage. The palm branch which she carries in her right hand is the attribute of martyrs in Western icono-graphy. The wheel upon which her left hand rests refers to the best known of her tortures. These Western attributes of the Saint were introduced in the East by the painters of the Cretan School of the 16th century. The panel belongs to a later phase of Catalan painting, which is of a high quality as seen in this work as well.[114] The elegant appearance of the Saint, evident in her pose, borrowed from French Gothic works, and in the luxuriousness of her garments, belongs to the climate of the International style. The same influence is seen in the gabled top of the panel as well as in the intricate pattern of punched decoration that embellishes the nimbus and borders the figure of the Saint. The link of the Catalan altarpiece with the consul of the Catalans in Damascus reveals the ties of the Monastery with Syria. The establishment of Western consuls at this time in the ports of the Eastern Mediterranean[115] had as a main purpose the unhindered travels of pilgrims in the Holy Land[116] and often also to the Monastery of Saint Catherine at Sinai.[117]

ICONS OF THE 15th CENTURY

The icons of the Sinai Monastery which can be dated to the 15th century are more numer-ous than those of the 14th century. From the first half of the 15th century, the collection of the icons at the Monastery includes mainly small works, as in the 14th century. To a certain extent, these works reveal a close dependence on the development of painting during the Palaeologan period. Even though not a single work can be dated from epigraphical evi-dence, it is certain that the greater part of the 15th - century icons at the Monastery can be placed in the second half of the century, after the overthrow of the Byzantine state by the Ottomans in 1453. The available evidence suggests that this was a period when the Monas-tery was at an economic height.[118] The new aesthetic appearance of the icons is a result of the systematic attempt to copy 13th-century panels at the Monastery. This tendency is in part due to the interruption of the flow of works and of artistic ideas from Constantinople. Into this chronological framework must be placed a number of icons which indicate the close links of the Monastery to the Christian Syrian and Arab communities of the Near East. Due to their folk character, these icons, which have not yet been studied, present additional difficulties as to their dating. More easily datable are a restricted number of works with Western features. Finally, an interesting group of icons from the second half of the 15th century are early examples of the Cretan School.

One of the magnificent small icons from the 15th century is the Virgin Glykophilousa (fig. 74)[119] in the variant of the Pelagonitissa, named after a celebrated icon in Pelagonia (Macedonia). The playful pose of the Child and his lively gestures form a contrast to the serious, sorrowful expression on the face of the Virgin. This contrast alludes to the meaning of this iconographic variant since, in both hymnographic and homiletic texts, the Virgin, in her laments during the Passion of Christ, evokes the remembrance of His infancy. Stylistically the work illustrates the main characteristics of the official Palaeologan art of the period. The hieratic austerity of the Virgin is in keeping with the conservatism of Palaeologan icon painting after a long period of experimentation during the 13th century. The facial characteristics are rendered with fine brown brushstrokes. The restricted shading and the modelling of the faces, predominantly with light ochre, create a transparent effect which gives the impression of oil painting. This technique and the small clusters of white highlights, which model the wrist and the fingers, indicate that the icon must be dated to the 15th rather than the 14th century. The subject and the small dimensions of the panel suggest that it was destined for private devotion. There is no indication that the work was painted at Sinai. It is more probable that it came to the Monastery from the central cultural zone of Byzantium, most likely from Macedonia, where the iconographic variant of the Virgin Pelagonitissa enjoyed great popularity.

The icon of the Lamentation (fig. 75)[120] exemplifies another trend of Late Byzantine painting that coincides with the beginning of the so-called Cretan School, which flourished from the second half of the 15th until the end of the 17th century. The scene is a careful composition formed by smaller units in a rigidly symmetrical structure. The theatrical approach to the scene, in which the setting plays a major role, already hints at its placement among the academic works of the Late Byzantine period. Other elements which elucidate the artistic identity of the panel are the fleshy faces with strong modelling, especially for the female figures, the unrestrained theatrical manner of the participants in the scene, the darker tones of the garments, and the white highlights which acquire metallic reflections. Certain sections of the outlines of the garments, such as the maphorion of the Virgin, provide indirect evidence for infiltrations from Western art. Western connections are even more obvious in the realistic rendering of certain details, such as the hair, the strong musculature of the body of Christ, its extensive shading in olive colour, the nails in the rungs of the ladder, the texture of the wood of the cross, the differentiation of Mary Magdalen from the other Maries by means of the bright red colour of her maphorion, and also the perspectival appearance of the crenellations and of other architectural features of the walls of Jerusalem. These realistic elements co-exist, nevertheless, with anti-naturalistic details, such as the decorative bushes with abundant chrysography in the leaves and the branches. A number of stylistic characteristics relate this icon to pictorial works of Constantinopolitan origin from the early 15th century, such as the wall paintings of the Pantanassa at Mistra (c. 1430). However, it has more features in common with a group of 'pre-Cretan' icons, dependent on the International Gothic style, as seen, for example, in the Nativity of the former Volpi Collection. These icons must have been painted in artistic centres where interaction with Western art can be taken for granted. Thus Crete may be proposed as the most likely place for the training of the painter of the Lamentation icon. This work could, however, have been painted at Sinai, a hypothesis supported by the decoration on the reverse side with successive bands of red wavy brushstrokes, and by the presence at the Monastery of another icon by the same painter with the depiction of Christ of Pity.[121]

The icon with the Great Deesis and various groups of saints (fig. 76)[122] carries an obvious Sinaitic stamp and, as in the case of a large number of Sinai panels, it revives in the 15th century the style of 13th-century icons preserved at the Monastery. In the upper most register is depicted the Trimorphon flanked by the Archangels Michael and Gabriel, and the Evangelists. In the second zone are five hierarchs and five prophets and in the third, ten martyrs. The fourth zone includes nine labelled monastic saints, John Climacus, Sabbas,

Euthymios, Ephraim the Syrian, Theodore the Studite, Pachomios, Arsenios, Paul of Thebes and Anthony, as well as nine anonymous monastic saints with the inscription, Oἱ ἅγ(ιοι) ἀβδάδων (sic) (the Holy Abbots), a selection, in other words, from the Forty Martyrs of Sinai. In the fifth zone are depicted, on the left, three patriarchs of the Old Testament, in the middle, Saints Constantine and Helen with the Cross, and, on the right, three female saints (one equal to the Apostles, Thekla, one martyr, Catherine, and one nun, Phevronia). In the middle of the lower border of the icon is depicted the donor, a monk with his hands raised in supplication. The composition shows an ideal gathering of holy figures according to the view of the Sinaitic monk-donor. This selection, in combination with the more or less correctly written inscriptions, indicates an ambitious work. As for the arrangement of frontal figures in superimposed registers, the composition copies the scheme of Menologion icons, perhaps those which present the saints of the calendar year in twelve individual panels (see fig. 30, for March). The manner in which facial features are rendered is reminiscent of works from the 12th and early 13th centuries. However, the faces are more oval-shaped and have a suave expression, their modelling in light tones gives the impression of porcelain, while great emphasis is placed on the luxuriousness of the garments by the use of abundant chrysography. In general the colours, which are blended and have a glazed quality, play a major role in the aesthetic appearance of this work as in many other icons in the Monastery from this period.

## POST-BYZANTINE ICONS (Cretan School)

Of the large number of icons housed at Sinai, and dated to the years following the conquest of Constantinople by the Turks (1453), few have been published. Their selection was not an easy one[1] since a scholarly catalogue has not yet been prepared, and contemporary restoration work has not been undertaken. Thus, the selection is based on the good preservation of the icons, on their aesthetic quality and on the relevance of their subject matter to Sinai.

The selected works belong mainly to the 15th through 17th centuries, the period of the birth and height of the 'Cretan School' in painting. It is known that the 15th century was a critical point in the formation of the art of the following two centuries. During the first half of the century, Constantinopolitan painters worked in Crete, while in the same period, others from the island went to the capital. This contact resulted in the elevation of the quality of painting in Crete and contributed to the birth of the art of portable Cretan icons. Thus, in Venetian-occupied Crete, the great art of Byzantium continued even after the collapse of the empire. Among others, the wall paintings by the Phokas family (mid-15th century) and even a few from the beginning of the 16th century, which are preserved on the island, are delicately worked, as are the portable icons.

Features of Cretan painting (of both wall painting and portable icons) were considered to be the adherence to the best traditions of the art of Constantinople, the dogmatic clarity of iconography, the scent of holiness given off by the works, their technical perfection, the nobility and the elegance in the restrained poses and gestures of the figures and, lastly, the spirit of Classicism which pervades the quiet, rhythmical compositions.[2]

These qualities exerted a magnetic attraction on the pious and conservative patrons (Orthodox and Catholic) of the Cretan painters of holy images. Since the authorities of Venice did not provide an obstacle, the demand for icons increased and their trade grew. Many artists painted icons, as may be deduced primarily from documents housed in the State Archives of Venice. Commissions of a vast number of icons with the same subject, which had to be ready in a short time had, as a consequence, the crystallization of subjects into types which resulted in the formation of 'common topoi'. Superior painters created icon-models, which were copied exactly or in variations.[3] Originality retreated and the virtuosity of the painters now became more important.

Cretan artists also accepted commissions from large monastic communities, such as those of Sinai, Mount Athos, and Patmos. In the case of Sinai, ties to Crete were close. In Chandax (Heraklion) the Sinaitic metochion of Saint Catherine blossomed. The later wooden templon of the katholikon of the Monastery (1612) was carved in Crete and its icons were painted by the Cretan artist Jeremiah Palladas.

The icons of the 15th century are distinguished by their excellent technique, but their subject matter is rather restricted, and the compositions lack originality and daring.[4] Although the painters sometimes introduce details from Western or Byzantine images, they are secondary elements only, and are adapted in their compositions.[5] When the artists resort to Western creations, they choose Gothic works of the 14th century.[6] Toward the turn of the 16th century, icons maintain technical excellence, the compositions gain new iconographic elements and later the iconography is enriched by new subjects.[7] Italian Mannerism does not leave the Cretan icon painters uninfluenced. During the 17th century, the number of imported Western elements increases and at some point the iconography becomes Western. Thus, Cretan painting responds to contemporary cultural currents as two worlds, Byzantium and the West, draw nearer. The close ties between Crete and Venice play a role in this rapprochement. Cretan artists drift between Western realism and Byzantine idealism, but their technique remains the same until the end. Colours continue to be dissolved in egg yoke, and the painters do not establish a single source of lighting. Each figure in the icon maintains its own inner otherworldly light. The transcendent heaven is still nearly always in gold, and the dimensions of the figures are in proportion to their importance.

It is difficult to discuss further the Cretan School in the years following the end of the 17th century, since works by its most important representatives no longer exist.[8]

Some of the icons of Sinai are the works of famous Cretan painters. One of the earliest, Angelos, has been identified, most probably correctly, as Angelos Akotantos of Heraklion (died 1457).[9] Consequently, his most active period must be dated within the second quarter and around the middle of the 15th century. The signature on his icons follows the type Χείρ Ἀγγέλου (hand of Angelos). More than forty signed and unsigned works are attributed to him.[10] The Palaeologan style dominates his compositions and his icons are distinguished by their great 'workmanship'. Since the painter seems to have had a close connection with the Sinaitic metochion in Chandax (Heraklion), it is natural to find his works also at Sinai.

In a small icon[11] with the Byzantine iconographic subject of the Deesis (fig. 77), the enthroned Christ is flanked by the Virgin and John the Baptist, who pray for the salvation of the world and evidently for the donor or the painter. Below, to the right, is the signature of the painter following the usual type.[12] The authenticity of this icon is unquestionable.[13] The finely worked figures of outstanding beauty radiate nobility and the Virgin's expression of sorrow reveals the lyrical mood of the painter.[14] I attribute to the same painter an unsigned icon (fig. 78), also with the subject of the Deesis.[15] Christ, this time standing, holds a closed Gospel. In this impeccable work, John the Baptist has been replaced by the elegant Saint Phanourios,[16] a favourite of Angelos, who painted him many times.[17] The finely detailed chrysography on the breastplate of the Saint realistically imitates swirling acanthus leaves. The portrait type of Christ is the same as in the preceding icon. The lyrical mood is again evident in the faces of the two supplicants.

The signature of Angelos is borne also by the icon (fig. 80) which represents the aged John the Evangelist in the opening of a cave, accepting divine illumination and dictating his Gospel to the young Prochoros.[18] It is difficult to question the authenticity of this work.[19] Behind the scribe there is a woven basket, suspended in mid-air, containing a set of scrolls. The same subject is encountered in a miniature from a codex written in 1415 in Crete[20] and was refined and repeated by Angelos in his later icons and wall paintings. In the Sinai icon, the drapery should be characterized as Palaeologan. We also detect a lyrical mood in the noble, delicate face of Prochoros.[21]

The formation of a variant of the Byzantine iconographic theme of the Presentation of the Virgin (fig. 81) is attributed to Angelos, according to the evidence of the signed icon of the Loverdos Collection (now in the Byzantine Museum in Athens).[22] This work resembles so greatly the unsigned icon of Sinai with the same subject[23] that I believe that it too can be attributed to Angelos.[24] The iconography of the Presentation is inspired by the apocryphal Protoevangelium of James. The icon follows Byzantine models and its style is in accordance with the Palaeologan tradition.

Certain unsigned icons from Sinai can be traced to the atelier of the famous Cretan icon painter of the 15th century, Andreas Ritzos (c. 1421-1492). Because of the high quality of his work, and perhaps through his teaching also, Ritzos is part of the renewal of traditional painting.[25] In his icons, with their charming colours, he does not avoid the 'artistic calligraphy' that is so characteristic of academic art.[26] It has been suggested that Andreas Ritzos must have been an apprentice in the workshop of Angelos Akotantos.[27]

Inside the Sanctuary of the great basilica, on the eastern side of the iconostasis, is situated an icon of the Archangel Michael, full-length, in military dress (fig. 79). I consider the gentle rendering of the face with rose-coloured cheeks to be very close to that of the Virgin Zoodochos Pigi of the Sinai Monastery.[28] It has been asserted that this icon displays characteristics of the art of Ritzos.[29] The working drawings *(anthivola)* of the Sinaitic work would have been used for other icons of Michael, such as that in Patmos.[30] I would date the Archangel of Sinai to the last quarter of the 15th century.

The Hodegetria icon (fig. 82), within whose borders are depicted half-length saints, also belongs, I believe, to the period of Ritzos (from his atelier?).[31] The gold background of the entire icon shines. The Virgin in this type, half-length as usual, supports the Child in her left arm. The original icon, considered to be a work of the Evangelist Luke, was located in the Church of the Virgin of the Hodegon in Constantinople, and was its protector. Noteworthy is the manner in which the maphorion in brilliant crimson descends, draped, from the left shoulder toward the right, hiding the chiton near the neck. The same arrangement occurs in the Hodegetria icon of the Serbian Orthodox community of Trieste, attributed to Andreas Ritzos.[32] The two icons resemble each other as much in the positioning of the figures as in the chrysography. Of the half-length figures in the border, we should note the Deesis in the upper section, with the Saviour[33] between Ioakeim and Anna.

In the Sinai Monastery is also located the icon of the Dormition of Basil the Great (fig. 83).[34] Four hierarchs, a deacon, a young reader, and, to the right, a group of cantors, who carry lit candles and wear unusual head-dresses, participate in the funeral *akolouthia* for the deceased.[35] Monks and nuns observe. On the open Gospel of the censing priest are written a pair of pericopes, both from the Gospel, according to John (8:31 and 5:17), mentioned in the funeral *akolouthia* for a priest.[36] In the background, a wall joins two structures, whose openings are rendered in correct perspective. A mask decorates the wall of the three-aisled edifice on the left.[37] Between the buildings two flying angels carry the swaddled soul of the Saint. From Byzantine times, an example of the Dormition of Saint Basil appears in an

11th-century miniature in Codex 14 of the Patriarchal Library of Jerusalem.[38] The drapery on the right-hand building is discreetly decorated with a band of pseudo-Cufic, which was considered a typical characteristic of Cretan icons of the 15th century.[39] In the figures, again, a few highlights emphasize brighter sections of the flesh. In the group of splendid figures on the left, there is a lively contrast between the lighted faces and the blackened garments. The icon can be dated to around the year 1500.

In the katholikon, inside the glass-case of the narthex, located to the right of the entrance, is an icon of a full-length Saint Anthony (fig. 88),[40] surrounded in the border by half-length figures of the Deesis (above) and of holy figures, including Saint Catherine, the holy Abbots of the Monastery, John Climacus and Anastasios, the Prophet Moses and the righteous Melchisedek. The selection of the saints of the border supports the hypothesis that the icon was made for Sinai or by commission of a Sinaitic monk. Below the feet of Saint Anthony is written the name of the painter: $Χεὶρ \ Δημητρ[ίου] \ ἱερέ[ως]$ (hand of the priest Demetrios). The priest Demetrios, most likely an important Cretan painter,[41] is known so far only through three works.[42] Based on the style of his icons, it can be stated that he lived at the end of the 15th or at the beginning of the 16th century.

Saint Anthony has a broad face as do the other saints of the border.[43] The inscription on his scroll is usual for icons of this saint. Melchisedek in the border is depicted naked with a hairy body.[44]

In the Chapel of John the Baptist, the splendid Sanctuary doors (fig. 90),[45] perhaps originally from an older templon of the katholikon, are divided into two zones, and are decorated in the upper section with the Annunciation and in the lower section with the Prophets Moses and Aaron. On the crowning element there is a half-length depiction of Christ-Emmanuel. The carved apex of the Sanctuary doors, in the drilled technique, recalls those of Patmos, with painted representations attributed to Andreas Ritzos.[46] They correspond, however, also to Sanctuary doors dating to the first half of the 16th century.[47]

Moses carries within a box-like vessel a half-length figure of the Virgin of the Burning Bush, and the stamnos.[48] The prophet resembles the Moses by Theophanes at the Stavronikita Monastery on Mount Athos even in the colour of his skin.[49] Pseudo-Cufic letters decorate the lining of the cloak of Moses and the mantle of Aaron,[50] who carries the staff, the 'flowering rod'. The Sanctuary doors must be considered a creation of the period of Theophanes.[51]

On the south wall of the katholikon hangs an icon of Saint Theodore Stratelates and Saint Theodore Teron (fig. 91).[52] Both figures wear military dress. The first holds an upright spear and supports a shield with the other hand. The second unsheathes a sword, while a rectangular shield, with convex surface, is suspended from his left forearm. Above, in the middle of the icon, is a half-length figure of the blessing Christ. The saints are tall with thin bodies. In this aspect, they surpass the military saints of the frescoes of Theophanes at the Stavronikita Monastery (1545-1546).[53] The portrait of Theodore Stratelates resembles that of the same saint at Stavronikita, who carries, in a similar manner, a shield with an identical emblem.[54] This tie to the works of the great painter leads to a dating of this beautiful icon to around the middle or the third quarter of the 16th century.

In the Chapel of the Burning Bush is located the unsigned and undated icon of the 'In Thee Rejoiceth' (pl. 93),[55] an illustration of the hymn chanted during the Liturgy of Basil the Great following the consecration of the Gifts. The composition is confined only to the main subject and is composed of two parts. In the upper section, inside a two-coloured aureole (red with gold rays), the enthroned Virgin and Child, surrounded by the choirs of angels, sit in front of a five-domed church which is bordered by trees. This portrayal is undoubtedly an effect of the characterization in the hymn of the Virgin as 'a hallowed temple and a spiritual paradise'. The deep blue sky is decorated with gold stars, the sun and the moon: 'all creation', which 'rejoices'.

In the lower zone, in successive rows is depicted the 'race of men'.[56] In the lower left and in larger scale are John the Baptist and the composer of the hymn, John of Damascus. In comparison with the icon of Klontzas on the same subject, which we shall see below, few figures are depicted. In the first row, however, are presented in the same order as in the Klontzas icon the hierarchs, with the prophets and, across from them, the apostles. The first of the Disciples, most likely Peter, resembles the same apostle in the Ascension and in the Dormition in the Stavronikita Monastery[57] and in the Last Supper in its refectory. The preservation of the work is good and the colours harmonious. I would date the icon, in agreement with M. Constantoudake-Kitromelidou, to the 17th century.

To the iconographic type of the Virgin of the Passion belongs the icon[58] with the inscription: *Mary, Mother of God. Lady of the Angels* (fig. 87). On the raised edge of the border, is inscribed: Μνήσθητί μου Κ[ύρι]ε. A little below is the date: Ā.Φ.Ο.Θ. (1579).

The type of the Virgin of the Passion was crystallized, as has been noted,[59] by Andreas Ritzos and enjoyed widespread popularity. To the right and the left of the Virgin and Child, in half-length, the Archangels Michael and Gabriel present to the Christ Child the symbols of his future Passion (the cross with the crown of thorns and the nails, the pot with vinegar, lance and sponge) in accordance with the specific epigram which corresponds to the composition: θνητὴν σάρκα ἐνδεδυμένος πότμον δεδοικὼς δειλιᾶ ταῦτα βλέπων.

The Sinai icon, despite its beauty, does not have the perfection of the works of Ritzos. It has been commented that its rendering is more linear and dry, its figures less expressive, the fingers without delineation.[60]

A large icon of the Presentation in the Temple (fig. 89),[61] with the traditional figures from the Byzantine period, adorns the west wall of the katholikon. To the right, standing on two steps and bending over, Symeon reverently holds the infant Christ who turns his body and extends his hand toward the Virgin, clad in a bright crimson maphorion. The rose-coloured himation of Symeon has broad highlights in yellow and olive. Between the Virgin and Symeon are closed Sanctuary doors and an altar with ciborium. According to the preserved inscription, the icon was painted by Damaskinos in 1571.[62] However, the icon is not characteristic of his art, and thus, despite its virtues, it is not acknowledged as his work.[63] The splendid luminous faces of the Sinaitic icon are reminiscent of figures of Theophanes.[64] The Presentation in the Temple would have been painted during the second half of the 16th century.[65]

From the end of the century must derive the icon of Sinai which bears the inscription: *The Massacre of Demetrios* (fig. 92).[66] The icon repeats a type described already by Mark Eugenikos in the 15th century.[67] In front of the saint is a group of soldiers who pierce him with lances. Two of them, who are not bearded, have long moustaches,[68] and all wear strange helmets. Three of the helmets have ostrich feathers in the back and one, a pair of delicate feathers in front.[69] The helmet of the first is encircled with jewels imitating acanthus leaves, as in the corresponding soldier in an icon of Cortezas (second half of the 16th century)[70] with the same subject. The tunic of Demetrios has numerous highlights.[71]

At the Monastery of Sinai there are also a number of works of Georgios Klontzas which imply some special relationship between the painter and the Monastery.[72]

Klontzas, a distinguished painter, was born in Chandax around 1540 and died in 1608.[73] Three of his four sons are referred to as painters. His atelier was located in the public square of Saint Mark, a central point of the city. His style, daring, and innovation distinguish him from fellow Cretan artists of his period. He was a connoisseur of the Venetian art of his day,[74] and his familiarity with Italian Mannerism is obvious. His figures are tall and agile and, as their number multiplies — even to excess — they smother the free space and express the painter's *horror vacui.* The restless Klontzas enriches the accepted types with secondary subjects, while the gold background is often replaced by colour.

In the Chapel of the Holy Fathers of Raithou and Sinai, an icon which represents the monastic life is situated on the proskynetarion (fig. 99).[75] It is divided into four horizontal zones. In the uppermost, is represented the Transfiguration of Christ with the ascent and descent from Tabor, which is depicted in traditional fashion with stepped rocks and small trees of a Western type. Below the Transfiguration is inscribed in black capital letters; Χεὶρ Γεωγίου (sic) Κλόντζα τοῦ Κρητ[ὸς] ΑΧΓ´.[76] The two middle zones illustrate a two-storey portico[77] with cells. Monks, with their prayer beads sit or walk conversing in a lively manner under the monastic arches. In the right corner of the upper portico is a chapel. In the lower zone, to the left, is painted a garden with streams and trees bearing fruit or blossoming, and to the right, a refectory with dining monks.[78] The majority of these are elderly with long beards. Their tall silhouettes, their lively discussion and movement, the Italian influences, the introduction of genre painting (e.g., the novice [?] who empties the food into bowls), the technique of the figures with large, bright surfaces, which contrast the shade, and finally, the original composition of the subject, do not leave any doubt that the creator of this graceful work is Klontzas.

Inside the Sanctuary above the templon and next to the icon of the Archangel Michael is placed another large icon with the theme 'In Thee Rejoiceth' (fig. 98).[79] The main subject is contained in the middle of the composition inside a rectangle crowned by a blue arch with the zodiac cycle in grisaille on its narrow surface. In the spandrels on either side of the arch is written the entire hymn 'In Thee Rejoiceth'. In the approximate middle of the rectangle is a circle containing the sceptre-bearing Virgin with the Child, on a throne of the Western type. The circle is surrounded by a band with inscriptions relating to the small icons arranged radially and containing subjects from the Old Testament (the stories of Joseph, Moses, the tower of Babel, Noah, the murder of Cain). The circle touches the choirs of angels at its top, and is bordered by the couples Ioakeim and Anna to left, and Elisabeth and Zechariah to the right, who stand in front of domed churches with Gothic elements. Below is painted 'the race of men' in horizontal, superimposed rows. The upper section of the rectangle, in a deep blue, stary heaven, presents a Gothic church with three domes. It is noteworthy how its side walls have not been drawn in proper perspective, but according to the manner which today would be called modern.

The centre rectangle is surrounded by twenty small icons of which seven, on the left side, depict subjects from the Old Testament considered prefigurations of the Virgin. The others, dedicated to her life, begin with her Presentation and end with the Nativity of Christ.

Innovative and prolific, the painter develops in many scenes the subject of the Annunciation, following most likely the iconography of the strophes of the Akathistos Hymn, and unites in the same composition the Journey to Bethlehem with the Census,[80] a rare subject in Post-Byzantine painting. Below the scene of the Journey to Bethlehem, half hidden by the frame of the icon, we can distinguish a signature with the name of Klontzas, and the date ‚ΑΧΔ´ (1604). Even if the authenticity of the signature can be doubted (it has been thought to be an addition by Kornaros, who wrote in another location how he renewed the work in 1778), the attribution of the icon to Klontzas, does not raise serious questions.[81] The figures are not long and slender and the technique of the faces is reminiscent of that of wall painting. A gold heaven is included: other scenes are enclosed according to the Western manner in rooms of which the ceiling and the walls are rendered in proper perspective. The mixture of Western and traditional elements is obvious. Klontzas painted the subject[82] on another occasion in an altered manner, evidence of his flexibility.

During the first half of the 17th century, the Sinaitic 'Papa kyr Silvestros' Theocharis lived in Heraklion. He was a conservative painter, distinguished by his technical capabilities, mainly in miniature works and copies of good models.[83]

On the north wall of the katholikon, on a shelf, is the icon of the Holy Ten Martyrs of Crete,[84] who were martyred in Gortyna in the period of the Roman Emperor Decian (fig. 94). They carry a cross, symbol of martyrdom, and wear chitons and mantles. Each one has his name written above his head or below his feet. The icon is unsigned. However, its similarity to the icon of the Holy Ten of Silvestros in the Metochion of Sinai in Zakynthos,[85] dictates the attribution of this icon to the same painter.

The priest Emmanuel Tzanes Bounialis of Rethymnon (1610-1690) lived in Venice from the year 1655 until his death. Thus, he had the opportunity to gain a solid knowledge of Western art. His known works today are in excess of 135.[86] Tzanes did not lack erudition and his art exemplifies, as has been remarked, the duality of Western and traditional elements. His skill as a miniaturist is evidenced by a small icon[87] in the 'gallery' of Sinai which presents the Virgin and Child (fig. 97), seated upon foamy, ash-white clouds (as is usual for Tzanes), and among the Prophets Moses, Aaron, Isaiah and Jacob, who hold scrolls with texts related to the Virgin. On the scroll of the Virgin is written a strange dialogue between herself and Christ. The restorer Kornaros in 1778 added (foreign to Tzanes) misspellings and the signature of the artist, and wrote incorrectly the date 1551, instead of the correct date of 1651, according to Xyngopoulos.[88] That it is a work of Tzanes is indicated by the style, especially as seen in the figure of Jacob.[89]

The Cretan priest Victor, who lived and worked in Heraklion, has a great reputation and a special relation to Sinai. His works, more conservative than his models, enjoyed great popularity, though they lacked originality. Victor also painted the banner of the flagship of Morosini. His authentic icons, which number 95, date to the years 1651 to 1697.[90]

One of his works which is preserved in the Sinai Monastery is a triptych (fig. 101)[91] which, when it is open, depicts in the central panel the enthroned Christ as High Priest with the symbols of the Evangelists. On the left sit the enthroned Virgin and Child with half-length prophets,[92] and on the right, John the Baptist. On the outer faces of the side wings are depicted respectively, Saint Catherine and the Annunciation. Below the left foot of the angel, the signature, χείρ Βίκτωρος (hand of Victor).

Of further interest is the central panel of a triptych[93] with the Enthroned Christ as High Priest bordered by the authors of the Divine Liturgy, Chrysostom and Basil (fig. 102). In the crown of the gilded wood carved frame, are depicted the three peaks of Sinai with the Monastery, the small monasteries and the churches of the area. To the left is Moses with the Burning Bush, and to the right is Saint Catherine (depicted frontally). The Giving of the Law by the Hand of God to Moses is illustrated, as well as the entombment of the body of Saint Catherine by angels.

The main composition is organized according to the usual iconographic subject of the Deesis. The hierarchs carry texts apparently of the liturgies which they wrote and give the impression that they are prepared to concelebrate with the High Priest.

The intense white highlights on the dark faces of the figures result in a lively contrast to the brown underpainting. The slender figure of Basil the Great is close to the rendering of the same saint by Theodoros Poulakis in the 'In Thee Rejoiceth' of Patmos.[94] The depictions in the crown resemble the corresponding figures of another triptych of the Sinai Monastery which is a work of Victor. Very similar also is the decorative sculpture of the frame.[95] Should this work then also be attributed to Victor?

On the proskynetarion in the narthex has been placed a small icon (fig. 100) with the inscription *Tο θεοβάδιστον όρως Σηνὰ (the God-Trodden Sinai mountain)*.[96] To the lower left is pictured the Monastery with its walls,[97] the katholikon with the apparition of the Burning Bush, the mosque with the minaret and the monks' cells. Monks have gone out of the open gate in order to receive the approaching Archbishop with his escort. In the background are the three peaks of the mountain. On the middle peak, where monks ascend the stepped footpath, is depicted the Giving of the Law to Moses and to the right, the entombment of the holy remains of Saint Catherine by two angels. In the foothills are small churches, 'kathismata', and metochia. Near the centre of the right side is the misspelled signature in red letters: *Χιρ Ειακοβου / Μόσκου* (hand of Iakovos Moskos).

Two dated icons of the painter are known, one in Paros (1704) and the other in Cyprus (1711).[98] Therefore the Sinai icon with its folk character also belongs in the first quarter of the 18th century. A similar representation of the Monastery has been published by George Soteriou.[99]

## ICONS FROM THE METOCHION OF THE SINAI MONASTERY IN HERAKLION, CRETE

Certain icons of the Cretan School which are located in the metochion of the Sinai Monastery in Heraklion are of great interest. In the representation of the Deesis (fig. 84) the peculiarity of the iconographic type is due to the fact that the traditional figure of John the Baptist, to the right of Christ, has been replaced by Saint Nicholas, whose selection may be related to the person who ordered the icon, or to the church to which the icon was given.[1] The inclusion of Saint Nicholas together with the three traditional figures of the Deesis, in an 11th- century Sinai icon, has been explained by the preeminent position which he holds in the hierarchy of saints.[2] This position perhaps justifies his replacing, under certain conditions, the Baptist, who is the third in the hierarchic order of the Christian scheme of salvation. The representation of the standing Christ, in frontal pose, who blesses with His right hand and holds a closed jewel-encrusted Gospel book in the left, derives from older Byzantine iconography and is repeated on a very limited scale in Cretan painting, which predominantly maintains the type of the enthroned Christ.[3] To the left, the Virgin turns toward Christ, inclines her head and extends her hands in supplication. Saint Nicholas, dressed in episcopal garments and bowing slightly toward Christ, has his hands crossed on his chest.[4] The faultless technical execution, the very delicate modelling in gradated tones of transparent colours, the geometric rhythm of the drapery with its intense reflections, which creates the feeling of sculpted form and emphasizes the monumentality of the figures with a controlled ethos, and also the highly decorated and tooled nimbi reveal that the work is by a Cretan painter of the late 15th century.

The rare iconographic representation of Symeon Theodochos ('Receiver of God') with the Christ Child in his arms (fig. 86) is known from a 13th-century Sinai icon and is thought to be a condensed form of the depiction of the Presentation in the Temple derived mainly from the miniatures in the margins of illuminated manuscripts.[5] From this medium, the iconographic type spread to icons and wall painting. One such example is the representation in the Vrondisi Monastery where, however, Symeon in half-length, turned to the right, gazes at Christ, whom he holds in his arms, as in the Sinai icon. In the full-length representation and in the manner in which Symeon holds the Child, the iconographic type in this icon is rendered differently from older representations. Formed by the technical methods of Cretan painting, with characteristic freedom of the brushwork, the venerable, elderly figure of Symeon assumes a clear portrait type, full of strength and realism, which is intensified by the penetrating and reflective sidelong glance. The portrait of Symeon is related to the figures of aged bishops in the icon of the First Ecumenical Council painted by Michael Damaskinos in 1591, which is located in the Sinaitic metochion of Saint Catherine in Heraklion. This link, as well as the resemblance of the figure of the robust young Christ to the Christ in the scene of the Vision of Saint Peter of Alexandria in the same icon, justifies the attribution of the work to Michael Damaskinos. Characteristic from this viewpoint is the realistic manner of rendering the veins of the hands and the temples of the elderly figures, both in the bishops of the icon of the Ecumenical Council and of Symeon in our icon. This realism reflects the painter's awareness of Italian art.[6]

The iconographic type of John the Baptist (fig. 85) derives from a model of the Palaeologan period which was also followed by Cretan painters in the 15th century. The very tall saint, depicted frontally, is dressed in sheep skin and a himation. His right hand is raised in blessing, and in his left hand he holds an open scroll with the well-known inscription in capital letters, *Repent, for the kingdom of heaven is at hand*, and a long staff that terminates in a cross. Characteristic of the origins of this iconographic type is the foreshortening of the lowered left arm as well as the absence of the paten with the decapitated head such as seen in the wall painting in the church of the Virgin at Sklaverochori, in the area of Heraklion, and in the icon painted by Andreas Ritzos, now in Tokyo.[7] It differs, however, from these specific models by the addition of open wings. The style and technique in modelling the flesh by means of brown underpainting and wheat-coloured highlighting, the great facility in the creation of volume and of the prominent cheekbones of the face (features which are seen also in the figure of Symeon), reinforce the attribution of this icon to Michael Damaskinos. This attribution is supported by the nearly identical dimensions of the icons (figs. 85 and 86) which confirm that they were originally part of the same iconostasis.[8]

The iconographic type of Saint Catherine, dressed in imperial garments, and enthroned between the symbols of wisdom and of her martyrdom, seems to have been formulated in Crete in the second half of the 16th century by Michael Damaskinos.[9] The older, well-known icon of this type, in the iconostasis of Saint Catherine at Sinai,[10] belongs to the Cretan painter and Sinaitic monk Jeremiah Palladas, who also elaborately signed his name on the icon of the Sinaitic metochion of Heraklion (fig. 96) between the spokes of the wheel of the saint's martyrdom.[11] The basic characteristics of this type, inspired by Italian models are: the contrapposto of the body, the position of the hand which holds the palm branch to her breast, the mantle with gold embroidered eagles trimmed with ermine, the gold-woven Venetian dress wrapped with the loros, the hair gathered by a gold snood according to the Venetian fashion, and the wooden cross with the Crucified Christ held by the saint in her left hand, which rests on the wheel of her martyrdom.[12] In the lower part of the icon, which has been trimmed in order to fit another iconostasis, are depicted the attributes of wisdom: a pair of compasses, an inkwell, and an astronomic globe. Together with these were lost the small gold monochrome representations of a throne and a lectern. The Sinaitic monk Jeremiah Palladas, even if he represented the conservative Orthodox circles of the period, accepted the already formed Western iconographic type of Saint Catherine, and transmitted it as a model for later painters.

The depiction of the military Saint Phanourios, full-length and seated on a throne, and treading on the body of a slain dragon, repeats faithfully the model of a Cretan icon of the 15th century in the Monastery of Valsamoneron which is linked to the great Cretan painter Angelos.[13] As in the iconographic model, the Saint is depicted in a rigid frontal pose (fig. 95), holding a spear in his right hand, and in his left, which supports the shield, a cross, which he stabs into the open mouth of the dragon. An angel crowns the victorious saint with a ribbon decorated with precious stones, and the Hand of God, descending from heaven, blesses him. The mention of the Monastery of Valsamonero in the donor's inscription, *Prayer of the servant of God, Parthenios monk-priest, Davygla in the Monastery of Valsamonero*, which was the centre of the penetration and dissemination of the cult of the new saint on Crete,[14] explains the faithful repetition of the iconographic model and confirms the continuation of the iconography in the later period.

*1. Christ Pantocrator. Detail of fig. 2.*

2

*2. Bust of Christ Pantocrator (84×45.5 cm.). Encaustic icon. First half of the 6th century.*

*3. Christ Enthroned (76×53.5 cm.). Encaustic icon. Beginning of the 7th century.*

5

4. The Virgin between
St. Theodore and St. George
(68.5×49.7 cm.). Encaustic
icon. 6th century.

5. St. Peter (92.8×53.1 cm.).
Encaustic icon. Second half
of the 6th century - first half
of the 7th century.

6. The Nativity of Christ. Centre of a triptych (32.6×19.7 cm.).
Tempera. 8th - 9th centuries.

7. Nativity, Presentation in the Temple,
Ascension, Pentecost. Centre of a
triptych. Fragment (36.5×14.2 cm.). Tempera.
9th - 10th centuries.

8. The Three Hebrew in the Fiery Furnace
(35.5×49.6 cm.). Encaustic icon. 7th century.

*9. The Crucifixion
(46.4×c. 30 cm.). Tempera.
8th century.*

141

IC XC

*11. St. Mercurius (42.2×32.7 cm.).*
*Tempera. 10th century (?).*

*10. The Ascension (41.8×27.1 cm.).*
*Tempera. 9th or 10th century.*

143

12. The Washing of the Feet (25.6×25.9 cm.). Tempera.
First half of the 10th century.

13. Two wings of a triptych. Left, Thaddaeus, St. Paul
of Thebes and St. Anthony; right, king Abgarus, St. Basil
and St. Ephraim (34.5×25.2 cm. with frame). Tempera. Middle
of the 10th century.

14. St. Philip (32.8×20.2 cm.). Tempera. Second half of the 10th century.

15. St. Nicholas with saints (43×33.1 cm.). Tempera. End of the 10th century.

16. Leaf of a tetraptych, menologion, with the martyrs of September, October and November (55×45 cm.). Tempera. Second half of the 11th century.

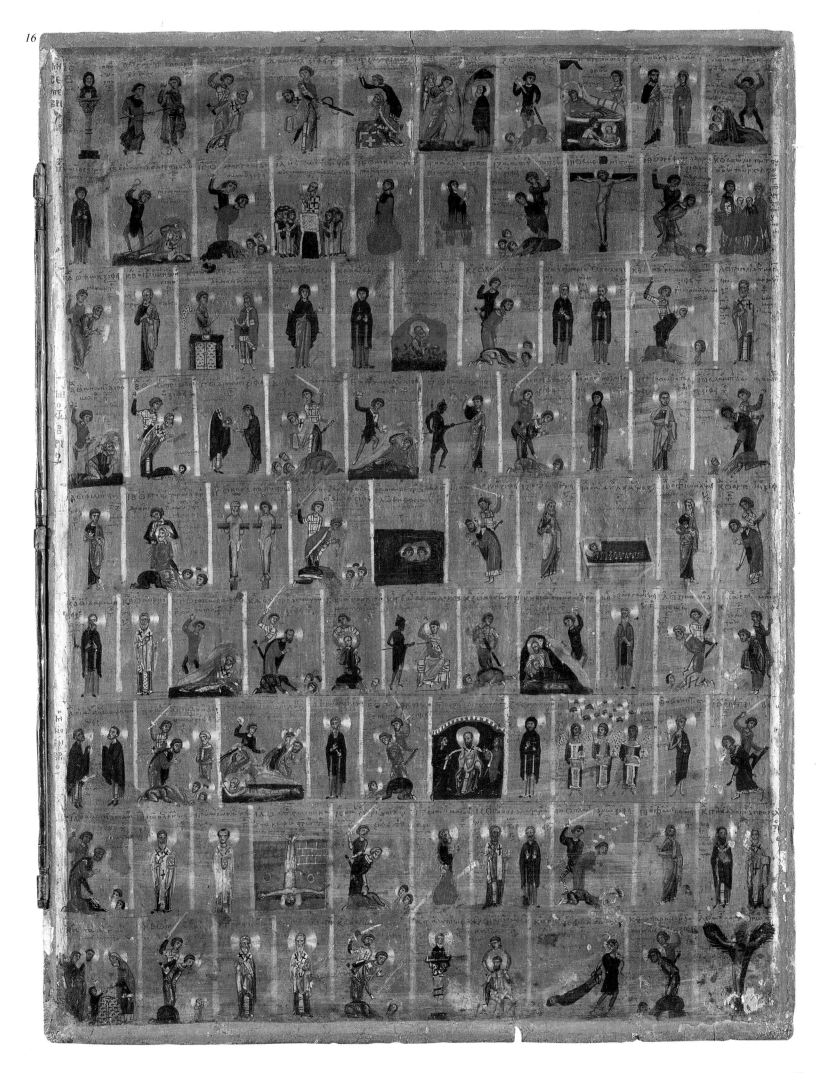

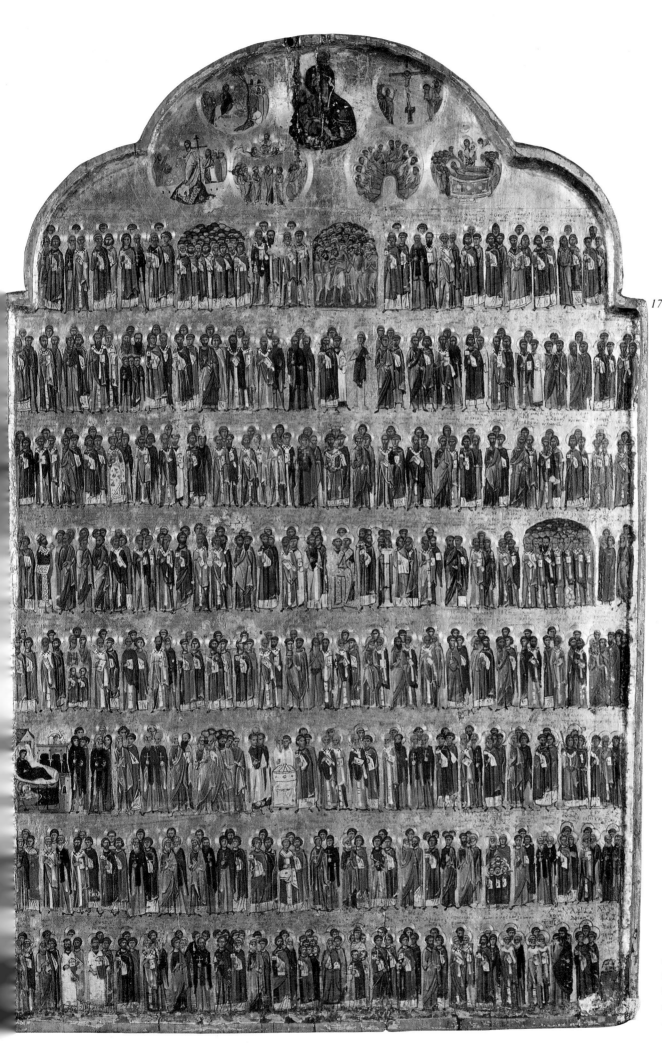

*17*

17. Diptych,
menologion of the
entire year (36×24 cm.
each leaf). Tempera.
Second half of the
11th century.

18

18. Nativity
and Infancy of Christ
(36.3×21.2 cm.). Tempera.
First half of the
12th century.

19. The Virgin Kykkotissa
surrounded by Christ in
Glory, Prophets and Saints
(48.5×41.2 cm.). Tempera
on wood. First half of the
12th century.

20. *Iconostasis beam with Miracles of Saint Eustratios (34.5×275 cm.).
Tempera on wood. Second half of the 12th century.*

*21. Miracle of Saint Eustratios:
The Healing of an insane
person. Detail of fig. 20.*

22. *Miracle of the Holy Five:*
*The Healing of the Woman*
*who was mute and motionless.*
*Detail of fig. 20.*

*23. Miracle at Chonae (37.7×31.4 cm.). Tempera on wood.*
*Second half of the 12th century.*

24. *The Heavenly Ladder (41.1×29.5 cm.). Tempera on wood.*
*Late 12th century.*

25. Two sections of an iconostasis beam with scenes from the life
of the Virgin and the Dodekaorton (41.5×140 and 41.5×159 cm.).
Tempera on wood. Last quarter of the 12th century.

26. The Nativity. Detail of fig. 25.

27. The Transfiguration. Detail of fig. 25.

27

28. Tetraptych with the Dodekaorton
(57×41.8 cm. – each one of the central panels –
49.6×38 cm. – each of the wings). Tempera on wood.
Late 12th century.

29. The Annunciation (61×42.2 cm.). Tempera on wood.
Late 12th century.

30. *Menologion icon for March (97×66.2 cm.). Tempera on wood.*
*c. 12th century.*

*31. Section of an iconostasis beam with scenes from the Dodekaorton (38.7×152.3 cm.). Tempera on wood. c. 1200*

*31*

*32*

*32. The Baptism. Detail of fig. 31.*

*33. The Raising of Lazarus. Detail of fig. 31.*

*33*

НЄГЄRСІСΘΛΑΖΑRΥ

163

34. *The Prophet Elijah (129.1×69 cm.).*
*Tempera on canvas. Early 13th*
*century.*

*35*

35. Sanctuary doors with the representations of Moses and Aaron (c. 127.5×35.5 cm. each side). Tempera on wood. Early 13th century.

*36. Moses before the Burning Bush (92×64 cm.). Tempera on canvas.*
*Early 13th century.*

*37*

37. *The Giving of the Law to Moses (88×65 cm.). Tempera on canvas.*
*Early 13th century.*

*38. Saint Phevronia (58×36 cm.). Tempera on wood. Second half of the 13th century.*

*39. Saint Theodosia (33.9×25.7 cm.). Tempera on wood. Early 13th century.*

*40. Saints Theodore Stratelates and Demetrios (64.2×50.2 cm.). Tempera on canvas. Early 13th century.*

*41. The Archangel Michael. Icon of a Great Deesis (54×45 cm.).*
*Tempera on wood. Early 13th century.*

*42. Christ. Icon of the Great Deesis. Detail (54.1×46.5 cm.).*
*Tempera on wood. Early 13th century.*

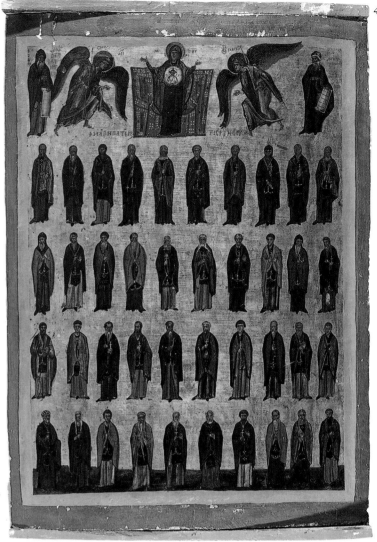

43. The Holy Fathers of Sinai (57.2×42.5 cm.). Tempera on wood. Early 13th century.

44. The Holy Fathers of Raithou (58.2×40.8 cm.). Tempera on wood. Early 13th century.

45. The Virgin of the Burning Bush flanked by four monastic Saints of Sinai (38.3×39.8 cm.). Tempera on canvas. Third decade of the 13th century.

46. Saint Catherine with scenes of her martyrdom (75.3×51.4 cm.). Tempera on wood. Early 13th century.

ΗΑΓΙΑ ΕΚΑΤΕΡΙΝΑ

47. *Saint Procopios (69×37.5 cm.). Tempera on canvas. Third decade of the 13th century.*

48. *The Virgin Blachernitissa flanked by Moses and the Patriarch
of Jerusalem Euthymios II (44.6×36.6 cm.). Tempera on wood. c. 1224.*

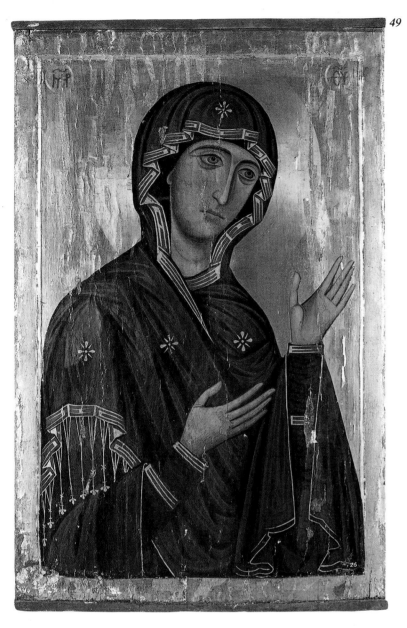

49. *The Virgin. Deesis icon (97.7×65.2 cm.). Tempera on canvas. Early 13th century.*

50. *Christ. Deesis icon (98×65.6 cm.). Tempera on canvas. Early 13th century.*

51. *Saint Nicholas with scenes from his life (82.2×57 cm.). Tempera on wood. Early 13th century.*

51

52. *Saint John the Baptist with scenes from his life (70.8×48.8 cm.).*
*Tempera on wood. Early 13th century.*

53. Saint Panteleimon with scenes from his life and martyrdom (102×72 cm.).
Tempera on wood. Early 13th century.

54. Triptych with the Hodegetria Aristerokratousa and scenes from her life
(112.5×81.5 cm. – central panel, 98.5×40 cm. approximately each of the wings).
Tempera on wood. Early 13th century.

55. The Virgin Hodegetria Aristerokratousa.
Central panel of the triptych of fig. 54.

*56. The Protomartyr Stephen (96.8×63.8 cm.). Tempera on canvas.*
*Early 13th century.*

57. *Saint George (35.7×29 cm.). Tempera on canvas.*
*Early 13th century.*

58. *The Crucifixion (38.5×28 cm.). Tempera on wood.*
*First half of the 13th century.*

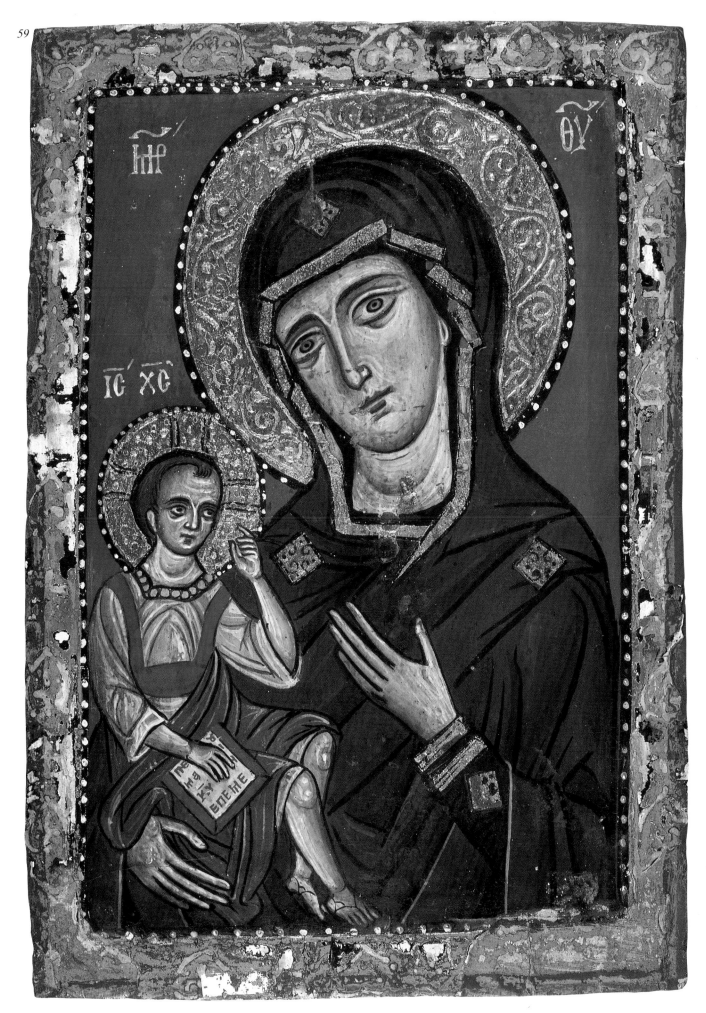

59. *The Virgin Hodegetria Dexiokratousa (38.6×26.9 cm.).*
*Tempera on wood. First half of the 13th century.*

60. *The Virgin Hodegetria Aristerokratousa (94×74.7 cm.).*
*Tempera on canvas. Last quarter of the 13th century.*

61. *The Virgin Blachernitissa (99.2×67 cm.). Tempera on*
*canvas. Last quarter of the 13th century.*

62. *The Virgin Hodegetria Dexiokratousa (74.7×52.8 cm.).*
*Tempera on wood. Last quarter of the 13th century.*

63. The Crucifixion. Front side of a two-sided icon (120×68 cm.). Tempera on wood. Last quarter of the 13th century.

64. The Anastasis. Reverse side of a two-sided icon (120×68 cm.). Tempera on wood. Last quarter of the 13th century.

189

65. Diptych. Saint Procopios and a variant of the Virgin Kykkotissa
(51.2×39.7 cm.). Tempera on wood. Last quarter of the 13th century.

*66. Saints Sergios and Bacchos. Reverse side of a two-sided icon (95×62 cm.).*
*Tempera on wood. Last quarter of the 13th century.*

67

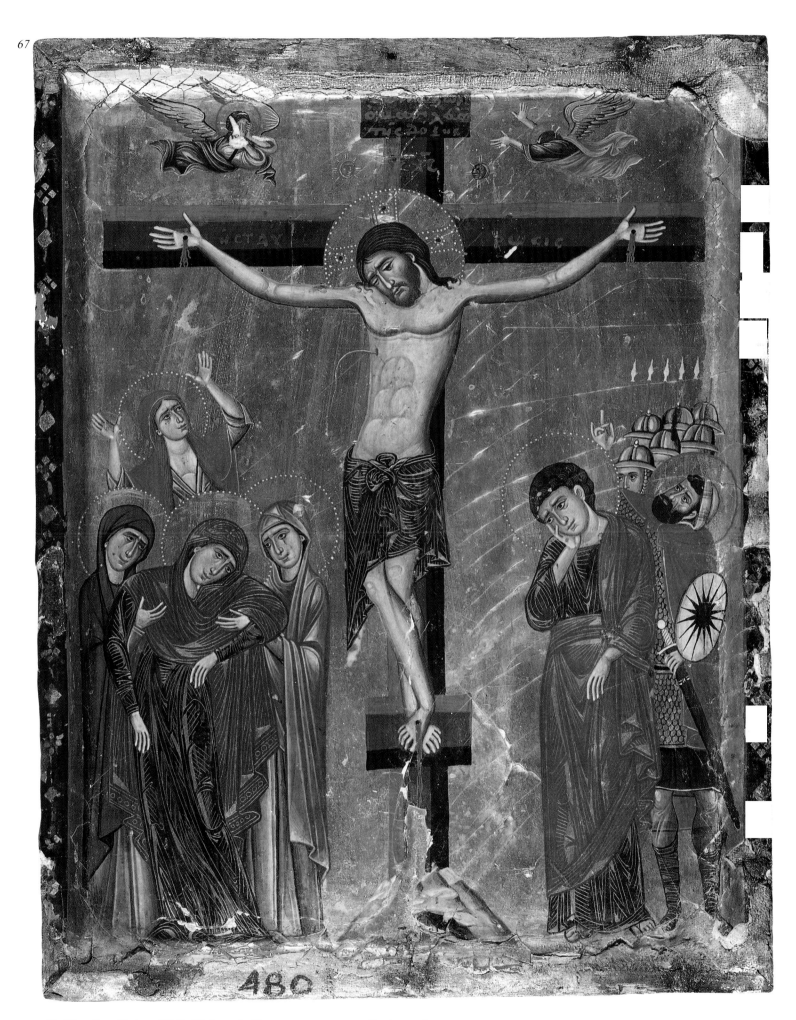

67. *The Crucifixion (33.7×26.6 cm.). Tempera on canvas. Last quarter
of the 13th century.*

68. The Nativity. Dodekaorton icon from an iconostasis (33.7×24.9 cm.). Tempera
on wood. Third quarter of the 13th century.

69. *The Baptism. Dodekaorton icon from an iconostasis (33.5×23.2 cm.). Tempera on wood. Third quarter of the 13th century.*

195

70. *The Forty Martyrs of Sebasteia (38.5×29.4 cm.). Tempera on wood.*
*Late 13th – early 14th century.*

71. *The Crucifixion and the Nativity (43.9×34 cm.). Tempera on canvas.*
*Late 13th – early 14th century.*

72

72. *Hexaptych with the Dodekaorton (31×13.5 cm. – each panel).*
*Tempera on wood. Around the middle of the 14th century.*

73

73. *Saint Catherine. Catalan Retable*
*of Martinus de Vilanova (128×56.3 cm.).*
*Tempera on wood. 1387.*

74. *The Virgin Pelagonitissa (28.5×18.9 cm.).*
*Tempera on wood. Early 15th century.*

ΜΡ ΘΥ
ΙC ΧC

ΘΕΠΙΤΑΦΙΟC ΘΡΗΝΟC·

75. The Lamentation (41.6×31.2 cm.). Tempera on canvas.
Early 15th century.

76. Great Deesis and saints (69.7×51.1 cm.).
Tempera on wood. Second half of the 15th century.

77. Deesis. Work of the painter Angelos (36.2×31.3 cm.).
Tempera. Around the middle of the 15th century.

78. Deesis with Saint Phanourios.
Work of the painter Angelos (24.4×16.9 cm.).
Tempera. Around the middle of the 15th century.

*79. The Archangel Michael. Work attributed to the painter Andreas Ritzos (114.2×63.7 cm.). Tempera. Second half of the 15th century.*

*80. Saint John the Theologian dictates his Gospel to Prochoros. Work of the painter Angelos (66.5×50.7 cm.). Tempera. Around the middle of the 15th century.*

ΓΑΓΙΑ ΤΩΝ ΑΓΙΩΝ

*81. The Presentation of the Virgin. Work attributed to the painter Angelos*
*(39.4×33 cm.). Tempera. Around the middle of the 15th century.*

82. *The Virgin Hodegetria with half-length saints (29.7×27 cm.). Work attributed to the atelier of Andreas Ritzos. Tempera. Second half of the 15th century.*

83. *The Dormition of Saint Basil the Great (39.5×32.8 cm.). Tempera.*
*Early 16th century.*

84. *Deesis with Saint Nicholas (97×80 cm.).*
*Tempera on wood. 15th century.*

85. *Saint John the Baptist. Work attributed to the painter*
*Michael Damaskinos (104×32 cm.). Tempera on wood.*
*16th century.*

86. *Symeon Theodochos with the infant Christ in his arms.*
*Work attributed to the painter Michael Damaskinos*
*(99×32 cm.). Tempera on wood. 16th century.*

87. *The Virgin of the Passion (81.2×62.4 cm.). Tempera. 1579.*

88. *Saint Anthony bordered with half-length saints.*
*Work of the painter-priest Demetrios (70×43.1 cm.). Tempera.*
*Late 15th – early 16th century.*

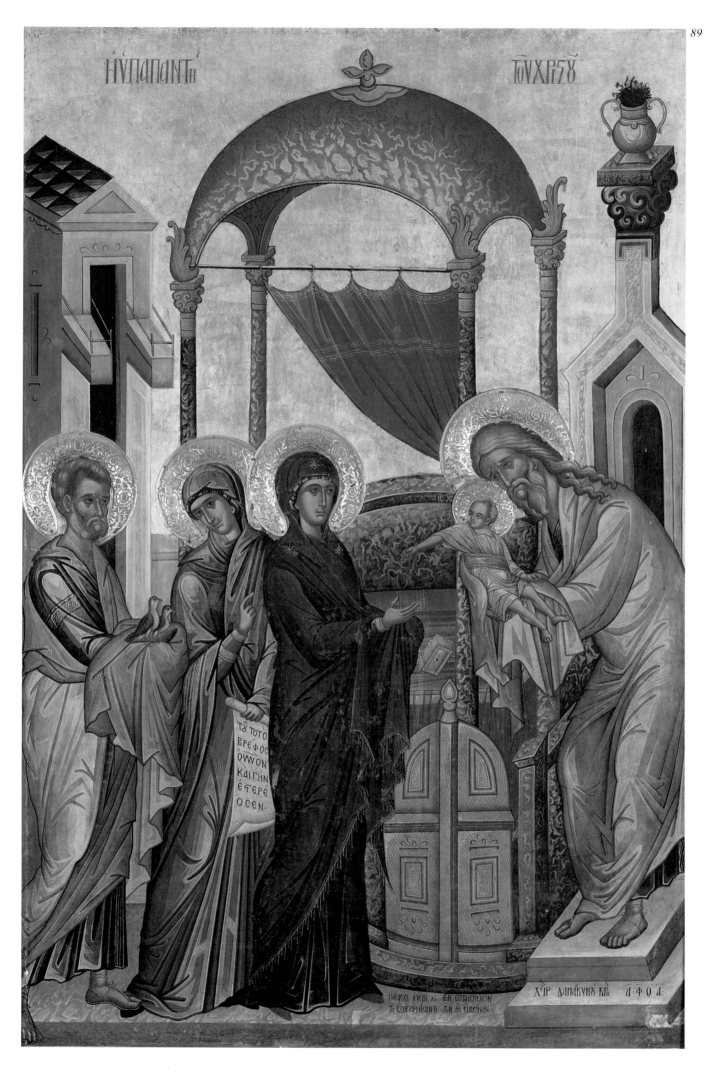

ΗΥΠΑΠΑΝΤΗ                                                   ΤΟΥΧΡΣΥ

ΤΒ ΤΟ ΤΟ
ΒΡΕΦΟΣ
Ο WON
ΚΑΙ ΓΗΝ
ΕΤΕΡΕ
Ο CEN.

89. *The Presentation in the Temple
(111×79 cm.). Tempera. Second half of the
16th century.*

90. *Sanctuary doors from the Chapel
of Saint John the Baptist (total dimensions
165×77.5 cm.). Tempera. 16th century.*

91. *Saint Theodore Stratelates and Saint Theodore Teron (91.8×55 cm.).*
*Tempera. Around the middle of the third quarter of the 16th century.*

*92. The Massacre of Saint Demetrios (74×59.5 cm.). Tempera.*
*Late 16th century.*

93. 'In Thee Rejoiceth' (52.5×39.5 cm.). Tempera. 16th century.

OI ΔΓΙΟΙ ΔΕΚΑ          Ο Ι ΕΝ ΠΚΡΤΗ

ΕΥΔΡΕΤΟΣ          ΠΟΜΠΙΟϹ          ΑΔΘΟΠΟΥϹ          ΒΑϹΙΛΙΔΗϹ

Ο ΑΓ ΘΕΟΔΥΛΟ          Ο ΑΓ ϹΑΤΟΡΝΙΝΟ          Ο ΑΓ ΕΥΠΟΡ          Ο ΑΓ ΓΕΛΑϹΙ          Ο ΑΓ ΕΥΝΙΚΙΑΝ

94. The Holy Ten, Martyrs of Crete. Work of the painter Silvestros Theocharis
(49.5×39 cm.). Tempera. First half of the 17th century.

95. *Saint Phanourios. Work of the painter Ioannis Kolyvas (89×66 cm.).*
*Tempera on wood. 1688.*

*96. Saint Catherine. Work of the painter and monk Jeremiah Palladas*
*(99×84 cm.). Tempera on wood. 17th century.*

97. *Full-length Virgin and Child with Prophets. Work of the painter*
*Emmanuel Tzanes Bounialis (12.5×10.6 cm.). Tempera. 1651 (?).*

98. *'In Thee Rejoiceth'. Work of the painter*
*Georgios Klontzas (106.5×81 cm.). Tempera. 1604 (?).*

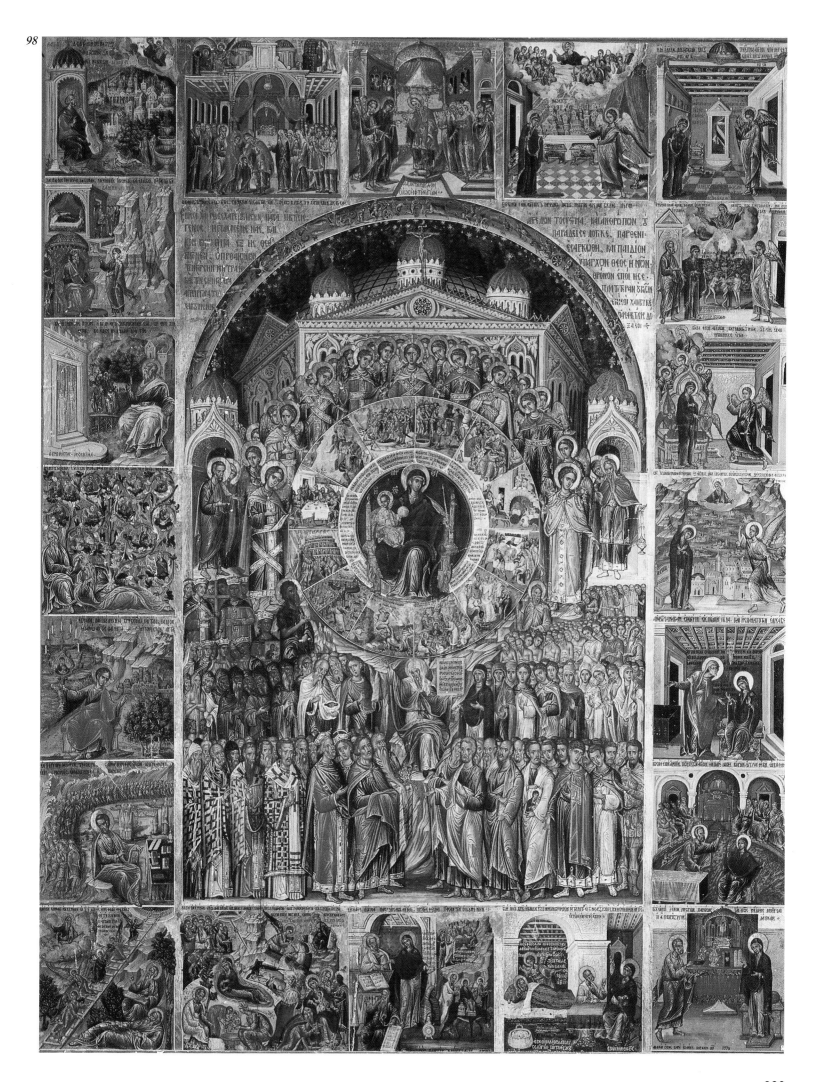

ΓΕΩΡΓΙΟ ΚΛΟΝΤΖΑ ΤΟ ΚΕΤ. ΑΧΓ.

100

TOΘCOB ΔΑΙΓON OPΩCCHN4

100. Sinai. Work of the painter Iacovos Moskos (39×28.6 cm.). Tempera.
First quarter of the 18th century.

99. Icon with the representation of monastic life. Work of the
painter Georgios Klontzas (63×39 cm.). Tempera. 1603 (?).

101

*101. Triptych with Christ as High Priest in the middle panel. Work of the painter Victor (dimensions, when open, approximately 31×40 cm.). Tempera. 17th century.*

102. *Middle panel of a triptych with Christ as High Priest,*
*Chrysostom and Basil. Work of the painter Victor (?)*
*(34×20 cm.). Tempera. 17th century.*

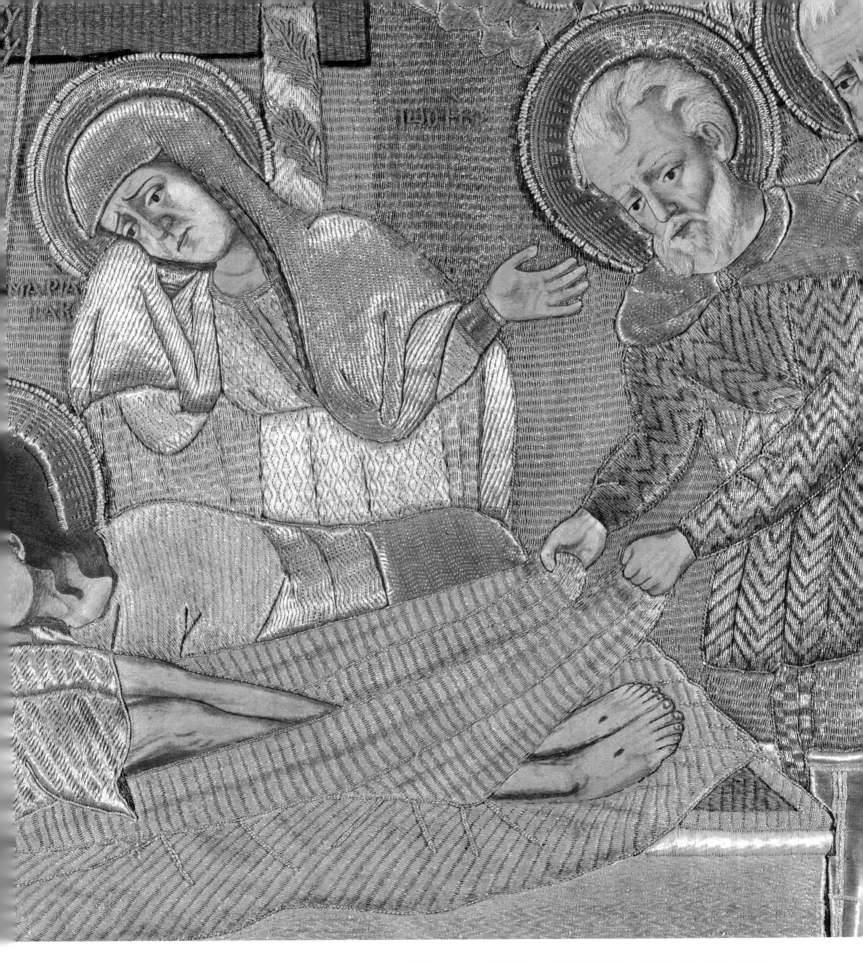

# CHURCH GOLD
# EMBROIDERIES

# CHURCH GOLD EMBROIDERIES

**M**oses on Mt. Sinai, together with the Tablets of the Law, also received commandments from God concerning the garments intended for *Aaron thy brother, and his sons with him... that they may minister unto me in the priest's office.* The command that special sumptuous vestments should be used by the priest, given to Moses on this sacred spot, has been devoutly observed here through the centuries. Tradition served to ratify those ancient commands: an imperial vow ascribed to the founder of the Monastery, the Emperor Justinian, laid down for its head: *my kingship honours him who for the time being presides in Sinai with the rank of hypertimos... and that he should be vested in such vestments as bishops wear* (P. G., vol. 86, I, l. 1149).

The peoples of the Orthodox world and the Christians of the West vied with each other in sending the richest vestments to the Monastery. Those of these which are presented here are the merest sample of the treasures of embroidery which Sinai possesses. The aim of this volume is not to deal with the subject exhaustively, but to prepare the material for a future publication. Thus, we have not given priority to a chronological account, but to the purpose and aesthetic value of the works dealt with. If for the monks of Sinai the Arabs were *an acerbic and bitter set of neighbours*, patriarchs and popes, kings and rulers of the West, princes of Russia, of Moldo-Wallachia, kings of Georgia have recorded their names as donors of these precious objects.

We have given particular emphasis to ecclesiastical gold embroideries coming from Vienna, a city with the closest links with the activities of Greeks abroad during the years of Turkish domination of their homeland. Particularly after the signing of the Treaty of Passarowitz (1718), the major commercial centre of Vienna exercised a powerful attraction upon the enslaved Orthodox. Among these were large numbers of Greeks from Macedonia, who lost no time in demonstrating, in a multitude of ways, their devotion to the land of their origin. Among their many benefactions are their gifts to the Church: gold and silver vessels and gold embroideries intended for use in the rites of Orthodoxy. Greek merchants, not only from the city itself but from other Orthodox communities throughout the Balkans placed orders with the flourishing workshops of Vienna for objects destined for the great centres of their Faith. A large number of these works have been preserved in the sacristies of monasteries, but some have found their way into museums. In many cases the name of the embroiderer has been recorded next to that of the donor, while others are known to us from the monasteries' codices.

The Monastery of Mt. Sinai has preserved a large number of such works, in excellent condition. Among them, the stoles (epitrachelia) (fig.15) embroidered by Christopher Zephar, who combined the roles of painter, engraver, book publisher, copper etcher and embroiderer and who is credited with a revival of Post-Byzantine art in the Balkans, stand out particularly. Works originating in Vienna bear the names of other well-known embroiderers and, in the case of the older embroideries, are marked by the characteristics and spirit of Baroque. In the mid 18th century the features of Rococo become apparent, while at the end of the century Classicism comes to the fore. Thus the alternation of the artistic styles prevailing at that period in Western Europe can also be traced in the art of gold embroidery. Sinai also possesses fine gold embroidery produced in the Constantinople of the Phanariots and in Crete; these carry on the tradition of an earlier style, that of Byzantine art.

## LITURGICAL VESTMENTS

*Aeres.* These are the veils with which the celebrant covers the sacred elements during the Eucharist. They are divided into the *small aeres* — separate covers for the chalice and paten — and the *great aer* which covers both sacred vessels. During the Great Entrance, the priest removes the great aer from the sacred vessels and places it on the shoulder of the deacon. The subjects embroidered on aeres, from the 12th to the 15th centuries, were the reception of the Holy Communion under the form of wine (chalice cover), its delivery under the form of bread (paten cover), the Lamb of God (*amnos*) and the Breaking of the Bread (*melismos*). At a later date, however, we have aeres with the Mourning at the Sepulchre whose liturgical character is brought out by inscriptions from the service for Easter Eve. The Sinai epitaphios-aer (fig. 2) is placed on the altar of the Monastery until Pentecost instead of the great epitaphios. It is embroidered completely in gold on red satin, apart from the Holy Shroud and the projecting garment of the Virgin. Christ lies on the red stone on which He has been anointed with myrrh. He is flanked by the Blessed Virgin, St. John and Joseph of Arimathaea, while tiny angels hover above the scene, weeping. In the background is the Cross of victory with the instruments of the Passion: the crown of thorns, the spear and the sponge. Above the cross is the text of the dismissal hymn of Matins for Easter Eve and this continues below the stone slab in fine capitals: *The honourable Joseph took down Thy immaculate body from the tree; wrapping it in a clean shroud and spices, he laid it to rest in a new tomb.*

The scene is surrounded by a narrow border, decorated with spiral flower motifs, with the head of an angel in the middle of each side and a stylized fleur de lys at the corners. This aer was, according to the codex of the Monastery, brought from Smyrna in 1768. It is, however, a work of an earlier date, belonging to the mid 16th century.

*Epitaphios.* This is the liturgical cloth used today in the Good Friday service. During the 'aposticha' hymns at Vespers, it is carried in procession out of the Sanctuary and round the church and is placed in a baldachin (or on a plain table on Mt. Athos), standing in the centre of the church, to be reverenced by the faithful. At Matins on Easter Eve, at the end of the Te Deum, it is placed on the altar, where it remains until Ascension Day, the Holy Liturgy being celebrated on it. Since the time of the Fall of Constantinople, following the introduction of the short hymns called 'enkomia' into the Good Friday service, the liturgical character of the epitaphios changed in the direction of narrative. It now bears a representation of the dead Christ, lying on the red stone and surrounded by the figures of the Lamentation at the Sepulchre: the Virgin, St. John, the myrrh-bearing women, lamenting, Joseph of Arimathaea and Nicodemus. However, the liturgical nature of the epitaphios has not been totally discarded in the workshops of monastic houses; the two types — liturgical and narrative — have been amalgamated, and in many cases, prophets have been added to the border, who, together with the Evangelists, who appear at the corners, symbolize the Church Triumphant. As to the Cross, which is to be seen in many epitaphioi of the amalgamated type, it here serves as a necessary condition of the Resurrection and the salvation of mankind. Monastic epitaphioi retain their liturgical inscriptions, which allude to the eschatological significance of the iconography, while those produced by the workshops of luxury art stress the theme of the Burial and the Lamentation.

On the Monastery's epitaphios of the year 1612/3 (fig. 3) the scene is embroidered on crimson satin, with the dedicatory inscription on dark blue satin. The background is spangled with stars. The events are enacted below a canopy with four small columns, only two of which are visible. In the foreground Christ lies on the stone on which He has been anointed with myrrh, while the Virgin, on the left, sits on a stool, holding the head of her dead Son in her arms. The other figures are symmetrically arranged: three of them bend over the dead Christ: John, Joseph and one of the Maries. Behind them are the two Maries, mourning, and Nicodemus. Above the scene is the inscription Ὁ ἐπιτάφιος θρῆνος ('The Mourning at the Sepulchre'), while at the two extremities above, the sun and the moon —cosmic symbols which serve as a guard of honour to the *King of Glory* as Christ is called in the inscriptions— are to be seen. Around the scene a narrow border bears words from an Easter Eve hymn, sung in the evening of Good Friday: *Thee who art clothed with light as with a garment Joseph took down from the tree with Nicodemus, and seeing Thee dead, naked, unburied, took up his tender lamentation saying 'O woe, sweetest Jesus'. In the year 1612/3.* This correctly-spelt inscription seems at first sight to be written in cufic characters. Are we to suppose that some learned monk of Sinai composed it in this way so that it too would resemble decoration? Decoration in the sculpture of Byzantine churches which strives to imitate cufic lettering is not unknown. At the four corners of the work, in the places usually occupied by the four Evangelists, the embroiderer has put four crosses.

This epitaphios has been embroidered with exceptional skill in rich materials: gold and silver wire alternate in the garments of all the figures and in the canopy; the wire is affixed with the familiar *kavaliki* stitch. The monotony of the colour of the metal wire is broken up by the painted gold thread which shapes the folds, red on the gold and ultramarine on the silver. On the naked parts of the body a delicate straw-coloured silk in *riza* stitch has been used. The outlines of the figures have been traced in a brown silk. The *kamares* stitch in gold and red is used for the *maphoria*. The haloes and maphoria of the Women at the Tomb, the outline of the canopy and the stars in the background are brought out by artificial seed pearls. This epitaphios narrates the historical scene of the Lamentation at the Sepulchre and it is only the inscription which bears witness to its liturgical character.

Originating in a Constantinople workshop, the epitaphios dated 1842, with a representation of the Lamentation and a canopy (fig. 6), is embroidered on mauve satin; this shows only in the narrow border, which bears the words of the dismissal hymn in capitals on three of the sides: *The honourable Joseph took down Thy immaculate body from the tree; wrapping it in a clean shroud and spices, he laid it to rest in a new tomb.* At the bottom, the frame is broader and bears the dedicatory inscription in two lines: *He who rules over the whole earth and the vault of heaven is seen lying in the grave. Constantios Bishop of Byzantium and Sinai now adorns with gold the tomb of the Lord, which before Joseph hewed in the rock. 1842.* The name of the embroideress can be seen in the bottom right-hand corner: *The work of Gregoria Costa Papa.*

The scene is set against the background of a flower-strewn plain, behind which stand a cross and the canopy of the Holy Sepulchre. The Blessed Virgin couches the head of Christ in her arms. On the opposite side Joseph of Arimathaea holds the edge of the winding-sheet, while in the centre John bends to kiss the hand of the dead Saviour. Behind John are the two Maries — Mary Magdalene and the mother of James — bearing spices, while the third, Mary of Clopas, standing upright behind the Virgin, corresponds to the figure of Nicodemus behind Joseph. Two Archangels with wings spread incline towards the dead Christ. In the corners, the four Evangelists are shown in bust form, each with his symbol. The scene of Lamentation is here combined with the Cross, which is decked with a crown of thorns and the other instruments of the Passion. The Cross also signifies the offering of the Crucified for the whole world, as St. John Chrysostom says: *For the Cross, terminating at the four extremities, means that God crucified is in all places and comprehends all bounds.* It is precisely this which the presence of the four Evangelists — or their symbols — at the corners of the material stresses. Thus the whole community of the faithful participates in the worship which centres around the holy altar, accompanying the commemoration of the sacrifice of Golgotha with hymns of triumph. The Cross, the instrument of condemnation, is at the same time a symbol of victory.

The embroidery, which covers the whole of the material, with the exception of the inscription, is in relief. Calvary has been rendered in a large variety of shades of green and brown, while the clothing, below the gold outer garments, is in grey, pink and ultramarine. In the case of the gold garments, the direction of the stitch leaves gaps which form the folds. The haloes of Christ and the Blessed Virgin are picked out with artificial seed pearls and those of the other figures with twisted silver wire.

Gregoria was an embroideress working in Constantinople, at the beginning of the 19th century; another work by her, a *podea*, is preserved on Mt. Athos at the Iviron Monastery. The donor of the epitaphios was the Ecumenical Patriarch Constantios I, former Archbishop of Sinai, nephew of Cyril I, Archbishop of Sinai. He occupied the patriarchal throne for only four years, but his brief term of office has been described as 'a period of brilliance'. He was, as N. Tomadakis has written, 'a man of letters and a philosopher such as few of the Patriarchs after the Fall of Constantinople have been'.

## PEPLA

**Podea.** This is a *peplon* (ecclesiastical drapery) serving as a hanging just below an icon. It is framed on its four sides by its *periphereia*, material in a strikingly different colour. It frequently has a fringe at the bottom. This form of peplon was much used in Byzantium and was even an object of veneration to which miracles were attributed; for example, the Emperor Alexius I Comnenos was cured of an illness after being wrapped in the podea attached to the icon of Christ of Chalke. There was also among the ranks of ecclesiastical office an *archon of the podea*, whose duty it was on major feast days, when the churches were thronged with people, to keep watch lest the precious stones with which the podea was adorned should be stolen.

Podees are mentioned in texts from the 12th century, but it would seem that they are of much earlier origin. This can be concluded from inventories of monasteries which refer to *vlattia* (rich purple fabrics) *of veneration* and the painted curtaining occupying the lower zone of church murals. Embroidered podees have a very much smaller place in church furnishings today than they did in the Byzantine age. They usually hang from the icon of the saint of the day or from that of the patron saint on the icon-stand, while in earlier times — and still in monasteries, as in Sinai — the podees were attached below icons which hung on the walls or below the icons of Our Lord on the iconostasis. Some podees adorn the icons only on feast days; in the 11th century at the Paniktirmon Monastery in Constantinople, a valuable fabric was intended *for the office of a podea on feast days*, while at the Eleousa Monastery in Macedonia, the inventory mentions *festal podees and everyday podees*. Podees are attached not only to icons but to *staurothekes* (repositories for portions of the True Cross). According to certain 'typika', the Gospel too is to be placed, on the first three days of Holy Week, on a lectern *with vlattion*. There is always a connection of form and content between the painted icon and the embroidered one of the podea. The most common colour of the silk used for podees was purple. Dedicatory inscriptions or invocations in calligraphy which itself constitutes decoration are usually to be found on the border of the podea; at one time, however, they occupied the greater part of it.

The podea of the icon of St. Catherine of 1763 from a Vienna workshop (fig. 5) is embroidered on red brocade. It has a broad border with gold embroidered stylized flowers. In the centre, two angels are translating the body of the Saint, wrapped in a shroud, from the top of the mountain to the Monastery. Christ hovers above the scene, wearing a crown of glory; he is flanked by the two cosmic symbols of the sun and moon. At the corners there are four seraphim and between the two angels, above, the words of the *megalynarion* hymn of the Saint: *Heaven has thy spirit, thy sacred body has been treasured up in Sinai; the city of Alexander has the blood of thy martyrdom. Wise Catherine, protect thy servants.* Below the Saint, in a decorative triangle, the dedicatory inscription in capitals can be seen: *By the aid of the very reverend kyr Ioannikios protosynkelos of Sinai and at the expense of kyr Ioannis Papapolyzos, 1763.* Ioannis Papapolyzos and his brother Alexandros were well-known benefactors of the Greek community in Vienna. The gift is noted in the Monastery's register.

The garments of the Saint are embroidered in silver thread and red silk, with the winding-sheet in ultramarine; the girdle which she wears is in gold wire, as are the wings of the angels. Her crown is of gold leaf and her necklace is formed by large and small spangles. The faces of the figures are portrayed with straw-coloured and grey silk, with points in red on the cheeks. The Pantocrator is embroidered in gold, with sea-blue and pink silks. Relief is achieved on the embroidery of the border by gilt wire and spangles; also in relief are the wings of the angels. Gold-woven fringes surround the work.

The epitaphios of St. Catherine, dating from the year 1805 and coming from a Viennese workshop (fig. 4) is embroidered on salmon-coloured brocade; the figures in the centre are in blue. The border on three of the sides has a stylized floral decoration, while the fourth, bottom, side is occupied by an inscription in capitals: *Favourably receive and graciously the sacred gift of thy divine icon from the miserable and wretched sinner, thy suppliant, Azarias, that is, protosynkelos of Sinai in memory of all those who gave their alms and applied their skills to this work wrought finely with excellence and joy, that we may have thee as the intercessor and protection of all these and of Georgios who makes the offering, Theodora, together with Kyrasti, likewise their parents, children, brothers and sisters, that they find mercy on that awful day and at the judgement which respects not persons and is impartial. We beseech thee, Virgin Catherine, that we may be granted this in that hour. In the year 1805, August 15.* This liturgical embroidery, which in some catalogues is referred to as a podea, was, in earlier times, used as an epitaphios of the Saint during the procession held as part of the service for her feast day. Today it adorns the marble chest containing her relics on that day and at other great feasts.

The central scene shows two mountain tops; on the one, on the left, Moses is receiving the Tablets of the Law, while on the right flying angels translate the relics of St. Catherine to the Monastery. In the centre is the chest, with the Saint and flying angels, of whom two are holding the shroud in order to cover her. In the heavens the Ancient of Days gives His blessing. In the foothills of the mountains can be seen the fortified Monastery, Moses with his flock, St. Catherine and, in the centre, the Virgin as the Burning Bush. Flanking this central scene are three small icons on each side with scenes from the life of the Saint.

This epitaphios is embroidered chiefly in silver thread and coloured silks, with gilt wire and spangles on the chest and delicate coloured stones on the crown and the orarion-like girdle of St. Catherine; artificial pearls are employed in the surrounding scenes. The faces are rendered by painting and the variety of the silken colours with their different shades makes this very successful; generally, however, the impression given is that this is a work of painting rather than of gold embroidery.

*Lavara.* The *lavaron* (banner) is a kind of flag. It consists of a piece of square or oblong fabric which hangs stretched from the cross-piece of a shaft and covers its length. It is used on certain feasts in churches, at religious processions and at the ceremonies of associations, societies and guilds. From ancient times, various peoples have hung the emblems of their gods on a shaft or spear and these have accompanied them on their military campaigns and at their religious ceremonies. The Greeks used such emblems from the time of Alexander the Great: red material on a javelin gave the signal for battle to be joined. According to tradition, the first Christian lavaron was that raised by Constantine in the battle against Maxentius in 312. This was a square piece of purple material, embroidered in gold and set with precious stones, which was attached to a long gold spear; on one side it had pictures of the Emperor and of his two sons. At the top of the spear, a golden crown surrounded the monogram of Christ, the *XP*, which from that time on replaced the eagle of pagan Rome. Another renowned Byzantine lavaron was the Holy Mandelion (a cloth with the imprint of the Face of Christ) of Edessa, which accompanied the Emperor Heraclius on his campaign against the Persians in the 7th century. Late Byzantine lavara usually show the patron saint of the church or monastery or of the guild or society or, again, scenes associated with the sacred spot to which they belong.

Sinai has two lavara: one of them depicting the Transfiguration and the other the Burning Bush. The first (fig. 17) is occupied, in the upper part, by a representation of Mt.

Tabor, with three peaks, with Christ standing in a round nimbus of light from which rays emanate; the Prophets Elijah and Moses are on the right and left, while at His feet there are four disciples instead of the usual three: Peter, James and John. The embroiderer has misinterpreted the design and has derived the extra disciple from Christ's ascent and descent of the mountain, shown by two separate figures. The border has a representation of the Great Deesis, together with the Apostles.

Here the central scene is embroidered on pink satin, while the satin ground of the border and terminations is of mustard colour. Bullion in the form of floral decoration divides the scene depicted from the border. On the garments and mountains the gold thread is faded; various colours are used, of which ultramarine is predominant. The faces and hair have been rendered in thick beige thread and the haloes with gold thread and paint. This work, like the banner of the Burning Bush, was probably embroidered by the Sinaitic donor Hilarion, who came from Ioannina, where there was a long tradition in gold embroidery.

*Pyle*. This is the name given to the curtain wich fills the gap above the low double doors of the central entrance to the Sanctuary, the 'Gate Beautiful'. In early Christian times, decorated curtains (*vela*) hung either from the four arches of the ciborium magnum (canopy over the altar) — the *tetravelon* — or only from the front one — the *katapetasma*. The latter recalls the Jewish Katapetasma (veil) which covered the Holy of Holies (Exodus 26: 31 - 33).

When sanctuary screens came to be erected, which coincided with the development of the *Proskomide* (ceremony of preparation of the eucharistic elements) and the introduction into the liturgy of the *Prothesis* (offertory at the credence table) and of the Great Entrance, the shaking of the tetravelon was preserved in the use of the great aer which succeeded it. The great aer is now wafted above the bread and wine during the recital of the Creed, while the katapetasma has been transformed into the pyle, filling the gap in the central entrance to the Sanctuary.

Pyles usually bear an embroidered representation of Christ as Great High Priest or of Christ giving His blessing by means of the chalice. There are many pyles with depictions of the patron saint of the church or monastery, such as the pyle with the Congregation of the Archangels in the Docheiariou Monastery and that with St. Nicholas at the Stavronikita Monastery, both on Mt. Athos. These rich hangings with the patron saint of the monastery on them served as icons: they were hung from the screen only on the church's patronal festival.

The pyle which depicts St. Catherine and scenes from her life (fig. 18), originating in Vienna and dated 1770, is divided vertically into three sections, the central one, showing the Saint herself, being the broadest (50×136 cm.). St. Catherine is shown sitting; in her right hand she holds a cross and in her left a palm branch and the wheel of her martyrdom. She wears a royal crown covered by her halo and, beneath her outer garment, a kind of *orarion* with crosses, reminiscent of the Byzantine *loros*, emblem of the patrician *zoste* (a high office held by ladies of the Byzantine court). Two angels are crowning the Saint, while the sun sheds its beams on her. Behind her, two peaks of the mountain are to be seen; on the one Moses is receiving the Tablets of the Law, while on the other are the relics of the Saint. On the two flanking sides there are six scenes from the life and martyrdom of St. Catherine, rendered with great vitality and alternating with divisions decorated with carnations and pomegranates.

A broad border extends across the full width of the embroidery. In the middle of this there is a depiction of the Monastery and of monks throwing bread from its walls to the Arabs, who respond by firing arrows. Below the picture of the Monastery, in a tablet with a silver ground and gold lettering, is the dedicatory inscription: *This holy pyle was dedicated to the honour of the saint and martyr Catherine on Mount Sinai by the most honourable kyrios Nikolaos Dimitriou of the province of Pelagonia and therein from his native town of Malovista in memory of his parents and of his own pious intention towards God. Made while the most reverend holy archimandrite kyrios, kyrios Jeremiah was travelling in*

*Vienna in 1770.* The Monastery's codex also bears witness to the gift of the pyle: *1770 October 1. The most reverend archimandrite kyr Jeremiah came from Germany, who after many persecutions and imprisonments there... barely escaped death... and brought a fine pyle for the katholikon of the monastery having depicted on it the virgin martyr Catherine in the middle and around her all her sufferings, all gold embroidered by use of a frame for a thousand groschen.*

The art of gold embroidery in the 18th century attempted to imitate painting or engraving. Thus, the Sinai pyle had an engraving as a model (see D. Papastratou, vol. II, nos. 404 and 407), in which the Saint is shown with all the details encountered here — the small icons and the scene with the Bedouin. All that is missing from the engraving is the floral decoration, which was regarded as a necessary feature of embroidery. The scenes have been embroidered by the use of a frame, precisely in the manner of Byzantine gold embroidery. Silk thread in a variety of colours with gold and silver wire give vitality to this embroidery. The Saint wears a sea-blue dress and red outer garment; her earrings and necklace are decorated with artificial seed pearls, while her girdle is in silver. The garments of the sacred figures have been rendered in gold thread and there is pure silver in the background of the flowers.

## VESTMENTS OF THE CLERGY

**Sakkos.** Today, the sakkos is the episcopal vestment par excellence of the Eastern Church. As in the case of the omophorion, it comes from the imperial wardrobe. The sakkos and the *sagion* are mentioned as imperial robes for the coronation and major feasts, such as Palm Sunday. It was towards the end of the Byzantine era that the sakkos passed into ecclesiastical use. A large number of sakkoi on Mt. Athos and Sinai are embroidered with cherubim and crosses with the monogram $\overline{IC}.\overline{XC}.\overline{NI}.\overline{KA}$ between their arms. In shape the sakkos resembles the dalmatic of the West: it is a short tunic with broad half-sleeves. The two rectangular parts of which it consists are sewn together at the shoulders and fastened at the sides with little bells ('tintinnabula'), reminiscent of the vesture of the Old Testament High Priest (Exodus 28), or sometimes with ribbons.

The sakkos of Cyril of Crete (figs. 24 - 25), a work of the 17th century, has a representation of Christ as the Vine on its front. Seated in the middle on a branch of the vine, He gives His blessing with both hands, while He has the Gospel open at His breast. He receives the blessing of the Ancient of Days and of the Holy Spirit; flanking Him, in the tendrils, are the Apostles, six on each side. The other side of the vestment has a representation of the Tree of Jesse: the Virgin, Holding the Holy Child, is sitting in the tree, while Jesse is lying at its root. Entwined in the tree's branches are prophets and forebears of Christ; they are holding unfurled scrolls. Above the Virgin, David is shown holding a sceptre. On the sleeves, the Evangelists, with their symbols, are shown in pairs. A border of spiral shoots runs round the vestment on both sides and extends to the large surfaces of the sleeves. On each side the sakkos has five gilt tintinnabula. The garments of the figures are rendered in gold thread combined with blue, green and cherry silks. The folds are formed by the direction of the embroidery. There were seed pearls in the halo of Christ (as there would have been in that of the Virgin). The decoration of the embroidery is completed with grey beads and spangles. The codex ascribes the sakkos to Cyril, one of the most vigorous and able of the Archbishops of Sinai, but it certainly predates the period of his archiepiscopate (1759 - 1790). It would seem, however, that in his time the vestments of the Monastery also underwent 'renovation'.

**Mandyas.** As in the case of other episcopal vestments, the mandyas (cope) was transplanted into the Church from the imperial court. The authorities tell us that during the ceremony of the coronation of the Emperor, as soon as the hymn of the Great Entrance started to be sung, the Emperor approached the credence table and vested in the sakkos (dalmatic), the diadem and *a mandyas of gold.* Others, however, take the view that the vestment originates in the monastic cowl. It is recognized, as a liturgical vestment from the

14th century. At that time, the bishops came to do homage to the Emperor wearing mandyes with *potamoi* (see below). Some authorities maintain that until the 17th century the mandyas was a robe and not a vestment, but the symbolism associated with it as early as the 14th century suggests that in all probability it was in fact a vestment.

The mandyas is a long cloak, dark blue or violet in colour, open in front and with or without a train. Its two edges are fastened in front at the neck and the feet with buttons. At its four corners it is decorated with square pieces of silk material, richly embroidered. The upper ones are called *pomata* and the lower ones *poloi*. On the pomata, which symbolize the Old and New Testaments, the Annunciation is usually depicted, while the poloi have seraphim or various floral patterns. Sometimes the poloi and pomata are occupied by the figures of the Evangelists, as in the case of the Sinai mandyas. Coloured bands, white or red, vertical or horizontal, usually three in number, cross the vestment at equal distances: these are the potamoi ('rivers'), which symbolize the spiritual waters of the divine teaching which is poured out from pole to pole.

The Sinai mandyas (figs. 19, 20-23), of the 19th century, belonging to Constantios, former Archbishop of Constantinople and Sinai, has pomata and poloi depicting the four Evangelists sewn on the purple silk. Three potamoi in gold braid encircle the vestment, which fastens in front with the same material. Of the Evangelists, Matthew and Luke are writing their Gospels, while Mark and John hold theirs open at their breasts. Matthew and John are shown as old, and Mark and Luke as young men. The embroidery which covers almost all the material sewn on to the mandyas lacks the delicacy of older work. The embroiderer has used virtually all the varieties of stitch, but making most use of the oblique *riza*, the *vereriki* and the *kamares*.

***Epitrachelion***. From the beginning of the 6th century, the epitrachelion (stole) was regarded as an indispensable vestment for the priest. It consists of a strip of material narrower than the pallium (*omophorion*), worn round the neck and with the two strips hanging down in front; these are usually fastened together by small bells or buttons. In more recent times the part around the neck has been cut in a circle. The stole symbolizes the yoke of Christ or the halter by which He was led to His Passion. The fringes along the bottom edge stand for the souls for which the priest will give an account on the Day of Judgement. Embroidered on the neck of the stole is Christ as Great High Priest in bust form, while down the two strips in front are Archangels, the Deesis or the Annunciation and, below these, prophets, apostles or bishops, martyrs or soldier saints, monastic or hymn-writer saints. Of these figures, some are shown full-length under single or triple arches, while others are in medallions occupied by one or three forms. Apart from the portrayal of single figures, scenes from the Gospel are also embroidered on epitrachelia. Those possessed by the Monasteries are notable for their special decoration. They have on them either gold-decorated liturgical inscriptions, such as *Hosanna* or *Blessed be God who has poured out His grace*, embroidered in a rounded capital script which is elegant and carefully executed, covering the whole of the surface of the vestment and replacing the usual figures, or liturgical abbreviations derived from the monastic *analavos* (a garment, decorated with emblems, worn by monks of the Great Schema), divided by decorative crosses.

The Monastery's 15th century epitrachelion (fig. 13) with scenes from the Christological cycle comes from Constantinople. The purple all-silk material which forms the ground is not completely covered by the embroidery as in stoles of this period, but adds its colour to the other rich materials, thus producing successful harmonies. The uninterrupted band of the vestment has embroidered on it in medallions and in pairs 18 scenes from the Christological cycle, while at the neck the Holy Trinity is shown in the form of the Hospitality of Abraham. The deep border above the fringe is decorated with patterns made up of quatrefoils, the gaps in which are filled with four-lobed rosettes and schematized double-headed eagles. It is noticeable that two of the feasts depicted are not in their right order, that is, the Presentation in the Temple after the Baptism and the Transfiguration at the end of the feasts.

The medallions are linked together by smaller circles filled with flattened crosses. The angles left are occupied by gardant birds drinking from a fountain and dragons, also gardant, with open mouths in front of fruit. The tails of each pair are intertwined in a heart-shaped pattern culminating in an acanthus branch.

On the two parallel last divisions, large quatrefoils interweave, leaving between them one rounded octagon each, decorated successively with schematized double-headed eagles and interlacing. At their centre, the quatrefoils contain a further octagon, free on all sides and decorated with a rosette. There are similar epitrachelia in the Vatopedi and Stavroniki-ta Monasteries on Mt. Athos. This one is bordered with a gold embroidered band. The outline of the designs has been worked in coloured silk thread, which in the majority of places is worn. The scenes from the Christological cycle are set against backgrounds of gold (the Crucifixion), gold and green (the Descent from the Cross), gold and blue (the Resurrection) or gold with dark green (the Hospitality of Abraham). On the edge of the last unit of decoration the name Matthew Priest-Monk, in monogram form, can be seen. The stole is trimmed with 14 tassels which hang from two rows of knots. The little bells which join the two hanging sides of the vestment are old.

The epitrachelion of Ananias, Archbishop of Sinai, a work of the year 1671 (figs. 14 and 16), is embroidered on red satin and consists of a continuous strip inscribed with the 'Hosanna' which is punctuated by cherubim and floral decoration which forms spirals and crosses. The embroidery ends in two vases with daisies. The dedicatory inscription in capitals which follows is embroidered on mustard-coloured satin which has been sewn on to the border of the stole: *Of Ananias, Archbishop of the Holy Mountain of Sinai, 1671.* Ananias became Archbishop of Sinai (1661-1671) following an agreement with the monks of Sinai imposing their terms upon him, but his demands that he should be addressed as *makariotatos* ('most blessed'), the innovations which he introduced and the privileges which he demanded should be assigned to him were not acceptable to the Sinaites and he was finally deposed from his orders by the Ecumenical Patriarch Methodios, which forced his resignation in September 1671. Later, however, he was again employed by the monastic community of Sinai on various missions.

Also among the vestments of the Monastery is a gold embroidered epitrachelion from Vienna (fig. 15), dated 1752. It consists of a strip with an opening cut around the neck which descends to the chest. This part is decorated with stylized vine branches and ears of corn, embroidered with gold thread in high relief. This is followed by three pairs of sacred figures under arches: the Annunciation, St. George and St. Demetrius and the Prophets Moses and Aaron. On the border, framed, there is the following inscription in capitals: *Offering of the servant of God Anastasios Moralis from the city of Kastoria. I dedicate this on Mount Sinai. 1752.* At the three extremities of the inscription it bears the words *by Christopher Ziphar* in monogram form. Christopher Zephar was a well-known artist —icon painter, engraver and embroiderer — of the period of Turkish domination. The works of embroidery ascribed to him are so numerous that we must suppose that he was personally reponsible only for the patterns.

This Sinai epitrachelion is embroidered on red satin in pure gold wire in high relief. On the garments of the figures, the gold stands out with silk in various colours: brown, bright green, russet, pink and blue. This vestment was made in Vienna for Anastasios Moralis, benefactor of the Greek community there.

***Orarion.*** The word orarion is derived from the Latin *orarium*, which in turn comes from *os-oris* (mouth). This derivation points to its original use: it was held below the mouth of those receiving Holy Communion direct from the chalice. It also has its earlier history in pagan dress; Pre-Christian art shows the priestesses of Isis wearing a shawl identical with the orarion.

During the Holy Liturgy the deacon holds the end of this stole in the fingers of his right hand. When he comes to recite the Lord's Prayer, during Holy Communion, he crosses the orarion over his chest and back, in imitation of the seraphim, who veil their faces before the Lord. From the 4th century writers describe the orarion as a piece of fine linen material, the badge of the office of deacon; draped over his left shoulder, it symbolizes the wings of the angels. It is for this reason that it is customary for cherubim or angels doing reverence or offering incense, or the triumphal hymn sung at the Offertory of the Holy Liturgy to be embroidered on the orarion. In monasteries the orarion, together with the representation of the heavenly powers, also has scenes or saints connected with the particular locality, such as, in the case of Sinai, the Burning Bush, St. Catherine or Moses.

A typical example is the orarion of Nikephoros of Crete (fig. 12), of the year 1748, embroidered in a Cretan workshop. It consists of a continuous strip of red satin, with a cross at the neck. Descending from this is floral decoration which is interrupted by three pairs of sacred figures: above Moses and Aaron, in the middle the Blessed Virgin as the Burning Bush and St. Catherine, and below the two deacons St. Laurence and St. Stephen. These figures are separated by two seraphim in floral interlacing. On the two parallel sides of the border there is an inscription on three lines: *By the charity of the pious Christians in the city of Rethymna 1748. of Nikephoros Archbishop of Sinai the Cretan by the aid of kyr Kallinikos bishop of Rethymna.* The garments and the haloes are embroidered in gold, the faces and bare flesh with white, painted silk, the features with brown silk and the lips with red. The garments and wings of the seraphim are embroidered in gold and silver thread, but at many points the gold has come away and only the yellow thread remains. Spangles and beads in red, blue and green complete the decoration of the embroidery. Below the golden cloaks, the dress of the Virgin is sea-blue with gold and that of St. Catherine pink and blue with gold.

*Sticharion.* The sticharion (alb) is one of the three vestments of the deacon, together with the orarion and the epimanikia; it is also common to all three degrees of holy orders. It is related, according to Josephus, to the long tunic worn by the Jewish High Priest (Flavius Josephus: *Jewish Antiquities*, Book III, Chap. 7). The sticharion is first mentioned as a liturgical vestment by Jerome, while St. John Chrysostom speaks of it as *a small gleaming white tunic* (P.G. 48, 745). Its original white colour symbolized purity and spiritual joy. For the Pseudo-Sophronius, the sticharion was a type of *the white-clad angels*. When this vestment is purple *like fire* it recalls, according to the Pseudo-Germanus, the words of King David in the Psalms: *who makes His angels spirits and his ministers a flame of fire.*

The 18th- century Russian sticharion (fig. 1) in the form in which we have it here — a long, narrow piece of velvet with a hole in the centre for the head — is rare even in Russia. The Sinai Catalogues describe it as an *epomis* (ephod). It is worn by the deacon only on the Feast of St. Catherine, as he holds the censer in one hand and the artophorion in the other. In the centre there is a depiction of the Monastery with two domes crowned with crosses; above the Monastery and between two peaks with chapels on them, we see amid foliage the Blessed Virgin in bust form with Christ on her breast, while a pencil of the sun's rays falls upon her. On the right of the Virgin, St. Catherine, standing, holds a palm branch, while the wheel of her martyrdom can be seen at her feet. On the left, in the corresponding position, Moses is shown with his staff in his hand and his flock at his feet, while at the other end of the vestment the deacon St. Stephen prays with his orarion held out in his raised hand. Small cherubim adorn the four corners of the sticharion. The inscriptions stating its origin are in Russian. The embroidery seems to be a copy of an engraving, as was usual in the 18th century. Its exact model, however, has not yet been identified; nevertheless a large number of icons on paper come close to it (see D. Papastratou, vol. II, no. 394).

*Epimanikia.* Epimanikia are the long cuffs worn by the clergy to cover the lower part of the sleeves of the alb (sticharion). Up to the 12th century, like the epigonation, they were an exclusively episcopal vestment, used in baptism for practical reasons. In the 15th century they are mentioned as being worn by priests as well, while after the Fall of Constantinople their use further extended to deacons. The epimanikia symbolize the fetters with which Christ was bound when brought before Caiaphas, a scene which in monasteries often appears on them. Sometimes their decoration bore no relation to their symbolism and was harmonized with the surface of the material: the Annunciation, scenes from the Dodekaorton, Christ with prophets, the Apostles Peter and Paul predominated in their iconography from the 17th century, until, in recent years, this has been simplified down to a cross on each epimanikion.

On the pair of epimanikia of the 17th century (fig. 7) from a Sinope workshop, two scenes appear below the arching with its denticulated curve: the Scourging of Christ and 'Ecce Homo'. On either side of the arch there is a vase from which plants climb, with two eagles perching in their branches. In the first scene Christ is shown bound to a pillar while His two tormentors scourge Him. At their feet is the head of John the Baptist, with a sword at the side, a feature which stresses that the sufferings of John forshadowed those of Christ. In the second picture, Christ, with hands bound and wearing a crown of thorns, is presented by Pilate to the crowd. The scenes are surrounded by a narrow border with floral decoration. The epimanikia are embroidered on red satin in gold and silver thread, while the columns and arches are in gilt silver thread, twisted with coloured silks. The plants in the vases are rendered in shades of green, pink, mauve and blue, and the garments of Pilate and the torturers in green, blue, pink and mauve. The faces have been formed with grey silk and the features with dark red.

*Epigonation.* The epigonation is derived from the soft *encheirion* (hand cloth) which hung from the girdle of clerics, like the napkin which hung from the belts of the nobles of Byzantium, which was in turn derived from the *mappula* or *mappa*, the cloth used by the consuls to give the starting signal at the games. In the 12th century the epigonation came to symbolize the towel worn by Our Lord when He washed the disciples' feet. Again, in the 15th century it acquired a new symbolism: *the victory over death and the Resurrection of the Saviour.* For this reason, it is in the shape of a sword and has embroidered on it, on its border, the verse from the Psalms recited by the priest as he dons it: *Gird thy sword upon thy thigh, O most mighty, with thy glory and thy majesty. And in thy majesty ride prosperously because of truth.* The scenes which most usually appear on this vestment are the Washing of the Feet and the Descent into Hell or the Resurrection, in the Western style, on later epigonatia. The figures are placed along the vertical diagonal of the vestment, but also appear arranged along the axes of the rectangle. In monasteries there may be other scenes connected with the special sanctity of the place, as, for example, the Burning Bush in Sinai or the Vision of John in Patmos.

On the epigonation showing Christ as 'Wonderful Counsellor' (fig. 8), from a Cretan workshop, dated 1720, Christ, in the centre, gives His blessing with both hands and is supported on seraphim. Although He is not shown with wings, His youthful appearance suggests the type of the Wonderful Counsellor rather than that of the Great High Priest. He is surrounded by floral decoration which forms circles with daisies and carnations. A narrow border frames the vestment and bears the Psalm verse and the date 1720. In the four corners the Evangelists are shown in bust form (Matthew appears only in the form of his symbol - an angel). The inscription on the border has been embroidered in the opposite direction to those of the Evangelists. In the case of the figures, the gold embroidery is well-preserved, while the flower decoration, in which silks of many colours have been used, is worn. Of the artificial pearls used in the haloes, most have fallen out. The style and the decoration point to a Cretan workshop.

The epigonation of Archbishop Cyril, of the year 1746, from a Constantinople workshop (fig. 9) is embroidered on red satin in rich materials: gold and silver wire and multi-coloured silk thread with artificial pearls and other coloured stones. The centre is occupied by a representation of the Blessed Virgin as the Burning Bush and, in the lower part, by a depiction of part of the Monastery's buildings. On the left, Moses can be seen with his flock, kneeling to loose his sandals and to enter on the holy ground. On the right, St. Catherine, standing, holds a cross. The figures are surrounded by a broad spiral plant pattern, at the edges of which two angels, shown full-length, hold the emblems of a bishop: the mitre in the middle, the cross and the pastoral staff crossed. The three corners on the right, left and top are occupied by angels in bust form and in clouds, while Aaron is shown in the bottom one. The design, which is dominated by the Baroque style, is a copy of a wood-cut, the plate of which is in the Monastery (see D. Papastratou, vol. II, nos. 397, 1699). The inscription above reads *The unquenchable Bush,* that in the left corner, *Remember, Lady, thy servant Cyril* and in the right corner, *the humble Sinaite. 1746.* The figures are in relief and the faces painted, while the garments are in gold with various shades of green and blue. This vestment is mentioned in the register of Cyril's property and in the Monastery's codex 2198 under *the year 1769.*

*Mitre.* In early Christian times, the ministers of the Most High were not permitted to cover their heads, and for that reason the introduction of the mitre provoked, in the East, strong reaction. In the Byzantine era, only the Pope of Rome and the Pope and Patriarch of the great city of Alexandria wore a mitre; we know from the records that at the Council of Florence the bishops of the East celebrated the Liturgy bare-headed. It was from the time that Cyril Loucaris, who as Patriarch of Alexandria had worn a mitre, became Ecumenical Patriarch (November 1620) that the wearing of the mitre spread in the Eastern Church. The Patriarch of Constantinople, as time went on, awarded the privilege of wearing the mitre to certain archbishops, until finally the practice became general for all metropolitans and bishops. The mitre is derived from the *kammelaukeion,* the crown, that is, of the Emperor in the time of the Comneni, referred to as a form of royal headgear by Constantine Porphyrogenitos. It is a cylindrical covering for the head made from woollen or velvet material, with *epithemata* (applied panels) of gold-embroidered silk. On the dome (*tepes*) there is a representation of the Holy Trinity under the form of the Hospitality of Abraham and on the sides Christ as Great High Priest or Our Lady in the type of 'Platytera' or scenes from the Christological cycle. Often the decoration includes the double-headed eagle, crowned, a patriarchal emblem after the Fall of Constantinople. Another form of episcopal headgear in use in monasteries is the soft cap, which has two flaps at the ears and bears the same decoration as the mitre, except for the double-headed eagle. The mitre symbolizes the crown of thorns with which the Jews crowned the Saviour to mock Him as a king. Bishops, wishing by the wearing of the mitre to demonstrate their devotion to the King of All, have it decorated with a variety of precious stones, which symbolize *the variety of the virtues of Christ.*

The cylindrical bishop's mitre (fig. 10) of the Monastery, belonging to the early 19th century, is embroidered on blue velvet. At the base there is relief embroidery, of which four bands link this with the flat surface above (tepes). In the four spaces left by the embroidery, radial medallions contain the symbols of the Evangelists. The decoration is completed by garlands and a cross of diamonds on the tepes.

The embroidered monastic cap of the year 1731 (fig. 11), from a Cretan workshop, bears on one of its sides Christ as Great High Priest and on the other St. Nikephoros in branching floral decoration, while the other two sides are occupied by Sts. Peter and Paul. On the tepes there is more flower decoration, this time with tulips. A calligraphic inscription in capitals runs round it: *Of Nikephoros Archbishop of Mount Sinai. 1731 September.* Its owner was Nikephoros Marthalis Glykys (1728 - 1747), one of the most distinguished of Sinai's bishops.

The richly-varied treasury of the Monastery's church textiles formed by its liturgical and priestly vestments and its decorative hangings, most of them with inscriptions, entrances the visitor not only with its wealth, its variety or its artistic value, but with the devotion of the faithful which prompted these dedications and offerings. It is impossible to conceive what Sinai meant to the enslaved Greek nation — and the whole of Christendom — without seeing the multitude of its works of art and the wealth of its offerings of devotion, drawn as they are from every corner of the Earth.

*1. Russian sticharion (epomis) (105×63 cm.), with representations of the Blessed Virgin as the Burning Bush, the Monastery, Moses and St. Catherine. 18th century.*

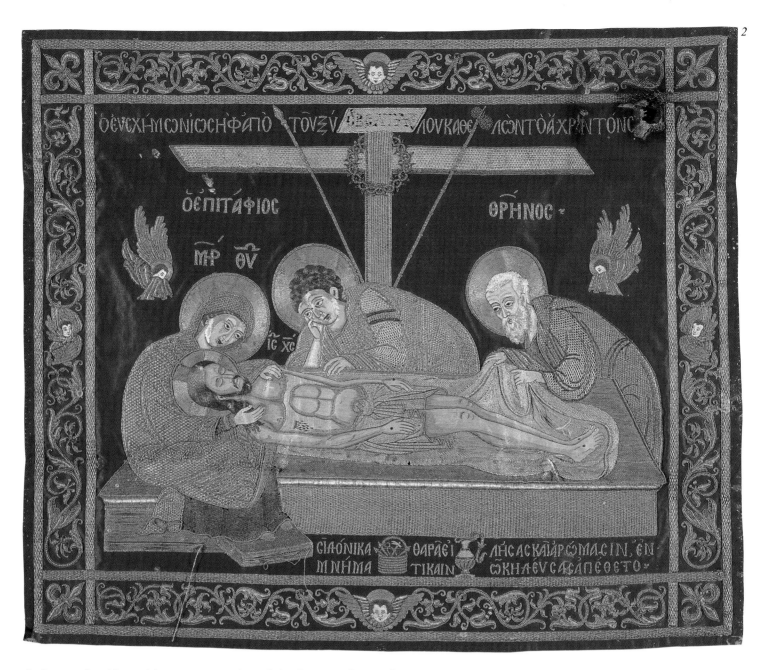

2. *Aer - epitaphios, with a representation of the Lamentation at the Sepulchre (63×53 cm.). From a Smyrna workshop. 16th century.*

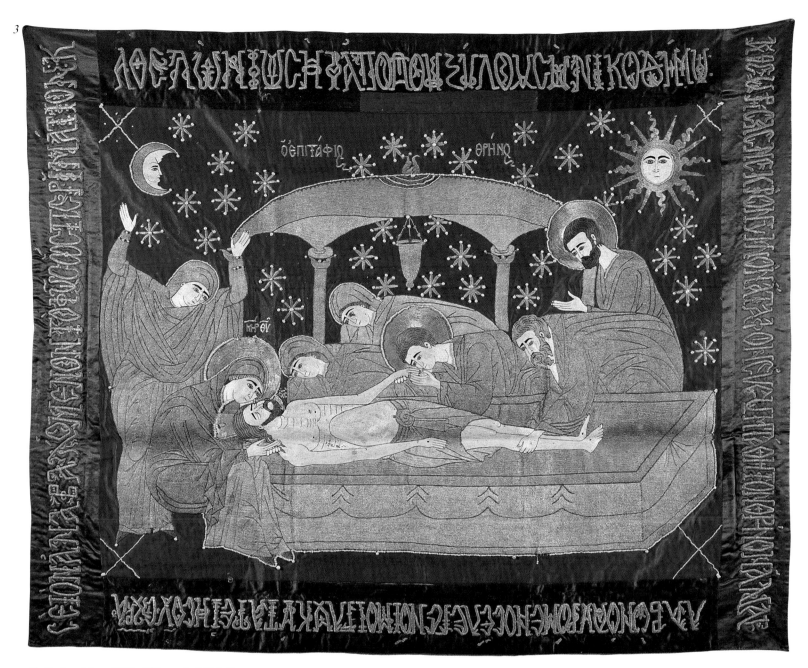

3. *Epitaphios (136×107 cm.). 1612/3.*

4. *Epitaphios of St. Catherine (139×68 cm.). Offering of the Protosynkellos of Sinai Azarias. From a Vienna workshop. 1805.* →

ΔΕΞΟΝ ΕΥΓΕΝΩΣ ΑΜΑΓΕ, ΧΑΡΙΕΝΤΩΣ ΙΕΡΟΝ ΔΩΡΟΝ ΤΗΣ ...ΗΣ
ΑΖΑΡΙΩ ΦΗΜΙ ΠΡΩΤΟΣΥΓΓΕΛΩ ΣΙΝΑΙΤΩ, ΕΙΣ ΜΝΗΜΗΝ ΑΜΑ ΠΑΝΤΣ
ΦΑΙΔΡΩΣ ΚΑΙ ΛΑΜΠΡΩΣ ΑΜΑΤΕ ΧΑΡΜΟΣΥΝΩΣ ΟΠΩΣ ΕΧΩΜΕΝ ΣΕ ΠΡ...
ΑΜΑ ΣΥΝ ΤΗ ΚΥΡΑΣΤΗ, ΟΜΩ ΓΟΝΕΩΝ, ΤΕΚΝΩΝ, ΚΑΙ ΑΔΕΛΦΩΝ ΤΕ, ΕΥΕ...
ΔΕΟΜΕΘΑΣΟΥ ΠΑΡΘΕΝΕ ΑΙΚΑΤΕΡ...
Εν έτει ...

246

5. *Podea, with a representation of St. Catherine (129×101 cm.). Offering of Ioannis Papapolyzos, benefactor of the Greek community in Vienna. From a Vienna workshop. 1763.*

6. Epitaphios (99×73 cm.). Work of the embroideress Gregoria and offering
of the Ecumenical Patriarch Constantios I. From a Constantinople
workshop. 1842.

*7. Pair of epimanikia (height: 24.5 cm., length: above, 27 cm., below, 32 cm.). From a Sinope workshop. 17th century. The scenes on them are: above, the Flagellation of Christ and, below, 'Ecce Homo'.*

*8. Epigonation with a representation of Christ as Wonderful Counsellor (31 cm. each side). From a Cretan workshop. 1720.*

*9. Epigonation with representations of the Blessed Virgin as the Burning Bush, Moses, St. Catherine and a part of the Monastery (25 cm. each side). Offering of Cyril, Archbishop of Sinai. From a Constantinople workshop. 1746.*

10. Cylindrical bishop's mitre (decorated with diamonds), with the symbols of the Four Evangelists in medallions; at the base, Christ and the Virgin and St. Catherine. Said to have belonged to Cyril, Archbishop of Sinai. Late 18th century.

11. Monastic soft cap, with representations of Christ as Great High Priest, St. Nikephoros and the Apostles Peter and Paul. Offering of Nikephoros Marthalis, Archbishop of Sinai. From a Cretan workshop. 1731.

12. *Orarion of Nikephoros Marthalis, Archbishop of Sinai, with depictions – in three pairs – of Moses and Aaron, the Virgin as the Burning Bush and St. Catherine, and St. Laurence and St. Stephen (282×9 cm.). From a Cretan workshop. 1748.*

13. *Epitrachelion of the priest-monk Matthew, with scenes – in medallions – from the Christological cycle (141×25 cm.). From a Constantinople workshop. 15th century. Detail.*

14. *Detail of the border of the epitrachelion in fig. 16.*

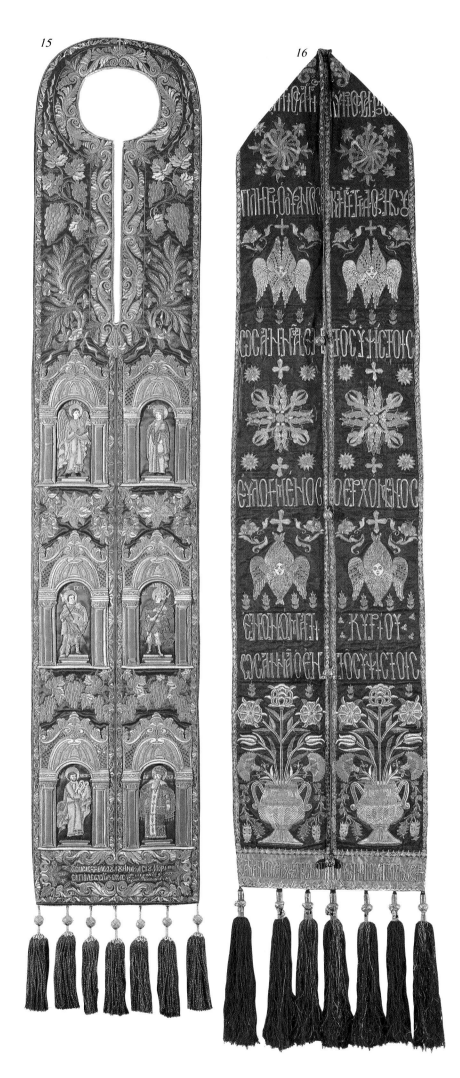

15. Epitrachelion, with depictions – in three pairs – of the Annunciation, St. George and St. Demetrius and Moses and Aaron (142×29 cm.). Work of Christopher Zephar and offering of Anastasios Moralis, benefactor of the Greek community in Vienna. 1752.

16. Epitrachelion, with embroidered inscription of the 'Hosanna' (137×16 cm.). Offering of Ananias, Archbishop of Sinai. 1671.

17. *Lavaron, with a representation of the Transfiguration (103×87 cm.).*
*Work of the Sinai embroiderer Hilarion (?). 1673.*

18. *Pyle of St. Catherine, with scenes from her life and*
*martyrdom (136×34 cm.). Offering of Nikolaos Dimitriou.*
*From a Vienna workshop. 1770.*

19

19. Mandyas, with representations of the Four Evangelists. Offering of Constantios, former Archbishop of Constantinople and Sinai. Early 19th century.

20 - 23. Pomata and poloi from the mandyas in fig. 19.

*24. Sakkos 'of Cyril of Crete', with a representation on the front of Christ as the Vine. 17th century.*

25. *The reverse side of the sakkos 'of Cyril of Crete', with a representation of the Jesse Tree. 17th century.*

# CHURCH
# METALWORK

# CHURCH METALWORK

The various items of metalwork which are to be found in the Monastery of St. Catherine will allow the reader to trace the lengthy journeys of the pilgrims who have come to Sinai, of the successive conquerors who have subdued it and protected it, of the monks leaving for the dependencies (*metochia*), on alms missions (*zeteies*), or for the courts of faithful rulers, benefactors and donors. Through this place, lying between three continents, have passed, over the centuries, soldiers, pilgrims and merchants; here interests, ways of life and faiths have clashed and have co-existed. Here we meet with craftsmen, techniques and styles; here works of art —offerings— have been laid up as treasure.

Many of the Monastery's treasures have been dedicated to it *at the expense and by the diligence* and *by the toil, labour and sighs* of the monks of Sinai. Others have found their way here as a result of the activities of the monks either in the course of their various missions or while they were based at the Monastery's dependencies in Cyprus, Crete, Western Greece, Serbia, Adrianoupolis, Moldavia and Wallachia and the Ukraine.[1] Frequently they co-ordinated the individual or collective offerings made *by the toil and at the charges of many devout Christians* and saw to it that these reached their destination. The monks of Sinai acted as intermediaries between the benefactors and the Monastery and, by extension, the saints venerated there. The dedicatory inscriptions make special mention of their *aid* and *assiduity*. In these inscriptions the local authorities, ecclesiastical and secular, also have their place: *most sacred* and *most holy* patriarchs, bishops and abbots, *most pious* emperors and *most noble* gentlefolk. The record of the name serves to mark the date of the offering and to increase the prestige of both donor and gift, while those thus named are indiscreetly enrolled among the recipients of the expected benefits: salvation of the soul and remembrance. Customs and habits of thought remain for centuries the same:[2] *1761 april. Let it be a perpetual memorial that I the hadji kyr Yiannos of Thessaloniki... went as a pilgrim to your holy monastery and devoutly brought a lamp of silver promising to send each year ten piastres for the oil for this lamp to be ever-burning in the holy bush on all feasts and sundays...*[3]

A large number of other works not described here provide, through the inscriptions on them, information on connections, centres and individual craftsmen, donors and mentalities. A *polykandelon* dated 1672 testifies to the skill of the craftsmen of Thessalonica, and a benediction cross, the gift of Arsenios III Patriarch of Peć (1682) and two lamps from Bečkerek (1672 and 1677)[4] to the Serbian presence. A benediction cross and a chalice from Tyrnovo (1674, 1782)[5] and a hanging oil lamp from Philippoupolis (1776) point to relations with the Bulgarian provinces. The workshops of Pontus are represented by two small polykandela (1671)[6] and Nizna in Russia by an imposing chandelier (1752), the work of *the master-craftsman Ioannis Zachariou.*[7]

The treasures of the Monastery of St. Catherine have followed the vicissitudes of the treasures of Orthodoxy: looting, sale in times of need, re-using of the metals. The codices of the Sinaitic dependency of Tzouvania in Cairo record their fortunes from the 16th century: *+ 1789, august: 8... we wrote to the holy monastery, and they collected all the useless silver-ware, and sent it to us in 36 okes, and let this be a perpetual memorial. We brought down a further 42 okes and they were all in all 78 okes, of which we kept an artophorion only, while we sold the rest at 10 piastres the dram by the hand of father raphael, and we received from this six thousand and seven hundred 32 piastres; there were 68 okes sold.*[8] In the course of the 'closures' of the Monastery which are recorded in the 17th century, the sacred vessels were hidden and very few remain exposed. In order to cope with difficult times, the monks had recourse to these hoards: *1606, February. We took out from the abditory silver in all of 16 and 63 drams... likewise a gold cup.*[9]

Church silver was not always regarded as works of art. An exception to this is the case of offerings of persons of rank, where the dimensions and quality, together with the name of the donor, lent them a special value. Silver objects were always valuable goods in practical terms, that is, capable of liquidation. Afterwards, when they were worn by use, cleaning and repairs, they were 'refined' in order to be used again as raw materials or in order to meet urgent financial needs: *1789. during the month of april we conferred in council many times as to how many old and useless pieces of silver had been in the sacristy for many years, chalices, patens, belts, plates, crosses, or which were not in any use and the dirt was corroding them from year to year hence we determined to melt them down, to obtain the pure silver, and to make lamps or other items in the holy monastery, and we summoned a craftsman secretly and refined them, and thirty eight okes were refined, 50 drams of not so pure silver.*[10]

The presentation which follows does not attempt, and anyway would not be able, to be exhaustive. Of the mass of objects for ecclesiastical use to be found in the sacristy, the katholikon and the chapels of the Monastery, very few have been fully studied. Systematic cataloguing would require a prolonged stay at the Monastery, which was not feasible in the context of the publication of this volume. Furthermore, with very few exceptions, the bulk of the archival material of the Monastery and its dependencies remains unknown. These factors have prevented a fully documented and composite review of the objects at the present time. The commentary on the works is based only on internal features (techniques, styles, inscriptions); the tentative conclusions here are of a provisional nature.

## BYZANTINE WORKS

There are very few works in metal remaining from the early centuries of the Monastery's life.[11] The bronze cross (fig. 2) from the period of the Monastery's foundation (6th century), which now crowns a screen (iconostasis) of a later date in the Chapel of the Holy Fathers is of interest for other reasons besides its date.[12] Its design, with flaring arms terminating 'in pairs of drops', is customary for crosses of the 6th and 7th centuries, as are the prickets on its horizontal arms, from which *pentelia* hung.[13] The obverse side is occupied by a quotation from Exodus (19: 16-18) and the dedicatory inscription. Of interest are the scenes engraved on the extremities of the arms: the divine presence is indicated on the upright by a heavenly sphere with stars, from which emerge the hands of God, one holding the Tablet with the Commandments, the other in a gesture of blessing or speech. Moses, on the left arm, depicted as young, is climbing Mount Sinai, his hands covered, in order to receive the Tablet; on the right arm he is stooping over his bent leg to loose his sandal in preparation for this momentous event.[14]

Weitzmann believes that the engraver took as his iconographic model the miniatures of manuscripts, and particularly *Octateuch*. It is his view that the high quality of the design and its transference on to metal are perhaps due to the engraver himself, whose rendering of it follows the style of the late classical art of the 4th and 5th centuries, with a Constantinopolitan work as a model.[15] Ševčenko, however, points out that the lettering most closely related to that of the inscription is encountered on objects of the 6th century from Syria and Palestine.[16] The original position of the cross was probably on top of the marble screen which the church appears to have had in the time of Justinian. There it functioned on the symbolic level, supplementing the idea of the revelation of divinity, which in the apse of the Sanctuary was expressed through the mosaic of the Transfiguration of Christ.[17]

From the Middle Byzantine period an enkolpion-reliquary for a fragment of the True Cross has been preserved. It is made of copper alloy and decorated with scenes in niello and inlaid silver. The obverse is occupied by a depiction of the Crucifixion, surrounded by the Annunciation and Visitation, the Baptism of Christ, His Birth and the Presentation in the Temple. On the reverse, in the centre, St. John is shown flanked by Sts. Cosmas and Damian, the Prophets Habakkuk[18] and Elijah, Sts. Andrew and Thomas, the Ascension and the Descent into Hell (Anastasis). In the inscription which runs round the narrow sides, its owner, Thomas, as a suppliant, invokes the protection of Christ, with the aid of the 'venerable wood' contained in it.

This *staurotheke* belongs to the category of historiated reliquaries.[19] The technical and stylistic relationships between these are close, and they are decorated with scenes from the Christological cycle, which includes subjects frequently employed from the early 6th to the early 8th centuries in the decoration of objects with a commemorative/prophylactic function: censers, wedding rings, bracelets, ampullae for oil from the Holy Land. The use of these enkolpia in the first Post-Iconoclastic period testified to orthodoxy of faith and the opposition of those who wore them to the Iconoclasts.[20]

Earlier scholars have ascribed to these works a Syro-Palestinian origin and have dated the most sumptuous of the enkolpia, the Fieschi Morgan staurotheke, to around 700. Today they are placed in the first quarter of the 9th century[21] and the theory of a connection with the Holy Land has been abandoned, while there is evidence that they were the products of workshops in Constantinople or, perhaps, Thessalonica, the only centres at that time which were in a position to produce such rich and innovative enkolpia.[22] The ascription of this origin and dating to the Sinai staurotheke receives support from another feature, the sense of variety of colour achieved by the parallel use of inlaid silver and niello, an aesthetic approach which in the period of the Macedonians had taken on a new lease of life in Constantinople.[23]

The greatest affinities of the Sinai enkolpion are with the Pliska and Vicopisano crosses, although its scenes are less clear and more summary, its figures more schematic and static and its workmanship less skillful. It is, moreover, the only one of the group with a depiction of the Visitation, a subject which indicates Pre-Iconoclastic preferences.[24] The niello sometimes picks out only the outlines or the details of the scenes and sometimes, alternating with the inlaid silver, is used on broad surfaces for the rendering of the bodies.[25] Although this is less valuable in terms of its raw material and inferior in quality of workmanship to other crosses of its type, it is not, nonetheless, a mass-produced work but the result of an order placed at high cost. This is confirmed by the rarity of enkolpia richly decorated with scenes as this is, with the studied combination of niello and inlaid silver, and the well-designed, long dedicatory inscription, with the invocation of its owner. Thomas, who, in addition to the healer saints Cosmas and Damian, discreetly contrived to have the saint after whom he himself was named portrayed at the end of the right arm.

Candelabra of high value are frequently depicted in Byzantine art. They are listed in church inventories and 'typika', and are mentioned as imperial offerings or as gifts to forcign rulers. Nevertheless, very few examples have come down to us.[26] The Sinai candelabrum (fig. 5), still in use today in the katholikon, is unique of its kind in its decoration and is of exceptional importance for the history of Byzantine metalwork.[27] Its six-lobed cast foot rests on three schematic griffins. The shaft is made up of hollow cast pieces and supports a disc with 12 candle-spikes, these being in all probability a later addition. The decoration, engraved on a ring-punched ground, includes peacocks, griffins facing one another and lions, some in medallions, as are busts of military saints, as well as animals in movement, very probably in a hunting scene; it is completed by geometrical and schematized plant motifs. L. Boura notes that in its individual morphological details it displays similarities with the so-called Amalfitan candelabra in the Megiste Laura Monastery on Mount Athos,[28] and these features are also met with in Islamic works of the 11th and 12th centuries.[29] In terms of style and execution, she links its engraved figurative and aniconic decoration, with its marked oriental character, in spite of some weaknesses, with two silver bowls, today in the Hermitage Museum, attributed to Constantinople workshops of the 12th century.[30] These features, which reflect the taste of the age for figurative decoration with movement and plasticity, are encountered not only in metalwork, but also in works of small-scale sculpture, textiles and ceramics.[31]

## WORKS FROM THE WEST

In describing his visit to the Monastery of St. Catherine in 1846, the French traveller Dumas mentions a detail which appears strange: 'As we left the church, we stopped to admire the doors. These are divided into square panels, each containing a work in enamel, exceptionally well-preserved and faultlessly designed...'.[32] It is difficult to accept this account as completely true. However, today, on the door of the katholikon an enamelled plaque, itself rectangular and once the central part of the cover of a sacred book, has been nailed. It shows Christ in Glory and comes from a Limoges workshop; it dates from approximately 1200.[33] We do not know whether a second enamelled plaque (fig. 1), today in the Pinakotheke of the Monastery, once also constituted a part of the decoration of the katholikon door. Its unusual proportions lead to the hypothesis that it was an icon or cover of the whole of the wood board of a book.[34] Christ, in a mandorla, sits on a backless throne, His feet on a footstool. He gives His blessing with His raised right hand, while in the left He holds a closed book. He is surrounded by the symbols of the Evangelists in bust form, in their traditional positions. The mountings on the metal sheets of the frame once held glass paste stones. The colour range of the enamels includes deep blue, turquoise and, to a lesser extent, red, white, azure, green, black, yellow and pinkish-mauve.

The Sinai plaque belongs to a group of works enamelled in the Limoges fashion, known as the 'star group'. Their chief characteristics are the enamelled forms on the gilded background with dense guilloché, with scattered stars which lack this form of engraving, the colour range and the unified coloured surfaces within the broad grooves, without many sub-divisions, a technique which used to be called 'plate peinture'.[35] Stylistic, iconographical and historical evidence connects the works belonging to this group with Central Italy, where, around 1215, we know that there were craftsmen who had been summoned to produce large works on the spot, using the technique of the Limoges enamels. It is very likely that the Sinai plaque was made there between 1225 and 1235, a period of lively interchange of ideas, works of art and craftsmen.[36] Such a hypothesis is supported by the inclination of the head of Christ with its sidelong gaze, the broad folds and the range of colours.[37] Its presence in the Monastery lies within the framework of the historical parameters, at a time when the Monastery sought, and obtained, the protection of Pope Honorius.[38]

The reverence in which St. Catherine was held by the royal family of France and its entourage in the 14th and the early 15th century is reflected in the depiction of the Saint in valuable works of art of the period[39] and in the chalice (fig. 8), presented by Charles VI of France (1380 - 1422) to the Monastery of St. Catherine.[40] Charles VI, 'the mad king', was famed for his love of luxury and his generosity.[41] His gift to the Monastery coincides with one of the difficult periods of his reign, one when the royal treasury had begun to be stripped of the valuable objects which his father, Charles V, had amassed.[42]

The silver gilt chalice has features of the 14th century: a bowl without a calyx, an eight-sided, star-shaped base and a spherical compressed knob with medallions.[43] The royal origin of the gift is stressed by the calligraphic inscription in Latin and Greek which runs round the base,[44] with the enamelled royal coat of arms on one of its sides, and the engraved or stippled fleurs-de-lys which adorn the whole of the chalice. Its Parisian origin is confirmed by the hallmark, the crowned lily.[45] The Crucifixion is depicted on a shield-shaped plaque, while on the medallions of the knob are the busts of Christ and some of the Apostles. The figurative decoration, produced by 'basse taille' technique, is covered by translucent enamels in green, blue, a warm yellow, violet, light and dark grey and brown, and pale pink for the flesh.[46] It was by the use of this technique, which had its roots in Italy, that the Paris goldsmiths of the 14th century created some of the finest secular and religious works. The Sinai chalice with its fleurs-de-lys and the subtlety of its enamels belongs in stylistic terms to the last decades of that century.[47]

## WORKS WITH WESTERN INFLUENCES

In the inventory of the sacristy of 1673 mention is made of a cross *in the holy bush, silver, Frankish work*.[48] This must have been the processional cross (figs. 6, 7), *the work of the hands of Alexios siropoulos*, still on the altar of this chapel.[49] The description 'Frankish work' expresses the attitude of the monks of the time towards a work in which Eastern and Western characteristics co-exist, a form of co-existence which even today strikes one as strange. Its design is unusual in its cross-shaped arms and the spherical knob with plant decoration and the monograms.[50] The obverse side is dominated by a figure of the Crucified,[51] in relief and realistic in accordance with the Eastern tradition, which is surrounded by enamelled medallions with the symbols of the Evangelists. Ranged around these are relief busts of Christ and the Evangelists.[52] The depiction of the Pelican in the Tree of Life[53] belongs to Western iconography, as does the full-length portrayal of the Virgin in profile, as she stands, gesturing, on the left narrow side of the cross, her head closely covered and decorative band[54] edging her dress[55]. The positioning of St. John on the right narrow side of the cross is similar. Enamelled medallions with scenes which precede and follow the Crucifixion, such as the Entry into Jerusalem, the Descent into Hell, the Ascension and Pentecost, modelled on Palaeologan iconography, complete, on the other side, the iconographic programme of this cross.[56] St. Catherine is depicted full-length and full-face, beneath a Gothic arch, in the type of Cretan painting of the second half of the 15th century.[57] Translucent enamels in black, dark violet and shades of blue, green and brown and opaque enamels in red and blue cover in part or completely the figurative and aniconic decoration in 'basse taille' and 'ronde bosse' techniques.[58]

The Sinai cross is a rare example of silver and gold work belonging to what is known as 'Crusader' art.[59] The faces, with their pronounced features and 'rolling' eyes,[60] the short veil worn by the Virgin,[61] the use of the profile position and the Gothic features[62] point to Cypriot painting of the second half of the 15th century.[63] The likelihood of such an origin is strengthened by the fleurs-de-lys, symbol of the Lusignans' rule,[64] on the enamelled additional decoration and the surname of the craftsman, indicating his Syrian descent, in an area where there was an important Syrian minority.[65] Two Gospel covers with Western characteristics and enamelled plaques, on which the Evangelists are depicted with inscriptions in Greek, provide evidence that the Sinai cross was not the only specimen of the translucent enamel technique in the Eastern Mediterranean.

A similar spirit, though expressed through different media, can be seen in a chalice with gilding (fig. 9), which is an amalgam of Gothic and Renaissance features. Its marked similarities with a chalice dated 1576 in the Megiste Laura Monastery on Mount Athos permit its dating to the second half of the 16th century. The chalice has a multi-lobed base with points between the lobes, a form which is encountered more frequently in Italian Late Gothic chalices.[66] Its pierced band also has a Gothic character. The knob of the chalice takes the shape of a six-sided building with pilasters at its edges[67] and the calix of the bowl has freely-placed acanthus leaves.[68] The fine foliage scrolls at the base of the chalice continue higher, on to the foot, forming twelve intersecting volutes which frame busts of Apostles in high relief and the symbols of the Evangelists making up the number of the Apostles. These figures too, with the slight turn of the body and the manner of rendering mass, the angle of the head and the halo in perspective, show evidence of Western models. Also deserving of attention is the figurative decoration of the knob, the Akra Tapeinosis between two worshipping angels in bust form, and the Virgin and Child, flanked by Moses and St. Catherine. Both subjects follow the iconographic models of Cretan painting of the second half of the 15th century.[69] The Sinai chalice is a robust work, clearly from the hands of an able craftsman who was acquainted both with Italian works and Cretan iconography.

The Cretan presence on Sinai is confirmed in the sphere of silverwork by an inscribed and hallmarked reliquary (fig. 13), the offering of Maximos Arpharas in 1619, *on pain of my curse, to be here perpetually in the monastery of Saint Catherine.*[70] The eight-sided reliquary rests on a circular base with engraved straps interweaving with plant decoration, also engraved, on a finely matted background. Its sides are occupied with full-length depictions of St. Catherine, Christ, St. Chrysostom, a relic of whom the reliquary contains, and the Virgin 'orans'. These forms, engraved and completely flat, alternate with seraphim on the remaining sides. The figures are surrounded by pierced strapwork and flower decoration. The Sinai reliquary, in its style and the manner of its decoration, which reflect the last phase of Mannerism, is directly linked to Venetian silverwork of the second half of the 16th and the beginning of the 17th century,[71] and is an example of the adaptation of a style in the service of local needs to the existing means of expression.[72] The reliquary is a highly important work; it brings to light the policy, unknown up to now, of the Venetian administration in Crete in the matter of the quality control of precious metals, it confirms archival evidence of the existence of metal workshops, it provides evidence of the influence of Venetian gold and silverwork on works produced in Crete and establishes a fixed point of reference for a series of other Cretan works, hallmarked and otherwise, to be found on Sinai and in other sacristies in the Aegean.

## WORKS FROM THE DANUBE PROVINCES

Thanks to the policy of protection pursued by the princes of the Danubian provinces, a climate of permanent relations with Sinai was established.[73] In 1540, Radu VII Paisie, Voevod of Wallachia, ceded by his chrysobull to the Monastery the sum of 10,000 aspers per annum.[74] A few years later, probably between 1542 and 1545, officials of the court of Wallachia, the Great Komis, the Great Dvornik Župan Koada and his sons Theodosis and Staiko,[75] also Župans, gave a casket (*kibotion*) (fig. 10) in the shape of a church with five domes.[76] Its figurative decoration includes prophets, bishops, soldier saints and hermits, ranged side by side in rectangular panels, a characteristic of the Wallachian workshops of the period.[77] The iconographic programme continues with the Sinaitic subject of the Transfiguration, the Deesis, the pillars of the Church, Peter, Paul and Andrew, other Apostles and seraphim. The decoration is completed by the interlacing, with Ottoman subjects and Late Gothic embellishments, which penetrated from the Dalmatian coast to the workshops of Herzegovina and from Transylvania to the Danubian provinces and remained in the Balkans until approximately the middle of the 18th century, together with other styles, sometimes employed side by side on the same object, as here.[78] This casket shows great similarities with the work of Dmitar from Lipova in the Sišatovac Monastery (1550-51).[79] Attribution to him would, however, be improbable, since the execution differs in the detail and the quality is inferior, particularly in the supplementary decoration.[80] Nevertheless, both kibotia are modelled on works belonging to the beginning of the 16th century.[81]

The memory of the piety and generosity of the Voevod of Wallachia Alexander II Mircea, his wife Ekaterini and their son Mihnea is perpetuated at the Monastery not only by the commemoration of their names as founders of the Chapel of St. John the Baptist,[82] but by their depiction as suppliants on the reverse of a valuable cover for a Greek manuscript of the 11th century (figs. 11, 12).[83] The Crucifixion and the Transfiguration, with its connection with Sinai, are the principal scenes on the boards; these are framed by rectangular panels containing busts of prophets, Evangelists, saints and anchorites. This cover, which is not the only one of its kind preserved in the Monastery,[84] has the characteristics of a group of works from Wallachian workshops of the 16th century: the lining up of the severe, inflexible, schematic forms, without mass, around the central scene, and low relief on the ring-punched background, which is decorated with schematic plant forms, to a greater or lesser degree influenced by Ottoman models.[85] We do not know whether the noble couple presented the manuscript together with this rich binding. A memorandum in another Gospel with valuable binding, the gift of Jeremiah Movilă, Prince of Moldavia (1595-1606), supplies information on certain customs of the time which perhaps held good for the gift of Alexander II of Wallachia: ...we took (the Gospel) down from the monastery to take it to Wallachia to silver it and for it to come back to the monastery again.[86]

In a different style, though more or less contemporary with the Gospel from Wallachia, is the gilt censer (fig. 14) which Roxandra, widow of Alexander Lăpuşneanu of Moldavia and guardian in his minority of her son Bogdan IV Voda, presented in 1569 to the Chapel of St. John the Baptist, as we are informed by the dedicatory inscription.[87] The censer rests on a cylindrical foot on a six-lobed base. On the shallow hemispherical bowl virtually the sole decoration is the dedicatory inscription in Slavonic. In contrast with the austere lower section is the high cast cover, on three levels, in the form of a church, with its complex pierced Gothic architectural decoration. The plain multi-faceted finial at the top serves to create a balance between the impressions given by the decorated and undecorated surfaces. The four-sided part of the handle, in contrast to the whole, has fine Ottoman flower ornaments. The Sinai censer belongs to a series of similar works known to date from the 16th (chiefly) and early 17th centuries, also depicted in the painting of the time,[88] inspired by the labyrinthine censers of the international Gothic style.[89] A severe structure and clearly-marked characteristics, features of the 16th century, are to be seen in the Sinai censer, without it, however, approaching in quality the better examples of its kind, the censer of the Banja Monastery at Priboj, for example, on which the latest view is that its probable origin is a workshop of Transylvania.[90]

The gilt church-shaped casket (fig. 15) must have formed a set with it. This was given to the Monastery by Georgios, Bishop of Radauţi in Moldavia, in the same year as the censer was given (1569).[91] The sides have cast plant decoration and, in two bands, the Greek dedicatory inscription. Three turrets with complex cast pierced Gothic architectural elements culminating in a plain finial and topped with a cross rise from the cover. The edge of the cover has plant decoration with Gothic crochets. The information which we have to date would place this casket as chronologically the first of a series with Late Gothic features, from the second half of the 16th century.[92]

WORKS OF THE 17th CENTURY

The 17th century is represented by a wealth of works of note. Enamel techniques, the sharp colour contrast of niello and gold and preference for precious stones, often imitation, are among the means of expression of the Ottoman climate which prevailed during that century. There must have been local workshops in the Balkans employing enamel techniques, probably the same ones which produced local jewelry. We know which some of these were, but not how long they were active, while others have not yet been identified.

A work typical of this atmosphere is a fine cross dating from 1626 (fig. 26), one of the best of its type. It was MADE IN THE YEAR 1626 JANUARY 25 IN ARTA PROTECTED OF GOD, according to the inscription on it.[93] On the body of the cross, of carved wood and of considerable quality, are depicted scenes with a multiplicity of figures from the Dodekaorton. Here the craftsman has attempted to introduce a sense of depth by emphasizing the architectural elements, using open-work in some scenes, a technique employed increasingly from the beginning of the 17th century.[94] The flanking side panels, with a dragon design, show prophets[95] and are supported by dragons in full relief. These hold in their mouths small icons bearing depictions of the Virgin and St. John the Theologian, features reminiscent of crosses on sanctuary iconostases.[96] The gilt mounting of the cross, covered with fine flower decoration of the Ottoman type and arabesques, is crowned by two turrets. The dedicatory and liturgical inscriptions are engraved on both sides of the shaft in small skillfully executed calligraphy. The exceptional quality of this refined work, the equal of the best examples of Constantinopolitan art,[97] points to a workshop of a high standard, a surprise for a city such as Arta, since no evidence has yet come to light that it was at that period an important gold and silver-smithing centre.

There are also marked references to Constantinople in a rich mitre (fig. 20), made *through contributions and expenditure of all the Christians of the city of Ioannina,* and while Parthenios was Metropolitan of Ioannina.[98] This *sacred* and *holy treasure* was given to the *most holy and most royal Monastery of the Holy Mountain of Sinai* in 1636. This mitre is stepped in a manner reminiscent of the papal tiara, a shape which also recalls the helmet of Süleyman the Magnificent, as depicted in Venetian engravings (1532 and 1535).[99] The figurative decoration includes the Deesis and Apostles in bust form below an arched arcade, prophets at full length in aedicules in the form of churches, St. Catherine and medallions with the symbols of the Evangelists. In this bold work with its rich aniconic decoration, the variety of its themes, techniques and materials, and the high standard of the execution, characteristics of Constantinopolitan art, such as the arabesques on the niello,[100] the way in which the plant decoration has been carried out and the plaques with their delicate flowers and polychrome stones, are recognizable.[101] Similarities of style and execution form a connection between this mitre and the cross discussed above (fig. 26), so much so that one wonders whether these two works have a common origin or whether they were made in different places, but by craftsmen who had served their apprenticeship at the same centre.[102]

Similarities of aniconic design are also apparent in a gilt chalice (fig. 25), an offering of Constantine and Kale in 1633.[103] The shape is reminiscent of the chalices with Late Gothic and Ottoman features, without figurative decoration, of the second half of the 16th century, as well as other ecclesiastical vessels, chiefly from the workshops of Herzegovina.[104] In the case of the somewhat heavy Sinai chalice, the Gothic elements, such as the multi-sided foot with the over-elevated multi-lobed base, are a mere echo. What dominates here is the dense, pierced, vegetal and floral Ottoman-type decoration, enhanced with enamelled rosettes and the multiplicity of colour of the nielloed cover, set with precious stones and pearls, which does not seem to match the rest all that well. Nor has the decoration the delicacy and clarity of the preceeding works; furthermore, the space has not been calculated correctly, with the result that the inscription on the base has remained incomplete. However, this type of chalice predominated in the first half of the 17th century in the workshops of the Balkans in local variations, not always successful.[105]

WORKSHOPS IN THE PHILIPPOUPOLIS AREA

The use of enamels in conjunction with filigree work plays a much greater role in a gilt five-domed casket (fig. 30) in the form of a basilica. It was presented to the Monastery in 1635 through the efforts of the priest-monk Anastasios of Crete and is probably the work of the craftsmen Daniel and Poullos, who have left their names in a discreet manner on the back.[106] Perhaps this is the object which is described in the inventory of 1673 as *a large (kibotion) of value the likeness of the katholikon*.[107] Certainly the present form of the katholikon of the Monastery, apart from the fact that it is indeed a basilica, bears little resemblance to that of the kibotion. However, the scenes depicted under the arches on the sides reveal that the majority of the saints depicted either have a direct connection with local cults, such as the Transfiguration, the Virgin as the Burning Bush between Moses and St. Catherine, the burial of St. Catherine, St. John Climacus and St. Anastasios of Sinai, or have chapels dedicated to them, such as the Prophets Moses and Aaron, the Three Hierarchs, St. Symeon Stylites, St. John the Baptist, St. Stephen and Sts. Constantine and Helen. These figures, unskillfully engraved, without details, are almost lost beneath the weight of the paradisal and symbolic decoration. The inspiration of the craftsmen went beyond their technical capabilities. The impression of multiplicity of colour is reinforced by the red and green satin which serves as a background for the open-work sections, the coloured stones, the turquoises and the seed pearls. Some of the architectural features are suggested by geometrical motifs, such as the pediments on the facade and the sides, or an effort has been made to render them in perspective, as in the case of the domes of the chapels flanking the Sanctuary. The oriental character of the casket is readily apparent, though Late Gothic features, such as the row of palmettes along the sides, the rose window in the higher central aisle and the animals on which the casket rests, are also present.[108] Another casket in the Bačkovo Monastery (1637) shows a number of similarities with the Sinai casket.[109] This fact permits the hypothesis that, although the craftsman whose signatures appears was not Greek, both these works have the same place of origin, perhaps Philippoupolis, an important centre for the production of filigree enamels in the 17th century, though not the only one.[110]

The technique of enamels, in conjunction with filigree ornaments and cast plaques, is also encountered in a five-domed censer (fig. 28), dedicated *through the aid* and *pains of Anastasios priest-monk of Sinai* and *by the hand of Phoresi*.[111] The disproportionately small cast and pierced foot is joined to the body of the censer by a multi-sided knob, a feature which is constantly encountered as the termination of the shaft in benediction crosses of the 17th century. The circular plaques with which the bowl is decorated, with the Sinaitic themes and the Evangelists, contrast with the rectangular plaques with their scenes from the Dodekaorton, which occupy the sides of the cover. The small domes, however, are not in harmony with the whole. Nevertheless, what catches the attention in this work is again its multi-coloured nature. This censer is from the point of view of iconography, technique and style linked with a group of Gospel covers of the 17th century with enamelled plaques in various combinations and arrangements. Most typical are the circular plaques depicting the Evangelists, which are in intaglio, virtually flat, and give the impression of woodcarvings. In one category, probably the oldest, the plaques are used either scattered about the cover or together with other cast figurative or aniconic Ottoman decorations and stones in flower-shaped mountings.[112] In another category, which seems to be of a later date, the plaques are framed by filigree work on an enamelled ground. The date of the high-point of this second type is suggested, for the present, by a Gospel cover in the Bačkovo Monastery in Bulgaria, dated 1686.[113] It is not impossible that the donor was the same Anastasios who presented the casket in 1635. The geographical distribution of the surviving Gospel covers indicated the probable location of the workshop which produced them, which might well be the same as for the casket. However, the identification of the centres which produced plaques and the trade in them from approximately the mid 17th to the mid 18th century remain an issue for investigation, since, it would seem, there were a number of workshops employing various styles, more or less in parallel, in the Balkans.[114]

The inscriptions which are incorporated into the mitre's decorative system (fig. 32) state that *the crown was made by the aid and at the expense of Nikephoros priest-monk of Crete and protosynkelos of Sinai*.[115] In these inscriptions the craftsman occupies a position of equal honour: *by the hand of Anastasios, 1678, in the province of the bishop of Lititza kyr Theodosius*.[116] This information is supplemented by a benediction cross presented to the Monastery a year earlier, in 1677, by the same Nikephoros, which was made by the same craftsman *in Voulgarochori*. This location is confirmed by an inscribed cross in the Megiste Laura Monastery on Mount Athos, the work of the same Anastasios. The aesthetic perceptions of the times dictated by the variety of colour here find expression in the gilt engraved panels with the Deesis and depictions of the Apostles, the filigree decoration on a background covered with light green and blue enamels, the studied alternation of multi-coloured stones, the pearls and the coloured material which serves as a background for the open-work sections. The fine, well-twisted wire is used with considerable exactitude, a merit which is lacking in the engraved decoration, in order to form the floral decoration, the secondary geometrical motifs and the inscriptions. It is not known what the relations of Anastasios from Voulgarochori were with Philippoupolis or with nearby Adrianoupolis, but the fact that for the open-work sections he used the delicate themes of Floral Baroque, the new fashion which from the mid 17th century prevailed in Constantinople,[117] shows that he followed the artistic trends of his times.

The ceremony of *artoklasia*, or *blessing of the loaves* is one which is performed, particularly in monasteries, with great pomp. The priest blesses the five loaves, the grain, the wine and the oil which are offered and the bread is then broken and distributed to those present.[118] For this ceremony, in wealthy churches, there were special vessels, called *artoklasies*. A particularly fine example is a monumental artoklasia (fig. 24) which *was finished in 1678 in the city of Sofia ... and was dedicated to the holy mountain of Sinai trodden of God in remembrance of the christians*.[119] The small cruets are intended for the oil and wine and the trays for the grain and the bread. Functionality is subordinated to the decorative conception in this complex work, without, however, the symbolic implications of the scenes presented being overlooked: the Virgin and the miracle of the multiplication of the five loaves, with the Virgin between Moses and St. Catherine, the Transfiguration of Christ and the Annunciation of the Virgin. Small double-sided icons, like banners, with symbols of the Evangelists, and seraphim reinforce the decorative character of the vessel. The iconographic programme is completed by scenes from the Dodekaorton, busts of prophets and bishops shown at full length. Among these, St. Metrophanes, first Bishop of Constantinople, and St. Sabbas, Archbishop of the Serbs, reflect traditions connected with the ceremony of artoklasia and the local cultus.[120] The figures, lacking plasticity, are traced in a somewhat schematic manner on the ruggedly punched background, some in low relief and others engraved, virtually flat. The tradition of Sofia is continued here, but with inferior qualitative results.[121] Nevertheless, the secondary decorative features, with their delicacy and accuracy of execution, give strength to the overall impression. The fine vegetal and geometrical subjects are worked in single or twisted wire on enamelled background, or, in contrast with the works of the period and the region, are filled, according to the Russian technique, with opaque enamels in light green, blue and azure on a background covered with very fine silver granules. The oriental nature of this imposing work is stressed by the Ottoman style of the cruets, the enamelled plant decoration, the details of construction and the multi-coloured nature of the vessel as a whole.[122] This work would have a claim to uniqueness, were it not for the existence of a virtually identical artoklasia presented in 1677 to the Megiste Laura Monastery on Mount Athos.

The enkolpion of the *humble Bishop Theophanes* (1663) (fig. 22) with its small painted icon within a metal frame is a further illustration of the strong preference for filigree enamels during the second half of the 17th century. The full-face busts of the Evangelists, St. John the Baptist, Archangels and bishops are contained in the pointed arches of the frame. The delicate filigree vegetal decoration, on an enamelled background, covers the frame and the back of the enkolpion. It is enriched with pearls, large turquoises and glass paste stones, out of proportion with the miniature character of the figures.[123]

## WORKS IN ENAMEL FROM CONSTANTINOPLE

An entirely different manner of employing enamels, in the representation of scenes and figures, is to be seen in a monumental casket, in the form of a church (fig. 23), *the work of Ioannis* originally presented (1672) to the Stavronikita Monastery on Mount Athos *through the aid and toil and sole expense of Ioakeim priest-monk*.[124] It remains unknown how this five-domed casket reached Sinai. The figures and scenes depicted on panels, attached by round nails to the two zones, are those customary on caskets, such as the Apostles Peter and Paul, or relating in some way to the Monastery, as in the case of the Vision of St. Nicholas, to whom the katholikon of the Stavronikita Monastery is dedicated.

The enamel technique here follows the principle of cloisonné enamels, but the cells which are used for the designing of the scenes and their details are formed with very fine, well-twisted wire and the enamels enclosed as unified colour surfaces are opaque, without reaching the same level as the cells. The colour range includes blue, azure, turquoise and light and dark green; flesh is rendered in off-white. The impression of multiplicity of colour is reinforced by the flowering branches, pointed up in niello, surrounded by delicate nielloed flowers of the Ottoman type. The firm structure of the work, the good proportions of the figures, the delicacy of the workmanship and the carefully thought-out details all confirm that the casket is the product of an important workshop. The same niello technique was used in Constantinople.[125] It was very common also in Muscovite gold and silver-smithing of the period and the connection lies in the stay in Moscow, between the years 1662 and 1667, of craftsmen from Constantinople.[126] Thus it is possible that this was where the casket was made. It is, moreover, an interesting work for a period when filigree opaque enamels were limited largely to aniconic decoration and very few works with figurative decoration produced by this technique are known.[127]

A small group of objects with a wealth of stones, not always precious, follows the aesthetic principles of the Ottoman court. These must have been pilgrims' offerings, since their aniconic decoration does not always suggest ecclesiastical use. Belonging to this group is an oval enkolpion (fig. 18) whose central jade plaque is encrusted with gold leaf and flowers in relief, each of which encloses one precious stone, perhaps emeralds and rubies. This technique, to which we owe some of the most impressive works of Ottoman art, was particularly popular from the second half of the 16th to the end of the 17th century.[128] The stones in their flower-shaped settings and the enamelled flower decoration on both sides of the enkolpion point to a dating in the 17th century.[129]

A second enkolpion (fig. 19), this time open-work and its front covered with gold leaf, is in the same spirit. The flower-shaped mountings with coloured stones arranged radially occupy the chief position, set against a background covered with green translucent enamels. The interstices are filled with delicate enamelled floral decoration. This spectacular style of the Ottoman court of the second half of the 17th century[130] also prevailed at the court of the Tsars of Russia, even in large-scale works.[131] Combined with figurative decoration, it lent lustre to the supreme symbols of ecclesiastical office: the staffs and mitres of patriarchs, and rich enkolpia. In the case of a belt buckle, which had also a liturgical use (fig. 17), the central circular part is flanked by two pierced sections with a leaf motif, all produced by the jewelled technique, enriched by a more complex combination of translucent, opaque and painted enamels, a fashion equally current in the second half of the 17th century.[132]

A pastoral staff with an ivory finial (fig. 36) is another example of the technique of inlaid, jewelled gold. The shaft is decorated with *fine shell of a sea conch (sedef), and Indian turtle (bağa).*[133] The use of valuable and exotic materials such as these had as its purpose the creation of a strong sense of colour.

Another pastoral staff (fig. 37), covered with azure and green enamels, in harmony with the turquoises which decorate its knots, testifies to the great extent of the use of filigree enamels. The quality of the workmanship, with the carefully executed details, and the small jade discs with the inlaid gold flowers and small precious stones point to the refined style of the capital city.[134] It is to the capital also that the pastoral staff (fig. 38) of the Abbot of Sinai Athanasius (1714), with its finial of ivory inlaid with gold leaf ornaments and gems, should be attributed. Delicate flower decoration — green champlevé enamels and enamels painted in white, azure, green and russet — cover the shaft.

## OTHER WORKS OF THE 17th CENTURY

Another approach to the vessel used for the artoklasia is illustrated by a work (fig. 33), presented to the Monastery in 1679, *by the pains and at the expense of many devout christians ...by the hand of the sinner Eustathios of Trikke in Thessaly.*[135] One of the loaves was placed in the receptacle with the tall foot and the spherical knob, while the wheat, the oil and the wine went into the spherical vessels which rest on dragons with plant-shaped tails. The three candles stood on the heads of the three upright lions which support the model of the Monastery, shown ringed by a low wall. The katholikon, the Chapel of the Burning Bush, the Holy Summit, where Moses received the Commandments and the summit of St. Catherine with her tomb are recognizable. The fantastic and symbolic elements, such as the dragons, the lions, the cypresses above the roofs and the peacocks on the wall of the facade, co-exist with the intention of providing a realistic reproduction of the site, in which the caravan with the camels has its place. In rendering the individual items, the craftsman has resorted to the means of expression of the Ottoman art of the times. The most characteristic are the pomegranates on the lower extremities of the tray, the dragons, the tulip-shaped candleholders, the decoration of the base and the lip of the tray and the open-work covers of the receptacles.[136] However, the work does not succeed in transcending the provincial level, in which the 'picturesque' finally predominates. It is, nonetheless, an interesting depiction of the Monastery, probably inspired by models which had been established since the mid 16th century, such as travellers' engravings, paintings and icons dealing with Sinai.[137]

*Cross carved by hand, silvered, gilt* is the term used to describe the benediction crosses at the end of the 17th century.[138] The Monastery has a large number of crosses of this category, from various workshops. In the case of the cross (fig. 34) donated to the Monastery in 1684 *by Makarios priest-monk of Crete*, the carved wooden part, with some perforation, belongs to the most simple type of the genre, with the Crucifixion and the Resurrection as the central scenes on each side, flanked by angels and Evangelists. Here too the mounting follows the trends of the times: a polygonal extremity, a braided band midway on the handle, filigree work on an enamelled background, in a version enriched with additional decoration in tulip form.

A variation on the carved cross as to the metal frame is provided by a cross dating from 1683 (fig. 35), the work of *Georgios Moukios from Stemnitsa in the Peloponnese*. The tentative appearance of the small circular base, with feet, which reminds one of the bases of lights and caskets in the shape of animals, the cast plant-shaped lateral decoration, reminiscent of dragons or birds, the small flowers on the surfaces of the sides and the champlevé enamels suggest models which had established themselves in the second half of the 17th century in Constantinople.[139] Of significance in this work is the origin of the craftsman, which is evidence, as early as the late 17th century, of the involvement of the inhabitants of Stemnitsa in this branch of metalwork, since up to now very few dated and inscribed works earlier than the 19th century from this source have come to light.[140]

## MAJOR CENTRES OF THE 17th CENTURY

It is still to the atmosphere of the 16th century that a gilt case for a Greek manuscript Lectionary (fig. 16) belongs. The case was given to the Monastery in 1604 by the priest-monk Ioakeim, from Crete, surnamed Skordilis.[141] The principal subjects, the Crucifixion and the Descent into Hell, without many figures and in front of a rudimentary natural or architectural background, occupy the obverse and reverse respectively. On the flaps which cover the side the Evangelists are shown in medallions, with the Virgin as the Burning Bush, between Moses and St. Catherine. These noble figures with their slender proportions, in spite of the stylization and the slight awkwardness in the movement of Christ, the expressive severe faces with the large eyes — another feature typical of Georgian art — and the complex linear folds have been rendered with multiple levels of relief.[142] The heads and hands are brought out most, so that the icon acquires greater depth. Different in style, but of almost equal importance is the net of flowering shoots with its simple and composite palmettes which is chased on a fine ring-punched field and runs round the frame and covers all the intervening surfaces.[143] This decoration, typical of Persian and Ottoman art of the 16th century, is also the feature which differentiates the style of eastern from that of western Georgia at that period.[144]

Augsburg is the place of origin of a shallow silver basin with gilding (fig. 39). It is not known whether it had a matching ewer. From the time of the Renaissance onwards such a set formed part of the furnishing of the houses of the rich, where it was used for the guests to wash their hands during meals.[145] At the same time, it had an ecclesiastical use.[146] In the age of Mannerism,[147] these vessels, sophisticated in design and decoration, remained the most imposing showpieces — as can be seen from contemporary paintings.[148] From the middle of the 16th century, the workshops of Germany supplied not only the courts of Europe's princes but also the rich burgess class with this commodity. This was the period in which Augsburg gained the lead over its rival Nurenberg, thanks to religious toleration and the trade in silver in Europe.[149] The Sinai basin with its elegant oval shape, a typical innovative feature of Augsburg,[150] belongs to the last phase of international Mannerism. Predominant in the decoration is strapwork interlacing with a festoon of fruit, cupids, heads of cherubim, and delicate flowering shoots.[151] These motifs, whose spread was due to the pattern books used by goldsmiths,[152] are rendered by means of lustrous gilt surfaces, flat or in sharp relief, on a background of a matt silver colour, thus achieving a sense of a harmonious painting. The basin bears the maker's mark of the workshop of Tobias Kramer,[153] the assay zig-zag groove and the stamp of the city of Augsburg.[154] Certainly this work is not one of the most impressive of its kind. What, perhaps, we find more striking today is its displacement from Western Europe into the orthodox monastic environment of the Sinai desert and its acceptance and use there.

The close relations between the Monastery and Russia, to which the archives testify, are also confirmed by a large number of icons *which*, Paisios, Metropolitan of Rhodes, informs us, *the monks would bring from Russia in the old times silvered and gilded with pure gold.*[155] The favour of the Tsars of Russia towards Sinai was expressed, inter alia,[156] by *a muscovite mitre with pearls* (fig. 31), given in 1642 by *Michael, faithful King of Muscovy.*[157] The mitre keeps to the older low cylindrical shape, derived from the cap worn in monasteries, and also follows the earlier style of decoration, as encountered in a gold-embroidered mitre of the 16th century at the Esphigmenou Monastery on Mount Athos.[158] The small gilded icons with the pointed arches and the geometrical framework show the Deesis with Christ as Great High Priest, Archangels, St. Peter and St. Paul and St. Nicholas. The small icons, figures engraved by an experienced hand, the row of pearls around each item which is sewn on and the stones with their flower-shaped settings fully reflect the aesthetic tastes of the period in the decoration of liturgical vestments.[159] Austere by comparison with other works contemporary with it, this mitre stands out for its balanced structure and the subtle, harmonious combination of the gold with the pearls.[160]

The slender, graceful forms of the Archangels Michael and Gabriel are encountered again engraved on the inside of the wings of a small silver gilt triptych (fig. 21), which contains a Russian enkolpion with a depiction of St. Catherine.[161] This is rendered in cameo, the material being grey-blue and dark brown chalcedony, with moderately high relief and soft curves, characteristics of Late Byzantine and Post - Byzantine art.[162] This small icon, framed in gold, is linked to a small cameo on which is shown, as was usual, the Holy Face.[163] Its frame in white enamel, forming a background for plant decoration either in the colour of gold or covered with enamel, translucent and opaque, is typical of the workshops of the Kremlin in the first half of the 17th century.[164] The same is true of the reverse, where the enamels, in more colours and ornamented with painted 'points', cover decoration in low relief on a background worked in gold.[165] The precious stones and large pearls, of regular shape, confirm that this small, delicately-worked enkolpion must be the product of the court workshops. It is not impossible that it had some connection with Tsar Michael or his entourage, as did other known works in gold of that period, decorated with the same enamel techniques, which were particularly popular in the 17th century at the court of the Tsar.[166]

Of exceptional interest and rarity is a cross for the blessing of water[167] from Transylvania (figs. 27, 29), which combines Orthodox tradition with the innovation of the measurment of time in a valuable portable clock, the possession of which was a privilege enjoyed at that time by few European bourgeois.[168] The clock, made in Kronstadt (Braşov) by the, in all probability, Saxon Michael Rener,[169] is protected by a special case[170] with cast lions and an open-work cover, crowned with a cross. On the bronze, silvered face the delicate engraved flower decoration in a silver colour, typical of the 17th century, is in harmony with the background of the reddish bronze.[171] The cross retains the typical features of its kind, with the usual scenes (Baptism and Crucifixion) on each side in fine open-work woodcarving, but is original for its period in its small base, which is in the same style but disproportionate in its size. Its gilt mounting is covered with delicate vegetal ornaments and small flowers in translucent azure and green enamels and opaque enamels painted on white, in pink, russet, yellow, blue and black, known as 'Transylvania enamels'.[172] The use of this technique was widespread in Transylvania in the second half of the 17th century, above all for the decoration of jewelry and utensils for secular use, chiefly in the Floral Baroque period. Narcissi and half-opened tulips with naturalistic petals and leaves, soft curves and high relief, as on the cover of the clock, were favourite subjects at the time in the workshops of the Saxon goldsmiths of Transylvania and they were used for the decoration not only of secular but also of ecclesiastical utensils.[173] This unique work belonged to the Abbot Ioasaph (1617 - 1660)[174] and served chiefly as a prestigious decorative item, since, of course, Sinai did not have the specialized craftsmen who would have been required for the maintenance and repair of the clock.[175]

## WORKS OF THE 18th CENTURY

We encounter the elegant style of Floral Baroque once more in a gilt buckle dating from 1716 (fig. 40), a stamped and inscribed work from Kronstadt (Braşov): *Stephan Weltzer de Corona fecit.* The allegorical renderings of Peace ('Pax') and War ('Bellum') suggest that it was not originally intended for ecclesiastical use, but for a man's velvet belt with metal rosettes sewn on at intervals, such as were worn by the Saxons of Transylvania.[176] It was, nevertheless, used by *bishop Meletios*, as the possessor's inscription informs us. To extol the benefits of Peace, the goldsmith shows her as a woman in archaic costume dancing to the sound of the cymbals which she is holding. War, with battle attire and equipment, seems to be approaching her threateningly. The sculptural effect conveyed by the correct rendering of the mass of the bodies is complemented by the faultless execution of the flower decoration, which is rendered by graduations of the relief, in which shiny and dull surfaces alternate.[177] These details are indicative of the experience of a craftsman such as Stephan Weltzer II, one of the most famous goldsmiths of his time.[178] This is evidenced in those of his works which have survived: a tankard in the Mannerist style, an oil lamp with Baroque floral decoration and an austere Gospel cover, donated by Constantine Brâncoveanu, Prince of Wallachia, to the Greek Church of St. John in Bucharest (1703).[179]

A work by *Georgi Mousi*, dated 1779 (fig. 41), is a representative example of a type of cross for the blessing of water. Typical of this category are the flanking dragons with heads at both ends of their bodies, the architectural features with the domes, the birds, the palmettes and the tulips at the ends of the arms. The wooden core is buried beneath the mass of the frame. The schematic plant decoration in fine twisted gilt wire, in contrast with 17th century crosses, is filled in with opaque light and dark green enamels and adorned with gilt 'granules', coloured stones, coral and pearls. The mounting of the Sinai cross is among the richest of this type, but it is also encountered in simpler versions.[180] The period at which it was prevalent was, to conclude from the examples currently known, the second half of the 18th century; nor was it confined to crosses, as can be seen from a *panagiarion* in the sacristy of the Monastery (fig. 42), belonging within the context of the same style and technique. On its carved disc is depicted the Root of Jesse with the Virgin in the type of the Platytera, one of the scenes typical in the decoration of panagiaria, in which the role of Mary in the Incarnation is stressed.[181] The iconographic type and the open-work suggest an 18th-century date. The system of chains with the pin shows that this panagiarion was used as an enkolpion, a symbol of high ecclesiastical office.[182]

The silver chandelier (fig. 43) which was made in 1752 in Ioannina *under the surperintendence of the most noble archon kyr Anastasios Karaioannis* was presented by the

Sinaitic archimandrite Germanos from Kastoria.[183] The shape of the chandelier follows the prevailing model of the times for multiple lights (with candles or lamps) with two or three tiers of branches, usually in the form of dragons, supported on a shaft with a double-headed eagle on top and round finial beneath.[184] The dense, slightly stylized, plant and floral decoration which covers, in low relief, the ball turnings of the shaft, is an expression of a local variation of the Floral Baroque which, depending, of course, on the locality, still had prestige during the 18th century.

Although somewhat heavy by comparison with other contemporary works,[185] this is, nevertheless, one of the very few of this period known which is signed and dated and is, consequently, of value for the history of Ioannina gold and silver work. It is, furthermore, important because it was made *by the labour of the goldsmiths the brothers Serbanos and Eustathios Sougdouris,*[186] scions of an old Ioannina family of men of letters and goldsmiths, as can be seen from a Gospel cover dated 1671 at the Simonopetra Monastery on Mount Athos, and, much more, from their reputation *that among the goldsmiths of the 18th century the patterns which they engraved, and still engrave, on their works they call Sougdouris flowers.*[187]

Sinai, Jerusalem, Mount Athos, Patmos: at the great centres of Orthodoxy, treasuries of Orthodox and European art, princes, bishops and simple believers, benefactors, artists and humble craftsmen, chapters of European history meet. The systematic study of their fate and what they contain will bring to light important features of which we are still ignorant.

1. *Enamelled panel, showing Christ in Glory (height 32.5 cm.). Limoges technique. Central Italy (?). c.1225-1235.*

2. Bronze cross (height 104 cm.), with engraved scenes from the delivery of the
Tablets with the Commandments to Moses, verse from 'Exodus' and
dedicatory inscription. 6th century.

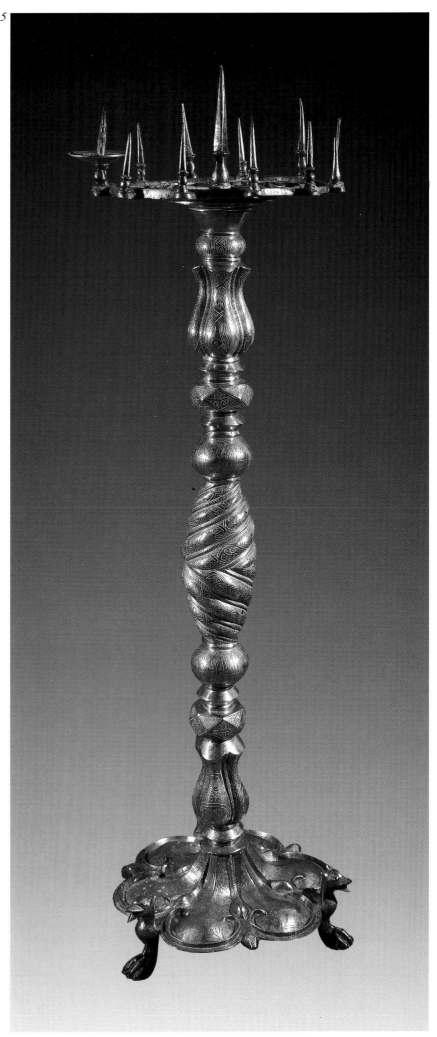

3-4. Bronze enkolpion-reliquary (height 13 cm.), with scenes from the Christological cycle worked in inlaid silver and niello. 10th century.

5. Bronze candelabrum (height 139 cm.), with engraved decoration of an oriental character and medallions showing saints. 11th-12th century.

*6. Silver gilt processional cross (height 57.5 cm.), with relief and enamel decoration worked in 'basse taille' and 'ronde bosse' techniques. Work of Alexios Siropoulos. Cyprus (?). Second half of the 15th century (?).*

7. The reverse side of the cross in fig. 6.

8. Silver gilt chalice (height 21.3 cm.), with translucent enamels worked in the 'basse taille' technique. Gift of King Charles VI of France. Parisian workshop. 1411.

9. Chalice (height 33 cm.), with Late Gothic and Renaissance features and relief figures from Cretan iconographic types. Silver with gilding. 16th century.

10. Silver gilt, church-shaped casket (height 31.7 cm.), with relief figures, Ottoman-type interlacing and Late Gothic ornaments. Offering of officials of the court of Wallachia. 1542-1545.

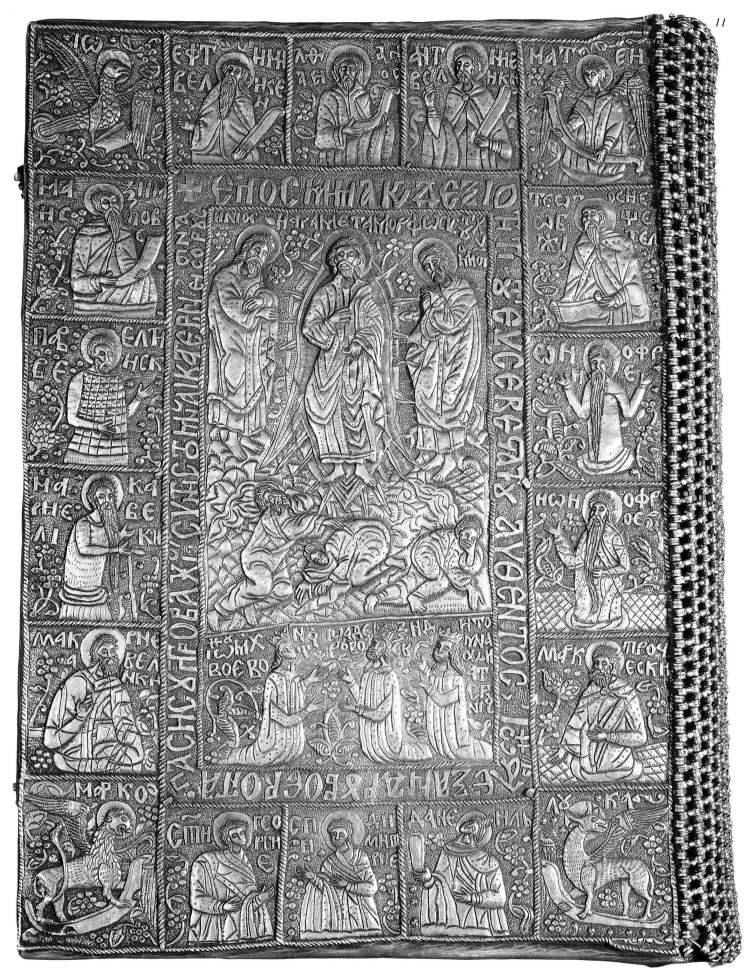

*11. Gospel cover (heigth 39 cm.), with a depiction of the donor, Alexander*
*II Mircea, Prince of Wallachia, and his family. Wallachian workshop. 1568-1577.*

*12. The reverse side of the Gospel cover in fig. 11.*

13. Reliquary (height 30,5 cm.), with open-work, engraved, figurative and aniconic decoration and features of Venetian silverwork. Stamped work of a Cretan workshop. 1619.

14. Silver gilt censer (height 31 cm.), with Late Gothic features. Offering of Roxandra, widow of Alexander Lăpuşneanu, Voevod of Moldavia, to the Chapel of St. John the Baptist. 1569.

15. Silver gilt church Shaped casket, with Late Gothic features (height 27.2 cm.). Offering of Georgios, Bishop of Radanţi in Moldavia. 1569.

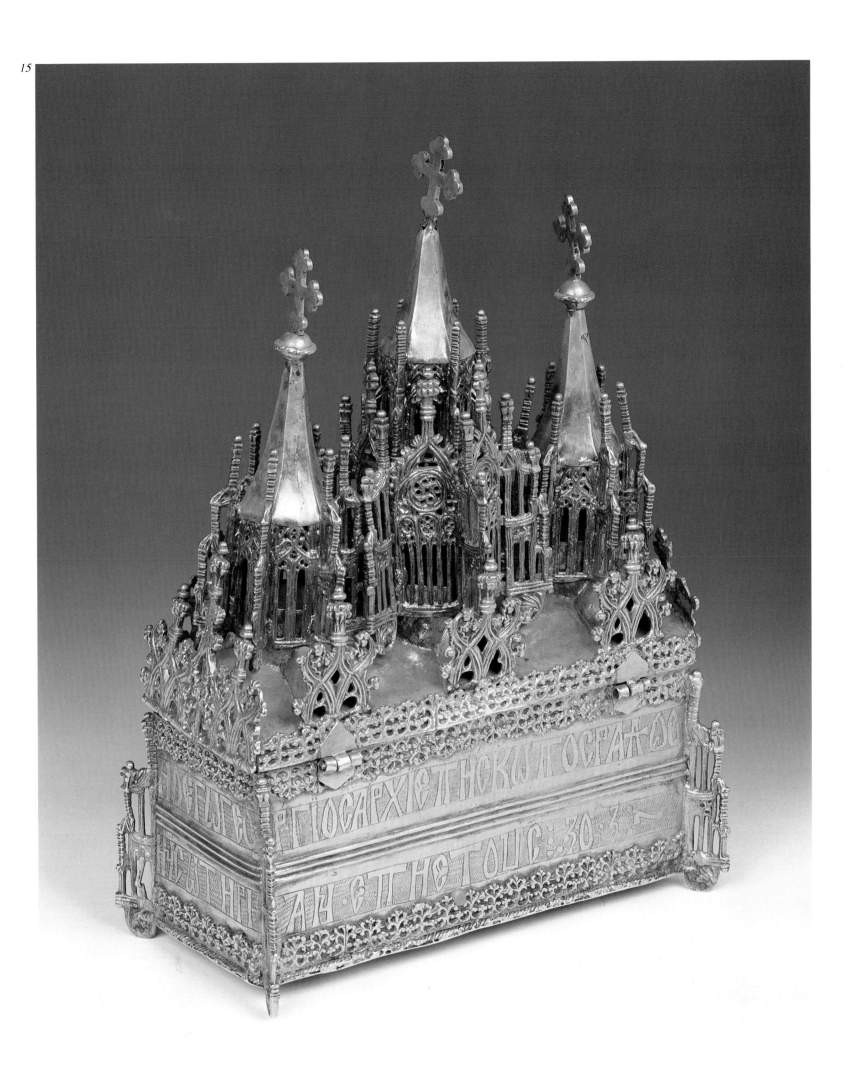

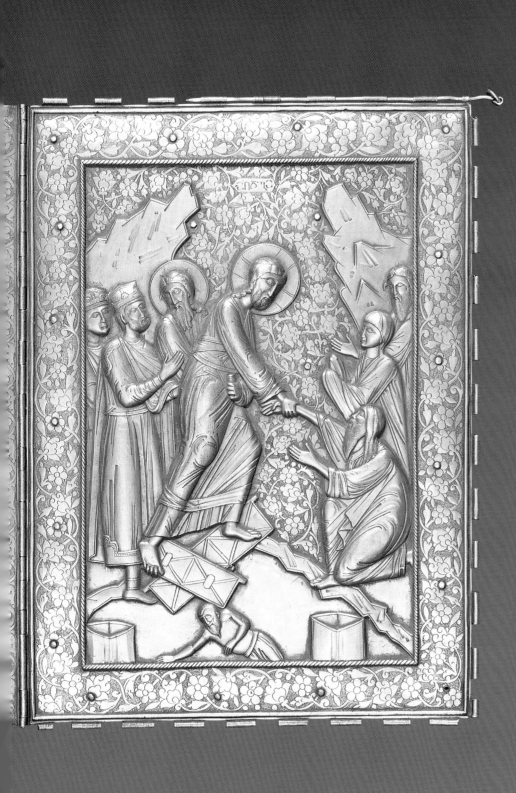

16. Silver gilt Gospel cover (height
30.5 cm.), with the Crucifixion and
Descent into Hell in relief and
engraved floral interlacing of an
Eastern type. Gift of the priest-
monk Ioakeim of Crete, surnamed
Skordilis. From a workshop in
eastern Georgia. 1604.

17. Silver and gold leaf buckle (height 30.5 cm.), decorated with plant  motifs by the jewelled technique. Opaque, translucent and painted enamels. From a Constantinople workshop. Second half of the 17th century.

18. Enkolpion of silver, gold leaf and jade with encrusted gold, precious stones and enamels (height 7.5 cm.). From a Constantinople workshop. 17th century.

19. Enkolpion of silver and jewelled gold leaf, opaque and translucent enamels (diameter 10 cm.). From a Constantinople workshop. Second half of the 17th century.

20. Silver gilt mitre (height 25 cm.), with figures in relief and aniconic decoration of an Ottoman character. Niello, turquoises, pearls, stones. Collective gift of the Christians of the city of Ioannina. 1636.

22

21. Silver gilt triptych, with engraved decoration (height 13 cm.). Contains a chalcedony enkolpion (height 10.5 cm.) with a representation of St. Catherine, set in gold and enamels. From a Kremlin workshop. Second quarter of the 17th century.

22. Enkolpion (height 8.8 cm.), with a small painted icon in a silver gilt frame, decorated with filigree enamels, turquoises, pearls and glass paste stones. 1663.

23. Silver gilt casket in the shape of a church, with enamelled figures and floral decoration in niello (height 42.5 cm.). Originally donated to the Stavronikita Monastery on Mt. Athos. From a Constantinople workshop (?). 1672.

*24. Artoklasia (height 52 cm.) of silver with gilding, figurative engraved and relief
decoration, filigree enamels, turquoises and glass paste stones. Collective offering.
From a Sofia workshop. 1678.*

*25. Silver gilt chalice (height 43.5 cm.), with open-work, aniconic decoration in the Ottoman style, enamelled rosettes and niello. 1633.*

*26. Silver gilt cross (height 52.5 cm.), with floral decoration and interlacing of Ottoman type, flanking dragons and small icons. Arta. 1626.*

27. Combined clock and cross (height 23.5 cm.), with mounting covered with painted enamels. Property of the Abbot Ioasaph. From a Transylvania workshop. A little before 1660.

28. Censer in the shape of a church (height 27.5 cm.), with cast, enamelled panels, filigree enamels and glass paste stones. 17th century.

29. Detail of fig. 27. The clock, the work of Michael Rener, in its case. From a Braşov workshop.

*30. Silver gilt church-shaped casket, with engraved figures (height 23 cm.). Enamelled and cast, open-work decoration of oriental character. Offering of the priest-monk Anastasios of Crete. Work of Daniel and Poullos. 1635.*

*31. Silver gilt mitre, with small engraved icons framed with pearls (height 20.5 cm.).*
*Gift of the Tsar Mikhail Fedorovitch. From a Moscow workshop. 1642.*

32. Silver gilt mitre, with engraved figures (height 20.5 cm.). Floral, open-work
decoration, enriched with filigree enamels. Offering of the Protosynkellos of
Sinai Nikephoros of Crete. Work of Anastasios. Voulgarochori. 1678.

*33. Artoklasia (height 40 cm.), with a model of the Monastery of St. Catherine, Moses receiving the Commandments and the tomb of the Saint. Silver with gilding, niello, enamels and coral. Collective offering. Work of Eustathios from Trikkala. 1679.*

34. *Benediction cross (height 22.7 cm.), with gilt mounting enriched with filigree decoration against an enamelled background, pearls and glass paste stones. Offering of the priest-monk Makarios of Crete. 1684.*

35. *Cross for the blessing of holy water (height 24 cm.), with silver gilt frame, decorated with champlevé enamels, pearls and coral and glass paste stones. Work of Georgios Moukios of Stemnitsa in the Peloponnese. 1683.*

*36-37. Pastoral staffs. Constantinople, 17th century, 36. Ivory inlaid gold and decoration of mother of pearl shell, turtle shell and ebony (height 166 cm.). 37. Silver pastoral staff, decorated with filigree enamels and jade, inlaid gold, turquoises and precious stones (height 160 cm.).*

*38. Pastoral staff of the Abbot Athanasios (height 163 cm.), with ivory finial, with inlaid gold and precious stones, shaft of copper, covered with champlevé and painted enamels. From a Constantinople workshop. 1714.*

*39. Silver basin with gilding, with engraved and relief decoration in the Mannerist style (diameter 45.5 cm.). From the workshop of Tobias Kramer. Augsburg. c. 1620.*

*40. Silver gilt buckle (length 23 cm.), with relief figures of Peace and War and decoration in the Floral Baroque style. Work of Stephan Weltzer II. Braşov. 1716.*

*41. Cross for the blessing of water (height 25 cm.), with frame of gilt silver, enriched with decoration in filigree, granules, enamels, pearls, coral and glass paste stones. Work of Georgios Mousis. 1779.*

*42. Wooden panagiarion (diameter 11.5 cm.), with Jesse Tree in low, open-work relief, set in silver gilt, filigree, granules, enamels, coral, pearls and glass paste stones. Second half of the 18th century.*

*43. Silver chandelier with gilding, two lines of branches and floral decoration in low relief. Offering of the Archimandrite of Sinai Germanos. Work of the brothers Serbanos and Eustathios Sougdouris. Ioannina. 1752.*

ILLUMINATED
MANUSCRIPTS

# ILLUMINATED MANUSCRIPTS

The illuminated manuscripts in Sinai, outstanding for their importance in terms of pictorial themes and aesthetic values, are distinguished from manuscripts in other monastic libraries. Throughout the centuries, they reflect the history of the Holy Monastery: they speak of the holiness of the site, the presence of the Arabs and their contribution to Christian art, the brilliance of Middle Byzantine art, book production in Sinai, the presence of the West, the importance of Crete for Sinai and for the relations of Hellenic art to the art of the West, and Sinai as centre of pilgrimage. Above all, these manuscripts are documents of faith.

Pilgrims in small groups or in streams journeyed through the arid desert to bring a gift from their hearts and to receive a blessing from the Monastery of the Holy Bush. Gifts in the form of manuscripts were customary. Written and illuminated under the light of yellow candles in a far-off place, a library or a monastic cell, these holy books, tarnished by time, had become relics and as such they belonged to a site that was full of relics. Of course manuscripts were written, copied and illustrated in Sinai. But above all the Holy Monastery was the recipient of relics and therefore the depository, treasurer, and guardian of holy books.

Some of these manuscripts were bequeathed to the Monastery by a dying man for the salvation of his soul; others were sent as means of supplication, prayers, for deliverance from the darkness of sin; or they were offered for the souls of loved ones who had departed from this earth; but also books were given as prayers for the loved ones who were still living. Still others were made and presented simply as precious gifts to God who had spoken to man on Mount Horeb.

Written in Sinai, or commissioned for the Monastery, or presented to it, these codices often contain *colophons* or notices stating often the wishes of the scribe or the donors. For example, in one of the most important, early illustrated Lectionaries in the Monastery (cod. 312), the scribe prays: *remember, O Lord, thy servant Eustathios, the presbyter, sinner and humble servant who wrote this Gospel with zeal.* Colophons or notes of this nature are repeated with variations in many of these manuscripts. Often, when a codex is brought as a precious gift, the Monastery is mentioned as that of the Holy Bush; or special mention is made of the holy relics of the Great Martyr Saint Catherine, the patron saint of the Monastery.

## MANUSCRIPTS PRODUCED IN SINAI. THE BEGINNINGS OF THE SINAITIC SCRIPTORIUM, THE PRESENCE OF THE ARABS

It is reported that when Justinian founded the Monastery, some books were brought presumably from Constantinople. Probably they were Psalters and Lectionaries needed for the Liturgy and the life of a monk. Among the extant illuminated manuscripts no one can be assigned to this far-off period. The earliest surviving codices with some kind of ornamentation were produced in the time of the Arabs, whose invasion in the 7th century separated the Sinai peninsula from the Byzantine empire. They provide us with the first evidence for book production in Sinai. These manuscripts are Psalters and can be dated to the 8th and 9th centuries. They are written on a hard parchment, in beautiful, majuscule script with titles and in some instances with texts written in two languages, Greek and Arabic, as seen, for instance, in codex 32, fol. 408$^v$. The illustration is limited to a simple interlace, or interlaced crosses, marking the title or the conclusion of a section, tinted in a color scheme which comprises red, deep olive-green, pale yellow and brown. These colours became a special feature of manuscripts produced in Sinai in various centuries and enabled the student to recognize the activities of a local scriptorium. Evidence in some of these manuscripts shows that they and their related copies, produced in subsequent years, were written and illuminated in Sinai. In one of them, the Psalter codex 32, cited above, the scribe signs his name in Arabic. He is Michael, priest in Sinai. Bilingual manuscripts with sparse ornament continued to be produced in Sinai. They contain other texts as well, for example, the Gospels, such as codex 116, which was written on paper in Sinai by a certain priest John c. 995/6.

However, not all these manuscripts were copied and illustrated in Sinai. Some were produced in nearby centres in Palestine, of which the most important was Jerusalem, the Holy City, with which Sinai had religious and artistic connections from the beginning as the study of the early icons in Sinai has shown. A case in point is the Lectionary codex 210 from 861/2 which was not written in Sinai. It has, however, all the characteristics of the Sinaitic manuscripts and belongs to the same group. A number of its missing quires were discovered among the new finds (Sinai gr. NE meg. Perg. 12), which had remained walled up in the fortress of Justinian until recently. The very beautiful ornament in one of its colophons, a new discovery, remains without any parallel in the art of the period. The antique character of the rinceau motif with the orange-red berries speaks of an earlier tradition which was spread in the early Christian world in the Mediterranean and which survived, in some forms, in certain works of the West in the time of Charles the Great.

From the 10th century we have two Sinaitic manuscripts sophisticated and imaginative in their illustration, even though in both of them the emphasis is on the ornament. The first one (codex 417), is perhaps the oldest copy with pictures of the *Heavenly Ladder*, a work written probably at the close of the 6th century by one of the greatest personalities of asceticism in the Eastern Church, John Scholasticus or Sabbaïtes, best known as John Climacus, after his great work, who fled to the Sinai desert for the love of God. Such was his holiness — he lived as an *anchorite* for 40 years — that the monks in Sinai invited him to become their abbot, an office which he held only for a short time. Out of his rich experience of hermetic life John composed his book which became a beloved reading for monks everywhere. In thirty steps, corresponding to the thirty years of Christ's age at his baptism, it leads from the renunciation of the world to perfection. Sinai has several copies of the work (codices 416-430) but not many with pictures.

The codex, presented here, contains (fol. 13$^v$) an ornamental ladder and a schematic, diagonal flight of steps, all numbered in accordance with the sequence of chapters, normally from top to bottom. This simple decoration may well be the earliest tradition of Climax illustration, before it was developed into a scene. The starting point of this scene, as we see in another Climax manuscript in Sinai (codex 423, fol. 10$^v$), from the 11th century, is the ladder beheld by Jacob (fig. 2) who is shown asleep at bottom of the ladder. Monks are climbing up, assisted by two angels, trying to reach Christ at the head of the ladder, who is ready to crown their struggle. This Ladder-scene does not seem to have existed prior to the 11th century. As an independent composition, it was dear to monastic communities and it was often depicted in the narthexes of great monasteries in Athos, Serbia and on the external walls of churches in Rumania. The lengthy description of the theme in the *Painters' Manual* by Dionysios of Fourna shows the importance attached to the theme by the Church. It was natural to attract not only painters and illustrators of manuscripts but icon painters as well — Sinai has a splendid 12th-century icon which includes not only angels guiding the monks but also demons causing the monks' dreadful fall (see Icons, fig. 24). The theme must have been known in the West as well, for, as it has been shown recently by Leopold Kretzenbacher, it is reflected in an illustration in the *Hortus deliciarum* by Herrad of Landsberg, written in the late 12th century. All these creations, regardless of the particular technical medium, were to serve as means of meditation for the faithful. Whether we have a simple Ladder illustration (as in codex 417) or a Ladder scene (as in codex 423), the symbolic meaning of the picture is clear. The ladder symbolizes the gradual spiritual improvement of man and the Christian way of life.

In codex 417, more important, however, is the portrait of the author (fol. 13$^r$) John Climacus, one of his earliest depictions. The great Sinaitic father, in a bust form, icon-like, is portrayed as an aged, bearded man with his hands held before him in prayer. In manner of presentation, the portrait reminds us of the many portraits enclosed in medallions in a manuscript of the *Sacra Parallela* of John of Damascus, now in Paris (Bibliothèque Nationale cod. gr. 923) from the 9th century. The rich, pearl-studded rinceau ornament of the frame, the abstract pattern of the design, the star-like motifs in the four medallions relate the work to monuments of early Muslim art in Jerusalem such as the famous Dome of the Rock. In addition, the ornament of the manuscript, found in several pages, betrays relations with Coptic art. Removed from the art of Constantinople this codex speaks of influences which had reached Sinai from the Islamic and Coptic worlds and had penetrated other artistic works in the area such as the early icons, now in the Monastery.

The second manuscript from the same period, codex 213, is a Lectionary, written in 967 by a certain presbyter Eustathios, *a humble sinner*, whom we have already mentioned. This codex has a long association with Sinai and it is known as the *Horeb Gospels*. In its several headpieces, initials, its fascinating vignettes, one sees imaginary compositions in which the griffin and the dragon predominate. These motifs, old in the repertory of art, in constantly renewed compositional renderings (for example, fol. 19$^v$ recalls representations of the Ascension of Alexander the Great), are all orientalized in character. They look like Sassanian products which, as it is well known, had a great impact on Byzantine ornamentation. The character of the illustration is aniconic. The ornament and the impressive titles serving as another form of ornament are most predominant. The only figural illustration is a bust of Christ (fol. 196$^v$) in a medallion. It is placed at the beginning of the Passion pericopes. The Horeb Lectionary is a marvellous example of a work illustrated in an area in which the restrain of the 'iconic' representations was necessary. That is, the codex presupposes an Islamic milieu.

These two codices, and others related to them, with their Islamic influences and aniconic elements speak of the Islamic surroundings in which the Monastery existed and they point to the fact that at that time, when the art of Constantinople under the Macedonian dynasty was turning to the great works of ancient Greece, the monks in Sinai were cut off from the artistic activities of the capital of the Empire. The tradition represented by these manuscripts remained strong in the Sinai scriptorium that was active down to the Post-Byzantine period. Works which came out of this scriptorium vary in quality and density of ornamentation.

After the Fall of Constantinople, when the relations of Sinai with Crete were intensified, the Sinai scriptorium produced a number of codices relating to works made in other monastic centres of the Orthodox world. Typical among them are a series of illustrated liturgies which, according to their colophons, were written and illuminated in Sinai by scribe-monks residing there. In them, one sees the abundant, florid, baroque-like, exaggerated ornamentations and figural initials relating to the contents of the liturgical texts. A splendid example, but not the only one, is provided by codex 1053, from the year 1668, which impresses the onlooker with the richness, minuteness and delicacy of the decoration.

## MIDDLE BYZANTINE ILLUMINATED MANUSCRIPTS IN SINAI

Cut off from the artistic activities of Constantinople, the Monastery of St. Catherine was destined to receive some great Constantinopolitan masterpieces, long after the City of Constantine had fallen into the hands of the infidel. Notes in some of these codices contain information regarding the entry of these manuscripts into the Monastery; other notes are not clear but imply the acquisition of a given manuscript after the Fall of Constantinople; there are also codices about the history of which we know nothing. But in most cases, we can safely say that these splendid illuminated codices reached the Monastery through its important *metochia* in various distant places such as Crete, Cyprus, S. Italy, Rumania.

One of the most beautiful examples of the art of Constantinople which should be dated about the year 1000, is a deluxe, large Lectionary (codex 204), indeed a 'jewel' in the Monastery's collection. The portraits of the four, standing Evangelists are great works of art (fig. 6). Beautiful and imposing as they are, in their renderings, stance, drapery, and the modelling of the flesh parts, they betray early models, which represented men of letters, dramatists and philosophers of classical antiquity. It was in them, it is well known, that the Christians sought the portraits of the four Evangelists. The slender proportions, the expressive faces, their elegance, the subtle colour, the effective use of the brushstroke speak of the high art of Constantinople at the time. Next to these figures, pointing to the revival of the classical in the Middle Byzantine period, and in fact opening the codex, are the standing figures of Christ and the Virgin Mary (figs. 3-4). In their rendering they are more austere and hieratic, more restrained. A great contrast, however, is presented by the figure of Hosios Petros (fig. 5), who in his physiognomic features, particularly his long beard, reminds us of Hosios Euthymios the Great. Evidence in the manuscript help us identify him as Hosios Peter of the Monastery of Monobata (Πέτρος ὁ ὅσιος, ὁ ἐν Μονοβά-τοις), whose memory is celebrated on February 9 and about whom the Synaxarion does not tell us much. This monastery is mentioned in Byzantine texts but its exact location within the borders of the Byzantine empire has not been agreed upon by scholars. The manuscript must have been made for and presented as a gift to this monastery.

These figures in antique drapes, looking into space, reveal an intense spirituality. Mary's depiction foreshadows the dematerialized style of the 11th century, while the spirituality of Peter of Monobata is both revealed and stressed by a linear design. His body is indeed hidden under the monastic garb.

A splendid example of an art which was much appreciated in the imperial court of Constantinople, this Lectionary has headpieces in gold, in innumerable, delicate variations, the designs of which reflect ornament found in Byzantine gold jewelry much sought after by the Europeans throughout the Middle Ages. There is no indication in the manuscript itself as to when it was added to the collections of the Monastery. Most likely it is a later gift, originally not intended for Sinai. The excellent state of its preservation, the lack of any traces of use and the peculiar relation of the text to the pictures — in fact the codex has only the title of each pericope and not the text — all this has led me to the conclusion that the codex was not to be used. From the beginning it was made as a holy relic to be kept in the treasury and to be carried around on Easter day, the monks being allowed to kiss its precious cover. The present, priceless covers are of a later date. The illuminations in this Lectionary, large as they are, each spreading over a full page, all placed at the very beginning of the book, recall icons and testify to the importance of this type of service book and to the interrelationship of the various artistic media.

It was in the Middle Byzantine period that the impact of the Liturgy on art became most predominant, manifesting itself in many ways, above all in the liturgical books of the Church. In the Lectionary itself the images underwent a transformation. The earlier narrative scenes, telling the events of Christ's life found in illustrated Gospels, were changed into monumental, full-page miniatures representing the Great Feasts that declared the essential doctrine of the Church.

Apart from the Great Feasts, Lectionaries may contain other themes of a clear liturgical significance. Among such themes, the most common one was the *Deesis*. In it Christ stands in the centre with His Mother and John the Baptist at His sides interceding to Him for mankind. This theme was normal for the beams of an iconostasis. In Lectionaries it was introduced at the very beginning of a codex and similar was the case of illuminated Gospels which came under the influence of the Lectionary.

A very impressive example of a Lectionary introduced by the Deesis theme, is the codex 208 (fol. 1ᵛ, fig. 7), dating from the 12th century. In the Monastery the codex is known as *Prince Alexander's Gospel* and it is considered to have been a gift to the Monastery by the prince of Wallachia in the 16th century, who commissioned the precious metal covers specifically for Sinai (the Metamorphosis in the centre is the subject of the glorious mosaic in the apse of the church). The middle part of the picture is given to the three protagonists with Christ in the centre, seated on a cushioned imperial throne. On the four corners are the busts of the four Evangelists, holding their Gospels and turning towards the centre. These busts may derive from an iconostasis beam. The change in style in these figures is evident. In comparison to the earlier Lectionary, the present images have greater degree of stylization and a more linear approach to features and details of drapery is in effect. Stylistically they relate to a group of icons in Sinai assigned by Kurt Weitzmann to Cyprus. Most likely the origin of the manuscript must be sought in the same island. It is one of the many examples in the Monastery which provides evidence of the veneration Sinai enjoyed among Christians everywhere.

Above all, it was the *homiletic* literature, the sermons of the Fathers read in the Liturgy, that attracted the illustrators. Sinai has some very beautiful and important examples of this type of liturgical book. The codex 364 with the Homilies of John Chrysostom on the Gospel of Matthew is chosen here because of its imperial portraits and their splendour. The manuscript, most likely written in Constantinople, came to Sinai as a present by Michael Ialynas, a member of the famous Cretan family of the Ialynas, in the 16th century. Another member of this family, Gerasimos Ialynas, was hieromonk and worked as copyist of manuscripts in the metochion of Sinai in Candia in the second half of the 17th century. The first illumination in the codex (fol. 2ᵛ, fig. 9), represents the Evangelist Matthew offering his Gospel to John Chrysostom who will interpret it in his homilies contained in the book. The Evangelist wears a light blue chiton and a light green himation, while John has a light brown sticharion and dark brown bishop's vestments. Matthew's stern expression and John's ascetic physiognomy, are familiar from their many various depictions. The composition belongs to the category of dedication pages found often in Byzantine book illumination. Deriving ultimately from a scene showing the Evangelists offering their Gospels to Christ, found in Gospels, it is a pictorialization on the title of the book. The inscription around the frame of the illustration refers to John and Matthew who intercede to God seeking serenity of life for the rulers represented on the next page.

The glittering imperial portraits (fol. 3ʳ, fig. 8) depict Constantine IX Monomachos flanked by the Empress Zoe and her sister Theodora. Above and in a mandorla is the figure of Christ from whose hands rays descend on the heads of Zoe and Theodora. The crown at the feet of Christ is destined for Constantine. Both empresses are crowned *Augustae*; the crowns designated for them are held by hovering angels. All three are in ceremonial costumes. Those of the women are distinguished by the shield-like *thorakion*, which has been studied by the late Maria Sotiriou. On the basis of these portraits the codex can be dated between 1042-1050, when Zoe died. It may have been presented to the

Monastery of Mangana in Constantinople which was founded by Constantine Monomachos shortly after he ascended to the throne in 1042.

The radiant trinity of the earthly rulers in their ceremonial costumes and regalia, in all their majesty and splendour, as the inscription around the border attests, ask for the protection of the Divine Trinity. There is a pictorial parallelism here between the celestial world and the world of the emperors sanctified by the special position given to them as chosen by Christ to serve Him and to rule the world in His name. Once more in this picture a change of style can be observed. The overall effect of the body is that of stiffness; the pose is hieratic which in essence stresses the ceremonial and freezes the represented sovereigns for eternity. The garments with rhythmic gold lines stress the lack of dimension, thus removing the sovereigns from the reality of this world. And yet Constantine, in this rendering, has the same features — rich, black hair, strong beard and moustache — seen in the famous mosaics in the gallery of the Church of St. Sophia in Constantinople. He is indeed individualized. This is not the case with the portraits of the Augustae which are rather stereotyped. The miniature combines the imperial ideology exalted by the applied style, with the splendour of the imperial court which had dazzled and bewitched both civilized people and barbarians whether in Sicily, Russia, Germany, Sweden or even Iceland.

A greater attraction, however, for the illustrators had the liturgical sermons, the *Homilies* of Gregory Nazianzenus, the great Cappadocian Father of the 4th century, reluctant Patriarch of Constantinople. A special interest in the work of Gregory was shown during the period of the Macedonian dynasty, during the Macedonian Renaissance. It was at that time that this new edition was produced which contained only sixteen of Gregory's sermons, chosen to be read in various feast days. Their illustrations stressed the liturgical character of the new book.

Among the several copies that have survived from the Byzantine period, Sinai has one of the most beautiful and richest surviving copies, which, in the opinion of this author, comes very close to the lost original creation of the 10th century. It is the codex 339, written between 1136-1155. According to a dedication in huge, gold, carefully written letters, and a colophon in verse, the manuscript is a Constantinopolitan product. It was made through the care of a certain Joseph who was abbot of the famous Monastery of Pantocrator in Constantinople. He presented it to the Monastery of the Pantanassa in the island of St. Glykeria, not far from Constantinople.

The portrait of Saint Gregory as author, inspired by Christ himself in his writings, has been placed at the beginning of the codex (fol. 4ᵛ, fig. 1). Gregory with an expressive and yet tense face, dressed as a monk, sits and is about to write his sermons on a piece of parchment which he holds with his left hand. The decoration of his large nimbus, at times found in portraits of the Evangelists, is most impressive. It imitates icons made of enamel. The depiction of Gregory as a monk and not as bishop shows how strong the influence of monasticism was on Constantinopolitan art. The architectural complex, the setting for the portrait of the author, is marked by the central, tripartite arch supported by two knotted, marble columns, and topped by domes and saddled roofs. Through the drum of the central dome, we see evidently the apse of a church on which the Virgin is represented holding the infant Christ in her lap. The image is similar to those found in Byzantine churches. The church has gardens and an atrium in the front with two fountains. In these gardens and the wall of the atrium, we recognize pictorial elements found in earlier manuscripts of the Homilies of Gregory such as the famous codex Paris gr. 510. Andreas Xyngopoulos, who has studied the problems of this frontispiece, has shown that the entire structure has derived from a similar composition found in the illustrated manuscripts of the Homilies of James of Kokkinovaphos in Paris and the Vatican and the liturgical scrolls of Athens and Patmos. Attempts to relate the complex to a specific building cannot be supported. In fact, what we see here are elements taken from real architecture, in this case a five-domed church, and put to a decorative use. Regardless the problems of the analysis of the various architectural elements, this type of frontispiece is important for another reason: it has influenced frontispieces in Russian manuscripts.

Each Homily is illustrated with more than one picture: a principal miniature and one or more secondary images in the margins of the page or in the figural initials. The choice of illustrations depends on the pericope or the synaxary of the day on which the sermon is read. In other words, they present to the viewer the theme of the feast. Thus we see the Great Feasts of the Church, the Anastasis, Nativity, Baptism (fols. 5$^r$, 91$^r$, 197$^v$, figs. 12, 10, 11).

In the Anastasis, Christ strides over a dark cave from left to right across the broken gates, nails and bars of hell. He approaches and seizes Adam with his outstretched right arm and raises him from a sarcophagus. Christ helds the patriarchal cross. This narrative, iconographic type, dates from the Pre-Iconoclastic period.

In the Nativity, we have the standard composition which became predominant in Byzantine art since the Middle Byzantine period. The main scene, in the centre, representing the actual Nativity, includes Joseph who, seated on a rock with his back turned to the infant and His mother, looks pensive, and in the foreground the Bathing of the Child. Two complimentary scenes have been added: the Adoration of the Magi on the left, and the Annunciation to the Shepherds to the right. All these scenes are treated seperately in the accounts of the Gospels and their illustrations. In the course of time, however, and under the impact of the Liturgy, these episodes were re-grouped and formed a feast picture. The change took place in the Lectionary in which these events were brought together in the pericopes for Christmas eve and Christmas day and on which the Christmas hymns were based. This is the typical illustration for the Christmas feast in Lectionaries.

The typical Byzantine feast picture has also been used for the Homily on Epiphany read on January 6, feast of Christ's Baptism. Christ, immersed in the river Jordan and turning slightly towards John, blesses the waters. The personification of the river, now flaked, sits probably on a dolphin at the feet of Christ. It is balanced by a small figure swimming in the water, on the opposite side. Three angels in familiar poses stand on the right bank of the river. On the left side of the composition, we see the disciples Andrew and John bearing testimony to Christ's Baptism. This is a reference to another episode in the Gospel (John 1:35) which has been combined with the main theme of Christ's Baptism.

Gregory, however, delivered a second Homily on Easter starting point of which was the vision of the prophet Habakkuk. Gregory imagines himself standing with Habakkuk and sharing his vision. He observed and saw *a man riding on the clouds, who was very tall and his countenance was like the countenance of an angel. His garment was like the luster of lightning that passes by... His voice was like the voice of a trumpet.* The illustrator of the codex Sinai 339 (fol. 9$^v$, fig. 16), has represented Gregory and the prophet sharing a vision. In the title miniature the youthful Christ-Emmanuel is seated on the arc of heaven within a mandorla carried by the four *zodia*, the Angel, Lion, Calf and Eagle which the Church Fathers interpreted as symbols of the four Evangelists. The principal elements of this composition are repeated in the initial *E* in which Gregory is shown as a teacher and the vision has been reduced to a bust of Christ.

But in the miniature set on the margin Christ is depicted as an angel surrounded by Archangels holding sceptres. This form of Christ, *Christos-Angelos*, based on biblical (Isaiah 9:6 and Malachi 3:1) and patristic texts presents Him as the messenger of the great counsel and messenger of the covenant. Christ is also the angel who spreads his wings over the faithful, as stated in the secret prayer recited by the priest, when he censes the *aer* (the veil) while covering the paten and the chalice, at the prothesis: *cover us, O Saviour, with the shadow of Thy wings.*

Both these compositions represent Theophanies with which Byzantine artists were familiar. They could see them on the apses of churches — a well-known example is the Vision of Hezekiel in the Church of Hosios David in Thessalonica — or in the illustrations of prefaces of Byzantine Gospels and in icons, all relating directly to the eucharistic liturgy. The iconographic types conveyed different theological concepts. In the Sinai illustrations, the artist presents Christ-Emmanuel, the Son of God, the Anointed of the Spirit, the Resurrection and the Life; while the Christos-Angelos expresses the eternal wisdom of God.

The illustrations chosen for Gregory's Homily on New Sunday (fol. 42ᵛ, fig. 14) are very significant. There are four distinct scenes. In the miniature above the title, Saint Gregory addresses Saint Mamas in whose church the sermon was originally delivered. In fact the sermon ends with a reference to the saint. Mamas is represented as a shepherd holding his staff and seated between two hills. The character of the composition points to a frontispiece that must have illustrated the Life of this saint or even a Synaxarion. Gregory's illustrator probably borrowed the scene from such a book.

The other illustrations, however, relate directly to the liturgy. The Incredulity of Thomas in the margin refers to the pericope of the day, Thomas Sunday, on which day Gregory's sermon is read in the church. This scene, too, must be a borrowing from another book (the event is not mentioned at all in Gregory's sermon), in this case a Lectionary in which the scene is common, illustrating the lection for the day. But the first Sunday after Easter, Thomas Sunday — which is the first Sunday of the ecclesiastical year — is called New Sunday. On this day the Church celebrates the Feast of the *Encaenia*, i.e. the dedication of the Church of the Holy Sepulchre in Jerusalem, which was instituted on September 13, the year 335. According, however, to the liturgical books of the Orthodox Church, the ceremony of the feast of the Encaenia is also the ceremony of the consecration of a particular church. The main rite in this feast is the anointing of the altar, described in detail in the *Euchologion*. Before the rite of the unction begins (the upper part of the Holy Table has by now been placed over the column), the bishop washes this column with a sponge and then, taking a jar containing the oil for anointing, he pours oil over the Holy Altar and forms three crosses with it. Following this, he spreads the oil of these crosses with his hands over the altar and makes crosses with this oil on the column as well. The illustrator has chosen to represent the bishop either in the act of washing the column with a sponge or, most likely, in the act of anointing it with holy oil.

To my knowledge this scene is unique and its importance is obvious. It illustrates with accuracy and detail a ceremony of the Middle Byzantine Church known from texts and from its survival in the Orthodox Church. The presence of this illustration in the Homilies of Gregory stresses their liturgical significance.

In the small, figural initial *E* there is still another liturgical scene related to the same feast. Gregory is teaching, being blessed by Christ; before him there is a small, domical church with a group of women worshippers participating in the ceremony of the Encaenia. Inside this church, we can clearly see a lit candle which plays a special role in the ceremony of the Encaenia and has a symbolic meaning. On the eve of the feast, a taper is lit in the church which must burn throughout the night. Next day, after a series of acts, described in the Euchologion, a new lamp, wick and oil are brought to the archpriest who, with his own hands, lights it, and then the church wardens are allowed to bring in lamps and candles and decorate the church. Church Fathers speak of the various symbolic meanings of this taper and of the lights in the church. In general, the flame of a taper or of an oil lamp is the symbol of the eternal clarity of heaven or a symbol of the light of heaven, or divine illumination, and in a particular way, the lamp that hangs over the altar at the Encaenia, according to Symeon of Thessalonica, indicates that the Church is the lamp of Christ.

We have discussed in greater details these illustrations in order to show the exceptional importance of this manuscript, and above all the impact that the liturgy had on the art of Byzantium after the crisis of Iconoclasm.

The richness, however, of this manuscript is not confined to the liturgical aspect of its illustrations. Gregory addressed a Homily to Julian the Tax Collector (not to be confused with the Emperor Julian the Apostate), who was unjust and indifferent to the plight of the poor for whom Gregory makes a strong plea. In the church, this Homily is read on December 21 and relates to the Gospel lection of the day (Matt. 18:31-36), which refers to the parable of the creditor and his debtor. Once more the illuminator displays great inventiveness. In the principal miniature (fol. 73$^v$, fig. 15), above the title with its multiple frames which impress us with the richness of the ornament, Gregory and Julian — the latter wearing the distinct hat of a 'civil servant' — are represented as writers. The one writes his sermon, the other the taxes. Both are accompanied by scribes that stand by, between the two protagonists. In an abbreviated form this scene is repeated in the initial $T$ and in the margin, next to it.

But on the upper part of the left margin, we have a scene taken from real life which provides us with an unusual insight into events of taxation in Byzantium. Julian, the Tax Collector, in his official costume, seated at one side of a table, demands the tribute. A scribe writes down the payments or debts on a piece of parchment, while another cleric, in the centre, weighs the coins deposited by one of the debtors on the table. At the opposite side of the table, two more persons stand by undecided, burdened with worries, waiting for the last word of mercy by the Tax Collector. And in the background, four more persons are coming down wearily to pay their tribute.

In the Homily delivered on the feast of the Seven Maccabees, Gregory speaks of their martyrdom, their tortures, praises their mother Solomone, extalls their suffering and places them among the saints of God who ended their lives by the hand of the executioner. The illustrator of the Homily (fol. 381$^v$, fig. 13) has represented the martyrdom of the Seven Maccabees, their mother Solomone and their teacher Eleazar — their portraits are in the initial $T$ — in great detail. The miniature has a narrative character, the events are depicted as described in the Fourth book of the Maccabees in the Old Testament, to which, most likely, these illustrations originally belonged. The represented details are not described by Gregory in his sermon. Fire, the throwing of the brothers on the wheel of torture, their casting in a hot cauldron, the presence of Solomone encouraging the boy to endure everything for the sake of his faith, the dislocating of their bones, the binding of the arms and hands with thongs, the dislocating of hands and feet — all these gruesome events have attracted the illustrator.

The inventiveness, however, of the Byzantine artist is best seen in the numerous figural *initials* in the sermons. Not related to the ideas of the Homilies, these initials serve a single purpose: to ornament the page and to give the artist the chance to express himself by recreating the ordinary in life, away from the official tradition of the Church. Nevertheless, all these initials have a thematic unity. They give us a glimpse of everyday life in Byzantium and speak of the approach of the Byzantine artist to the written page. A great variety of charming birds and fascinating animals, in imaginative compositions, real and fantastic, many of them recalling decoration of Canon tables in illuminated Gospels, all depicted with great power of observation and great love, adorn the pages. Amusing genre scenes, relating to circus spectacles, acrobats, animals which are able to dance skilfully and amuse audiences with musical instruments (figs. 17-22) recall popular shows in Constantinople and other cities of the vast empire. Such shows usually took place in the hippodrome during the intermission of the main races or other athletic games to divert the attention of the spectators and calm down the excitement of the various political parties. They even recall acts performed in the theatre in the streets of the cities.

These genre scenes bring to mind the *marginalia* found in Western Medieval manuscripts, mainly of the Gothic period, in the 13th century and later, and the sculptural programmes of the great Gothic cathedrals in the West, in which even a dentist's chair had a special place. The Church Fathers fought strongly against secular spectacles of any kind. But the artists ignored these admonitions, because through the figural initials and the ornament they expressed their own freedom, beyond the boundaries of religious tradition.

But God's creatures and man's activities on this earth had another, deeper meaning for the Byzantine artist. All these creatures manifested God's world, his creatures in time. With these pictures, the artists, in their own way, followed the teachings of the great Fathers of the Church who in their love of God and by His grace had sanctified everything. It was God's infinite world that the artists praised. Considering these genre scenes and the principal illustrations in this manuscript of Gregory's Homilies, we realize the two poles, between which the Byzantines lived, the paradox of Byzantium, liturgical mysticism on the one hand, and love for the exuberant side of life on the other. In fact it was the artist who redeemed the Byzantines from this paradox. The painter by preserving the elements of triviality and giving another form of life to the initial, lifted up the lower life into the realm of art and made the higher life more tangible.

Other types of manuscripts from this period, produced in Constantinople, have found a place among the treasures of Sinai. From the books of the Old Testament a favourite book of the Byzantines was the *Book of Job*, a book of suffering and contemplation, which was often illuminated. Among the several copies which have survived time, it seems that only the one in Sinai (cod. 3) was made in Constantinople in the 11th century, probably in the famous Monastery of Studios. It is distinguished by an elegant style and a persistent, extensive use of gold hatching for indicating highlights. The products of the Studios Monastery, including this Job manuscript, reflect an artistic tendency relating to a monastic movement which represented a reaction against the strong hellenism of the Macedonian Renaissance. This reaction, in terms of style, took the form of employing effective artistic means in order to dematerialize the body.

In essence, this book, accompanied by the commentary of Olympiodoros, the 6th century deacon from Alexandria, is a dramatic poem, indeed one of the great literary works of all time, with special appeal upon the faithful in general and the monks in particular. For, above all, it stresses the mystery of suffering, constancy and deliverance. According to Church Fathers, the Patriarch Job is the symbol of God's deliverance of man.

In the Sinai Job, all illustrations are found in the 'Prologue' of the book and follow the tragic events in sequence. The pictorial presentation of the story begins with Job and his wife depicted as an imperial couple within a palatial setting (fol. 7$^r$, fig. 25). He is dressed in the purple and she wears a crown. Both are seated on imperial, precious, jewel-studded thrones and are conversing with one another. The walled city on the left, which in typical Byzantine fashion is marked in its centre by a cross bearing dome of a church, provides the topographical reference of the events. It is the land of Ausis in which *there was a certain man whose name was Job* (Job 1:1)

Another illustration presents Job's flocks, all mentioned in the text, sheep, camels, oxen, asses, grazing in idyllic pastures (fol. 8$^r$, fig. 24). Among them a dog is hunting a hare and two bulls are butting. These motifs, Kurt Weitzmann has shown in an important book on Classical book illumination, have been taken from books illustrated in antiquity such as the *Cynegetica* by Pseudo-Oppian or Aelian's book *De natura animalium*, both from the 3rd century of our era.

The development of the story continues. The happy banquet of Job's children, seven sons and three daughters, is depicted in a scene that gave the chance to the illustrator to observe details of Byzantine furnishings, a beautiful table with gold rims and rich covers, utensils, a bowl and a cup in gold, precious vessels with which servants scoop wine (fol. 17$^v$, fig. 23). In addition to eating and drinking, there are exuberant, male dancers who perform for the delight of all those present. The miniature offers us a good insight into an aristocratic house and a banquet in Byzantium.

But it did not take long for this happiness to be shuttered by a series of disasters. When the days of the banquet were completed, horrible events followed. In their depiction the miniaturist renders the drama effectively. Bold colours, wide, quick brushstrokes create an art of expressionistic qualities. On fol. 18$^v$, fire falls from heaven upon Job's herd: *it burnt up the sheep, and devoured the shepherds* (Job 1:16). Only one escaped to announce this second disaster to Job. Frightening, fiery tongues are emitted from a blue sky, ironically carrying gold stars, and devour shepherds and herd.

After a series of other disasters, there comes the Devil who *went out from the Lord and smote Job with sore boils from his feet to his head* (Job 2:7). Naked as he is, his broken body covered with boils, Job, the smitten man, sits on a heap of dung facing his wife (fol. 26ʳ, fig. 26). She brings him food but, fearful of approaching too near, she presents it on the end of a long stick. At the same time she pulls her veil over her nose with a realistic gesture which foreshadows narrative details found in comparable scenes in Late Byzantine art, most common of which is the Raising of Lazarus.

But Job is not alone in all this. His faith in God sustains him. He finds also consolation in his friends who will journey from far away to offer him their support, share his grief, lament with him: *His three friends having heard of all the evil that was come upon him, came to him each from his own country* (Job 2:11). His third friend, Sophar the king of Minaeans, dressed in royal garments and riding a horse, escorted by a vanguard — a horseman carrying a banner — rides to visit Job (fol. 29ᵛ, fig. 27). The miniature is remarkable for the power of observation, the colour scheme and minuteness in the execution. It reflects everyday events. One thinks of imperial parades, military expeditions — all common occurrences in the life of the Byzantines.

Professor Stella Papadaki-Oekland, who has studied all the extant Job manuscripts in an important study, has drawn attention to the illusionistic backgrounds, the shimmering skies in most of these miniatures, legacies of the antique. This codex remains unique in the type of illustration it contains and Papadaki-Oekland believes that it was produced as a kind of special relic and that it was preserved as such in Constantinople.

All these manuscripts, presented thus far, are manifestations of the artistic activities in Constantinople and other areas of Byzantium during the second golden age of its civilization. We should not think, however, that the Sinai scriptorium has remained inactive. Trends and features that marked its beginnings, pointed out earlier, continue to appear during this period as well. However, artistic activities in Sinai take diverse forms and there are manuscripts which are more ambitious and constitute landmarks in book illumination. One of them is the *Christian Topography* written by Cosmas Indicopleustes at Alexandria between 547 and 549. The Sinai copy (codex 1186) belongs to the early part of the 11th century and among the extant copies this is the richest, illustrated one. A number of its miniatures are not found in other copies. In another copy, now in the Laurentian Library in Florence, Cosmas is referred to as monk. This information, however, has not been confirmed. In fact, he was a merchant who, in the early part of his life, travelled widely as far as India and Ceylon. Apparently he kept notes of the places he had visited, and described plants and products. It seems to have known the colony of monks that had settled in Raithou, and that he had visited on foot the Burning Bush in Sinai, although the Monastery is not mentioned by name. Prompted by his friend Pamphilos, Cosmas decided to 'publish' his travel experiences, almost twenty five years after the completion of his journey. In essence, the work he produced was nothing else but an interpretation of the *Octateuch*. Its value, however, lies not in the area of hermeneutic but in that of topography. The first copy of this work, which was accompanied by drawings, diagrams and relevant illustrations, is now lost. The reconstruction of this copy through the various extant copies is indeed most complicated problem, the discussion of which does not belong here. However, there is an agreement as to the system of illustrations, apparent in the copies, which must have been applied to the archetype as well. Whenever a reference was made to a holy site or an event, a relevant scene was introduced, which in most cases, possibly, had already been used in books of the Old and New Testaments. In other instances in which such borrowings were not possible or applicable, scientific illustrations and diagrams were introduced. As example of the first category, we reproduced here the Vision of Moses and the Receiving of the

Law (fol. 75$^v$, fig. 29). It belongs to a group of miniatures the themes of which are found in the Octateuch and which have been studied by Professor Doula Mouriki. On the lower corner of the illustration, we see Moses prostrated within a cloud towards Mount Sinai from which tongues of fire are issued. Above and to the right, Moses is represented once again ascending the peak of the mountain to receive the Tablets of the Law from the hand of God, while turning to the Israelites who are represented in groups at the feet of the mountain, gesticulating in astonishment and pointing to the tabernacle. The illustration is narrative and from the artistic point of view, it should be noted that everything is represented against the white parchment and that the use of gold is sparse.

It is generally agreed that the cosmographic diagrams were invented for the original manuscript of the work. All these diagrams present various aspects of the Byzantine image of the world which is *geocentric* and not *heliocentric*. In this image we see naive ideas found in literal interpretations of the Old and New Testaments and in the culture of the ancients in general.

According to these ideas, the earth is the dwelling place of man; the heavens is the habitation of higher spiritual beings. The heaven is always thought as a vault or a series of vaults. But the earth, seen by Cosmas is a flat disc. Cosmas believes this to be true because neither in Africa nor in Asia had he discovered any curvature of the earth. Most of the cosmographic diagrams, found in this codex and its relatives, must be understood within the context of these ideas.

When the illustrator presents the side view of the cosmos, the inhabited earth, set in the middle of the universe, takes the form of a mountain which swims in a primeval ocean (fol. 65$^r$, fig. 31). The firmament — στερέωμα — divides the lower heaven from the upper one which takes the form of a blue arch representing the ocean of water, above the firmament.

In another illustration, we see a map of the world and Paradise (fol. 66$^v$, fig. 28). In this case the earth is in the form of a rectangle which is marked in its four inner sides by the ocean. The waters penetrate the land and form *the Roman, the Arabic and the Persian gulfs* as well as the Caspian sea. In the waters of the ocean and within medallions are personifications of the winds blowing horns — all identified by inscriptions. To the extreme right, to the east part of the earth, is the Garden of Eden.

In another cosmogram (fol. 69$^r$), the various schemata depicted earlier, are brought together in another form. The earth and the ocean are enclosed in a chest-like structure. The sides of this chest represent the walls of heavens; its vaulted lid is the upper heaven where Christ dwells. This is the realm of the Kingdom of Heaven. Inside the chest, above and around the mountain of the earth, one sees the sun rising and setting.

However, what moves over the earth is set to motion by angels. Thus, the illustrator, following the text, in the image of the motion of the stars depicts standing angels arranged in a zodiac-like circle (fol.181$^v$, fig.30). Each one of them holds in his hands a gold constellation which corresponds to a month inscribed outside the circle. Within an inner circle, winged angels raise and lower the sun and in the following circle, one sees the rising and setting moon. The mountain in the centre, and above all its peak, indicate the uninhabited, northern part of the earth, while the earth proper is shown on either side of the mountain in the form of vertical pillars.

The inhabited parts of the earth are marked by creatures, trees and plants that produce fruit according to the seasons. Of these, we single out the charming gazelle, the exotic birds and the palm trees (fol. 146$^r$, fig. 32).

In all these miniatures, there is a linear quality, an angularity in the rendering of the figures, and as we have already pointed out, a sparse use of gold, and a particular application of colours which are strong but without lustre. All these features set this work apart from Constantinopolitan products. We believe that the codex was most likely produced and illustrated in Sinai.

The lack of elegance, apparent in the Cosmas codex, a particular characteristic of monastic spirit, is found also in the illustrations of the *Heavenly Ladder* by John Climacus. We have already commented on the author and the text. The 10th-century example, which was presented earlier, contains the schematic ladder and the portrait of the author. But since the 11th century, a number of manuscripts with this text were illuminated, each, however, varying considerably in its illustration. Sinai has manuscripts which differ in the density of the illustrations and their quality.

In one of them (codex 418) from the 12th century, which was probably written and illustrated in Sinai, there are several pictures for the thirty chapters corresponding to the thirty rungs of the Heavenly Ladder. In these illustrations, we see allegories, personifications of vices and virtues, visions, everyday life scenes of monks and anchorites — all these in many ways parallel the vices and virtues represented in Western art, best seen in the portals of the cathedral of Notre Dame in Paris and at Amiens.

In undertaking the difficult task to climb the ladder a monk is aided by his virtues or is pulled down by his vices. In the illustration of the chapter on Slander, Homily 1, we see the slandering monks (fol. 124$^r$). Behind an aged, seated monk, who addresses a young one, stands another young monk who whispers in the ear of the old man. Apparently he is accusing slanderously the meek brother. In the chapter on Poverty, Homily 17, the illustrator represents the glorification of the poor man (fol. 164$^r$). He is seen as a seated, bearded monk who wears a loose garment which leaves his right shoulder uncovered. His poverty is further suggested by his bare feet. He is attended by angels one of whom places a wreath on the monk's head; the other who stands behind places a sceptre in his hand. The wreath and the sceptre are symbols of the glory achieved by the man who endures poverty. For, in this chapter, John says that the monk who is poor is ruler of the world.

The ascent of the ladder is difficult. To reach the top where Christ is awaiting the victorious monks, to avoid temptations which pull them down, the monks must keep vigilance, they must pray constantly. This is the theme of the illustration for the chapter on Prayer, Homily 10 (fol. 269$^r$). Within the interior of a church, standing before a ciborium which is the one set over the altar, a monk is reading from a book placed on a lectern; on the left, two monks are kneeling and an old bearded monk prays with uplifted hands; at the extreme right, another monk is also praying. Other monks are seated, as if meditating on the lesson read from the pulpit. Their prayers are addressed to the icons of the Virgin Mary and Christ which are the *despotikai* icons placed on the iconostasis of a church.

These and several other illustrations in this codex are vivid representations of monastic life and above all of the struggles of the monk to achieve perfection and union with Christ. It is possible that many of these scenes are borrowings from an earlier, lost cycle illustrating the life of Syrian anchorites, which became the source for Byzantine artists who attempted to illustrate books of monastic contents such as the famous romance of *Barlaam and Joasaph*. On the other hand, it is possible that the pictorial cycle for the Climax manuscripts was invented in Constantinople in the 11th century, when monasticism had become an important stream in the thought world of the Byzantines, especially under the impact of the writings of Symeon the New Theologian. Whatever the origins of the cycle may be, it matters little. The overall composition of the pictorial cycle stems out of the monks' meditation on the text of John Climacus. The Sinai codex 418, is one of the three chief manuscripts of the Climax and the latest of them, which are in Princeton and in the Vatican.

## SINAI, CRETE AND THE ART OF THE WEST

In general, Sinai has always had relations with the West through its *metochia* and the pilgrims who never ceased flowing to the Holy Land. These relations entered another phase at the beginning of the 11th century, when three fingers from the hand of Saint Catherine were taken in a reliquary and laid on the altar in the abbey of the Holy Trinity at Rouen, in

Normandy. This event was of great significance for the cult of Saint Catherine, the medieval world in general and the Monastery in particular. There were also relations with the West on another level of a more particular nature: the exchange of ideas between Sinaitic fathers and great religious personalities of the West. For example, pope Gregory the Great (590-604) corresponded with John Climacus and other fathers of Sinai and in one of his letters expressed the wish to visit Sinai and 'stay there permanently'. These connections meant also gifts made to the Monastery often in the form of works of art.

After the taking of Jerusalem by the Crusaders in 1099, and the setting up of the Kingdom of Jerusalem, Sinai became a see suffragan to the bishop of Petra. Eventually, a colony of Latin monks lived in the Monastery which, however, continued to enjoy the protection and help given to it regularly through the centuries. It was at this time, in the 13th century, that the Church of St. Catherine was founded in Crete out of which came the famous Sinaitic school, which, according to some scholars, was to play an important part in the history of hellenism. These historical changes had an effect in the production of icons in the Monastery which show strong western influences as Weitzmann has shown in a series of studies of these icons. Such influences are not strong in the illuminated manuscripts produced in this period in Sinai or in the area of Palestine. Western influences can be detected in details, for example, in the nimbi which at times can be studded or rayed. Most important is the use of the brushstroke; in general, the flesh parts are softer and the drapery is more plastic in its modelling than it is generally in Byzantine manuscripts. On the whole one can speak of a more 'painterly' style.

These tendencies can be seen in codex 198, written in paper, which contains the Four Gospels and dates from about the middle of the 13th century. The repertory of its illustrations is the usual one: canon tables, portraits of the four Evangelists and ornamental headpieces. The three Evangelists are depicted seated but John is standing (fol. 199$^v$, fig. 36). Instead of dictating the text of the Gospel to Prochoros, still holding in his left hand an open codex with the beginning of his text written on it, John blesses with his right a kneeling monk whose name is inscribed on the tower-like structure to the right side of the composition. The inscription reads: *[supplication] of the monk Germanos.*

This composition is surely an adaptation of a common image found in illustrated Gospels, that of John dictating to Prochoros, known since the 11th century. The stylistic changes, mentioned above, can be observed in John's portrait. He is dressed in the traditional *chiton* and *himation*, the modelling of the drapery, however, is soft; it is achieved by brown shadows and soft highlights. Smoothness and plasticity are observed in his hair and beard with delicate gradations of tone in light blue and white. His nimbus is defined by a red-dotted circle and rays in the tradition of 'Crusader style'. On the other hand, the kneeling monk wears a brown *sticharion* — the usual colour for monks in the Eastern Church — but his *phelonion* is olive green and his headdress is western. The monk's portrait representing the donor is expressive but less detailed in its execution than John's portrait; it has however, physiognomic features such as the slightly bent nose, the thin moustache and the beard. Spatharakis, who has studied this miniature, in attempting to explain the presence of Germanos before the Evangelist John, considered several possibilities. The simplest one with several parallels would be that Germanos had special veneration for the fourth Evangelist and considered him to be his patron saint.

Whatever the reasons for the commission of this codex may be, the manuscript speaks of the piety of the Christians and the contribution it has made — like all holy relics — to Christian art. Despite the western influences this manuscript is not a western product. It has strong relations with 13th - century Crusaders' icons and most probably it was produced during this period in Palestine.

Drastic departures from the Canon of Byzantine iconography are not common in manuscripts of this period. In a 13th- century Sticherarion, codex 1216, illustrated with a series of feast pictures and portraits of saints, all executed in wash, the Koimesis picture can serve as an example of an iconographic departure (fol. 149ʳ). The arrangement of the groups differs from the traditional one. The Apostles do not surround the bier on which the body of Mary is laid but they are standing on one side only. They are balanced by a group of Archangels on the opposite side. The best parallel for this iconography is a contemporary iconostasis beam at Sinai, which, as Weitzmann has shown, was executed by a Western and most likely Venetian master. This Sticherarion may also be the work of a Latin artist. Other elements strengthen this possibility. Most important is the emotional expression of Christ more typical of the art of the West than of Byzantine art. Furthermore, the strange, rolling eyes relate the work to Crusader icons.

Another manuscript leading us to the art of the West is the Psalter and New Testament, codex 2123, dated in 1242. In its original state it has nothing to do with the imperial portraits that have now been included in its illustration. Among its original miniatures there is a portrait of Paul which includes a long sword, set against the frame of the miniature, the attribute of his martyrdom. This feature is unknown in Byzantine art but it is familiar in the art of the West. The figure style is soft, plastic, sharp folds are not longer present in the drapery.

Much later, and before the codex reached Sinai, at the end of the 16th century, several other miniatures were added. In another study, I have produced evidence to show that these added illustrations were executed by a painter who worked probably in Venice and who was familiar with Cretan and Italian art of the time. The portraits of the Emperors Michael VIII (fol. 30ʳ, fig. 34) and John VIII (fol. 30ᵛ, fig. 33) Palaeologi were added at that time. John's portrait, the Emperor who went to Ferrara and Florence in an attempt to unite the divided Church, is related to portraits of the Emperor made by the Italian artist Pisanello, who had met the Emperor personally in Ferrara in 1438 and who has given us a description of him. The Emperor shown in profile wearing the *skiadion*, a red mantle and a white open collar, is accompanied by an inscription written after the addition of the portrait to the manuscript, repeating the old-known formula applied to imperial portraits: *John in Christ God, faithful king, the Palaeologan.* This manuscript is a precious document for the relations of Cretan and Italian art.

Sinai possesses several manuscripts which were produced in or are related to Crete, during the last years of the Byzantine empire and after the Fall of Constantinople. Some of them are illuminated. A special place must be given to a Sticherarion, codex 1234, from the year 1469. According to its colophon, it was written by the priest Plousiadenos from Candia. It is known that he was a follower of Bessarion and a strong supporter of the union of the Churches at the Council of Florence. The codex was written in Venice, in the prosperous and culturally active colony of the Greeks, the centre of which was the Church of St. George. Most of its miniatures represent the Great Feasts of the Church such as the Annunciation (fol. 284ᵛ, fig. 35). Compositions and style show affinities with Cretan icons. The pictures are traditional in iconography but innovative in the softness of style and the delicate movement. They testify to the versatility of Cretan artists who could easily paint both manuscripts and icons and whose role in the history of Greek art has been a vital one. On the one hand they continued the Byzantine tradition long after the Fall of Constantinople, and on the other they were able to accept the innovations of the art of the West without becoming subservient to it. These were the forces that shaped and formed the great masterpieces of El Greco.

As we go through the centuries following the loss of Byzantium, we realize that the activities of Sinaitic monks pertaining to illustration of manuscripts are diminished. The produced codices are repetitive; finally the 'scriptorium' closes its door. Many reasons may account for this decline. The invention of typography and its dissemination, the fact that icons seem to have become more important than manuscripts, the problem of recruiting monks, may be some of these reasons. Sinai has become increasingly more the recipient of manuscripts.

The strong artistic relations of Sinai with Crete (apart from manuscripts, Sinai has frescoes and hundreds of icons painted by Cretan artists) and through Crete with the West, had not brought an end to the relation of Sinai with the East or other centres of the Orthodox Church. Sinai had remained the meeting place for eastern and western pilgrims. After the Fall of Constantinople, the Voevods of Wallachia and Moldavia first and the Russian Tsars later became the protectors of the Orthodox Church which was in captivity. This protection took the form of many gifts to the Monastery which included illuminated manuscripts. In many ways these gifts are similar to those presented by these rulers to other centres of the Greek Church, above all to the monasteries of Mount Athos and Jerusalem. Greek manuscripts and beautiful metal book-covers, codices written in slavonic, most of them produced by Greek masters, and icons coming from Russia and every part of the Orthodox world were presented to the Monastery of Saint Catherine.

This presentation has only suggested the richness of the illuminated manuscripts in Sinai. Their value is manifold. They have given us an insight into the production and illustration of manuscripts by Sinaitic monks which in the course of centuries varied in intensity and quality, but which remained, nevertheless, uninterrupted. They testify to the Christian piety and the fame which Sinai had everywhere. In these manuscripts we have followed the history of the Monastery, but also we learn much about great artistic centres, Constantinople, Cyprus, Crete.

At the same time the transmission of themes and forms from one medium to another, and above all the relation between manuscripts and icons, alluded to in many instances, prove to us the impossibility of isolating one medium from the other, whether manuscripts, icons or monumental art. Each one of them penetrates the other, each one loses its own particular role and autonomous existence in order to create another work of art, which is that of the Liturgy. The word and its message, pictorialized in the illuminated manuscripts, constitute only one component of this new work of art.

In all this, it should be remembered that the Sinaitic monks who have given the world their spiritual legacy of the prayer of the heart, while they offered hospitality to pilgrims from East and West and enjoyed the trust of the Muslims, they did everything possible to preserve these treasures as holy relics — for such they are — to this day.

*1. Homilies of Gregory Nazianzenus (32.3×25.4 cm., codex 339).*
*Gregory is about to write his Sermons, parchment (fol. 4ᵛ). 1136-1155.*

ὁ ἀββᾶ ἰωήη ἡγουμένου τοῦ σιναίου ὄρους.

λόγος ἀσκητικός περὶ τῆς ποιμαντικοῦ

βίου ἀποτοπαγτῆς. ὃν καὶ ἀπέστειλε τῷ

ἀββᾶ ἰωάη ἡγουμένου τῆς ραϊδοῦ προ

τραπεὶς παρ' αὐτοῦ συντάξαι:

τοῦ ἀγαθοῦ καὶ ὑπεραγαθοῦ καὶ σωπαρα

δοῦ ἡμῶν θῦ καὶ δεσπότου, καὶ ὁη γὰρ

δὶ κ θῦ παρ ὁ τὸ τῶ τῶ ἀβρααπ τασ ἀρθ

δαι. τασ τασ τῶ πατῶ αὐτοῦ κτὶ τῶ θξ τὰ

λοτ καὶ· αὐτοῦ ὁ τα λο τ ὑπο θ ξ ω ματὶ ἡ

ελιῶ τασ ποσ. οἱ μὲν ὑ ὁ οἱ πα τοῦ φίλοι· οἱ

δὲ τρ ὑ δοιοδοῦλοι· οἱ δὲ ἀχ ρ διοι· οἱ δὲ ἐ πᾶν

τη λη ἀ τοσ θ ξ υ ωρ μετιοι· οἱ δὲ· εξ καὶ αἰο θε

ρ δ σ· ὁ πα σ ἀρ τ λικοι· καὶ φη ρι ο υμ βι

λ α ρ ι σ ο υ λι μ ἀ τ· οἱ ἰ δι α τα ώ ἱ θρ α υ κεφα

λ ι απ τρ ἰ θ ὑ τα οι λη φα μ β η. πασ τασ πρι

αὐτου μοθρ αι σ τ θ κ αι αι ο ο μα τοῦσ

οἱ ο λ α σ · γη λ ο ι ο υ ὁ δ ο δ ο ι οἱ ο σ οπασ τα σ τ

το λ θη με α υ αιτο υ σ κρ ο ο λ α αι α ι ωα ρ σα

μ τα σ πα σ ο υ π τα σ ε α ι ο υ τασ ε πι ἡ σ ε ρ πα σ ·

μ τι σ π σ π ασ ο υ λο γ ο υ σ ε λ ο γι ο υ σ ι

δο σι α τα σ ε ζ μ ο ι α η σ υ ο ι σ ο τ ι · τα σ πα σ

ὁ ἰάκωβ

3. Lectionary (30×22.5 cm., codex 204). Christ (p. 1). c.1000.

4. Lectionary (codex 204, p. 3). The Virgin Mary. c.1000.

5. Lectionary (codex 204, p. 5). Hosios Peter of Monobata. c. 1000.

6. Lectionary (codex 204, p. 10). The Evangelist Mark. c. 1000.

329

8. Homilies of St. John Chrysostom on the Gospel of Matthew (33.7×25.5 cm., codex 364). The Emperor Constantine IX Monomachos between the Empress Zoe and her sister Theodora (fol. 3ʳ). 1042-1050.

9. Homilies of St. John Chrysostom on the Gospel of Matthew (codex 364, fol. 2ᵛ). The Evangelist Matthew offers his Gospel to St. John Chrysostom. 1042-1050.

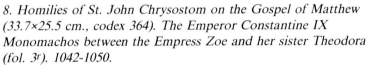

7. Lectionary (39×29.5 cm., codex 208). Deesis (fol. 1ᵛ). 12th century.

331

*10. Homilies of Gregory Nazianzenus (codex 339, fol. 91ʳ).*
*Nativity. 1136-1155.*

332

Λο͞ζ Η̄·

✝ ΤΟ ΥΑΥΤΟΥ ΕΙΣ ΤΑ ΑΓΙΑ ΦΩ ΤΑ ✝

ἀλιμ ἰ͞ϲ ὁ β́μος,
ιεαὶ το ἀλιμιᾶ ϟή
ριομ· μιᾶ τήριομ·
οὐ ιεάτω ατ η λόμ
οὐ δὲ τ ιεοομομ· οὐ
δὲ τῆϲ ἐχλιωνικῆϲ
το ἀμιϲ ιεαὶ μβ́
οὐ τω γαρ ἐγο διεα
λῶτα ελιάμομ

σβμμαι· ὁι μαι δὲ·
ιεαὶ τὸ ῥά φρρ
μοιώ τω μέ ιεαϲ·
ἀλ λαμιᾶ τήριομ
ιή λόμ τό ιεαὶ
θεῖομ, ιεαὶ τῆϲ ά
μω λαμπρότητ
ωρχεμομ· ιε ταρ
γιατῶρ φωΐτωμ

---

11. *Homilies of Gregory Nazianzenus (codex 339, fol. 197ᵛ).*
*The Baptism of Christ. 1136-1155.*

12. *Homilies of Gregory Nazianzenus (codex 339, fol. 5ʳ).*
*The Descent into Hell. 1136-1155.*

13. *Homilies of Gregory Nazianzenus (codex 339, fol. 381ᵛ).*
*The Martyrdom of the Seven Maccabees. 1136-1155.*

† ΤΥΑΥΤΥ ЄΙϹ ΤΗ Ν ΚΑΙ ΝΗ Ν ΚΥΡΑΚΗ Ν

ΚΑΙ ЄΙϹ ΤΟ ЄΑΡ · ΚΑΙ ЄΙϹ ΤΗ ΜΑΡΤΥΡΑ ΜΑΜΑΝΤ :·

14. Homilies of Gregory Nazianzenus (codex 339, fol. 42ᵛ). In the title
miniature St. Gregory is addressing St. Mamas. The other illustrations represent
the Incredulity of Thomas, the rite of the consecration of a church and
St. Gregory teaching at a domed church. 1136-1155.

15. *Homilies of Gregory Nazianzenus (codex 339, fol. 73ᵛ). In the title
miniature St. Gregory and Julian the Tax Collector are represented as authors.
In the margin an ordinary taxation scene in Byzantium. Julian, seated
at a table, demands the taxes from the debtors. 1136-1155.*

Λό̄ γ   B̂

+ έτεροс єic τ̀ο ἀ̔γ̔ιον π̀ас · єʹυπῗ

οἱ τ̄ηс φυλα          ὁ ή̄ μβρομ τὶο
κ̄ησ μ̄ουτη̄          δεδο μ̄ ῡ η̄ c μοι
οο μαι · φ̄ η̄ οϊ       σαρὰ τοῦ τῆ c
ὁ θα μ̄ άς τος        ἑ̔ ξουςί̔αc ἱ̇ α̇ ξ
α μ̄ β̄ ἁ λω ὑ μ̄    θεωρίαc · καὶ ἀ̇
κ̄ ά̔ ρ ο μ̄ εζϊ̈ ̔αυτο̄ῦ    ποςκο σἁ ὁ̇ ο̇ c

338

16. Homilies of Gregory Nazianzenus (codex 339, fol. 9ᵛ). St. Gregory participates in the Vision of the Prophet Habakkuk. In the title miniature the young Christ-Emmanuel is seated on an arc of heaven. In the margin Christ is shown as Angel surrounded by Archangels carrying sceptres. 1136-1155.

17

18

19

20

21

22

17-22. Homilies of Gregory Nazianzenus (codex 339, fols. 318ᵛ, 43ʳ, 123ᵛ, 74ʳ, 132ᵛ, 81ʳ). Initials (O, E, Δ and M) illustrated with charming birds and fascinating animals, real and fantastic, in imaginative compositions revealing the Byzantine artist's unlimited imagination. 1136-1155.

23. *The Book of Job (35×24 cm., codex 3). The banquet of Job's sons and daughters (fol. 17ᵛ). 11th century.*

24. *The Book of Job (codex 3, fol. 8ʳ). Job's herds grazing in idyllic pastures. 11th century.*

*25. The Book of Job (codex 3, fol. 7ʳ). In a palatial setting Job and his wife are conversing with one another. 11th century.*

*26. The Book of Job (codex 3, fol. 26ʳ). Devastated by a series of disasters and smitten by the Devil, Job sits naked on a heap of dung and receives food from his wife who is, however, afraid to approach him. 11th century.*

*27. The Book of Job (codex 3, fol. 29ᵛ). Sophar, the king of Minaeans, escorted by a vanguard, rides to meet Job, in order to offer him support in his misfortunes. 11th century.*

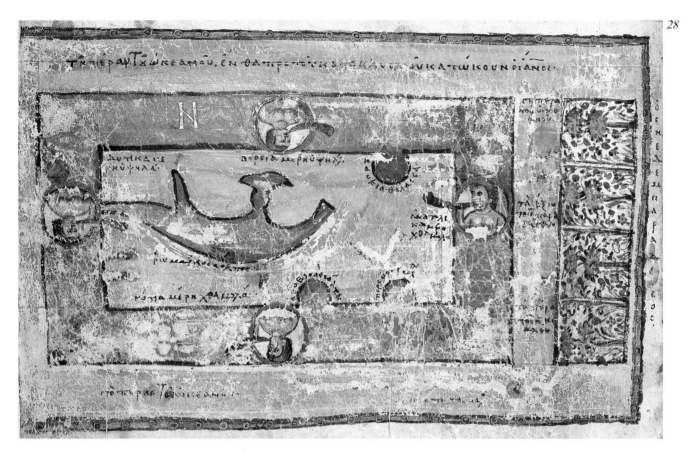

28. The Christian Topography by Cosmas Indicopleustes (27×18.5 cm., codex 1186).
Map of the world and paradise with personifications of the winds over the waters
of the ocean (fol. 66ᵛ). Beginning of the 11th century.

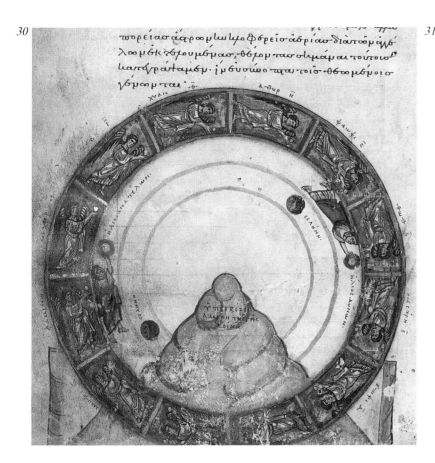

30. *The Christian Topography by Cosmas Indicopleustes (codex 1186, fol. 181ᵛ). The motion of the stars with angels standing in a zodiac-like circle. Beginning of the 11th century.*

31. *The Christian Topography by Cosmas Indicopleustes (codex 1186, fol. 65ʳ). The earth is shown as a mountain swimming in the primeval ocean. Beginning of the 11th century.*

29. *The Christian Topography by Cosmas Indicopleustes (codex 1186, fol. 75ᵛ). The Vision of Moses and the Receiving of the Law. Beginning of the 11th century.*

32. *The Christian Topography by Cosmas Indicopleustes (codex 1186, fol. 146ʳ) Gazelle, exotic birds and palm trees. Beginning of the 11th century.*

33. *Psalter and New Testament (16×12 cm., codex 2123), of the year 1242.*
*The Emperor John VIII Palaeologue, a later miniature (fol. 30ᵛ), was added to the codex*
*in the 16th century.*

34. *Psalter and New Testament (codex 2123, fol. 30ʳ), of the year 1242. The Emperor Michael VIII Palaeologue, a later miniature, was added to the codex in the 16th century.*

35. *Sticherarion (24×15.5 cm., codex 1234). The Annunciation (fol. 284ᵛ). 1469.*

36. *Four Gospels (17.3×12.5 cm., codex 198). The Evangelist John and a donor-monk (fol. 199ᵛ). 13th century.*

γραφος
αχαρι
ρὶθηέ
ὁδῶ ἀμ
ῳ καθέ
Αλληευ
αυτου·

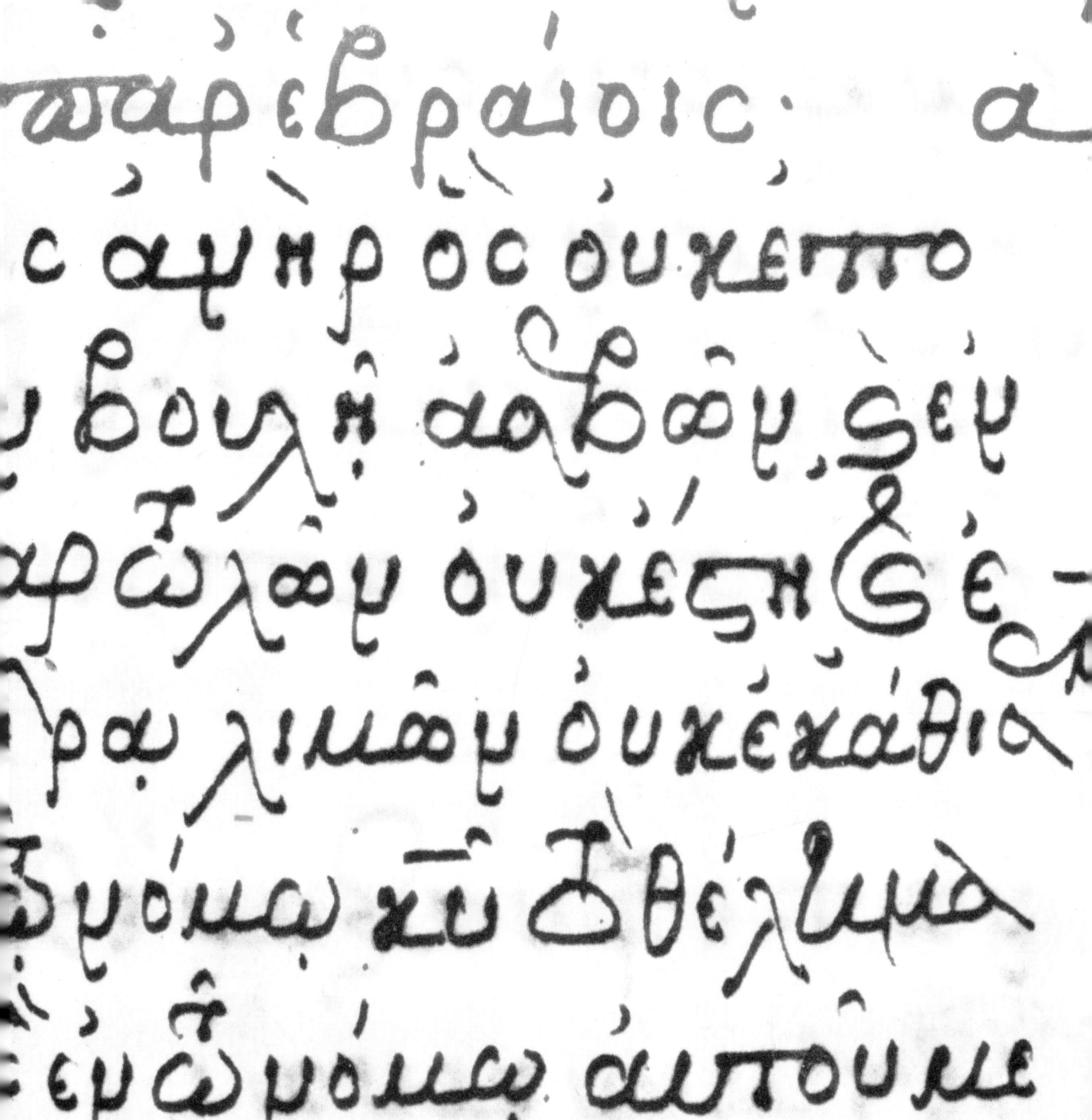

παρεβραιοις· α

ς αμηρ ος ουκεππο

υβουη τ̄ αφθωμ ς ε

αφ̄λ̄ωμ ουκεξ ς ε

ρα λιμωμ ουκεκαθια

βρομα κ̄ν̄ Θ̄ θελημα

εμφρομω αυτου με

# THE LIBRARY AND THE ARCHIVE

T he Holy Monastery is not, and never was, only a centre for the practice of the simple religious and ascetic life. All those who, whether in the past or still today, have sought refuge in the inaccessible Sinai desert have been people in search of the heremetical Christian life and, at the same time, the torch bearers of civilization and of learning in both theory and in practice. It is therefore not in the least bit strange that the Monastery of Sinai should boast one of the finest Library collections of manuscripts, a distinguished Library of printed books and an impressive Archive.

The special character of the Sinai Library depends on far more than the impressive number of manuscript codices — the recent discoveries added 1,000 new items to the 3,329 manuscripts already in the old collection — embracing also the wide range of types of Greek manuscript and a diversity of languages.

The Library houses more than 3,000 Greek manuscripts in addition to 700 Arabic, 266 Syriac, 86 Georgian and 80 Slavonic texts, as well as a handful of Armenian, Latin, Persian, Polish, Ethiopian and Coptic. The broad selection of languages found in the collection is unique amongst monastic libraries and it certainly reflects both the fortunes of the Monastery in the many centuries of its history, and the multi-facetted reverberations of its spiritual influence in the many countries where the Monastery maintained flourishing metochia.

## THE LIBRARY

The Library is distinguished not only by the large number of manuscripts but also by the age of many of these. A number of Greek manuscripts date to the earliest Byzantine period, before the 8th century. Amongst them is the famous *Codex Sinaiticus*, one of the most important manuscripts of Holy Scripture, the most important to transmit a text of the Old Testament, the New Testament and of the Apostolic Fathers. Dated to the middle of the 4th century, the manuscript is written in a classic example of one particular style of majuscule Greek script, the so-called Biblical. If this codex is not one of the fifty Bibles which Constantine the Great ordered Eusebius of Caesarea to have made for distribution to the churches of Constantinople, it is certainly derived from a direct copy of one of these fifty (fig. 7).

The *Codex Sinaiticus* has undergone a number of ignominious adventures. In 1844, the German scholar K. Tischendorf with the help of certain monks discovered 43 leaves of the codex, which he removed and presented to the Library of the University of Leipzig. In 1859, after making misleading promises to the monks, he succeeded in removing all the remaining leaves which he presented to the Tsar of Russia. The Monastery was undoubtedly aware of the misappropriation, and still lays claim to the manuscript; it is on record that it had only been given to Tischendorf to show to the Tsar and for Tischendorf's own use as a basis for publication. He had the right to make use of the manuscript, but no proprietary rights were conceded, as Archbishop Cyril clearly stated in a letter to Tischendorf sent from Constantinople in September 1867, and as the latter acknowledged. However, not only was the manuscript never returned, but in 1935 it was sold by the Soviet Union to Great Britain for the sum of £100,000. From then on it has been in the British Museum (catalogue number B. Mus. Add. 43725). The Monastery, nevertheless, still claims it. In the course of recent discoveries of new finds, a small number of leaves came to light, thus enabling the Monastery to display at least a small part of the original priceless treasure until such time as the rest of the codex is returned to Sinai.

Amongst the oldest manuscripts at Sinai are codices written in majuscule script, ranging in date from the 8th to the 11th century. There are more than forty of them, and the Monastery ranks as one of the largest holders in the world of manuscripts of this kind. Amongst them is Ms. 210, dated to 861/2 and written in Palestine in a beautiful majuscule 'ogivale inclinata' script. Another of the very old texts is Ms. 213, written in a majuscule 'ogivale diritta' script, and completed in Southern Italy on 30 January 967. Sinai Ms. Arabic 116 was written in 995/6 in Greek with an Arabic translation, the Greek part in majuscule. More important, however, is the fact that it was written on bombazine and penned at Sinai itself. It is amongst the oldest dated Greek manuscripts on bombazine, bearing a very typical colophon which reads: *Remember, O Lord, Thy Servant John, presbyter on Mount Sinai the son of Victor from Dammiette. Let God's Will be done.*

A large number of dated codices survive from the 11th century such as the parchment Sinai codices in minuscule script listed below: 448 from the year 1004, 736 of 1027/28 or 1028/29, 231 from the years 1034-1041, 223 of 1038/39, 364 from 1042-50 and 319 of 1048. Sinai codices 595 and 624 form part of a gift to the Monastery made in 1048/49: *Remember, O Lord, Thy unworthy servant, Pachomios, who offers here a gift to Thy All-pure Mother on the Holy Mount of Sinai, a Menaion for all the year in four parts of three months each.*

From the middle of the 11th and the beginning of the 12th century onwards the dated manuscripts in the Library increase in number. Of particular note is Sinai 257, a bombazine manuscript of 1101/2 written in minuscule script with this very typical colophon: *God is the beginning and end of all things. Finished by my hand, Peter the monk and presbyter of (the Holy Mount) Sinai in the year 1101/2. O reader, pray to the Lord for me. O Christ, Thee alone Who art merciful, save me, Peter.*

In addition to the directly dated manuscripts is a large number of texts which can be indirectly dated and are assigned to the 9th - 12th centuries. Tradition, repeated in various histories of the Monastery and in travellers' accounts, tells of the manuscript codex given to the Monastery by the Emperor Theodosius III (715 - 717); it is known as the *Theodosian Lectionary*, a Gospel Book written in majuscule gold letters on thin, very white parchment, and held in a magnificent silver binding. The manuscript (Sinai 204), cannot, however, date to the 8th, but must belong to the 10th or 11th century. It contains seven miniatures and its luxurious appearance seems to have been purposely executed so as to make possible its attribution to the last Emperor prior to Iconoclasm (fig. 3).

Amongst the valuable manuscripts which the Library exhibits are many containing illuminations described in the section devoted to illuminated manuscripts in this volume, as, for example, the Book of Job (Sinai 3) the manuscript of Cosmas Indicopleustes (Sinai 1186) and manuscripts of John Climacus (Sinai 275, 418).

In addition to these manuscripts, with their impressive miniatures and other decoration, Sinai 108, the *Psalter of Kassiani*, is of especial beauty. The small paper codex (14×8 cm.) is written in two columns and made up of only six pages on which all one hundred and fifty Psalms have been written in tiny letters. One line of one column, for example, succeeds in accommodating the following text from Psalm 1: *Blessed is the man that walketh not in the counsel of the ungodly, nor standeth in the way of sinners, nor sitteth in the seat of the scornful.* This Psalter does not, of course, have any connection with the famous poetess of Byzantium, Kassiani, but is of a much later date, of the 14th or 15th century.

Sinai 2246 is of particular interest to the Monastery, containing a collection of Latin and Italian decrees and decisions of the Doges of Venice, mostly relating to the Sinai metochia on the island of Crete and covering the entire period of Venetian rule over the island. Amongst the majuscule manuscripts, particular mention should be made of the *Uspenskij Psalter*, the largest part of which is today in Leningrad where it was taken by the notorious 'collector' of manuscripts, Porphyrios Uspenskij. Fortunately, however, other leaves from this same codex have turned up amongst the new finds and thus it is now beyond doubt that the Psalter had been stolen from the Monastery.

The range of content amongst the Library manuscripts is interesting. First place, of course, is held by manuscripts of the Holy Scriptures, in different sizes and of different types, such as: manuscripts of the Old Testament, the New Testament, Psalters, the Prophets, Lectionaries, Acts of the Apostles and even manuscripts containing commentaries on various books of the Bible. More than 400 manuscripts contain texts of the Divine Liturgies (of John Chrysostom, St. Basil the Great, and of the Presanctified), Menaia, Triodia, Pentecostaria, Oktoechoi, Theotokaria, Heirmologia, Horologia and Kekragaria. Also of particular importance are the Kontakaria, which date to the 11th and 12th centuries and may be compared with the famous Patmos Kontakaria. The Tropologia manuscripts at Sinai are also of note since they have preserved the original format of these books which contain the liturgical canons in the same way as the Kontakaria preserve the hymns.

Some 200 manuscripts contain Services in celebration of saints — a large number of them, of course, in celebration of St. Catherine. Some recount the lives and the martydom of saints, others are Menologia. Euchologia — that is manuscripts which could be used for various Services (sanctification, litanies, intercession, prayers for various natural phenomena and events) — are also preserved in some number (70). Of the roughly 300 musical manuscripts, many belong to the Middle and Later Byzantine periods; in other words, they are direct examples of Byzantine notation. Of especial merit are the 12th-century Sticheraria. In more than 300 manuscripts we find texts of the Church Fathers and Byzantine authors such as Sts. John Chrysostom, Basil, Gregory Nazianzenus, Pseudo-Dionysios the Areopagite, Gregory of Nyssa, Ephraim the Syrian, John of Damascus and John Climacus. No monastery library can be without works pertaining to ascetics some of which are by the great Ascetics themselves. In fact, about 100 manuscripts transmit the works of: Makarios the Egyptian, Maximos the Confessor, Isaac the Syrian, Abba Dorotheos, Palladios, Symeon the New Theologian; others contain tales of hermits and maxims of the Fathers. Because the spiritual growth and well-being of the monks was paramount, a large number of manuscripts are Kyriakodromia, containing sermons from the Gospels, the Acts of the Apostles or homilies based on the feast of the day. Most of the Kyriakodromia preserved at Sinai mention the name of the Patriarch of Constantinople, Philotheos Kokkinos (1353-1354, 1364-1376), once a monk at St. Catherine's. The number of purely theological tracts is also important, especially those of a polemical nature of which there are about one hundred. The *Typika*, i.e. the documents which set out liturgical order and the order of services, are of great use to the monks since they laid down the way in which their liturgical duties were to be performed. Only a small number, 20 or so, are preserved in the Monastery. Several scores of manuscripts with the Canons of the Church (Nomocanons) have survived, used mostly by the monks who departed to live at the metochia and whose holiness often meant that they would be called upon to intervene and settle the disputes and differences arising between inhabitants of the surrounding areas. Historical works, many of them pertaining to ecclesiastical history, like the work of Eusebius of Caesarea, or Chronicles are also represented. Particular mention should be made of the twelve volumes of the famous history of Athanasios Comnenos Ypsilantis written in 1752, contained in a unique manuscript, codex 1395. Works of the classical Greek authors are also preserved at the Monastery, very few earlier than the 13th or 14th century; most of these are dictionaries or books for school use. Many date to the 16th or 17th century.

The Sinai manuscripts are mostly written on parchment or paper; there are 400 and more parchment manuscripts, while the papyri are very few and will be described in the relevant section (see p. 356). Most of the manuscripts are in fact in book form, although some 150 are scrolls, providing the Library at Sinai with one of the most important collections of scrolls in the world. The few examples of palimpsests are exceptionally interesting since the first text to be written was subsequently erased to be replaced by another in a different language.

The Library at Sinai is also important for the styles of writing represented in the manuscripts. It is, in a sense, a museum with an example from each period and every stage in the history of the Greek literary hand. There is the majuscule script called Biblical, the Alexandrian script, the 'ogivale majuscule' which has two sub-divisions, the 'inclinata' and the 'diritta', and the large liturgical majuscule. Every known type of minuscule script is to be found, from the earliest pure style to the minuscule hand of the 18th century; many peculiarities can also be found amongst them.

It is reasonable to ask where the manuscripts in the Library came from; were they written in the Monastery, or did they arrive from elsewhere? Was there a scriptorium? The oldest uncontested dated manuscript written at Sinai is Sinai Arabic 116, bearing the year 995/6, and containing a Greek text of the New Testament with an Arabic translation. Another which was certainly written at the Monastery is no. 257, dating to 1101/2. From the mid-12th century, and even more in the 13th century, the evidence for the copying of manuscripts at Sinai becomes firmer. Codices 754 (dated to 1177), 817 (of 1258), 94 and 203 (dated to 1293) were written here. It is therefore safe to speak of a scriptorium at Sinai from the end of the 10th century.

However, many much older manuscripts are preserved at the Monastery, as for example the Codex Sinaiticus of the 4th century or the manuscript of John Climacus of the 7th or 8th century. Were these also written at Sinai, or were they brought from elsewhere, and when? There can be no categorical answer. We know that several manuscripts, earlier than the 12th century, were written outside the peninsula and arrived later at the Monastery. Codex 210, the oldest dated manuscript (861/2) was written in Palestine and was certainly in Sinai by the 14th century. Sinai 213, dated to 967, was written in Southern Italy by the presbyter Eustathios and was brought to the Monastery in the 12th or 13th century by Archbishop Makarios. Sinai 448, of the year 1004, came from Raithou in 1637.

From the middle of the 13th century however, the copying of manuscripts increased at Sinai. Thenceforth we have a long series of Sinaitic scribes, such as Germanos, Archbishop of Sinai in the 13th century, Matthew Rodaios (1495), Galaktion the deacon (1682), Pangratios the hieromonk, Kyprios (17th century), Athanasios of Naussa (1695, 1701), Nikephoros Marthalis Glykys, later Archbishop of Sinai (1706), and many others. A succession of Cretan scribes also copied texts, either at the metochion at Chandax in Crete, or at Sinai itself.

Sinai manuscripts also record the names of well-known copyists who worked outside Sinai, but whose manuscripts later came into the Monastery's possession. Many of them came from Southern Italy or Sicily, where many manuscripts were copied, many of which may have originated in the metochion at Messina. Others arrived from a variety of places in the Greek East (Bethlehem, Trebizond, Jerusalem, Damascus etc.). We also find copyists who sign their work, but give no indication as to the place where the manuscript was written, such as Solomon the deacon (8th - 9th century), George 'anagnostis' (12th - 13th century), Nicholas 'anagnostis' (12th - 13th century), and Nikephoros Moschopoulos (1303). Women too are listed amongst these scribes, for example Eirene Theodorou Agiopetritou who copied Sinai 1256 in 1308/9, Maria Krousaropoula who copied codex 940 in 1531, and Melanie the nun in Leontopolis who in 1612 copied Codex Sinaiticus 2006.

All the manuscripts discussed above written either in the 'kathismata' or the metochia in the desert, or in Cairo, reached the Monastery directly. Some must have been made as gifts, or by way of the many metochia scattered across different countries, as information in the codices themselves tells us.

Many of the scribes dedicated their manuscripts to the Monastery. There are, however, other, different dedications and donations, such as that of Nikephoros Moschopoulos who dedicated the Sinai codex 206 in the following words: *The wretched Nikephoros, once Metropolitan of Crete, hereby dedicates this Gospel Book copied and adorned by his hand to the Monastery in Phokaea bearing the name of [Saint] Athanasios so that the sword of the Ismalite may cease to be wielded, as a redemption of sin. Pray for him and the salvation of his soul. In the month of March during the First Indiction, in the year 1303.*

Unfortunately it was not possible to drive the Turks out of Phokaea as Nikephoros Moschopoulos had hoped and so he changed his mind, offering the manuscript to Sinai instead: *Since the terrible sword was not lifted, the aforesaid Metropolitan of Crete dedicates this work to the Monastery of Sinai, that which stands near the Bush.*

Other manuscripts were presented by Klemes, Archbishop of Sinai, in 1514 and others by Maximos Margounios in his will of 1602.

The existence of a scriptorium and the evidence of manuscript donations presupposes the existence of a library. It is unfortunate that the various references to it all date from a much later period. The historian Procopios had nothing to say on the subject. However, the presence of intellectuals at Sinai, such as Cosmas Indicopleustes, John Climacus, Anastasios the Sinaite and Anastasios of Antioch (who may be the same person) argues also for the presence of books. These writers all make reference to the Early Fathers as well as to the ancient Greek authors, and it is diffucult to accept that they knew such works by heart. Given that these authors lived at Sinai, they must have had books with them, and these books must have been stored somewhere. Independently, therefore, of the incontrovertible evidence for a scriptorium at the Monastery from the 10th century onwards, we should accept that there was a library of manuscripts even before that time. It is scarcely a tenable proposition that all the old manuscripts, dating from the 4th century onwards and today in the Monastery's possession, reached the Monastery later, namely after the 10th century. It is also unlikely that the Monastery had neither books nor library, the more so since it is situated in such an isolated and inaccessible region.

Many pilgrims and many who were simply visitors to the Monastery have, from time to time, provided us with written accounts, but they never speak of a library or indeed of books. They include not only the Anonymous of Placentia, who visited the Monastery around 570, but many others who, from the 14th century onwards, came in increasing numbers. On the other hand Vitaliano Donati, who journeyed to the Monastery in 1761, offers very detailed information about the Library and its contents: 'In this Monastery I found a huge quantity of parchment manuscripts, many of which had been placed in a library, others tossed into a filthy cupboard. Almost all are of parchment, and most of them are Greek. Many of the Fathers are there, and Commentaries on the Scriptures, various codices containing the Lives of the Saints, some histories and some writings of other sorts. There are a few which seem to be older than the 7th century, especially one Bible, on beautiful parchment, quite large, fine and square, written in rounded and very beautiful characters. Then in the church is a very beautiful Greek Gospel Book, also with round gold letters, which must also be very old. In addition to the Greek codices there are many others, in Arabic, Syriac, Georgian, Ethiopian, Slavonic and other languages. I did not see anything in Italian. Amongst the codices higher up I spied some examples of ancient Greek music and many longer manuscripts with a liturgical purpose (i.e. scrolls)'. Vitaliano Donati had therefore seen an organized library; it was in fact the building which Nikephoros Marthalis, Archbishop of Sinai, had erected a few decades earlier.

Immediately after his elevation to the archiepiscopal throne Nikephoros Marthalis Glykys bestirred himself about the organization of the Monastery, especially over the construction of a library. He himself tells us: *After seeing the manuscripts I found scattered about and neglected, some in cupboards, others in niches and cells, my conscience stabbed me and I put them into the care of the overseeer of books, the most learned of holy teachers, the protosynkellos Kyr' Isaias, who after much labour and care gathered all the books up from every corner, listing them in proper order, and arranging them as seemed best in a library, according to the judgement of the aforementioned Kyr' Chatzis Philo-theos, a monk from Prokonnesos, and after much reflection on the matter by the master Kyr' Symeon and all the brothers. May the Lord have mercy on them. Done between March and June 1734.* After the Library building had been completed an inscription was placed in its wall. It reads: *The library was erected by the efforts and support of the much loved and respected Archbishop of Sinai, Nikephoros, and the work of the builder Philotheos, monk of Sinai, and of Symeon. May all readers remember them, 1734.*

However, it seems that the Library was not the only building in which the monks continued to keep their manuscripts. The *Description of Sinai*, written in 1817, tells us that: *on the left of the passage, before you go down into the narthex, is the synodikon and four rooms belonging to the Archbishop and a second library of valuable books.*

Conditions of life at Sinai made it difficult for an open library to function. Frequent attack and closures often made it necessary for the monks to abandon the Monastery, forcing them to hide the books and the manuscripts. This, however, is the very reason why the Monastery has succeeded in preserving so many of its manuscript treasures.

The first person to draw up a catalogue of this wealth seems to have been Cosmas, later Patriarch of Constantinople. It was headed: *1734 in the month of July: A Catalogue of the books found [in the Monastery] that have come to be used by us which have been collected from various places, and here collected into one [body], where they have been classified. Cosmas of Sinai.* Nikephoros Marthalis had also charged the monk Isaiah with the drawing up of a catalogue. More systematic attempts at cataloguing were undertaken during the 19th century, first by Porphyrios Uspenskij in 1845 and 1854, later published in two volumes by V. Beneševic, and then by the Russian archimandrite Antoninos who in 1850 drew up another list, which formed the basis of V. Gardthausen's catalogue. The Sinai monk Andronikos Bryonides undertook to fill the gaps in this work. Kenneth Willis Clark made a catalogue of the microfilms of the manuscripts photographed by the American Mission of 1948-49, and a summary catalogue of all the manuscripts housed at Sinai has been published by M. Kamil. Recently, in addition to the devoted interest shown by Archbishop Damianos, the Hegumen of the Monastery, the hieromonk Demetrios Digbas-sanis, former librarian of the Monastery, has busied himself very systematically with the care of the Library, and has also drawn up a concordance of the different inventory numbers of the manuscripts as well as a supplementary catalogue.

The discovery of a great quantity of manuscripts in 1975 represented an event of the first order. While work was in progress on clearing and restoring the northern Justinian wall, a large amount of manuscripts (on papyrus, parchment and paper) was found in the earthen fill of a collapsed room immediately below the chapel of St. George. The then sacristan, the renowned archimandrite Sophronios, to whom we owe the discovery and the immediate care and collection of the new finds, describes the course of events in scrupulous entries of a diary which he kept day-by-day. The state in which the manuscripts were found was cause for despair — detached leaves, torn fragments, rollers of scrolls, bindings un-stuck from their codex, as well as whole bound volumes. Following the immediate conser-vation work administered by the monks under the direction of Father Sophronios and subsequently thanks to the special missions from the National Library of Greece, the material was sorted and arranged on a provisional basis. Most of the new finds are Greek manuscripts, though some are foreign language texts. The first attempts at sorting estab-lished that there were at least 1,100 separate manuscripts, whether fragmentary or com-plete, more than 800 of which were Greek, the rest being Arabic, Georgian, Syriac, Slavon-ic, Ethiopian, one Latin and one Hebrew. It is significant that a third of the finds were preserved as complete codices. It is also worth noting that there are more than 120 scrolls. Also of importance was the discovery of manuscripts written in majuscule. The new finds, which range in date from the 4th to the 18th century, are particularly fine in that they mostly demonstrate old styles of majuscule and minuscule script. Even more significant was the discovery of fragments of manuscripts already known, such as leaves from the famous Codex Sinaiticus, of a majuscule manuscript of John Climacus (the oldest known copy of whose work is already in the possession of the Monastery), leaves of the famous Uspenskij Psalter and leaves of a 9th-century manuscript containing the first five books of the *Iliad* with a commentary in simpler language.

It appears that the manuscripts discovered in 1975 had been hidden after the erection of the Library by Nikephoros Marthalis in 1734 since they were deemed no longer 'of use'. It is quite probable that these were the manuscipts seen by Donati in 1761, thrown carelessly in a cupboard, in addition to those he saw arranged neatly in Marthalis' Library. Many scholars, both Greek and foreign, have studied the Sinai manuscripts, including, to name a few, Th. Volidis, C. Amantos, N. Livadaras, Em. Pantelakis, V. Gardthausen, G. Garritte, I. Ševčenko, N.P. Kondakov, L. Tardo and others.

Dishonesty on the part of many foreign visitors has not been unknown at the expense of the priceless treasures of the Library. Many foreigners have stolen and looted precious manuscripts. They have not confined themselves only to theft, but have cut the miniatures from manuscripts which they have thus mutilated. Consequently, by one means or another, manuscripts which once belonged to the Sinai Library are now in foreign repositories, mostly in Leningrand, Leipzig, Oxford, Vienna, the British Library, the Marciana in Venice, and elsewhere. Such behaviour has made the monks adopt a cautious attitude to foreigners, and to impose strict surveillance over students who wish to examine the material. Cl. Sicard's comment, made in 1720, is typical: 'We especially desired to enter the library in order to study the manuscripts there to our satisfaction. The monks had some hesitation about unlocking for us, because they maintain they are always suffering some loss of their books. Indeed, they claim to have lost a lot. But despite these losses that they complain of, the library is particularly rich, especially in Greek manuscripts, Arabic, Syriac, Ethiopian and other languages. But all these books, manuscripts and other documents have been moved about so much that today they are in great disorder. We would have needed far more time to have acquired even a nodding acquaintance'.

Despite the many invasions of the desert by successive waves of peoples, destruction by natural and other phenomena (earthquakes, floods, fires), and occasional lootings, the Library of Sinai still retains its most precious treasures, the manuscripts. This is largely due to the vigilance and ceaseless interest of the monks through which the heritage of Hellenism and Orthodoxy, priceless for civilization in general, has been preserved until today. The Library at Sinai, as indeed the whole Monastery, now has the services of trained monks and is furnished with modern equipment — a specialist photographic laboratory, a conservation laboratory. The Library has been systematically organized and enriched with modern reference books. It can benefit and help scholars wherever they are and whenever they wish, without requiring them to travel to the Monastery. After 1951, when the building adjoining the south wall of the Monastery was completed, the Library was transferred to its upper floor. From its new home, the Library can now serve the needs of scholarship as well as constitute a centre for Greek and Orthodox culture of international standing.


THE PAPYRUS COLLECTION

Papyrus as a suitable writing material was employed for some four thousand years (from 3000 B.C. to A.D. 1000) and was still favoured even in the 2nd century A.D. when parchment, which was both cheaper and easier to handle, began to come into use for the same purpose. When the first monks arrived at Sinai from Egypt papyrus, curiously, was not in general or systematic use in the Monastery. This explains why there was never a significant number of papyri, although those that survive form a notable collection alongside the multitude of magnificent manuscripts in the Library.

The existence of many of the papyri at Sinai became known last century when J. R. Harris published two of them, containing the Psalms of David, in his book *The Biblical Fragments from Mount Sinai* (London 1890); and in 1894 A. Smith produced a catalogue of the Syriac manuscripts at the Monastery. Reference is made to this corpus of papyri in the earliest catalogues of the Monastery's manuscripts produced by Cosmas, Archbishop of Sinai in 1704, and by Isaiah the monk in 1734 and others. Beside this old collection made up of 42 texts and 12 fragments, we now have a new assemblage, containing Greek, Arabic and Syriac papyri which came to light in 1975 when part of the contents of the old Library was discovered. The latter collection is made up of 83 pieces and 10 fragments as well as 4 other attached fragments which came from the binding of Codex 213. With the addition of these new finds, which included important and interesting texts, the Monastery can claim to hold one of the world's finest collections of papyri. In 1988 a team of scholars, including the Director of the Papyrological Institute of the Austrian National Library, Assistant Professor H. Harrauer and the Institute's Conservation Officer, Mrs Andrea Donau, set about the task of restoring a large number of papyri; the result was a steady increase in their total number. The work has not yet come to an end, and so figures given here should not be regarded as final.

Amongst the papyri restored in 1988 was one leaf which contains part of Psalm 108; along with three parchment leaves (10×10 cm.) of 6th-century date reproducing part of Psalms 112-114, it was fixed with many nails to small boards. Individual psalms written on separate leaves of papyrus or parchment and nailed onto plaques were often attached to walls in houses to induce their residents to prayer.

Eight papyrus leaves, written in Latin and Greek script of the 6th century A.D., are of exceptional interest; their content is very typical — legal problems pertaining to monastic life, together with information about the Law book of the Roman Jurist Ulpian who flourished c. A.D. 200. For example: *Ob Donationes. R[esponsum] cod[icis] Ulp[iani].* i.e. 'On donations. The Verdict from the works of Ulpian: Concern yourself not with this, but...'. This provides an illustration of the deep significance of Roman Law; these leaves pose further questions which touch on the Law in relation to the life of the monks, making it probable that we are looking at a manual or handbook with problems of a legal nature concerned with every day life of the fathers and brethren of the Monastery. The questions are phrased in Latin, probably due to their being drawn from a source in that language, namely the codex of Ulpian. The answers, however, are given in Greek; the reason for this is a problem whose solution is awaited.

Roughly one hundred papyrus leaves in Georgian script were preserved in very bad condition within a wooden chest. The edges of the pages are badly charred, perhaps due to great heat during a fire. The conservation team mentioned above has done what it can. The script suggests a date of the 9th century at the latest. These are the only papyri in either Georgian script or language yet known.

Of great importance for the early history of the Sinai Monastery are the Greek Archival papyri. Five papyri, unstuck in 1988 from a bundle of yellowed scraps, date to the end of the 6th or the beginning of the 7th century. They are therefore contemporary with the first fifty years of the Monastery's history. Most of them are accounts. In one of them the sender writes: *I sent you a fish to fry.* Another acknowledges the receipt of 226 measures of wheat, and another states that *my lady mother* begs for exact information.

Papyrus strips have also been observed in the bindings of Greek, Arabic and other manuscripts; their detachment will add new and interesting finds to the already substantial collection in the Monastery Library.

## THE ARABIC MANUSCRIPTS

The Arabic language manuscripts at the Monastery are all concerned with Orthodox Christian texts with the exception of a very few devoted to the exact sciences, mostly medical texts. They constitute a treasure-house for the history of the Orthodox Church and of Arab Christian literature throughout the Near East. They form the largest, oldest collection of manuscripts with an Orthodox Christian subject matter in Arabic. These were originally books given to the Monastery or brought by the monks themselves from other monastic centres in Palestine, Syria and Egypt. They were either copied at the Monastery from codices which had become worn or were ordered to be copied for use elsewhere in the Arab-speaking world. These texts were translated from Greek originals to assist the immediate liturgical and spiritual needs of Orthodox Arab - speaking monasteries.

It was deemed suitable that the collection of literary Arab manuscripts and documents should be housed in the modern and spacious Library; official and private documents as well as correspondence in Arabic are kept in the Archive and thus will be treated separately in that section.

The many interesting subjects for study presented by this collection, both codices and documents, include the actual materials on which they were written (note that bombazine codices using flax as a raw material exist here and date two and a half centuries earlier than paper's first appearance as a medium for the written word in Europe). The shape, binding, and script are also significant although the manuscripts' date of composition, provenance and contents are of more concern to the study in hand.

The collection of Arabic manuscripts from both the Old and the New Collection numbers more than 700 parchment and paper codices and about 1,400 paper and parchment records. The oldest dated codex is the parchment Codex no. 16 in the New Collection, dated 859; next in order is the parchment codex no. 110, of the Old Collection dated to 867. The parchment and partly palimpsest manuscript no. 504 known as the *Codex Arabicus* dating from the 9th century, does, however, bear traces of 8th-century cufic lettering underneath the more recent text. We therefore have the oldest known codices with Christian subject matter in Arabic script. According to the decree issued by Omar Ibh El-Khatab (634 - 644) to govern the Christians, they were not permitted to use Arabic: 'The Christians shall not read, write nor use the Arabic language'.[1] With the passage of time, of course, this prohibition lost its force and ceased to be regarded as valid. The Christian secretaries in the service of the state were the best available and were thus quite irreplaceable; neither was it possible that the Arab Christians should cease to use their mother tongue. Hence, by the 9th century in Egypt, we have arrived at a situation where Greek and Coptic were being replaced by Arabic. From then on Arabic prevailed amongst the Copts and, similarly, amongst the Orthodox Arabs; Arabic was also in use parallel with Greek as the ecclesiastical language.

While in general the condition of the parchment manuscripts is good, that of the paper manuscripts varies from satisfactory to poor. Leaves are missing from the beginning and ends of most of the codices because of frequent usage. These are the very pages on which the date is usually found, so that very few codices preserve any indication to permit dating. On the basis of such evidence as we do possess, the bulk of the collection has been dated to the 9th-13th centuries. It is clear that the lack of writing material made it necessary on several occasions to scratch off the surface of older parchments in order to use them a second time. Indeed, on several occasions several pieces of parchment have been sewn together to make a larger sheet. The fact that the manuscripts often contain mention of heavy penalties for their lending or removal from the Monastery, and even from one chapel to another within the enclosure, is proof of the great material and spiritual value which the isolated monks of Sinai attached to these books.

The script in most of the codices is not of outstanding merit; only a few are calligraphic.

The language is the demotic of the time and only rarely eloquent. The amount of ornament-ation in relation to the number of manuscripts is limited. Only a few codices boast full page miniatures (figs. 11, 12) or other decoration such as illuminated capital or initial letters. The explanation for this may be that these manuscripts were not intended as gifts, but mainly for daily use in the Services.

Whenever translation occurred, it was from Greek into Arabic. We learn from the various notes and marginalia that the manuscripts originated from different monastic centres in Syria, Palestine, Sinai and Egypt. The subject matter of the codices includes books of the Old Testament, such as Genesis, Exodus, Leviticus, the books of the Prophets Daniel, Jeremiah, Isaiah, the Psalms of David, the Book of Job and others; from the New Testament are copies of the Gospels and the Acts and Epistles of the Apostles. Included amongst the liturgical texts are Lectionaries, Horologia, Triodia, Euchologia, Synaxaria, Discourses, Instruction Manuals, Saints' Lives, Martydoms and Encomia especially those of Palestinian, Syrian, Egyptian and Greek ascetic Fathers, together with works of Dogma, Literature and Philosophy, some chronicles and medical texts; in other words, books which would have been useful for the daily services, for spiritual improvement, the instruction of novices and the cure of various illnesses. Although the preservation of these manuscripts is to some extent due to the dry climate of the area, their survival is also in large measure due to the respect in which they were held, and the care which the monks took of them as part of their sacred inheritance.[2]

## THE SYRIAC MANUSCRIPTS

The substantial collection of Syriac manuscripts in the Library of St. Catherine's Monas-tery is unique in that it is the only large collection of Syriac manuscripts which are of Orthodox provenance;[1] thus the famous extensive collections of Syriac manuscripts in the British Library and the Vatican Library both largely originate from the Syrian Orthodox (Jacobite) Monastery in the Desert of Sketis.

The manuscripts range in date from the 5th to about the 15th century, the earlier ones containing biblical books or writings of the Fathers (both Greek and Syriac), while the later manuscripts, from about the 10th century onwards, are almost entirely all liturgical. Many of these manuscrips will have been written in North Syria and Mesopotamia, and been brought to the Monastery by monks or pilgrims from those areas; a considerable number of the 12th and 13th-century manuscripts, however, were actually written in St. Catherine's Monastery or its vicinity, and the scribes have left dated colophons explicitly stating this.

Undoubtedly the most famous manuscript is a palimpsest, known as the *Codex Sinaiti-cus Syrus* par excellence: the upper writing of this manuscript contains the Lives of various holy women, and the scribe has left both his name (John the Stylite) and date (A.D. 778); much more important, however, is part of the 5th-century underwriting, which preserves the text of the earliest Syriac translation of the Gospels, known as the 'Old Syriac', probably made in the 3rd century.[2] Only the other (incomplete) manuscript of this version survives, and these two 'Old Syriac' Gospel manuscripts are of particular importance for the early history of the New Testament text; their readings are regularly cited in critical editions.

Several other early biblical manuscripts, belonging to the 6th and 7th centuries, are to be found in the collection; among these is the earliest surviving Syriac manuscript of III Maccabees.

During the 4th to 7th centuries an astonishing number of translations into Syriac were made of the Greek Fathers, and these are well represented in the Monastery's collection: thus there are early manuscripts (often incomplete) of St. Basil's Commentary on the

Hexaemeron, St. Gregory of Nyssa's Commentary on the Song of Songs, St. John Chrysostom's Homilies on St. Matthew's Gospel etc. Of particular importance (fig. 14) are the only surviving manuscripts of the Apology of Aristeides (the Greek original of which is only known from its re-use in *Barlaam and Joasaph,* attributed to St. John of Damascus) and of the 6th-century Syriac translation of the corpus of writing ascribed to Dionysios the Areopagite (otherwise known from a late 7th-century revision). Greek monastic writings include works by Evagrios, Makarios, Neil, Abba Isaias, the Egyptian Fathers, and Anastasios of Sinai; the Syriac translation of St. John Climacus' writings is to be found in two manuscripts, and one wonders whether the translation may not even have been made at St. Catherine's Monastery.

The native Syriac Fathers are represented by St. Ephraim, John the Solitary, Jacob of Serugh, Isaac of Antioch, and St. Isaac the Syrian (whose works were translated into Greek at the Monastery of St. Sabbas in the 8th century). Among the abundant liturgical manuscripts is the only known example of musical notation in Syriac.

Rather surprisingly a number of late Classical Greek writers in Syriac translation are also represented: thus there are three works by Plutarch, one by Lucian, and various sayings of Pythagoras, Theano and other philosophers.

Besides the Syriac manuscripts, St. Catherine's Monastery also possesses a large proportion of the surviving texts in the dialect known as Christian Palestinian Aramaic or Palestinian Syriac. Almost all these are fragmentary, and they date from about the 6th to the 13th century. The manuscripts comprise monastic writings, Lectionaries (two are complete), and liturgical texts; all are translated from Greek.

The new finds, discoverd in 1975, have added considerably to the Syriac collection.[3]

## THE GEORGIAN MANUSCRIPTS

The Monastery's large collection of Georgian manuscripts is of great importance, not only for the history of Georgian language, liturgy and literature, but also for Greek patristic literature, seeing that many of the manuscripts are of great antiquity. The texts which they contain belong to the earliest period of Georgian literature (up to c. 980), and the translations from Greek date from a time prior to the 7th-century translation activity associated with Mount Athos (Iviron Monastery).

Of particular importance is a unique papyrus Psalter, of the 7th or 8th century. Two manuscripts bear dates in the 9th century (one of these, dated 864, was copied at the Monastery of St. Sabbas), and fourteen belong to the 10th century. Several of the manuscripts were copied on Sinai by Georgian monks, such as John Zosimos (originally from St. Sabbas) who was active between 949 and 987. Many of these early manuscripts contain texts not known elsewhere. Among the many translations from the Greek Fathers are works by Ammonas, Antonios, Athanasios, Basil, Ephraim, Evagrios, Gregory of Nazianzus, John Chrysostom and others; there are also many Lives of Saints.

The new finds of 1975 have now augmented the collection of Georgian manuscripts considerably.

## THE SLAVONIC MANUSCRIPTS

The Conversion of the Slavs in the 9th century was a very decisive step in the process whereby Byzantine civilization would become a culture of universal significance. From that period on, all the bubbling intellectual and cultural activity of the Empire would leave a lasting impression on the Slavonic world. The leading monastic centres (Mount Athos, Jerusalem, Sinai) have preserved for us a sharp picture of this reality, for in all these places traces of the Slav presence exist even from the 10th century alongside the Greek element. Examples of the spread of Slavonic Christianity can also be found at Sinai where the Slavonic manuscripts form a sizable and noteworthy collection of some 80 items and remnants of old codices. They are of great value, for they preserve part of early Slavonic literature from the 10th and 11th centuries and go right up to the Late Byzantine period. Their pages clearly record the efforts of the Slav monks to participate in the monastic and wider intellectual horizons of the Greek monasteries.

The new finds of 1975 included Slavonic manuscripts (complete codices as well as sections or fragments of lost manuscript books) totalling 41. The oldest of these, an Euchologion, two Psalters, a Menaion and a Missal, preserve the original Glagolitic alphabet which the brothers Cyril and Methodios devised to render the Holy Scriptures into the Slavonic tongue (fig. 16). These texts give us a faithful translation and record of the undeviating observance of the Byzantine liturgical tradition.

The rest of the manuscripts are written in Cyrilic, in the majuscule Byzantine script which the Slavs adopted as early as the 10th century and which became widespread from the 11th. In this group we have a considerable number of Psalters, amongst them part of two very old Psalters, one Serbian, the other Russian, and also Euchologia, Menaia, Services, Missals, Apocrypha and works of the great Ascetics and the Church Fathers.

Such a notable collection of Slavonic manuscripts at Sinai has engaged scholarly interest and has been interpreted in various ways. Up till now, however, no one has been able to give a certain answer as to how and when these manuscripts arrived here. The only thing which can be said with certainty is that some of them reached the Monastery Library long after their having being written and were initially used elsewhere, while some were the gift of pilgrims and still others were used to help the Slav monks who from time to time settled at St. Catherine's to lead a solitary life there, side by side with the Greeks.[1]

## THE ARCHIVE

The well-endowed Archive constitutes a very important section of the Library of the Monastery; it contains codices, loose leaf documents, letters, files, etc. which emanate not only from the Monastery and its numerous metochia throughout the world, but also from the ecclesiastical and temporal rulers of different countries. The Archive therefore contains documents written in languages other than Greek. The variety of content makes the Archive invaluable and the study of this material has revealed fascinating information about the history of the Monastery and its metochia, as well as about its relations with different Churches and with foreign states.

In chronological terms the material is not very equally distributed. The researcher is not, for example, likely to experience the joy of discovering an imperial chrysobull with the signature of the founder Justinian, or of other, later emperors, or sigillia of patriarchs of Constantinople. The Greek section of the Archive preserves very few documents of the Byzantine period which shed light on the relations of the Monastery with Constantinople, the centre of Hellenism until 1453. This is largely because of the occupation of the peninsula from the 7th century, which cut every administrative contact between the Monastery and the capital of the Empire. Such documents as chanced to exist were destroyed during the attacks of the barbarians or disappeared through other causes. The oldest Greek document to survive dates to the 15th century and is a brief letter from the Ecumenical Patriarch Gennadios to the monks and brethren at Sinai.

By comparison, the Arabic section of the Archive contains documents which inform us about the relations of the Monastery with the Arab chiefs and with the centres of the Islamic world from a very early date. For example, copies of the 'Achtiname' (the Holy

Testament) are preserved, that is, the first guarantee given by Mohammed which, according to tradition, the Prophet himself sanctified by stamping his palm over it (fig. 18). The copies date to the 16th century when the original was given to the Sultan Selim I after he conquered Egypt in 1517.

From the 16th century until today the material in the Archive is rich and valuable being, as we have already said, in many languages besides Greek, and coming from the many metochia of the Monastery throughout the world. The Sinaite 'metochiates' or itinerants served as gatherers of a variety of information and news which appears in the correspondence with the Monastery or in their personal diaries. From the 17th century the metochia of the Monastery in Constantinople, and from the 16th century, those in Cairo (Tzouvania), also developed important archives, all with very fine collections of Arabic and Turkish documents essential for the understanding of the Monastery's transactions with the administrative organs of the Ottoman Empire, especially in Egypt. A number of documents also originate from metochia in Moldavia, Cyprus, Crete and elsewhere.

The foreign language Archive contains Latin documents (from the 13th century), Spanish (from the 16th century), Venetian (from the 14th century), Italian, German, English and French; amongst the latter is the famous Guarantee given by Napoleon Bonaparte of 1798 (fig. 25). There are also documents in the Iberian language, namely modern Georgian, for example documents of the Iberian princes Heraclios and George from the years 1772 and 1780, documents in Russian (imperial chrysobulls and synodical seals) (fig. 21) and in Wallachian (chrysobulls and sigillia) (fig. 24).

However, the largest number of non-Greek documents are in the Arabic Archive of the Monastery. This is divided into a purely Arabic section with more than 1,000 items, and an Ottoman section containing documents written in Turkish with Arabic script. The oldest Arabic document belongs to the period of the Fatimids, and was perhaps written in 1106; the oldest Turkish document dates to 1496.

These documents deal mostly with the Monastery's relations with political authorities. They consist of the following: a) documents issued in favour of the Monastery or its metochia by local Egyptian authorities and dealing with matters within Egypt (deeds of ownership, mortgages, transfer deeds etc.); and b) documents pertaining to more general and important matters concerning the Monastery's interests within and without Egypt, more specifically the famous ordinances issued by the Caliphs, the supreme political authority of the Islamic state. Of these, only a few original documents have been preserved; others survive in verified copies. All these documents were issued on the basis of the Achtiname. Thus some of the later copies bear, apart from a depiction of the Monastery and Mt. Sinai, the imprint of a palm and five fingers, namely the symbol of the Prophet Mohammed and his blood relatives Fatima, Ali, Hasan, and Hussein. Documents of the Fatimids, the Ayyubids and the Mamelouk Caliphs from the 12th century A.D. and thereafter have been preserved in their original form or as copies.[1]

These documents are mostly indulgences dealing with the protection of the Monastery, the monks, the safe conduct of pilgrims, the security of the Monastery's religious and financial independence and that of its foundations and property in various parts of the realm, together with their exemption from the legal and tax system of the Islamic state. In all these documents one can follow the attempts made by the monks to preserve and increase the Monastery's property and to secure exemption from tax and other obligations to the state. These documents constitute a valuable source for the Monastery's history, the study of Islamic state institutions and that of the general history of the area.

This material is either in *codex* form or in ***unbound*** documents. The codices divide into:

*Avantaria*, in which the possessions of the Monastery and the metochia are written.

*Katasticha*. Account books where the Monks recorded their daily expenses whether in the Monastery or metochia, together with leases, purchases, expenses involved in the upkeep of plots of cultivatable land. In this category we may also include the personal diaries of the itinerant archbishops and monks, and of the Oikonomoi of the Monastery, or of the Hegoumenoi, as the heads of the Sinaite metochia were usually styled.

*Other codices.* These preserve copies of letters from the 16th century until today from various ecclesiastical or political figures, the originals of which are no longer extant. The same codices also record the decisions of the archbishops or Chapters to send Sinaite monks to metochia on itinerant visits or on journeys to collect funds.

*Praxeis.* Acts recording the decisions of the Chapter of the Monastery.

*Monachologia.* Lists the monks at the Monastery, their date of tonsure and taking of vows.

From 1897, there are volumes containing the impressions of various visitors and pilgrims.

The unbound volumes are similarly numerous, making up a large part of the Archive. They may be the original official documents sent to the monks or copies of such documents which the Monastery despatched. These include:

*Chrysobulls, Lead seal* or *Wax seal documents.* Documents sealed with gold (Chrysobulls), lead (Molyvdobulla) or Wax (Kerobulla) despatched by Russian emperors, the princes of Georgia or the rulers of Moldavia. None of these documents is earlier than the 17th century.

*Patriarchal Sigillia* (Seal-Bearing Letters). Most of these are lead or wax sealed. Few examples exist, and are dated to the 17th century and after.

*Apantachousae* (Circulars). Archiepiscopal documents of Sinai or of other hierarchs, with the purpose of requesting financial support for the Monastery. These documents also begin from the 17th century (fig. 20).

*Various letters*, which form the official correspondence of the Monastery with its metochia and various ecclesiastical and political authorities.

*Miscellaneous Documents*, relating to various subjects of interest to the Monastery.

The systematic arrangement of the Archive is under way; it will, however, require some time to complete.


## PRINTED BOOKS

The great amount of printed books at the Monastery make up one of the most important monastic libraries. The older part (books up to 1972) has more than 8,000 volumes while the newer section (books from 1973 onwards) has more than 5,000. The intellectual output of Antiquity, of Byzantium, of the period of the Ottoman occupation as well as that of more recent times, are all represented. The accumulation of the older volumes, which are the more important, was due to the erudite and bibliophile nature of many Sinaite archbishops and monks, as well as to gifts and purchases. The more scholarly brethren owned their own personal collections which they then bequeathed to the Monastery. We do not know exactly when the collection of printed books was first organized. Dedication notes in the books suggest that it may have been during the 16th century.

The books cover a wide time span and were printed in a variety of places. The Old Section contains some incunabula (books printed up to March 25, 1501), such as the first edition of the *Comedies* of Aristophanes (Venice, 1498), of the *Mega Etymologikon* (Venice, 1499) (fig. 26), the *Scholia on Aristotle's Categories* by Simplicius (Venice, 1499), and the *Souidas* or *Suda* (Milan, 1499). There are also many old prints (books printed between 1501 and 1600) produced by the presses of Aldus Manutius, for example his 1502 edition of the Plays of Sophocles, the 1503 edition of the Plays of Euripides, the 1504 Orations of Demosthenes, the 1513 edition of the Works of Plato, and the 1518 Old and New Testament. There are also books printed by the presses of Florence, Rome, Padua, Paris, Frankfurt, Basle and Leiden. There are plenty of books printed after 1600 and many contemporary works. Together with the books of liturgical nature — Gospels, Menaia, Psalters, Triodia, Paracletica — which were produced largely by the Greek presses in Venice, the Sinai monks enriched their library with minor works of Philosophy, History, Medicine, Mathematics along with works of a dogmatic nature and Canon Law. One may marvel at the range of editions of Homer, of the classical playwrights and poets, the distinguished editions of the great Church Fathers (figs. 27, 28), the various Dictionaries, the Grammars, the manuals of logic and letter-writing, the many editions of the Philological Encyclopaedia of Ioannis Patoussas, and the works of foreign literature such as the plays of Molière.

The wide-ranging subject matter reveals the existence of a monastic community whose intellectual preoccupations presuppose systematic training which the Sinaites had often acquired at the monastic School on Patmos, though not exclusively there. Names of owners, dedicatory notes, commentaries and observations on the book's content all attest to the fact that the monks studied their books, lent and even sold them to each other, before they were finally deposited in the Monastery library. Additionally the Archbishop, or the Dikaios and the Council of the Fathers lent the Library's printed books to the brethren to assist them in their studies, recently on condition that they were returned. One may therefore say that we are talking about an accessible Library, a working, living element in monastic life. Of course, not all the brethren were educated men. Nevertheless, the *ex libris* in many books record the names of the learned monks, better or less well known, such as Nektarios later Patriarch of Jerusalem, Nikephoros Marthalis, Archbishop of Sinai, Constantios, subsequently Patriarch of Constantinople, the Cretan monks Gregorios Melissinos, Ioannikios Pyros, Makarios, Hilarion and Anastasios, Christopher from Macedonia and others. The Library also contains books which belonged to famous scholars, such as Maximos Margounios, Bishop of Kythera, Gabriel Severos, Bishop of Philadelphia, Nikolaos Mavrocordatos and others. The part played by the metochia should not go unmentioned, for many of their inhabitants ('*metochiarides*') were bibliophiles and amassed admirable collections.

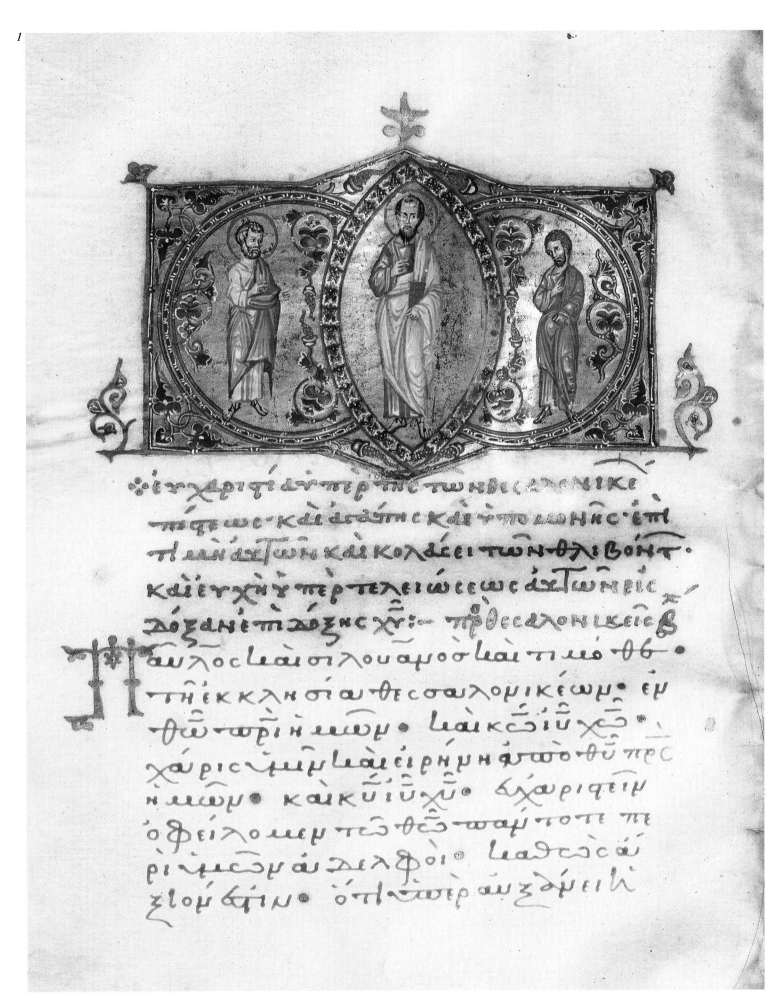

*1. Acts of the Apostles (21×16 cm., codex 275, f. 279ᵛ). The Apostle Paul between the Apostles Timothy and Silouanos. Parchment. Minuscule script. 11th century.*

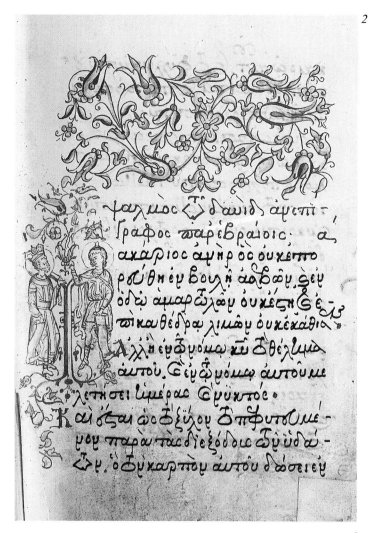

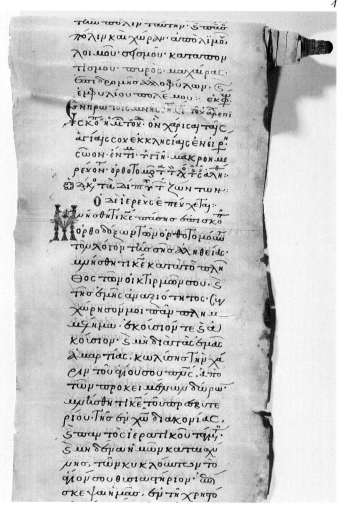

2. *Psalter (24×17 cm., codex 74, f.1). Heading, illuminated initial letter. Bombazine. Minuscule script, by the hand of Jeremiah the Sinaite of Crete. 1619/20.*

3. *Lectionary (28×21.5 cm., codex 204, f. 161ʳ) The 'Theodosian Lectionary'. Subheading ('gate'), double initial letter. Parchment. Majuscule biblica script. 10th-11th century.*

4. *Scroll and roller (32.3×19 cm., New Finds, no. E6). The Liturgy of St. Basil. Illuminated initial letter. Minuscule script. 12th century.*

5. *Readings from the Book of Genesis (25×19 cm., codex 7, f. 1ᵛ-2). Heading and initial letter. Parchment. Majuscule 'ogivale diritta' script. Donated by the monk Constantios Lependrenos. 10th-11th century.*

6. *The 'Uspenskij Psalter' (16×14.5 cm., New Finds, no. ΜΓ33). Parchment. Majuscule 'ogivale inclinata' script. 862/3.*

5

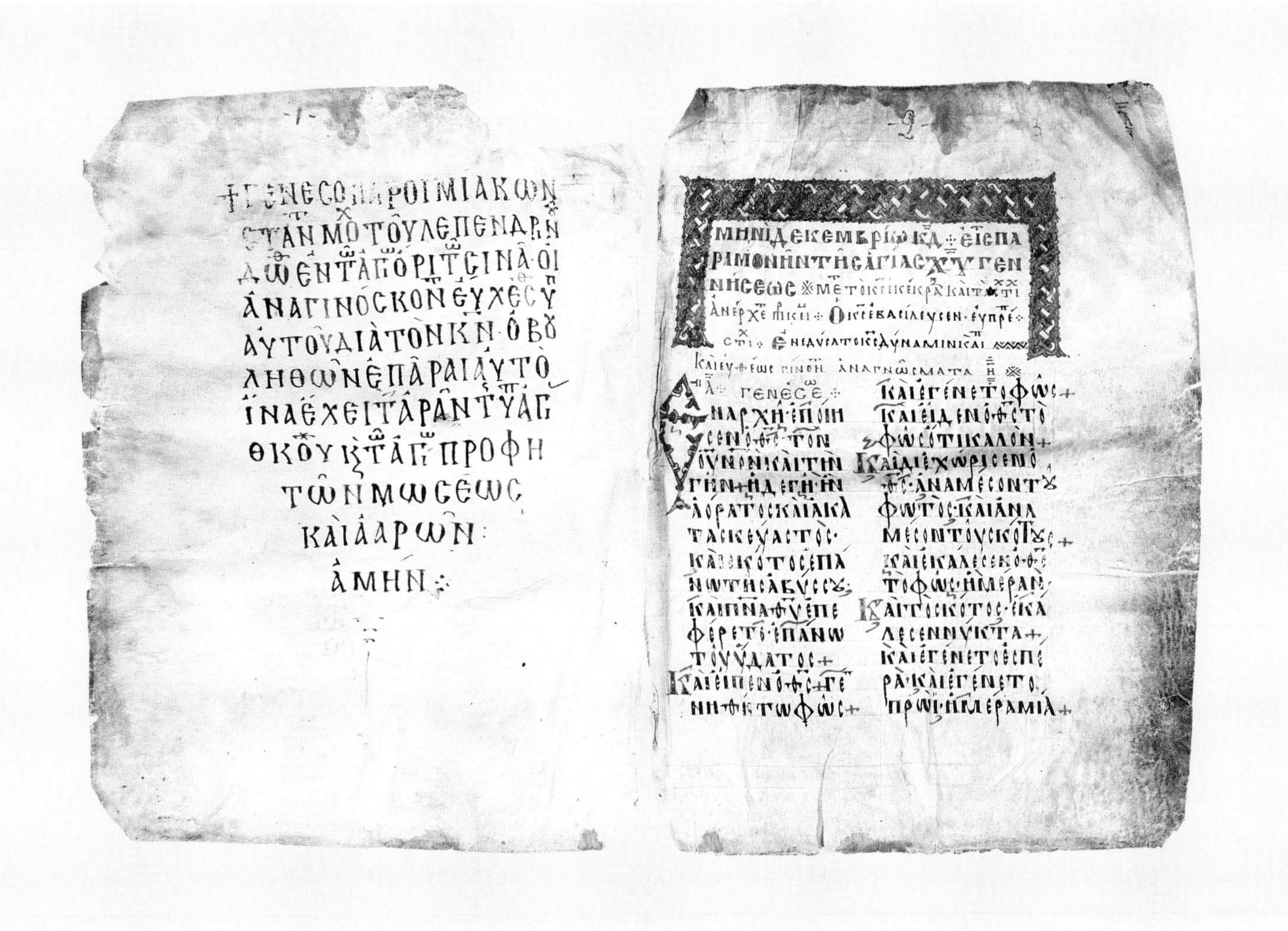

6

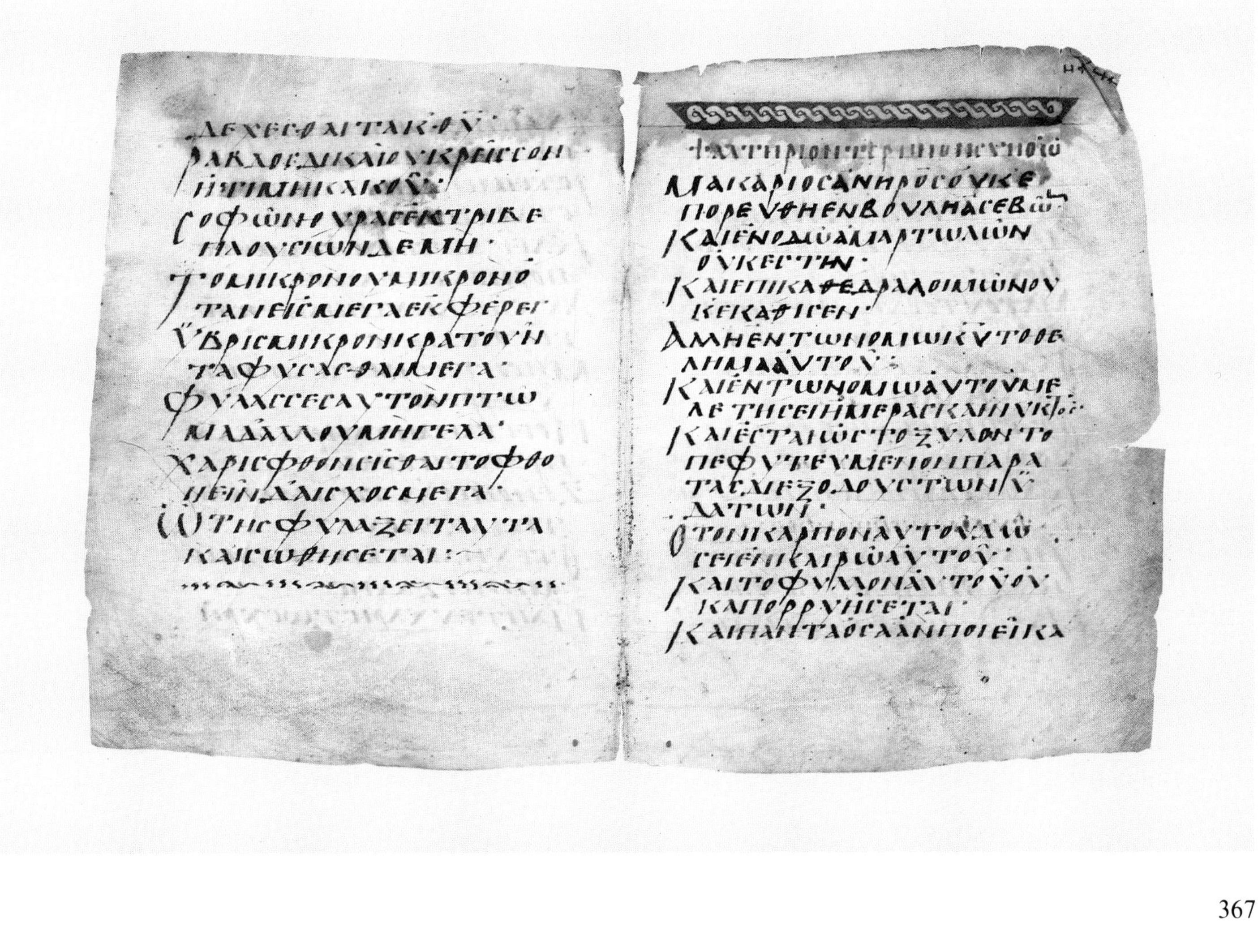

7. *Holy Bible - The Apostolic Fathers. 'Codex Sinaiticus' (36×32.5 cm., New Finds, no. ΜΓ1). Majuscule biblica script. Middle of the 4th century.*

8. *Papyrus fragment: Old Testament (Chronicles). 7th century.*

9. *Papyrus fragment. Part of a verse from the hymn of the Three Children and verses from the New Testament including the Gospel according to Luke (1:47 and 54-55). 6th or 7th century.*

10. *Parchment codex, Arabic (26.7×18.5 cm., New Finds no. 52). The Apostle Paul's Epistle to the Romans. 9th-10th century (?).*

11. *Paper codex, Arabic (30.5×20.5 cm., Old Collection, no. 343, f. 13ʳ). St. John Climacus. 1612.*

12. *Lectionary. Parchment codex, Arabic (20.5×15.7 cm., New Finds, no.14). Full-page depiction of St. John the Evangelist. 9th century.*

صورة سلم الفضايل والرهبان الصاعدين في درجا العمل وقتال الشياطين لهم وهبوط المتواينين الى الجحيم

13. *Paper codex, Arabic (30.5×20.5 cm., Old Collection, no. 343, f. 13ᵛ).*
*The Heavenly Ladder. 1612.*

16

14. Syriac manuscript (25.6×17.5 cm., no. 16, f. 56ʳ). Apology of the philosopher Aristeides to the emperor Hadrian. The full text is preserved only in Syriac translation in this manuscript. The original Greek text is lost. The manuscript also contains translations of works of Plutarch and Lucian. 8th century.

15. Syriac manuscript (24.6×17 cm., New Finds, no. M24, part of Syr. 28). Miniature illumination with a portrait of King David at the beginning of the Syriac translation of the 'Book of Kings' (III). 7th century.

16. The first page of a Slavonic Sinaitic Euchologion in 'glagolitic' script (14×11.1 cm.). Beginning of the 11th century.

17. *Syriac manuscript (17.5×13 cm., no. 111, f. 258ʳ). Paracletic Canon (Hymn of Intercession) to the Theotokos. Anthology written on Mt. Melan (Karadağ, near Antioch) in 1242.*

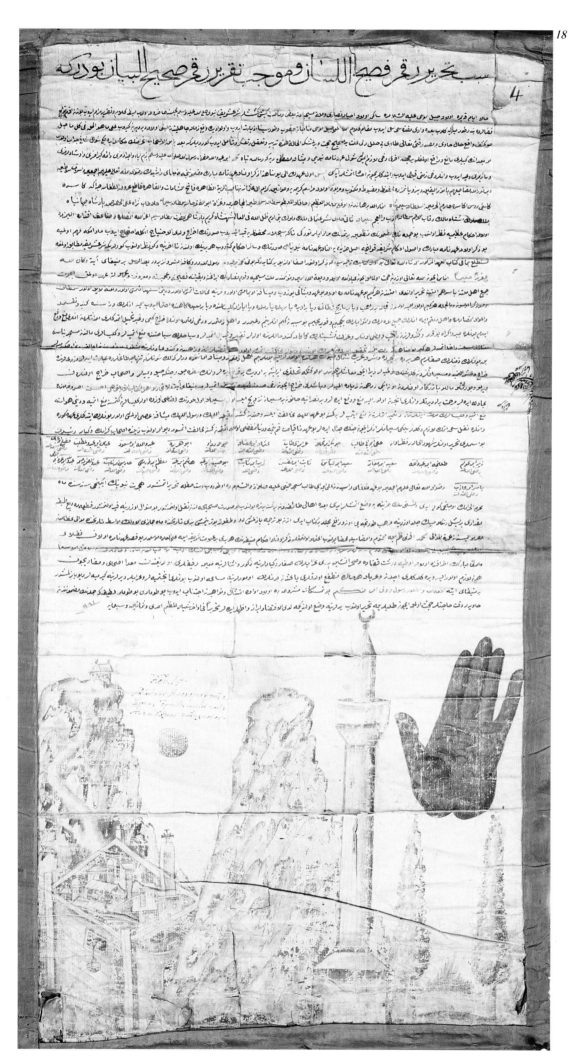

18. Turkish document, no. 4, paper (70.4×38.1 cm.). 'Achtiname' for the Sinaitic metochion at Chania. 1858.

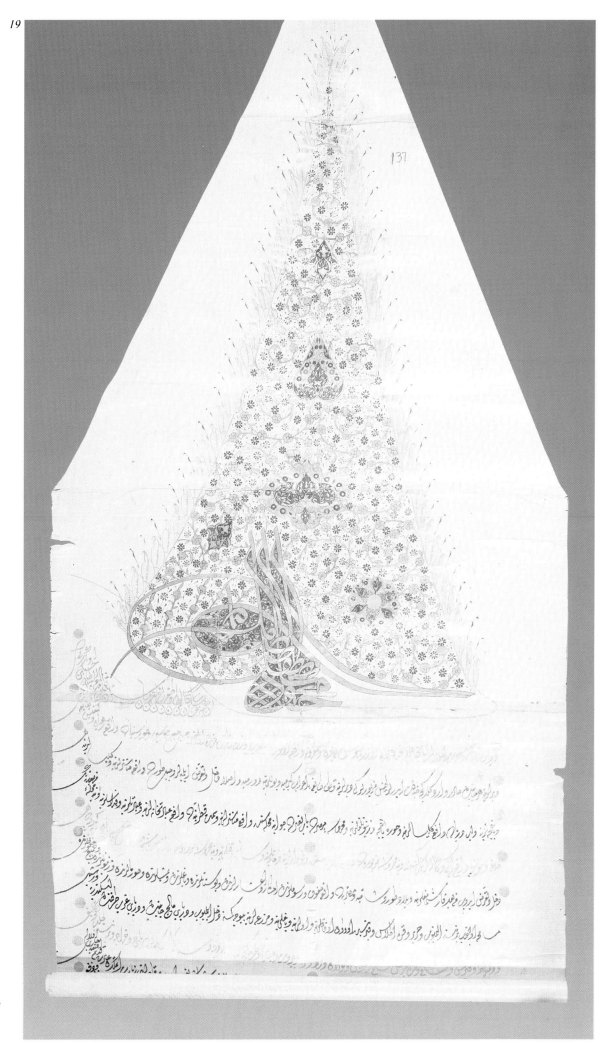

*19. Turkish document, no. 137, paper (46×12.5 cm.). Decree of Ibrahim Pasha of Egypt. The 'Tougra' (the ornate emblem and signature of the Pasha) appears at the top. 27th April, 1668.*

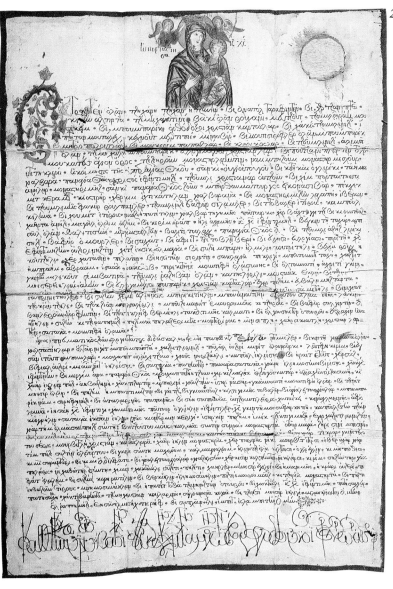

20. Paper document (73×51 cm.). 'Apantachousa'. Circular written in Turkish with Greek characters.

21. Slavonic chrysobull of the Tsar of Russia, Theodorovich Michail, no. 4-89, parchment (64.1×55.1 cm.). 1630.

22. Lead seal from a bull of a Greek document no. 4-28 (sigillion of the Ecumenical Patriarch Parthenios). Obverse with a depiction of the Virgin with Christ. 1643.

23. Seal depicted in fig. 22. Reverse. Bears the inscription: 'Parthenios, by the Grace of God, Archbishop of Constantinople, New Rome and Ecumenical Patriarch'.

24

25

24. *Rumanian document of the Voevod of Hungro-Wallachia John Constantine Basharaba. Parchment (38.5×30.4 cm.). Bears the seal in sealing wax within a metal covering. 1689.*

25. *French document, no. 241, paper (41.1×26.3 cm., p. 1). Decree assuring the Monastery's rights and privileges with the personal signature of Napoleon Bonaparte. 1798.*

26. *A page from the 'Mega Etymologicon'. The edition of 1499 produced by Nikolaos Vlastos and Zacharias Kalliergis. (Qto.).*

27. *An example of a rare printed scroll. 'The Liturgy of St. John Chrysostom'. Venice 1549.*

28. 'Works of St. John Chrysostom'. Frontispiece of the edition by Henri
Savile, printed at Eton, England, in 1613 (Qto.).

# GEOGRAPHICAL DISTRIBUTION OF THE PAST
# AND PRESENT METOCHIA OF THE MONASTERY
# OF ST. CATHERINE AT SINAI

**SINAI PENINSULA**
Pharan*
Raithou*
Island of Jotavi (*Tirān*)
Aila (*between Aqaba and Elat*)

**EGYPT**
Cairo*
Alexandria*
Damietta (*Dumyāt*)
Rosetta (*Rashīd*)
Suez

**PALESTINE (ISRAEL)**
Jerusalem
Joppa (*Jaffa*)
Gaza
Petra

**SYRIA**
Damascus
Laodicea (*Latakia*)

**LEBANON**
Beirut
Tripolis*
Tyre

**CYPRUS**
Nicosia*
Paphos
Vasilia* (*in Kyrenia*)
Rizokarpasso
Psevdas
Ha-Potami

**GREECE**

THRACE
Ferrai

MACEDONIA
Thessalonica*
Serrai
Edessa
Naoussa
Verroia
Florina
Kassandra
Misdanion

EPIRUS
Ioannina*
Parga
Arta

CENTRAL GREECE
Athens*
Piraeus
Episkopi Talantiou
Livadia
Volos
Tanagra
Euboea
Messolongi

THE PELOPONNESE
Kalamata
Kyparissia
Philiatra
Nauplion
Argos
Epidaurus
Aegion
Patras

ISLANDS
Andros
Zakynthos*
Kerkyra (*Corfu*)
Leukas
Lesbos (*Mitylene*)
Cephalonia
Samos
Santorini
Skopelos
Syros
Paros
Rhodes
Chios

CRETE
Heraklion*
Rizokastro
Chania*
Ierapetra

**TURKEY**
Constantinople*
Adrianople (*Edirne*)
Ainos (*Enez*)
Artake
Rodosto (*Tekirdağ*)
Imbros (*Imroz*)
Smyrna (*Izmir*)
Vourla
Attaleia (*Antalya*)
Kioutacheia (*Kütahya*)
Tarsus

**RUSSIA - GEORGIA**
Kiev
Bessarabia
Tiflis (*Tbilisi*)

**RUMANIA**
Bucharest
Iaşi
Galaţi
Timişoara
Rimniko (*Rîmnicu*)
Martzineni
Focşani
Formosa or Balika

**YUGOSLAVIA**
Belgrade
Sarajevo
Monastir (*Bitola*)
Tomblitsa

**BULGARIA**
Philippoupolis (*Plovdiv*)
Tyrnovo (*Veliko Tŭrnovo*)

**ITALY**
Venice
Livorno
Sicily

**FRANCE**
Rouen
Trèves
Lyon

**INDIA**
Calcutta
Bombay

*An asterisk (\*) indicates metochia which belong today to the Monastery.*

# GLOSSARY

*Achtiname*, the 'Testament' of the Prophet Mohammed, given by him to the monks of the Sinai Monastery, in order to protect them from danger and exempt them from heavy taxation.

*aer*, a gold-embroidered liturgical veil, used for covering the eucharistic vessels.

*Akathistos* (Hymn), a hymn of 24 strophes (oikoi), sung, all standing, on the Saturday of the 5th week in Lent, in honour of the Virgin Mary. It was probably written in the 6th century and a second prelude was added to it at the beginning of the 7th century.

*alms mission* (*zeteiai*), fund raising missions by itinerant clergy. This practice was instituted by the Orthodox Church during the period of Turkish rule to enable it to meet its economic needs and obligations.

*analavos*, a garment decorated with emblems, worn by monks of the Great Schema.

*Anapeson*, the depiction of the Christ Child reclining with His head in His right hand. Normally, the figure is accompanied by two adoring angels in a deesis pose and, more rarely, by the Virgin. The theme is inspired by a prophecy of Jacob *(... laying himself down he slept as a Lion and as a Lion-cub...*, Gen. 49.9).

*anthivolon*, a template produced by the hagiographer based on older models. The pattern to be applied was outlined on the anthivolon with small perforations. An application of charcoal dust on the anthivolon thus left the desired pattern.

*archimandrite*, an honorary title given by the patriarch or a bishop to *hegoumenoi* (abbots) and important *hieromonks* (priest-monks).

*argyronima*, thread, usually silk, with two very thin strips of silver or imitation silver foil wound round it, often loosely enough to allow the coloured silk core to show through.

*artoklasia*, the vessel where five loaves of bread, oil, grain and wine are placed during the ceremony bearing the same name, which takes place on the eve but also on the day of Great Feasts.

*artophorion*, the vessel where the eucharistic bread is kept for use in extraordinary circumstances.

*avantarion*, codex in which are written the possessions of the monastery.

*basilica*, a church usually longitudinal, and composed of a nave and aisles.

*Bema*, the central section of the Sanctuary of a church, where the liturgy is performed.

*Canon tables*, concordance of events in the Four Gospels arranged in tabular form, established in the 4th century by Eusebius of Caesarea.

*chiton*, Greek garment fastened on the shoulders and tied around the waist, usually worn as an undergarment.

*chlamys*, mantle or cape held by a clasp over the right shoulder, serving as outermost garment.

*chrysobull*, an imperial decree, granting privileges, written on a *parchment* scroll, with an attached gold (= *chryso*) seal from which the decree type takes its name.

*chrysonima*, the same as *argyronima* but with gold or gilt foil instead of silver.

*ciborium*, a domed canopy standing above the altar on four columns.

*closure*, the forced closure of the Monastery and the removal of the monks to another place in time of invasion.

*colobium*, short sleeveless tunic worn by Christ in early representations of the Crucifixion.

*Deesis*, a representation of Christ flanked by the Blessed Virgin and John the Baptist, interceding for the salvation of mankind, on either side of Him.

*Descent into Hell* (*Anastasis*), Resurrection. In Orthodox iconography the *Anastasis* is represented by the scene of Christ's Descent into Hell.

*Dikaios*, a monk chosen each year in a monastery, competent to act with the authority of an hegumen.

*Dodekaorton* (Twelve Feasts), the twelve most important episodes in the life and death on earth of Christ and His Mother (Annunciation, Nativity, Presentation in the Temple, Baptism, Transfiguration, Raising of Lazarus, Entry into Jerusalem, Crucifixion, Anastasis, Ascension, Pentecost, Dormition of the Virgin); in particular, such a set of icons on the *iconostasis* and elsewhere.

*Dormition*, of the Virgin, the death of the Blessed Virgin, similar to the Assumption in the West.

*double-headed eagle*, symbol of the Byzantine Empire.

*enamels*, a) 'champlevé: opaque enamel is placed within sockets carved into metal (usually copper). After firing, the enamel is polished down to the level of the metal.
b) 'basse-taille': The pattern is engraved or chased in gold or silver and then covered with translucent enamel, so as to be visible below it. The depth of the relief determines the intensity of the colours.
c) 'ronde bosse': the enamel covers with successive layers irregular or convex surfaces of gold or silver. Opaque white enamel is predominantly used. This technique was perfected by Parisian goldsmiths in the second half of the 14th century.

*Encaenia*, the ceremony of the consecration of a church.

*enkolpion*, pectoral medallion, pendentive, worn by ecclesiastical dignitaries.

*Entrance*, Little, a procession of the priest carrying the Gospel Book through the church to the altar in the Divine Liturgy, corresponding to the introit in the Western rite. The Great Entrance is the offertory procession in the Divine Liturgy, in which the bread and wine are brought from the *prothesis* through the naos to the altar.

*epigonation*, a lozenge-shaped piece of stiff material, suspended at the corner by a ribbon and hung at knee-height worn by ecclesiastical dignitaries.

*epimanikion*, a gold-embroidered vestment covering the foreams of the priest.

*Epitaphios*, the holy shroud used in reenacting the burial of Christ on Good Friday. It bears a representation of the dead Christ.

*epithema*, applied panel of gold-embroidered silk.

*epitrachelion*, strip of cloth worn around the neck of the priest and falling in front of the breast.

*Etoimasia* (Hetoimasia), 'Preparation', representation of a throne with a Gospel Book on it and the symbols of the Passion and sometimes the Dove, symbolizing the Second Coming.

*Eucharist*, The consecration of the Bread and Wine in the Orthodox Liturgy.

*Euchologion*, a prayer book, containing the order of prayers for the seven sacraments, and other prayers for various occasions.

*Gospel Lectionary*, the book with excerpts (lections) of the Four Gospels rearranged so as to conform to the sequence in which they will be read in the church over the course of the year. A *Lectionary* begins with the passage of St. John, read on East Sunday, and continues in order: Matthew, Luke, Mark.

*hegoumenos*, the head of a religious community, the first person of authority in a monastery, roughly equivalent to 'abbot'.

*heirmoi*, original ecclesiastic hymns with musical notation.

*Heirmologion*, a book which contains the *heirmoi*.

*hieromonk*, a monk who is also a priest (priest-monk).

*himation*, a garment consisting of an oblong piece of cloth draped over the left shoulder and around the body.

*Horologion*, a book containing the daily offices.

*hypertimos*, a title given to distinguished Metropolitans of the Eastern Church. It is still kept today as an honorary title without, however, conferring specific rights or authority.

*iconostasis*, partition with doors, covered with icons in a fixed order, which separates the nave from the Sanctuary in an Eastern Orthodox church. Similar to a chancel screen.

*initial* (letter), a large letter beginning a text, a division or a paragraph.

*kathisma*, dependency of a monastery.

*katholikon*, monastery church (the main church, if more than one).

*Kontakarion*, book containing *kontakia*, i.e. ecclesiastical hymns.

*Liturgy of the Presanctified*, the liturgy in which the consecrated Host of the previous liturgy is used during Lent, except Saturdays, Sundays and the day of Annunciation (if it falls during Lent).

*mandyas*, a long outer garment resembling a cope or cloak.

*maphorion*, a tunic, of Syrian origin, covering the head and the shoulders, worn by women.

*megalynarion*, ecclesiastical verses sung during feasts of Our Lord or the Virgin — and exceptionally — or name days of the saints.

*Melismos*, the breaking of the Bread. Iconographical type of the Christ Child in a paten, on the altar, which is usually depicted in the Bema conch.

*Menologion*, a) Ecclesiastical book containing the Lives of the Saints in the series in which they appear in the Festal Calendar. Manuscripts of Menologia were often illuminated with depictions of the saints and scenes of feasts; b) A type of icon usually in several panels, with portraits of the saints and more rarely with feast scenes according to the order of the liturgical year.

*metochion*, an extraterritorial possession of a monastery, whether a dependent cell or an estate, usually with its own church or chapel.

*mitre*, an episcopal cylindrical head-cover of wool or velvet — or metal —, with applied panels of gold-embroidered silk.

*narthex*, a vestibule or portico at the west end of an Orthodox church.

*Octateuch*, the first eight books of the Old Testament.

*omophorion*, the distinguishing vestment of a bishop. It consists of a broad band that encircles the shoulders of the prelate, with one end falling in front and the other behind.

*orarion*, the deacon's stole, worn hanging over the left shoulder.

*palimpsest*, writing material which has been used more than once, the earlier text having been erased.

*panagiarion*, a small, initially deep, disc made of semi-precious stone, ivory or metal for the raising of the Host (Artos) in honour of the Theotokos during a special service. From the 14th century it was also used as an enkolpion, a symbol of high ecclesiastical rank.

*Pantocrator* ('All powerful'), epithet of Christ. A stern-featured representation of Christ as 'Ruler of All', as found in the dome of most Byzantine churches.

*parchment*, the skin of a sheep, goat or other animal, prepared as a writing material.

*paten*, a dish or plate used in the Eucharistic service.

*Pentecostarion*, book containing the offices used during the period from Easter to the 8th day after Pentecost (Whit Sunday).

*pentelia*, suspended decorative elements such as pearls, precious stones, small crosses, and letters with symbolic associations.

*phelonion*, the bell-shaped chasuble, worn by the priest.

*podea*, ecclesiastical decorated drapery, hung below the icons.

*poloi*, applied panels of gold-embroidered cloth sewn on the lower corners of an episcopal vestment.

*polykandelon*, a silver or bronze support for several smaller lamps.

*pomata*, the same as poloi but sewn on the upper corners of the vestment.

*potamoi* ('rivers'), the two fringes at the end of a vestment.

*Prodromos*, the 'Precursor' or 'Forerunner', St. John the Baptist.

*Proskomide*, the first part of the Orthodox liturgy, in which bread and wine are offered to God before they are consecrated.

*Prothesis*, a) the Offertory ceremony at the beginning of the Divine Liturgy; b) an apse or recess at the east end of a church, north of the Bema, in which the Offertory ceremony takes place.

*pseudo-cufic*, imitation of a form of Arabic script for decorative purposes.

*pyle*, the curtain which fills the gap of the Central entrance to the Sanctuary, above the low double-doors.

*Red Stone*, a holy relic for the Byzantines. The stone had been brought to Constantinople from Ephesos by the Emperor Manuel Comnenos, who carried it himself from the Boukoleon harbour to the Pharos church. On the Emperor's death and internment in the Pantocrator Monastery, the plaque was removed thither. From this time, artists became accustomed to depict it in representations of the Threnos (Lamentation).

*sakkos*, the most widely used vestment of a bishop, a short tunic with wide half-sleeves.

*scriptorium*, the workshop of copyists of manuscripts.

*sigillion*, patriarchal edict.

*skete*, an idiorrhythmic community consisting of monks living in houses outside the parent monastery.

*staurotheke*, reliquary for a fragment of the True Cross.

*sticharion*, priestly vestment common to all ranks. A footlength chiton with sleeves, worn under all the other vestments.

*stichera*, short hymns following verses from the Psalms in the Divine Office.

*Sticherarion*, book containing stichera, i.e. short ecclesiastical poems.

*Synaxarion*, book containing short notices about saints or feasts, arranged according to the calendar.

*synthronon*, in the church, the bench or benches reserved for the clergy arranged either in a semicircle (sometimes amphitheatrically) in the apse, or in straight rows on either side of the Bema.

*templon*, see *iconostasis*.

*tetravelon*, decorated curtains hung from the four arches of the ciborium.

*thorakion*, ovoid piece of cloth, part of the attire of Byzantine empresses.

*tirtiri* (gold or silver bullion), a very fine coil of gold or silver wire that can be cut off at the required length and is attached to the ground material by a thread passing through the hollow centre.

*Triodion*, book containing the proper services for the period beginning the 4th Sunday before Lent to Easter Eve.

*troparion*, a short hymn.

*Typikon*, a) a book containing rules and rubrics for the divine offices; b) a book containing the rules and regulations of a monastery.

*vlattion*, rich Byzantine purple fabric.

*Voevod*, a title assumed by the rulers and princes of Moldavia and Wallachia, formerly the title of a military commander or civilian governor.

*zodia*, the symbols of the Evangelists: eagle, lion, angel, calf.

# ABBREVIATIONS

*AA* = Άρχαιολογικὰ Άνάλεκτα.
*AAA* = Άρχαιολογικὰ Άνάλεκτα Άθηνῶν.
*ΑΔ* = Άρχαιολογικὸν Δελτίον.
*AE* = Άρχαιολογικὴ Έφημερίς.
*CArch* = Cahiers Archéologiques.
*DOP* = Dumbarton Oaks Papers.
*ΔΧΑΕ* = Δελτίον Χριστιανικῆς Άρχαιολογικῆς Έταιρείας.
*ΕΕΒΣ* = Έπετηρὶς Έταιρείας Βυζαντινῶν Σπουδῶν.
*ΘΗΕ* = Θρησκευτικὴ καὶ Ήθικὴ Έγκυκλοπαιδεία.
*OCP* = Orientalia Christiana Periodica.

Amantos, *Σύντομος ίστορία* = C. Amantos, *Σύντομος ίστορία τῆς ίερᾶς Μονῆς τοῦ Σινᾶ, Έλληνικά*, Supplement, no. 3, Thessalonica 1953.

Belting, *Bild und Kult* = H. Belting, *Bild und Kult. Eine Geschichte des Bildes vor dem Zeitalter der Kunst*, Munich 1990.

*Βυζαντινὴ - Μεταβυζαντινὴ Τέχνη* = *Βυζαντινὴ καὶ Μεταβυζαντινὴ Τέχνη (Byzantine and Post-Byzantine Art)* (exhibition Catalogue), Athens 1986.

Chatzidakis, *Icônes* = M. Chatzidakis, *Icônes de Saint-Georges des Grecs et de la collection de l'Institut*, Venice 1962.

Chatzidakis, «Recherches» = M. Chatzidakis, «Recherches sur la peinture de Théophane le Crétois», *DOP* 23-24 (1969-70), pp. 311-352.

Chatzidakis, «Τοιχογραφίες Σινὰ» = M. Chatzidakis, «Τοιχογραφίες στὴ Μονὴ τῆς Άγίας Αἰκατερίνης στὸ Σινὰ», *ΔΧΑΕ* per. 4, 6 (1970-72), pp. 205-232.

Chatzidakis, *Σταυρονικήτα* = M. Chatzidakis, *Ό Κρητικὸς ζωγράφος Θεοφάνης, οί τοιχογραφίες τῆς Ί. Μονῆς Σταυρονικήτα*, Mount Athos 1986.

Chatzidakis, *Έλληνες ζωγράφοι* = M. Chatzidakis, *Έλληνες ζωγράφοι μετὰ τὴν Άλωση (1450-1830)*, I, Athens 1987.

Eckenstein, *History of Sinai* = L. Eckenstein, *A History of Sinai*, London 1921.

*Εἰκόνες Κρητικῆς Σχολῆς* = Nano Chatzidakis, *Εἰκόνες Κρητικῆς Σχολῆς - Μουσεῖο Μπενάκη (Icons of the Cretan School - Benaki Museum)*, Athens 1983.

*Εἰκόνες Πάτμου* = M. Chatzidakis, *Εἰκόνες τῆς Πάτμου, (Icons of Patmos)*, ed. National Bank of Greece, Athens 1977 (engl. ed. 1985).

Forsyth 1968 = G. H. Forsyth, «The Monastery of St. Catherine at Mount Sinai. The Church and the Fortress of Justinian», *DOP* 22 (1968), pp. 3-19.

Forsyth - Weitzmann, *The Monastery* = G. H. Forsyth - K. Weitzmann, *The Monastery of St. Catherine at Mount Sinai: The Church and Fortress of Justinian* (Ann Arbor, The University of Michigan), n.d. [1973].

Galey, *Sinai* = J. Galey, *Sinai and the Monastery of St. Catherine*. Introd. G. H. Forsyth and K. Weitzmann, Massada, Israel 1980.

*Holy Image* = *Holy Image, Holy Space, Icons and Frescoes from Greece*, ed. Greek Ministry of Culture, Byzantine Museum of Athens, Athens 1988.

*IEE* = *Ίστορία τοῦ Έλληνικοῦ Έθνους (History of the Hellenic Nation)*, Athens 1970-80.

Jorga, *Byzance* = N. Jorga, *Byzance après Byzance*, Bucharest 1971.

Kartsonis, *Anastasis* = A. Kartsonis, *Anastasis, The making of an Image*, Princeton 1986.

Mouriki, «Thirteenth-Century Icon Painting» = D. Mouriki, «Thirteenth - Century Icon painting in Cyprus», *Griffon* N.S. 1-2 (1985-86), pp. 9-80.

Mouriki, «Four Thirteenth - Century Sinai Icons» = D. Mouriki, «Four Thirteenth - Century Sinai Icons by the Painter Peter», *Studenica et l'art byzantin autour de l'année 1200* (Colloques scientifiques de l'Académie Serbe des Sciences et des Arts, vol. XLI, Classe des Sciences historiques, vol. 11), Belgrade 1988, pp. 329 - 347.

Rabino, *Le Monastère* = M.H.L. Rabino, *Le Monastère de Sainte - Catherine du Mont Sinaï*, Cairo 1938.

Soteriou, *Εἰκόνες* = G. and M. Soteriou, *Εἰκόνες τῆς Μονῆς Σινᾶ*, vol. I (plates), Athens 1956, vol. II (text), Athens 1958.

*St. Catherine's Monastery* = *The Monastery of St. Catherine on Mount Sinai*, ed. by the Monastery of Sinai, Glyka Nera, Athens 1985.

Weitzmann, «Thirteenth-Century Crusader Icons» = K. Weitzmann, «Thirteenth-Century Crusader Icons on Mount Sinai», *Art Bulletin* XIV (1963), pp. 179-203.

Weitzmann, «Icon Painting» = K. Weitzmann, «Icon Painting in the Crusader Kingdom», *DOP* 20 (1966), pp. 51-83.

Weitzmann, «Proceedings» = K. Weitzmann, «The Mosaic in St. Catherine's Monastery on Mount Sinai», *Proceedings of the American Philosophical Society*, 110, no. 6 (1966).

Weitzmann, «Byzantium and the West» = K. Weitzmann, «Byzantium and the West around the Year 1200», *The Year 1200: A Symposium*, The Metropolitan Museum of Art, N. York 1975, pp. 53-73.

Weitzmann, *Icon* = K. Weitzmann, *The Icon, Holy Images–Sixth to Fourteenth Century*, N. York 1978.

Weitzmann, *Ikonen* = K. Weitzmann, *Ikonen aus dem Katharinenkloster auf dem Berge Sinai*, Berlin 1980.

Weitzmann, *Studies* = K. Weitzmann, *Studies in the Arts at Sinai*, Princeton 1982.

Weitzmann, «Crusader Icons» = K. Weitzmann, «Crusader Icons and Maniera Greca», *Byzanz und der Westen. Studien zur Kunst des Europäischen Mittelalters*, ed. I. Hutter, Vienna 1984, pp. 143-170.

Weitzmann, «Icon Programs» = K. Weitzmann, «Icon Programs of the 12th and the 13th Centuries at Sinai», *ΔΧΑΕ* per. 4, 12 (1984-86), pp. 63-116.

Weitzmann et al., *Frühe Ikonen* = K. Weitzmann, M. Chatzidakis, Kr. Miatev, Sv. Radojčić, *Frühe Ikonen – Sinai, Griechenland, Bulgarien, Jugoslawien*, Munich 1965.

Weitzmann et al., *The Icon* = K. Weitzmann, G. Alibegašvili, A. Volskaya, M. Chatzidakis, G. Babić, M. Alpatov, Th. Voinescu, *The Icon*, N. York 1982.

Weitzmann - Ševčenko, «Moses Cross» = K. Weitzmann - I. Ševčenko, «The Moses Cross at Sinai», *DOP* 17 (1963), pp. 385-398.

Xyngopoulos, *Κατάλογος* = A. Xyngopoulos, *Κατάλογος τῶν εἰκόνων τοῦ Μουσείου Μπενάκη*, Athens 1936.

Xyngopoulos, *Σχεδίασμα* = A. Xyngopoulos, *Σχεδίασμα ίστορίας τῆς θρησκευτικῆς ζωγραφικῆς μετὰ τὴν Άλωσιν*, Athens 1957.

# NOTES - BIBLIOGRAPHY

\* Apart from the select bibliography provided for each chapter, a general bibliography on Sinai can be found in Sp. D. Kontoyiannis, «Γενικὴ βιβλιογραφία περὶ Σινᾶ», in *Πανηγυρικὸς τόμος ἐπὶ τῇ 1400ῇ ἀμφιετηρίδι τῆς Ἱερᾶς Μονῆς τοῦ Σινᾶ*, Athens 1971, pp. 335-566 and «Συμπλήρωμα εἰς τὴν Γενικὴν περὶ Σινᾶ βιβλιογραφίαν», in *Θεολογία* 43 (1972), pp. 773-791.

## ARCHITECTURE

**1.** R. Pococke, *A Description of the East and some other countries*, vol. I, London 1743, p. 149 ff., fig. 56. An improved plan, now in the Library, was drawn up in 1813 and published for the first time in Rabino, *Le Monastère*, p. 10, fig. 4.

**2.** Forsyth-Weitzmann, *The Monastery*, plates. Forsyth 1968, p. 3 ff., and pl. 1; see also P. Grossmann, «Neue baugeschichtliche Untersuchungen im Katharinenkloster im Sinai», *AA* (1988), p. 543 ff.

**3.** In particular from Egeria (Etheria), the Aquitanian pilgrim from Jerusalem; text ed. in: P. Geyer, *Itinera Hierosolymitae saeculi IIII-VIII*, 1898 (repr. 1964), p. 37 ff., esp. pp. 39-45.

**4.** The first researches were carried out by Israeli scholars; see Y. Tsafrir, «Monks and monasteries in South Sinai», *Qadmoniot* 9 (1970), pp. 2-18 (in Hebrew). J. Finkelstein, «Byzantine monastic remains in the southern Sinai», *DOP* 39 (1985), p. 42 ff.

**5.** Ammonios, *Narrationes* 2 (ed. D. G. Tsamis, Thessalonica 1989), p. 194 ff., esp. p. 196, and Egeria (Etheria) (ed. P. Geyer), p. 42 ff.

**6.** Ammonios, op. cit., 4.20, p. 216 and Grossmann, *AA* (1988), p. 557.

**7.** Recently P. Grossmann, «Early Christian ruins in Wādī Fayrān», *ASAE* 70 (1984/85), p. 75 ff.

**8.** Eutychios of Alexandria, *Annali* (*CSCO* 472 [1985], new edition and German translation of selected passages by M. Breydy), p. 89.

**9.** The tradition which ascribes the building of this tower to the Empress Helen is unfounded. The Empress never visited this region and when the monk Julian of Saba visited Mount Moses in the reign of the Emperor Julian (360-363) he met no one (Theodoretos, *Hist. rel.*, 2.13). Even less plausible is the view that anchorites were already established there in the lifetime of St. Helen.

**10.** Several examples from Kellia as quoted by D. Weidmann in: R. Kasser, *EK 8184, Survey archéologique des Kellia (Basse-Égypte). Rapport de la campagne 1981*, Louvain 1983, p. 412 ff.

**11.** H. C. Butler, amongst many examples in Syria, notes only two towers with an entrance on the first floor; idem, «Syria», *Publication of the Princeton University Archaeological Expeditions to Syria in 1904-5 and 1909, III, Architecture, section B. Northern Syria*, Princeton 1920, p. 84, fig. 92 ff. (Iʿgāz) and p. 138, fig. 160 (Qūkabā).

**12.** A similar solution is put forward by Butler, op. cit., *II section A*, p. 115, fig. 93, and for Sabḥāh tower (Ḥaurān).

**13.** Procopios, *De aedificiis*, 5.8; Eutychios, *Annali* 253 (=*CSCO* 472 [1985], new edition and German translation by M. Breydy), p. 88 ff. For a critique of the two texts see P. Mayerson, «Procopios or Eutychius on the construction of the Monastery at Mount Sinai: which is the more reliable source?», *Basor* 230 (1978), p. 33.

**14.** There is otherwise no explanation for the misunderstanding of Procopios who described the Monastery as if it were a fortress.

**15.** In a military fortress the corner towers were used for posting cannons, see S. Johnson, *Late Roman Fortifications*, London 1983, p. 38 ff.

**16.** This was established and published for the first time by I. Demakopoulos in *ΔΧΑΕ* 3, ser. 9 (1977-79), pp. 261-301.

**17.** Demakopoulos, ibid., pl. 107a. More windows of this sort must exist further to the east, but this section is still deeply buried.

**18.** Examples of similarly shaped windows have been noted in the eastern ends of the church at the Monastery of Shenute at Suhāğ; see P. Grossmann, «New Observations in the church and sanctuary of Dayr Anbā Šinūda — the so-called White Monastery at Suhāğ», *ASAE* 70 (1984-85), p. 69 ff.

**19.** See the examples of the installations of anchorites in Kellia: J. Jarry in: F. Daumas - A. Guillaumont, *Kellia I Kôm 219*, Cairo 1969, p. 58 ff. (room 19) and p. 76 (room 42).

**20.** T. F. Mathews, «'Private' liturgy in Byzantine Architecture: toward a re-appraisal», *CArch* 30 (1982), p. 125 ff., fig. 8 ff.

**21.** For the siting of latrines in the antique military camps see H. v. Petrikowitz, *Die Innenbauten römischer Legionslager während der Prinzipatszeit*, Opladen 1975, p. 106.

**22.** A detailed description of the church gives Forsyth 1968, p. 7 ff.

**23.** Towards the end of the 19th century a bell tower was added to the northern tower.

**24.** Forsyth holds a different view: Forsyth 1968, p. 11, note 13.

**25.** More photographs are in Forsyth-Weitzmann, *The Monastery*, pls. 43-57.

**26.** I. Ševčenko, *DOP* 20 (1966), p. 262, inscripts. 3-5.

**27.** See also Forsyth-Weitzmann, *The Monastery*, p. 8.

**28.** The missing panels were detached in the 10th century and re-used for the steps in front of the choir stalls.

**29.** Forsyth - Weitzmann, *The Monastery*, pl. 89A.

**30.** Procopios in his *De aedificiis* V9 brings still the original name 'Theotokos'.

**31.** This is clear from the inaccessible middle floor of the tower.

**32.** It is quite incomprehensible to me how Forsyth (Forsyth 1968) in p. 11, note 13 regards these irregular niches as original. Similarly, there is no truth in the suggestion of T. F. Mathews in *CArch* 30 (1982), p. 130 that the masonry on the inside of the wall consists of rubble and that for that reason the niches must be the real ones.

**33.** Forsyth, in Forsyth 1968, places its building immediately after the completion of the nave.

**34.** Good examples of how the porch might have looked are to be found in the side doors of the mortuary church 'extra muros' at Korykos; see E. Herzfeld - S. Guyer, «Meriamlik und Korykos», *MAMA* II (1930) p. 130 ff, figs. 133, 134 and in the chapel of Batūta in Northern Syria, H. C. Butler, *Early Churches in Syria* (repr. 1969), p. 200, fig. 204.

**35.** The accepted view of Forsyth (Forsyth 1968), p. 13 ff. and G. Descoeudres, *Die Pastophorien im Syrisch-byzantinischen Osten*, Wiesbaden 1983, p. 21 ff. for the liturgical use of them as an ambulatory has thus to be refused.

**36.** Forsyth 1968, p. 5 remarks 'but it could have been before 1216', and p. 14 'key to plan in fig. 2'.

**37.** References on the period of the Persian attacks are to be found in R. Solzbacher, *Mönche, Pilger und Sarazenen*, Altenberge 1989, p. 277 ff.

**38.** Theodoretos, *Hist. Rel.*, 2.13.

**39.** Ed. P. Geyer, *Itinera Hierosolymitae saeculi IIII-VIII*, 1898 (repr. 1964), pp. 1-5 must be the same church as Egeria saw and described as the 'ecclesia non grandis', op. cit., p. 39, pl. 24; the view of Solzbacher, op. cit., p. 410 ff., fig. 5 that the ruins of the larger church visible today belong to the one built by Julian, cannot be upheld, since by the date of his visit there would not have been the time to construct a larger church.

**40.** This relationship is reported by Eutychios, *CSCO* 472 (ed. Breydy) 253 (in translation p. 89), but it is also concluded by the archaeological evidence.

**41.** According to V. Benešević, *Byzantion* 1(1924), p. 149, note 1, this event took place on 11.12.1782.

**42.** L. Prévost, *Le Sinaï hier... aujourd'hui*, Paris 1936, fig. on p. 281.

**43.** For the reconstruction of the Justinian church see P. Grossmann, *ASAE* 72 (1987) (forthcoming) and idem in *Actes du XIe Congrès International de l'Archéologie Chrétienne, Lyon 21-28 Septembre 1986*, Paris 1989, vol. II, p. 1906, fig. 28; another somewhat faulty plan is published by Solzbacher, op. cit., p. 410, fig. 5.

**44.** Solzbacher, op. cit., p. 411.

**45.** Thus the 6th-century dating suggested by Forsyth 1968, p. 7 cannot be supported.

**46.** The older refectory may have stood in the same place, described in 1217 by Meister Thetmar, see S. de Sandoli, ed. *Itinera Hierosolymitana crucesignatorum (saec. XII-XIII)*, vol. III, p. 277, Latin text with Italian translation.

## MOSAICS

**1.** The early reproductions by drawings, lithographs and photographs which were quite unsatisfactory are described by the author in Weitzmann, «Proceedings», pp. 393-405.

**2.** K. Weitzmann, in Forsyth - Weitzmann, *The Monastery*.

**3.** The restorer was Ernest Hawkins, known through his activities at the Saint Sophia at Constantinople. His work at Sinai is described in Weitzmann, «Proceedings», p. 397 ff.

**4.** That this facility of using in the same work of art different modes of expression is by no means due to special gifts of the Sinai mosaic's artist; that it was commonplace in Byzantine art at various times and in different media, has been discussed by K. Weitzmann, «The Classical in Byzantine Art as a Mode of Individual Expression», in *Byzantine Art, An European Art. Lectures*, Athens 1966, p. 151ff. and esp. p. 170 and figs. 124-125.

**5.** For Jonah, e.g., Forsyth - Weitzmann, *The Monastery*, pl. CXIX A; cf. the miniatures in the Turin codex Bibl. Nat. cod. B.I. 2 (H. Belting and G. Cavallo, *Die Bibel des Niketas*, Wiesbaden 1979, pl. 7).

**6.** Forsyth - Weitzmann, *The Monastery*, pl. CXIX B.

**7.** K. Weitzmann, «The Mandylion and Constantine Porphyrogenitos», *CArch* 9(1960), p. 182 and figs. 17 and 19.

**8.** Forsyth-Weitzmann, *The Monastery*, pls. CLXXII-CLXXIII.

**9.** Ibid., pls. CXXII-CXXIII.

**10.** Ibid., pls. CXXIV-CXXV.

**11.** Weitzmann (note 4), *Byzantine Art, An European Art. Lectures*, pp. 171-172 and figs. 132-134.

**12.** L. Ginzberg, *Legends of the Jews*, vol. 3, p. 119, and vol. 6, p. 50, note 259.

**13.** Weitzmann, «Proceedings», p. 400 and fig. 15.

**14.** E. Dinkler, «Das Apsismosaik von S. Apollinare in Classe», *Wissenschaftliche Abhandlungen der Arbeitsgemeinschaft für Forschung des Landes Nordrhein - Westfalen*, vol. 29, Cologne and Opladen 1904, p. 26 and fig. 3. Here the difference of the two mosaics is clearly defined.

**15.** K. Weitzmann and H. L. Kessler, *The Frescoes of the Dura Synagogue and Christian Art*, Washington, D.C.: Dumbarton Oaks 1990, p. 34 ff. and figs. 41-42; p. 52 ff. and figs. 74-75; p. 170 and figs. 201-202.

**16.** Forsyth - Weitzmann, *The Monastery*, pl. C.

**17.** Rabino, *Le Monastère*, p. 30 and p. 105, note 57.

**18.** Forsyth-Weitzmann, *The Monastery*, pls. CXXX, CXXXII A and CXXXIII A.

**19.** Ibid., pls. CXXXI, CXXXII B and CXXXIII B. K. Weitzmann, «The Jephthah Panel in the Bema of the Church of St. Catherine's Monastery on Mount Sinai», *DOP* 18 (1964), p. 63 ff.

**20.** K. Weitzmann, *The Monastery of Saint Catherine at Mount Sinai. The Icons. I: From the Sixth to the Tenth Century*, Princeton 1976, pls. I ff.

**21.** Weitzmann, «Icon Programs», p. 63 ff.

## WALL PAINTINGS

**1.** *Exodus*, 3.2.

**2.** The important contributions of Kurt Weitzmann to Byzantine art history are well known and include, amongst other studies, a presentation on the 'side-chapel of Justinian' and the two encaustic paintings of the Sanctuary. Cf. Forsyth -Weitzmann, *The Monastery*, and K. Weitzmann, *The Icons, I. From the sixth to the tenth century*, Princeton 1976. An equivalent contribution has been made by Manolis Chatzidakis who published the conch mural of the Chapel of St. James, as well as corresponding mural in the Chapel of the Prophets and Saints. Cf. «Τοιχογραφίες Σινᾶ», pp. 205-232, pls. 71-84.

**3.** Forsyth - Weitzmann, *The Monastery*, p. 17 and pls. CXXXIV-CXXXV.

**4.** Cf. parallel works: N. Drandakis, «Παναγία ἡ Δροσιανή», in the series *Βυζαντινὴ Τέχνη στὴν Ἑλλάδα: ΝΑΞΟΣ* (supplement M.Ch.), pls. 13-16; and A. and J. Stylianou, *The Painted Churches in Cyprus*, London 1985, the Theotokos of Moutoulla (1280), pp. 323-330.

**5.** *Exodus*, 3 and 4.

**6.** Chatzidakis, «Τοιχογραφίες Σινᾶ», p. 212.

**7.** Ibid., p. 206.

**8.** Ibid., where mention is made of an icon of St. Andrew between the Apostles Peter and Paul (pl. 81), as well as a series of eight icons (pls. 83-84).

**9.** Ath. Paliouras, *Βυζαντινὴ Αἰτωλοακαρνανία*, Athens 1985, p. 236 and pl. 59.

**10.** M. Garidis, *La peinture murale dans le monde Orthodoxe après la chute de Byzance (1450-1600) et dans les pays sous domination étrangère*, Athens 1989, pp. 41-44, and pls. 57-59.

**11.** Ath. Paliouras, «῾Ο Κύπριος ζωγράφος Συμεὼν Αὐξέντης καὶ τὰ καλλιτεχνικὰ ρεύματα τοῦ 16ου αἰώνα», in *Πρακτικὰ Β΄ Διεθνοῦς Κυπριολογικοῦ Συνεδρίου*, Β΄, Nicosia 1986, pp. 591-600 and pls. 1-18.

**12.** The present condition of the archives of the Monastery of St. Catherine do not enlighten us as to whether other sections of the refectory were decorated in the 16th century. The short time period between the Second Coming (1573), with which the painting probably started, and the Hospitality of Abraham (1577), with which it probably ceased, allows us to conclude that the work was executed between 1573 and 1577.

# ICONS

## EARLY ICONS (FROM THE 6th TO THE 11th CENTURY)


M. Chatzidakis, «An Encaustic Icon of Christ at Sinai», *Art Bulletin* 49 (1967), pp. 197 ff.

G. Galavaris, *The Icon in the Life of the Church* (Iconography of Religions, XXXIV, 8), Leiden 1981.

E. Kitzinger, «On Some Icons of the Seventh Century», *Late Classical and Medieval Studies in Honor of A.M. Friend, Jr.*, Princeton N. J. 1955, pp. 132 ff.

K. Weitzmann, «The Jephthah Panel in the Bema of the Church of St. Catherine's on Mount Sinai», *DOP* 18 (1964), pp. 341 ff, repr. in *Studies in the Arts at Sinai.*

—, «Byzantine Miniature and Icon Painting in the Eleventh Century», *Proceedings of the XIIIth International Congress of Byzantine Studies, Oxford 1966*, London 1967, pp. 20 ff. (repr. in K. Weitzmann, *Studies in Classical and Byzantine Manuscript Illumination* ed. by H. L. Kessler, Chicago 1971).

—, «Loca Sancta and the Representational Arts of Palestine», *DOP* 28 (1974), pp. 31ff., repr. in *Studies in the Arts at Sinai.*


## ICONS FROM THE 12th TO THE 15th CENTURY

**1.** Ioannis painted the hexaptych with four panels of the Menologion, one of the Last Judgement, and one depicting iconographic types of the Virgin, miracles of Christ, scenes from his Passion, and feast scenes. Soteriou, *Εἰκόνες*, I, figs. 136-143 and 146-151. II, pp. 121-123 and 125-130. The hexaptych may be dated to the early 12th century.

**2.** For Ioannis Kornaros, see mainly N. B. Tomadakis, «᾿Ιωάννης Κορνάρος Κρὴς ζωγράφος (1745-1796?)», *Κρητικὰ Χρονικὰ* 2 (1948), pp. 253-264. S. Sophokleous, «Νέα στοιχεῖα γιὰ τὴν παραμονὴ καὶ τὸ ἔργο τοῦ Κρητικοῦ ζωγράφου ᾿Ιωάννη Κορνάρου στὴν Κύπρο», *Κυπριακαὶ Σπουδαὶ* 50 (1986), pp. 227-251.

**3.** For brief information about Pachomios, see K. Weitzmann, in Galey, *Sinai*, p. 90.

**4.** The Western elements which characterize a group of Sinai icons are attributed by K. Weitzmann to Crusader ateliers. See Weitzmann, «Thirteenth-Century Crusader Icons». Weitzmann, «Icon Painting». Weitzmann et al., *The Icon*, pp. 201-207. Weitzmann, «Crusader Icons».

**5.** E. G. Rey, *Les colonies franques de Syrie aux XIIe et XIIIe siècles*, Paris 1883, p. 90. Cf. Amantos, *Σύντομος ἱστορία*, p. 35.

**6.** The oldest and most important document detailing the possessions of the Monastery is a Papal bull issued by Pope Honorius III to the Archbishop of Sinai Symeon in August, 1217, with which the Pope placed under his own protection all the properties of the Monastery in the Sinai peninsula, in Egypt, Palestine, Syria, Crete, Cyprus, and in Constantinople. These privileges were renewed by later Papal bulls. In approximately the same period Venetian protection was added, as proven by a number of documents. See especially G. Hofmann, «Sinai und Rom», *Orientalia Christiana* IX (1927), pp. 218-297. Also G. Hofmann, «Lettere pontifice edite ed inedite intorno ai monasteri del Monte Sinai», *OCP* XVII (1951), pp. 283-303. A. Mercati, «Nuovi documenti pontifici sui monasteri del Sinai e del Monte Athos», *OCP* XVIII (1952), pp. 89-112. Cf. Amantos, *Σύντομος ἱστορία*, especially pp. 35-40.

**7.** P. Huber, *Die Kunstschätze der Heiligen Berge*, Pattloch 1987, p. 184, fig. 23 (in colour) and fig. 146.

**8.** For the Cyprus icons of the 13th century, see especially A. Papageorgiou, *Icons of Cyprus*, Geneva 1969. A. Papageorgiou, *Byzantine Icons of Cyprus*, Benaki Museum, Athens 1976. Mouriki, «Thirteenth-Century Icon Painting». For the properties of the Sinai Monastery in Cyprus see Hofmann, «Sinai und Rom» (as in note 6), pp. 243, 248-249, 253, 256-260, 265, etc. See also Mouriki, «Thirteenth-Century Icon Painting», pp. 72-74 (including earlier bibliography).

**9.** For the properties held by the Monastery in Crete, see Hofmann, «Sinai und Rom» (as in note 6), pp. 243, 245-252, 255-256, 260-262, 265, 267, etc. Cf. Amantos, *Σύντομος ἱστορία*, pp. 36-40.

**10.** Icons with Latin inscriptions: 1) the icon of the Apostles Paul, James, the Protomartyr Stephen, Laurence, Martin of Tours, and Leonard of Limoges (early 13th century). Soteriou, *Εἰκόνες*, I, fig. 202. II, pp. 182-183; 2) The Maiestas Domini (13th century). K. Weitzmann, «Four Icons on Mount Sinai: New Aspects in Crusader Art», *Jahrbuch der Österreichischen Byzantinistik* 21 (1972), pp. 291-292, fig. 11; 3) Side panels of a triptych depicting the Apostles Peter and Paul (late 13th century). Weitzmann, «Icon Painting», p. 65, fig. 31; 4) The two-sided icon with the Crucifixion on the front side and the Anastasis on the reverse-Latin inscriptions only in the Crucifixion (late 13th century). Weitzmann, «Icon Painting», pp. 64-65, figs. 27 and 28. See also note 89 and fig. 65. Icons with Greek and Latin inscriptions: 1) Icon with the Virgin of the Burning Bush between Moses and the Protomartyr Stephen (13th century). Soteriou, *Εἰκόνες*, I, fig. 197. II, pp. 179-180; 2) The Hodegetria of the central panel of a triptych with scenes from her Life on the side panels (early 13th century), note 56 and figs. 54, 55; 3) The icon of the Hodegetria with nimbi in relief (late 13th century). Mouriki, «Thirteenth-Century Icon Painting», pp. 63-64, figs. 26 and 40. See also note 84 and fig. 60. Icons with Greek and Arabic inscriptions: 1) Prophet Elijah by the painter Stephanos (early 13th century). Soteriou, *Εἰκόνες*, I, fig. 74. II, pp. 88-89. See also note 43 and fig. 34; 2) Prophet Moses by the painter Stephanos (early 13th century). Soteriou, *Εἰκόνες*, I, fig. 75. II, pp. 89-90; 3) Icon of the Presentation in the Temple (13th century). The title of the scene is in Greek and Arabic. A fragment of a Syriac inscription is preserved in a section of an icon of the Crucifixion (early 13th century). There are Greek and Georgian inscriptions on a hexaptych (see note 1), which was painted by the Georgian monk Ioannis Tsochabi according to the evidence of an unpublished invocation in Georgian on the Last Judgement panel. Ioannis was also the donor of this work. Greek and Georgian inscriptions also exist on the icon of St. George and a Georgian King whom I identify as George Lacha (1213-1222), thus dating the panel to the early 13th century. For this icon see Soteriou, *Εἰκόνες*, I, fig. 152. II, pp. 131-132. The collection of icons at Sinai also contains a tetraptych depicting the Great Deesis and various hagiographic figures, among which are certain Georgian saints. The inscriptions are only in Georgian, and the work came as a gift from Georgia in 1780, according to a long text on the reverse sides.

**11.** For example, a triptych of the second half of the 13th century depicting the Deesis, saints, and the Annunciation. K. Weitzmann, «Fragments of an Early St. Nicholas Triptych on Mount Sinai», *ΔΧΑΕ* 4, 4(1964-65), p. 16, figs. 11 a-c. On the upper right-hand spandrel of the central panel is an inscription dedicating the icon on behalf of Bishop Germanos, most likely of Sinai, with the stipulation that the icon remain hung in the hermitage of Saint Makarios. Failure to do so, according to the inscription, would result in the loss of the eternal kingdom. In the icon depicting the enthroned Virgin and Child, the Burial of Moses, and John the Baptist with the Feast of Herod, also from the second half of the 13th century, an Arabic inscription translates a biblical passage. For the icon, see Weitzmann, «Thirteenth-Century Crusader Icons», pp. 190-192, fig. 15. In the Last Judgement from the second half of the 13th century and in a small icon of the 15th century with the same subject, the name Hades is inscribed in Arabic. For the first icon, see Weitzmann, «Icon Painting», p. 58, figs. 14 a, b. For the second, see Galey, *Sinai*, fig. 106.

**12.** Cf. Eckenstein, *History of Sinai*, p. 131.

**13.** 1) The icon of Abraham and Melchisedek (early 13th century). The kneeling donor is labelled: ᾿Αβραάμιος ἐπίσκοπος τοῦ Σινᾶ ὄρους [καὶ] τῆς Ραϊθοῦ (Abraamios, Bishop of Mount Sinai and of Raithou). K. Weitzmann, «A Group of Early Twelfth-Century Sinai Icons Attributed to Cyprus», *Studies in Memory of David Talbot Rice*, Edinburgh 1985, pp. 54-55, pls. 21 and 22c. (the icon is dated here to the early 12th century); 2) The large icon with the Giving of the Law to Moses and with scenes of his life on the border (early 13th century). Weitzmann, «Icon Programs», pp. 97-98 fig. 28. A bishop Antonios of Sinai is depicted in the icon with the Heavenly Ladder (Weitzmann, *Icon*, p. 88, pl. 25) but I do not believe that he is the donor of the icon.

**14.** According to chronological order the icons are: 1) the hexaptych by Ioannis (beginning of the 12th century). Greek inscriptions mention the name of the monk on the reverse sides and one inscription in Georgian on the main side of the Last Judgement panel includes the first and last name of the donor, revealing that he is a Georgian. The same monk is depicted in proskynesis in front of the enthroned Virgin on the panel with various iconographic types of the Virgin, scenes from the miracles and the Passion of Christ, and feast scenes. He is depicted standing in the panel of the Last Judgement; 2) The Archangel Michael (early 13th century). Soteriou, *Εἰκόνες*, I, fig. 159. II, p. 139. Anonymous monk; 3) The Giving of the Law to Moses (central panel of a triptych, early 13th century). Soteriou, *Εἰκόνες*, I, fig. 161. II, pp. 141-142. Monk with the inscription: Ἅγιε τοῦ Θ(εο)ῦ βοήθησον τὸν δοῦλον σου Πέτρον μοναχόν; 4) Saint George with scenes of his miracles and martyrdom (early 13th century). Monk-priest with the inscription: Αγιε του Θ(εο)ῦ βοῆθι τὸν σων δοῦλον Ιω(άννην) μ(ονα)χ(όν) κε ἡερέαν τὸν ἐκ πόθου κτισαντα την σην ηκονα τον ηβερον, Soteriou, *Εἰκόνες*, I, fig. 167. II, pp. 149-151; 5) Saint George with scenes from his miracles and martyrdom (late 13th century). Soteriou, *Εἰκόνες*, I, fig. 169. II, pp. 154-155. Monk with the inscription: Ποιμὴν μοναχός; 6) Saint Nicholas with scenes from his life, miracles, the Deesis and saints (late 13th century). Soteriou, *Εἰκόνες*, I, fig. 170. II, pp. 155-157. Two monks with the inscriptions: Κλῆμος and Πημήν; 7) Side wings of a triptych with Saints George, Theodore Teron, John of Damascus, Ephraim the Syrian, Sabbas and Onouphrios (early 14th century). Soteriou, *Εἰκόνες*, I, figs. 62-63. II, pp. 77-78 (here dated to the 11th-12th century, but the correct dating has been made by Buchthal). On one wing appears a half-erased inscription containing the word deacon; 8) Triptych with the Dodekaorton, the Burning Bush, and saints (15th century). Soteriou, *Εἰκόνες*, I, fig. 220. II, pp. 193-194. On the reverse side is an inscription which includes the word 'economos'; 9) The Virgin Hodegetria between Ioakeim and Anna (second half of the 15th century). Soteriou, *Εἰκόνες*, I, fig. 164. II, pp. 143-144. Anonymous monk; 10) Great Deesis with saints (second half of the 15th century). Soteriou, *Εἰκόνες*, I, fig. 221. II, pp. 194-195. See also note 122 and fig. 78. Anonymous monk.

**15.** 1) The Giving of the Law to Moses (early 13th century). Soteriou, *Εἰκόνες*, I, fig. 160. II, pp. 140-141. Anonymous donor with Arab head-dress; 2) Moses and Aaron (13th century). Soteriou, *Εἰκόνες*, I, fig. 162. II, pp. 142-143. Donor with the inscription: + Δέ(ησις) Θεοδωσίου του Σαλουστίου; 3) The enthroned Virgin and Child (second half of the 13th century). Soteriou, *Εἰκόνες*, I, fig. 171 (by mistake fig. 172 was also attributed to the same icon). II, pp. 157-158. Anonymous donor with Arab head-dress; 4) Saints Theodore Stratelates and George (second half of the 13th century). Weitzmann, «Icon Painting», p. 80, fig. 64. Donor with the inscription: Δέ(ησις) τοῦ δουλου του Θ(εο)ῦ Γεῶργιου του Παρισι.

**16.** Namely nos. 1 and 4 in note 14, and nos. 1 and 3 in note 15. The icons that can be attributed to non-Greek donors may also include a panel of the Dodekaorton datable to the beginning of the 13th century. The inscription on the reverse side of the panel is: Δέ(ησις) Μουσελέμ ἀναγνόστου κε παντ(ὸς) τοῦ λαοῦ αὐτοῦ. ᾿Αμή[ν]. ('Prayer of Mouselem, reader, and of all his people, amen'). A detail with the Crucifixion has been published by Weitzmann, «Icon Painting», pp. 53-54, fig. 5. He attributes the icon to a Crusader atelier of Jerusalem and dates it around the middle of the 12th century.

**17.** The icon with Saint Sergios on horseback (end of the 13th century). Soteriou, *Εἰκόνες*, I, fig. 187. II, p. 171.

**18.** Soteriou, *Εἰκόνες*, I, figs. 74 and 75. II, pp. 88-90.

**19.** Soteriou, *Εἰκόνες*, I, fig. 158. II, pp. 138-139. Mouriki, «Four Thirteenth-Century Sinai Icons», pp. 329-347, figs. 1-12, 14-21.

**20.** See Weitzmann, «Icon Programs».

**21.** I owe this view to his Beatitude the Archbishop of Sinai Damianos.

**22.** Perhaps one of the oldest testimonies is by Jacques de Vitry (+1244). Cf. Eckenstein, *History of Sinai*, p. 147. Information on the renaming of the Monastery from the 14th century is provided in A. Guillou, «Le monastère de la Théotokos au Sinaï», *Mélanges d'Archéologie et d'Histoire*. École Française de Rome (1955), p. 223.

**23.** One example is the icon with the Virgin Blachernitissa between Moses and the Patriarch Euthymios II who died at Sinai in 1224. See note 60 and fig. 48. For the icon of St. George and of a Georgian King, see Soteriou, *Εἰκόνες*, I, fig. 152. II, pp. 131-132. According to the accompanying inscription, the figure is: [ΓΕ]Ω[ΡΓΙΟC] ΠΙCΤ(ὸς) ΒΑCΙ(λεύς) ΠΑC(ης) ΑΝΑΤΟ(λῆς) Ο ΠΑΓΚΡΑΤΟΥΝΙΑΝΟC. The king has been identified by Beneševič as David IV (1089-1125) and by George and Maria Soteriou as George III (1156-1184). Soteriou, *Εἰκόνες*, II, p. 132. In a paper delivered at the Fifth International Symposium of Georgian Art (Pavia, 1986) I suggested that the depicted monarch is George Lacha (1213-1222).

**24.** See Amantos, *Σύντομος ἱστορία*, pp. 42-43. It would be strange that the ecumenical policies, particularly of Manuel I, with daring initiatives toward Latin-occupied areas of the Near East did not leave an impression also on the great Orthodox monastery.

**25.** The painted decoration of the reverse side of icons with alternating strips of wavy brushstrokes in red and blue-black is not confined to Sinai, since it is encountered many times in other areas such as Cyprus and Mount Athos. It is the systematic use of this technique and the method of its application which suggest that this feature has a local character. It should be noted that no investigation has been made into the type of wood employed in each case.

**26.** Width of the border: 1 cm. Thickness: 2 cm. The reverse side is painted in a brown colour which has faded for the most part. Some of the inscriptions of the scrolls have been repainted in a later period. Soteriou, *Εἰκόνες*, I, figs. 54-56. II, pp. 73-75 (dated to the late 11th - early 12th century). Weitzmann et al., *The Icon*, p. 17, colour detail on p. 48 (dated between 1050 and 1100). Belting, *Bild und Kult*, pp. 326, 328, 330, figs. 174 and 178.

**27.** The inscriptions on the scrolls of the figures are: John the Theologian: Πάντα δι᾽αὐτοῦ ἐγένετο κ(αὶ) χωρὶς αὐτοῦ ἐγένετο οὐδὲ ἐν ὁ γέγονεν ('All things were made by him; and without him was not any thing made that was made') (John 1:3). John the Baptist: Οὗτο(ς) ἦν ὅν εἶπον ὁ ὀπίσω μου ἐρχόμενο(ς) ἔμπροσθέν μου γέγονεν ὅτι πρῶτός μου ἦν) ('This was he of whom I spake, He that cometh after me is preferred before me; for he was before me') (John 1:15). Paul: Ι(ησοὺ)ς Χ(ριστὸ)ς χθὲς κ(αὶ) σήμερον ὁ αὐτὸς καὶ εἰς τοὺς αἰῶνας ('Jesus Christ the same yesterday, and today, and for ever') (Hebrews 13:8). Peter: Σὺ εἶ ὁ Χ(ριστὸ)ς ὁ υἱ(ὸς) τοῦ Θ(εο)ῦ τοῦ ζὸντος ('Thou art the Christ, the Son of the living God' (Matthew 16:16). Moses: Παρελθὼν ὄψομαι τὸ ὅραμα τὸ μέγα τοῦτο ('I will now turn aside, and see this great sight') (Exodus 3:3). Jacob: κ(αὶ) ἰδοὺ κ[λ]ίμαξ ἐστηριγμένη ἐν τῆ γῆ ης ἡ κεφαλὴ αφηκνε[ĩ]το εἰς τὸν οὐ(ρα)νόν ('And behold a ladder set up on the earth, and the top of it reached to heaven' (Genesis 28:12). Aaron: 'Η ράβδος αὕτη ἡ βλαστήσασα παρθ(ενικό)ν τόκον ('The man's rod whom I shall choose, shall blossom' (paraphrase of Numbers 17:5). Symeon: Κ(αὶ) σοῦ δε αὐτῆς τὴν ψυχὴν διελεύσεται ῥομφαία ὅπως αν αποκαλυφθω[σ]ι[ν] ἐκ πολλ(ῶν) καρδιῶν διαλογισμοὶ ('Yea, a sword shall pierce through thy own soul also, that the thoughts of many hearts may be revealed') (Luke 2:35). Zechariah: Εὐλογητὸ(ς) ὁ Θ(εὸ)ς τοῦ [Ισρ]αὴλ ὅτι ἐπεσκ(έ)ψατο κ(αὶ) ἐποίησεν [λ]ύτρωσιν τῷ λαῶ αὐτοῦ ('Blessed be the Lord God of Israel; for he hath visited and redeemed his people') (Luke 1:68). Anna: Τοῦτο τὸ βρέφος οὐρανό(ν) καὶ γῆν ἐστερέωσεν ('This child has established heaven and earth') (the classic verse for the scroll of Anna from the second half of the 12th century on, without origin in the New Testament). Elisabeth: Ιδοὺ ώς ἐγένετω τοῦ ἀσπασμοῦ σου εἰς τὰ ὦτ(α) μου ἐσκήρτησ[ε]ν τὸ βρέφος [εν] ἐν ἀγαλλιασει ('For, lo, as soon as the voice of thy salutation sounded in mine ears, the babe leaped in my womb for joy') (Luke 1:44). David: ᾿Ανάστηθι Κ(ύρι)ε εἰς τὴν ἀνάπαυσίν σου σὺ καὶ ἡ κιβωτός τοῦ ἁγιάσματός σου ('Arise, O Lord, into thy rest; thou, and the ark of thy Strength') (Psalms 132:8). Isaiah: Καὶ ἀπεστάλη προς με ἕν τῶν σεραφείμ ('Then flew one of the seraphims unto me') (Isaiah 6:6). Ezekiel: Καὶ εἶπε(ν) Κ(ύριο)ς πρός με. ἡ πύλη αὕτη κεκλεισμένη ἔσται ('And the Lord said unto me; this gate shall be shut') (Ezekiel 44:2). Daniel: Εώρακας εως ὅτου [-ε]τμήθη λίθος ἐξ ὄρους ἄνευ χειρῶν ('Thou sawest toll that a stone was cut out without hands') (Daniel 2:34). Habakkuk: ῾Ο Θ(εό)ς ἀπὸ Θεμὰν ἥξη καὶ ὁ ἅγιος ἐξ ορους κατασκίου δασέος ('God came from Teman and the Holy One from Mount Paran') (Habakkuk 3:3). Solomon: ῾Η σοφία ωκοδόμησεν εαὐτῆ οικον κ(αὶ) υπη(ρεισεν) ('Wisdom hath builded her house') (Proverbs 9:1). Balaam: ᾿Ανατελλεῖ ἄστρ(ον) ἐξ Ιακώβ κ(αὶ) ἀναστήσεται ἄν(θρωπ)ος ἐξ ᾿Ιούδα ('There shall come a Star out of Jacob, and a Sceptre shall rise out of Israel') (Numbers 24:17). Gideon: 'Ιδοὺ απερίδωμαι τὸν ποκον τον ερ[ί]ον ἐν [τῷ] αλῳ[νι]('Behold, I will put a fleece of wool in the floor') (Judges 6:37). Joseph: ᾿Εγὼ του προφητι κελεύσματι θηο υπο αγγέλου πεπεισμέ (paraphrase of Matthew 1, 24). The majority of the above texts emphasize the mystery of the Incarnation. Of primary significance for the interpretation of the subject matter is the inscription ΙΩΑΚΕΙΜ Κ(αί) ΑΝΝΑ ΕΤΕΚΝΟΓΟΝΗCΑΝ Κ(αὶ) ΑΔΑΜ Κ(αὶ) ΕΥΑ ΗΛΕΥΘΕΡΩΘΗCΑΝ (from the Hymns of the celebration of the Birth of the Virgin) above the corresponding figures.

**28.** The dimensions of the panel indicate that it might have been meant to be situated in a chapel of the Virgin in the Monastery or that it was commissioned for the individual prayers of an important figure in the hierarchy of the Monastery, most likely the Archbishop of Sinai.

**29.** First section: Width; 136 cm. Height; 34.5 cm. Width of the border: 3.5-6 cm. Thickness of the board (with the border): 3.5 cm. (without the border: 2.9 cm.). Second section: Width: 139 cm. Height: 34.5 cm. Width of the border: 3.5-6 cm. Thickness of the board (with the border): 3.5 cm. (without the border: 2.9 cm.). The reverse sides are decorated by successive vertical bands with alternating red and blue-black wavy brushstrokes. Soteriou, *Εἰκόνες*, I, figs. 103-111. II, pp. 109-110 (dated late 11th-early 12th century). Weitzmann, «A Group of Early Twelfth-Century Icons» (as in note 13), pp. 52-53 and pls. 20 a-b. See also Weitzmann, *Studies*, IX, pp. 250-251, figs. 20a-b. Weitzmann, *Icon*, pp. 36, 78, pl. 20 with colour detail. K. Weitzmann, *Ikonen*, Berlin 1980, no. 8 with colour illustration. K. Weitzmann, «Illustrations to the Lives of the Five Martyrs of Sebaste», *DOP* 33(1979), pp. 108-110, figs. 28-39 (dated to the early 12th century). Weitzmann, «Icon Programs», p. 67.

**30.** See Weitzmann, «Icon Programs», p. 67.

**31.** Left section. Width: 140 cm. Height: 41.5 cm. Right section. Width: 159 cm. Height: 41.5 cm. The reverse sides are decorated with successive vertical bands with alternating red and blue-black wavy brushstrokes. Soteriou, *Εἰκόνες*, I, figs. 95-102. II, pp. 105-109 (dated to the second half of the 12th century). Weitzmann, «The Classical in Byzantine Art, as a Mode of Individual Expression», *Byzantine Art, An European Art, Lectures*, Athens 1966, p. 170, fig. 130. Weitzmann, «Byzantium and the West», pp. 59-62, figs. 14, 17, 20, 22, 24 and 30. Weitzmann, *Icon*, pp. 36, 38, 86, fig. VII, pl. 24 (colour detail with the Transfiguration). Weitzmann et al., *The Icon*, p. 18, with colour illustration on p. 58 (detail). *St. Catherine's Monastery*, fig 122. Weitzmann, «Icon Programs», p. 70.

**32.** Width of the border: 4 cm. (approx.). Thickness of the board: 3 cm. The reverse side is decorated with successive vertical bands of alternating wavy brushstrokes in red and blue-black. Soteriou, *Εἰκόνες*, I, figs. 112-116. II, pp. 111-112 (dated to the 13th century). Weitzmann, «Byzantium and the West», pp. 59-63, figs. 15-16, 18-21 and 23. Weitzmann, *Icon*, pp. 36, 101 and pl. 31 (colour detail with the Raising of Lazarus). *St. Catherine's Monastery*, fig. 144. Weitzmann, «Icon Programs», pp. 75-80, figs. 8-14 (dated to the early 13th century).

**33.** Width of the border: 4.5 cm. Thickness of the board: 2.6 cm. On the reverse side, traces of decoration with bands of wavy brushstrokes. Soteriou, *Εἰκόνες*, I, fig. 65. II, pp. 79-81 (dated to the mature Comnenian period). Weitzmann, «The Classical in Byzantine Art» (as in note 31), pp. 166-167, fig. 126. Weitzmann, *Icon*, pp. 36, 82, and pl. 22 (in colour). D. Mouriki, «Stylistic Trends in Monumental Painting of Greece during the Eleventh and Twelfth Centuries», *DOP* 34-35 (1982), p. 114. Weitzmann et al., *The Icon*, p. 18, with colour plate on p. 57. *St. Catherine's Monastery*, fig. 116. Weitzmann, «Icon Programs», p. 71 (dated to the first half of the 12th century). Belting, *Bild und Kult*, pp. 279, 304, 305, 310, fig. 166.

**34.** Width of the border: 5 cm. Thickness of the board: 1.8 cm. On the reverse side a continuous decoration of circular designs which enclose crosses. Rinceaux and pearls complete the decoration. The colours are deep brown, ochre, and white. Weitzmann, *Frühe Ikonen*, pp. XIII, XX, LXXX-LXXXI, colour plate on page 19. Weitzmann, *Icon*, pp. 35, 88, and pl. 25 (in colour) (in the second study the work is dated to the first half of the 12th century). *St. Catherine's Monastery*, fig. 144. Belting, *Bild und Kult*, pp. 304, 305, fig. 165.

**35.** The advantageous position held by the Archbishop of Sinai in the icon, evidently during the period in which it was painted, excludes the likelihood that he himself gave the commission of the work to a painter from the Monastery. It is possible, however, that the icon was ordered as a gift for the Archbishop by another person.

**36.** 61×42.2 cm. (without the later strip of wood on the lower part). Width of the border: 3 cm. Thickness of the board: 3 cm. On the reverse side continuous decoration of circular borders which enclose crosses. Deep brown, white, and ochre have been used. K. Weitzmann, «Eine spätkomnenische Verkündigungsikone des Sinai und die zweite byzantinische Welle des 12. Jahrhunderts», *Festschrift für Herbert von Einem zum 16. Februar 1965*, Berlin 1965, pp. 299-312, with colour plate on p. 305 and black and white details in plate 70. Reprinted in Weitzmann, *Studies*, no. X. Weitzmann, «The Classical in Byzantine Art». (as in note 31), pp. 169-170, fig. 131. K. Weitzmann, «Various Aspects of Byzantine Influence on the Latin Countries from the Sixth to the Twelfth Century», *DOP* 20(1966), p. 24, fig. 41. Weitzmann, *Frühe Ikonen*, pp. XVI, LXXXII, and pl. 30. W. F. Volbach and J. Lafontaine-Dosogne, *Byzanz und der christliche Osten. Propyläen Kunstgeschichte*, Berlin 1968, III, pp. 178, 180, pl. 44. Weitzmann, «Byzantium and the West», pp. 58-59, figs. 12 and 32. Weitzmann, *Icon*, pp. 36, 92 and pl. 27 (in colour). Weitzmann et al., *The Icon*, p. 19, with colour plate on p. 62 (the icon is dated to the late 12th century). Belting, *Bild und Kult*, pp. 304, 310-312, 646, fig. 167.

**37.** See Weitzmann, «Eine spätkomnenische Verkündigungsikone», op. cit., p. 302, and H. Maguire, *Art and Eloquence in Byzantium*, Princeton 1981, pp. 46-52.

**38.** The dimensions of the work suggest its use as a proskynesis icon for the Feast of the Annunciation on March 25. In the absence of another icon of the Dodekaorton of the same dimensions and style at the Monastery, it would be unwise to hypothesize that the icon belonged to a Dodekaorton set from a templon.

**39.** The central panels: Left. Height: 57 cm. Width: 41.8 Width of the border (upper and lower): 2.6 cm. Thickness of the board: 1.8 and 3 cm. Right. Height: 56.6 cm. Width: 41.6 cm. Width of the border (upper and lower): 2.6 cm. Thickness of the board: 2 and 3 cm. Side panels: Left. Height: 49.8 cm. Width: 38.8 cm. Thickness of the board: 6 cm. Right. Height: 49.4 cm. Width: 38 cm. Thickness of the board: 6 cm. Reverse sides of the central leaves. Pattern of continuous circles which enclose crosses, surrounded by cryptograms: $\overline{\mathrm{E}}$[$\overline{\mathrm{E}}$], $\overline{\mathrm{E}}$ $\overline{\mathrm{E}}$, $\overline{\mathrm{IC}}$ $\overline{\mathrm{XC}}$ $\overline{\mathrm{NI}}$ $\overline{\mathrm{KA}}$, $\overline{\mathrm{AP}}$ $\overline{\Pi\mathrm{C}}$ $\overline{\mathrm{MC}}$ $\overline{\mathrm{CT}}$, $\overline{\Phi}$ $\overline{\mathrm{X}}$ $\overline{\Phi}$ $\overline{\Pi}$. Reverse sides of the wings. On each one, a cross bordered by cryptograms. The colours of the decoration are: ochre, black, red-brown, olive and white. Soteriou, *Εἰκόνες*, I, figs. 76-79. II, pp. 90-92 (dated to the middle or the second half of the 12th century). L. Hadermann-Misguich, *Kurbinovo*, Brussels 1975, I, brief mentions. II, figs. 51 and 52 (dated to the late 12th century).

**40.** Width of the border: 3.5 cm. Thickness of the board: 3.1 cm. Reverse side. Superimposed bands of alternating wavy brushstrokes in red and blue-black. Soteriou, *Εἰκόνες*, I, figs. 126-130 (February, May, June). II, pp. 117-119 (dated around the 12th century). Weitzmann, «Icon Programs», pp. 108, 109-110, 112, figs. 37 and 39 (January) (dated to the early 13th century). Belting, *Bild und Kult*, p. 283, fig. 159 (February).

**41.** Weitzmann, «Icon Programs», passim.

**42.** The most characteristic instance concerns ten small icons of the early 13th century depicting the Virgin Kyriotissa or Virgin of the Burning Bush — according to the local name —and a saint who entreats the Virgin. For these works, see Weitzmann, «Loca Sancta and the Representational Arts of Palestine», *DOP* 28(1974), p. 53, figs. 48-49 (reprinted in Weitzmann, *Studies*, no. II, p. 39, figs. 48-49).

**43.** Width of the border: 5.7 cm. Thickness of the board: 3.2 cm. The reverse side is decorated with superimposed bands with alternating wavy brushstrokes, red and blue-black. Soteriou, *Εἰκόνες*, I, fig. 74. II. pp. 88-89 (dated to the late 12th century). Weitzmann, «The Classical in Byzantine Art» (as in note 31), pp. 172-173, fig. 135. Weitzmann, «Byzantium and the West», pp. 63-64, 68, figs. 25 and 37. Weitzmann, *Icon*, pp. 36, 97, pl. 29 (in colour). Galey, *Sinai*, figs. 55-56. Weitzmann, «Icon Programs», p. 102, fig. 32 (dated around 1200).

**44.** See Soteriou, *Εἰκόνες*, I, fig. 75. II, pp. 89-90.

**45.** Soteriou, *Εἰκόνες*, II, p. 90. Weitzmann, «Icon Programs», pp. 102, 103.

**46.** Leaf with the depiction of Moses. Height: 127.5 cm. Width: 36.2 cm. (at the bottom). Leaf with the depiction of Aaron: Height: 127 cm. Width: 34.8 cm. (at the bottom). Thickness of the board: 2.7 cm. The reverse sides have Post-Byzantine representations of the Annunciation and again depictions of Moses and Aaron. Chatzidakis, «L'évolution de l'icone aux 11e-13e siècles et la transformation du templon», *Actes du XVe Congrès International d' Études Byzantines. Athènes 1976. I. Art et Archéologie*, Athens 1979, pp. 355-356, pls. XLIV, 18 and 19 (dated to the 12th century, most likely early 12th century).

**47.** The ancient garment, the open scroll in the left hand and the gesture of speech with the right hand are reminiscent of representations of prophets in Byzantine domes. Due to the confusion created by the open scroll of Aaron, which does not belong to his iconography, his name was added two times on the scroll, even though it had already been written next to the head of the figure.

**48.** 92×64 cm. (with the two added wooden strips above and below). Width of the border: 5.8 cm. Thickness of the board: 3 cm. On the reverse side are traces of superimposed bands of alternating red and blue-black wavy brushstrokes. Soteriou, *Εἰκόνες*, I, fig. 160. II, pp. 140-141 (dated to the 11th-12th century). Weitzmann, *Icon*, pp. 36, 75, pl. 18 (in colour) (dated to the 12th-13th century).

**49.** There is a half-erased inscription in the upper right corner which gives the verse from *Exodus* 3:4 [Ε]ΚΑΛΕCΕΝ ΑΥΤΟΝ [ΚΥΡΙΟC ΕΚ Τ]ΟΥ ΒΑΤΟΥ [ΛΕ]ΓΟΝ ΜΩCΗ [Ο Δ]Ε ΕΙΠΕΝ ΤΙ Ε[CΤΙΝ; Ο ΔΕ ΕΙ]ΠΕΝ ΜΙ...('God called unto him out of the midst of the bush and said, Moses, Moses. And he said, Here am I').

**50.** 88×65 cm. (without the wooden strips above and below, which have fallen off). Width of the border: 6 cm. Thickness of the board: 3 cm. On the reverse side are traces of superimposed bands with alternating red and blue-black wavy brushstrokes.

**51.** For example, of the German Thietmar, who visited the Monastery in 1217. *Mag. Thietmari Peregrinatio. Ad fidem codicis Hamburgensis.* Ed. J. C. M. Laurent (Hamburg 1857). Cf. Eckenstein, *History of Sinai*, p. 151. Cf. also G. H. Forsyth in Galey, *Sinai*, note 3 p. 187.

**52.** Width of the border: 2.4 cm. Thickness of the board: 2 cm. The reverse side is undecorated, covered only with gesso. The subject and the dimensions of the icon indicate that it was intended to be placed on the proskynetarion on the feast day of the Saint. *St. Catherine's Monastery*, fig. 127.

**53.** Width of the border: 4 cm. (upper and lower) and 3 cm. (on the sides). Thickness of the board: 1.7 cm. On the reverse side red-brown Cross of Golgotha with the formula IC XC NI KA.

**54.** Width of the border: 3 cm. Thickness of the board: 3.8 cm. The reverse side is decorated with superimposed bands of alternating red and blue-black wavy lines.

**55.** See note 23.

**56.** Central panel: width of the border: 3.8 cm. Maximum thickness of the board: 3.9 cm. The reverse side of the central panel has decoration of superimposed inscribed half lozenges, red and blue-black on a gesso layer. The reverse sides of the wings have been painted in a red colour. In each one, two differently sized foliate crosses in a grey colour, one above the other. On the left are preserved only the ligatures IC XC. On the right, IC XC NH KA and Φ X Φ Π. Side wings: D. Mouriki, «Περὶ Βυζαντινοῦ κύκλου τοῦ βίου τῆς Παναγίας εἰς φορητὴν εἰκόνα τῆς Μονῆς τοῦ ὄρους Σινᾶ», *AE* (1970), Μελέται, pp. 125-153, pls. 44-47.

**57.** The scenes of the Life of the Virgin in the wings of the triptych are: Ioakeim's Offerings Rejected, the Departure of Ioakeim and Anna from the Temple, the Prayer of Ioakeim in the Desert, the Prayer and Annunciation to Anna in the Garden of her House, the Meeting of Ioakeim and Anna, the Birth of the Virgin, the Virgin Caressed by her Parents, the Presentation of the Virgin in the Temple, and the Annunciation to the Virgin at the Well. Two enigmatic scenes follow which I believe to depict the Reproof of the Virgin and of Joseph by the High Priest, and finally the Annunciation.

**58.** For example, the handling of the gold for the reflection of light and the manner in which the reverse side of the central panel is treated. The last characterizes Saint Panteleimon (fig. 57), the Hodegetria Dexiokratousa of the early 13th century, and the Virgin of the Burning Bush with a Patriarch of Jerusalem (the last is repainted).

**59.** The Holy Fathers of Sinai: 57.2 cm. (without the wooden strips) ×42.5 cm. Width of the border: 2.2 cm. Thickness of the board: 2.5 cm. The Holy Fathers of Raithou: 58.2 cm. (with the original wooden strips) ×40.8 cm. Width of the border: 2.7 cm (without the upper wooden strip) and 1.8 cm. (on the sides). Thickness of the board: 2.5 cm. On the reverse sides a different variation of the foliate cross with the ligatures IC XC. The Holy Fathers of Sinai: Soteriou, *Εἰκόνες*, I, figs. 153-154. II, pp. 134-135 (dated to the 12th or 13th century). Galey, *Sinai*, fig. 57 (in colour) (here dated by Weitzmann to the 13th century). The two icons were almost certainly intended to be placed in the Chapel of the Holy Fathers on the southeast side of the katholikon, the positions which they have even today.

**60.** Added border with wooden strips 3.3 cm. in width: Thickness of the board with the border: 1.8 cm. On the reverse side, a Greek cross in red-brown colour and with the formula IC XC NH KA within circles. The bishop on the icon, who has not a nimbus, is identified by an inscription. He is Euthymios II of Jerusalem, who died at Sinai on December 13, 1224, and was buried there, according to the evidence of a long inscription in Greek and Arabic on the north wall of the small chamber to the north of the Bema. Soteriou, *Εἰκόνες*, I, fig. 158. II, pp. 138-139 (dated on the basis of the portrait of Euthymios). Mouriki, «Four Thirteenth-Century Sinai Icons», pp. 329-331, 335-337, figs. 1, 2, 3-4, 16, 18.

**61.** Width of the border: 3.2 cm. Thickness of the board: 2.5 cm. On the reverse side a Greek cross in red-brown colour with the formula IC XC NH KA within circles. Soteriou, *Εἰκόνες*, I, figs. 155-156. II, pp. 135-137 (dated to an Early Byzantine period). Mouriki, «Four Thirteenth-Century Sinai Icons», pp. 331-332, 337-341, figs. 7-10.

**62.** For biographical information related to the four Saints, see Mouriki, «Four Thirteenth-Century Sinai Icons», pp. 338-341.

**63.** Width of the border: 3 cm. Thickness of the board: 3 cm. The reverse side is decorated with the Cross of Golgotha in a red-brown colour and with the formula IC XC NH KA within circles. Below, the inscription CTAYPOY CTACIC. Mouriki, «Four Thirteenth-Century Sinai Icons», pp. 333-335, 343-344, figs. 5-6, 14-15, and 20.

**64.** I owe this observation to Father Daniel of the Sinai Monastery.

**65.** 96.8 (without the later wooden strips) × 63.8 cm. Width of the border: 4.2 cm. Thickness of the board: 2.8 cm. The reverse side is decorated with superimposed bands of alternating red and blue-black wavy brushstrokes. Weitzmann, «Icon Programs», p. 106, fig. 35 (dated to the late 12th or the early 13th century).

**66.** Exceptions to the Sinai material from the early 13th century are three similar icons with the Archangel Gabriel and the Apostles Peter and Paul. No other panel from the same set has been identified. See Weitzmann, «Icon Programs», p. 87, figs. 18 and 19.

**67.** Christ: Width of the border: 2.1 cm. Thickness of the board: 2.1 cm. Archangel Michael: Width of the border: 2 cm. Thickness of the board: 2.5 cm. The reverse sides are decorated with superimposed bands of alternating red and blue-black wavy brushstrokes. Recently I identified the icon of John the Baptist from the same set. Soteriou, *Εἰκόνες*, I, fig. 72 (Michael) and 73 (Gabriel). II. pp. 87-88 (dated to the end of the 12th century). Weitzmann, «Icon Programs», p. 89, fig. 20 (Michael), 21 (Virgin) and 22 (the icon of Christ before the removal of the later layer) (dated to the late 12th-early 13th century).

**68.** Christ: Width of the border: 4.2 cm. Thickness of the board: 3.2 cm. Virgin: Width of border: 4.3 cm. Thickness of the board: 2.9 cm. The reverse sides in both icons are decorated with superimposed bands of alternating red and blue-black wavy brushstrokes. The icon of Christ has been published in Chatzidakis, «Évolution de l'icône» (as in note 46), pp. 360-361, pl. XLVIII. 24 (dated to the 12th century). K. Weitzmann, *Ikonen*, no. 18 (with colour illustration) (dated to the second half of the 15th century). Galey, *Sinai*, fig. 94 (in colour). H. Belting. *The Image and its Public in the Middle Ages. Form and Function of Early Paintings of the Passion* (English edition), New York 1990, fig. 51 (published as an icon from Nicosia and dated to the 12th century).

**69.** These are the icons of Christ Philanthropos and the Orant Virgin from Saint Neophytos near Paphos and the icons of Christ and the Virgin Hodegetria from the Panagia tou Arakos near Lagoudera. Papageorgiou, *Byzantine Icons of Cyprus*. Benaki Museum, Athens 1976, nos. 4-7.

**70.** Width of the border: 10.8 cm. Thickness of the board: 2.2 cm. On the reverse side traces of superimposed bands of alternating red and blue-black wavy brushstrokes. Soteriou, *Εἰκόνες*, I, fig. 166. II, pp. 147-149 (dated to the 12th - 13th century). Galey, *Sinai*, fig. 70 (in colour). Weitzmann, «Crusader Icons», p. 154, fig. 13. Weitzmann, «Icons Programs», p. 95, fig. 25 (dated to the late 12th - early 13th century). Belting, *Bild und Kult*, p. 426, fig. 227.

**71.** The icon was most likely placed near the relics of the Saint in the Bema. Cf. Weitzmann, «Icon Programs», pp. 95, 97.

**72.** Width of the border: 9.5 cm. Thickness of the board: 3 cm. The reverse side is decorated with superimposed bands of alternating red and blue-black wavy brushrokes. Soteriou, *Εἰκόνες*, I, fig. 165. II, pp. 144-147 (dated to the late 12th century). K. Weitzmann, «Fragments of an Early St. Nicholas Triptych on Mount Sinai», *ΔΧΑΕ* 4, 4(1964-66), 1967, pp. 6-9, fig. 6 and colour plate. Reprinted in Weitzmann, *Studies*, no. VIII, pp. 216-219, fig. 6. Weitzmann, «Thirteenth-Century Crusader icons», p. 196, fig, 21. Chatzidakis, «Évolution de l'icône» (as in note 46), p. 187, pl. XXXIX. Weitzmann, *Icon*, pp. 36-37, 104 and pl. 33 (in colour). N. Ševčenko, *The Life of Saint Nicholas in Byzantine Art*, Turin 1983, pp. 29-31, figs. on pages 182-192. Galey, *Sinai*, fig. 93 (in colour). Weitzmann et al., *The Icon*, p. 20, colour plate on page 67. Weitzmann, «Icon Programs», p. 100 (dated to the early 13th century).

**73.** For example, the icon with St. Theodore Stratelates and Saint Demetrios (fig. 42).

**74.** In all likelihood the icon was intended to be placed in the Chapel of Saint Nicholas which existed until recently within the south side of the walls of the Monastery. See Ševčenko (as in note 72), p. 164. Weitzmann, «Icon Programs», p. 100.

**75.** Width of the border: 10.5 cm. Thickness of the board: 2.8 cm. The reverse side is decorated with lozenge-shaped designs in red and blue-black on gesso. K. Weitzmann, «The Selection of Texts for Cyclic Illustration in Byzantine Manuscripts», *Byzantine Books and Bookmen. Dumbarton Oaks Colloquium 1971*, Washington, D. C. 1975, p. 85, fig. 23 (before cleaning) Weitzmann, «Icon Programs», p. 101, fig. 29 (before cleaning) (dated to the early 13th century).

**76.** The inscriptions of the scenes, which are partially covered by a later strip of colour which borders the icon are: [῾Ο ἅγιος ῾Ερμόλ]αος παραλαμβάνον τον αγιον Παντελεήμ[ονα]. Ο αγιος Πα[ντελεή]μον μαν[θά]νον τ[ην ἰα]τρικιν. ῾Ο ἅ(γιος) με σ τόν απο. ῾Ο ἅ(γιος) ανασ[τ]ον τόν πέδαν. ῾Ο ἅ(γιος) αποκτενον τόν ὤφιν. ῾Ο ἅ(γιος) Παντελεήμον βαπτιζόμενος. ῾Ο ἅ(γιος) καταργίζον τά ι[δω]λα. ῾Ο ἅ(γιος) ιώμενος τον τι[φλόν). Ο (αγιος) αναστον τον [π]α[ράλυτον]. ῾Ο ἅ(γιος) κεόμενος. ῾Ο ἅ(γιος) Παντελεήμ(ον) εν το πιρί. ῾Ο ἅ(γιος).. [θη]ριομαχ.. ῾Ο ἅ(γιος) ριπτόμενος ης τιν θάλα[σ]αν. ῾Ο ἅ(γιος) ξίφει τεληουτε. ῾Η κη[δεία] τοῦ ἁγίου.

**77.** The scene which shows Panteleimon and Ermolaos before a snake is not taken from the account of the martyrdom of the Saint by Symeon Metaphrastes, but from the narrative of another Passion of the Saint by an anonymous author. See *Hagiographica graeca inedita*, ed. by B. Vatysev, St. Petersburg 1914, p. 42. It is interesting to note that the two introductory scenes of the cycle tamper with the narrative, showing Panteleimon being taught medicine not by his real teacher, Euphrosynos, but by his spiritual father, Ermolaos.

**78.** The icon was most likely intended for the Chapel of Saint Panteleimon, which in older times existed outside the walls of the Monastery. Cf. Weitzmann, «Icon Programs», p. 101.

**79.** Width of the border: 9.7 cm. Thickness of the board: 2.5 cm. On the reverse side, superimposed bands of alternating red and blue-black wavy brushstrokes. Soteriou, *Εἰκόνες*, I, fig. 168. II, pp. 152-154 (dated to the early 13th century). Weitzmann, «Icon Programs», pp. 99, 100. Belting, *Bild und Kult*, p. 289, fig. 160.

**80.** Cf. R. Janin, «Les Géorgiens à Jérusalem», *Échos d'Orient* 16 (1913) pp. 211-212. The icon was probably intended to be placed in the Chapel of Saint John the Baptist within the enclosure of the Monastery. Cf. Weitzmann, «Icon Programs», p. 99.

**81.** Width of the border: 2.2 cm. Thickness of the board: 1.3 cm. The background of the icon was originally covered with metal revetment. The reverse side was covered with gesso. Galey, *Sinai*, fig. 71 (in colour) (dated here by Weitzmann to the 14th century). *St. Catherine's Monastery*, fig. 129.

**82.** For example, an icon of Christ-Emmanuel and one other of Christ.

**83.** Width of the border: 2.8 cm. The painting has been strengthened by the addition of a wooden support, which was added during recent restoration. Soteriou, *Εἰκόνες*, I, fig. 200. II, p. 181.

**84.** Width of the border: 4 cm. Thickness of the board: 2.8 cm. On the reverse side are traces of superimposed bands of red wavy brushstrokes. Mouriki, «Thirteenth-Century Icon Painting», pp. 63-64, figs. 26 and 40.

**85.** One section of the Greek ligatures was destroyed and replaced by later writing.

**86.** Width of the border: 5.3 cm. Thickness of the board: 3 cm. The reverse side is decorated with a continuous design of red brushstrokes.

**87.** The two other icons are the Sanctuary doors with the Annunciation in the Chapel of the Zoodochos Pigi, and the Archangels Michael and Gabriel. See Weitzmann, «Fragments of an Early St. Nicholas Triptych» (as in note 72), fig. 13. *Monastery of St. Catherine*, fig. 120.

**88.** See especially Weitzmann, «Icon Painting».

**89.** Width of the border: 3 cm. Weitzmann, «Thirteenth-Century Crusader Icons», pp. 183-185, figs. 5-6. Reprinted in Weitzmann, *Studies*, no XI, pp. 295-297, figs. 5-6. Weitzmann, «Icon Painting», pp. 64-65, figs. 26-28. Reprinted in Weitzmann, *Studies*, no. XII, pp. 338-339, figs. 26-28. Weitzmann, *Icon*, pp. 37, 114 and pl. 38 (in colour). Weitzmann et al., *The Icon*, pp. 204-205 and colour plates on pp. 225 and 227 (dated to the third quarter of the 13th century). O. Demus, «Zum Werk eines Venezianischen Malers auf dem Sinai», *Byzanz und der Westen. Studien zur Kunst des Europäischen Mittelalters*. Ed. I. Hutter, Vienna 1984, pp. 131-142, pls. XLVI, XLVII.

**90.** Weitzmann, «Icon Painting», p. 64.

**91.** Width of the border: 1.2 cm. Thickness of the board: 2.8 cm. The reverse side has been covered with a red colour on gesso.

**92.** Panel of Procopios: 51×39.7 cm. Panel of the variant of the Kykkotissa: 51×39.7 cm. Width of the border: 5.5 cm. Thickness of the board: 3 cm. The reverse sides are decorated with superimposed bands of wavy red brushstrokes. Soteriou, *Εἰκόνες*, I, figs. 188-190. II, pp. 171-173 (dated to the 13th century). Weitzmann, «Icon Painting», pp. 66-68, figs. 33-40. Reprinted in Weitzmann, *Studies*, no. XII, pp. 340-343. Weitzmann, *Icon*, pp. 37, 112 and pl. 37 (in colour). Weitzmann, «Crusader Icons», p. 150, pl. LV, fig. 8. Weitzmann et al., *The Icon*, p. 205, colour plate on p. 227 (dated to the third quarter of the 13th century). Belting, *Bild und Kult*, pp. 375, 378, fig. 205.

**93.** See Weitzmann, *Icon*, p. 112. Weitzmann et al., *The Icon*, p. 205.

**94.** Nativity. Width of the border: 1.7 cm. Thickness of the board: 2.7 cm. The reverse side is decorated with superimposed bands of red-brown wavy brushstrokes on gesso. Baptism. Width of the border: 1.8 cm. Thickness of the board: 2.9 cm. The decoration on the reverse side is as in the Nativity. Icon of the Nativity. K. Weitzmann, «Four Icons on Mount Sinai: New Aspects in Crusader Art», *Jahrbuch der Österreichischen Byzantinistik* 21 (1972), pp. 289-290, fig. 10. Reprinted in Weitzmann, *Studies*, no. XIII, pp. 397-398, fig. 10.

**95.** Height: 33.5 cm. Width of the preserved section: 10 cm. Width of the border: 1.6 cm. Thickness of the board: 2.1 cm. Soteriou, *Εἰκόνες*, I, fig. 176. II, pp. 163-164 (dated to the first half of the 13th century).

**96.** Soteriou, *Εἰκόνες*, I, figs. 185, 186. II, pp. 170-171 (dated to the 13th century). Galey, *Sinai*, fig. 99 (in colour). Weitzmann, «Crusader Icons», pp. 148-149, pl. LIII, figs. 3-4. *St. Catherine's Monastery*, figs. 125-126. Mouriki, «Thirteenth-

Century Icon Painting», pp. 67-69, figs. 63, 64.

**97.** The second processional icon in the Monastery depicts the Hodegetria on the main side and the Crucifixion on the reverse side. Its present state is a repainting by Ioannis Kornaros.

**98.** Weitzmann, «Icon Painting», pp. 71-72. Reprinted in Weitzmann, *Studies*, no. XII, pp. 345-346.

**99.** Weitzmann, «Icon Painting», p. 71. Reprinted in Weitzmann, *Studies*, no. XII, p. 345.

**100.** See Mouriki, «Thirteenth-Century Icon Painting», p. 71.

**101.** Hodegetria. Width of the border: 2.5 cm. Thickness of the board: 2 cm. On the reverse side, which has been covered with gesso, there are superimposed bands of red-brown wavy brushstrokes. Weitzmann, «Icon Painting», p. 78, fig. 61. Reprinted in Weitzmann, *Studies*, no. XII, p. 352, fig. 61. Mouriki, «Thirteenth-Century Icon Painting», pp. 64-66, fig. 6. Crucifixion. Width of the border: 2.5 cm. Thickness of the board: 2 cm. On the reverse side the same decoration as on the Hodegetria icon.

**102.** The miraculous icon at the Monastery of the Hodegon at one point exhibited, on the reverse side, the Crucifixion as suggested by various testimonies. The combining of the subjects of the Virgin and Child and the Crucifixion has parallels in Western art. See Belting, *The Image and its Public* (as in note 68), fig. 81.

**103.** Width of the border: 3.3 cm. Thickness of the board: 2.8 cm. On the reverse side, which has been covered with gesso, there is a double red cross. Galey, *Sinai*, fig. 64 (in colour).

**104.** Added border from four wooden strips, 2.7 cm. in width. The reverse side has been covered with gesso, while the four spandrels have been painted over with a red-brown colour and added bands in a deep red-brown. I warmly thank my colleague Helen Evans, for interesting comments on the 'Armenian' elements of the icon.

**105.** The black attendant first appears in Western art in the relief of the pulpit by Nicola Pisano in the Cathedral of Siena (c. 1270). Only after the 14th century, does the third Magus adopt the characteristics of a black. See P.H.D. Kaplan, *The Rise of the Black Magus in Western Art* (Studies in Fine Arts: Iconography, No. 9), Ann Arbor 1985, especially pp. 85-101.

**106.** To the masterpieces of the Monastery from this period belong the side wings of a small diptych with representations of martyrs and of monks, a section of an icon with the portraits of the Apostles Peter and Paul and St. John the Theologian, and the diptych with the Hodegetria and the Descent from the Cross. Soteriou, *Εἰκόνες*, I, figs. 62-63, 225 and 234. II, pp. 77-78 (a dating of the work close to 1300 has been proposed by H. Buchthal, «Notes on Some Early Palaeologan Miniatures», *Kunsthistorische Forschungen O. Pächt zu seinem 70. Geburtstag*, Vienna 1972, pp. 39-40.

**107.** Soteriou, *Εἰκόνες*, I, figs. 208-213, 214-217. II, pp. 189-191.

**108.** Soteriou, *Εἰκόνες*, I, fig.223. II, p. 196.

**109.** Width of the border: 1 cm. Thickness of the board: 1 cm. Soteriou, *Εἰκόνες*, I, figs. 214-217. II, pp. 190-191. *St. Catherine's Monastery*, fig. 130 (in colour): Annunciation, Nativity, Entry into Jerusalem, Crucifixion.

**110.** Added border, width: 2.4 cm. Thickness of the board (without the border): 2.2 cm. With the border: 4.2 cm. The reverse side is undecorated and bears the signature of the painter. A. Soler i Palet, «Un retaule catala del monestir del Sinai», *Estudis Universitaris Catalans* VI (1912), pp. 92-94. J. Couyat-Barthoux, «Sur une peinture catalane du XIVe siècle trouvée au monastère du Sinaï», *Anuari del Institut d'Estudis Catalans* V (1913-1914), pp. 729-733.

**111.** Bernardo Maresa, citizen of Barcelona, was appointed consul on November 13, 1385 by King Peter, while the end of his service was on August 23, 1390. A. Lopez de Meneses, *Los consulados Catalanes de Alejandria y Damasco en el Reinado de Pedro el Ceremonioso*, Zaragoza 1956, p. 183.

**112.** Ibid., p. 132.

**113.** I warmy thank Delpfim Santos and Toby Baldwin for their help in the reading of the inscription.

**114.** See, for example, J. Sureda, *El Gotic Catala I. Pintura*. Barcelona (n. d.).

**115.** A colony of Catalan merchants was established in Syria in a period when the Catalan presence in the Eastern Mediterranean was very strong. See also K. M. Setton, «The Catalans and Florentines in Greece, 1380-1462», in K. M. Setton and H. W. Hazard, ed. *A History of the Crusades*, III. Madison, Milwaukee, London, 1975, p. 267.

**116.** Eckenstein, *History of Sinai*, p. 156.

**117.** Ibid., pp. 155-164.

**118.** For the economic height of the Monastery in the second half of the 15th century, see Amantos, *Σύντομος ἱστορία*, pp. 38-39. Z. N. Tsirpanlis, «Ὁ Ἰ. Πλουσιαδηνὸς καὶ ἡ σιναϊτικὴ ἐκκλησία τοῦ Χριστοῦ Κεφαλᾶ στὸ Χάνδακα», *Θησαυρίσματα* 3 (1964), especially pp. 8-12. Cf. Chatzidakis, «Τοιχογραφίες Σινᾶ», p. 229. For certain characteristics of the Sinaitic workshop of icons and monumental painting of the second half of the 15th century, see Chatzidakis, op. cit., pp. 224-229.

**119.** Width of the border: 1.4 cm. Thickness of the board: 1.4 cm. The reverse side is covered with gesso and cloth. Soteriou, *Εἰκόνες*, I, fig. 235. II, pp. 205-206 (dated to the early 15th century). G. Babić, «Il modello e la replica nell'arte bizantina delle icone», *Arte Cristiana*, no. 724 (1989), p. 74, fig. 21.

**120.** Added border, width: 1.7 cm. Thickness of the board with the added wooden strips: 2.6 cm. The reverse side is decorated with dense superimposed bands of red-brown wavy brushstrokes on gesso.

**121.** The subject and the dimensions of the icon of the Lamentation suggest that it had a determined function in the church, most probably to be placed on the proskynetarion during Holy Week (especially on Good Friday when this particular theme was the focal point of the Akolouthia).

**122.** Width of the border: 4.1 cm. Original thickness of the wood: 3.9 cm. The reverse side is covered with gesso. Soteriou, *Εἰκόνες*, I, fig. 221. II, pp. 194-195. *St. Catherine's Monastery*, fig. 145 (in colour).

## POST-BYZANTINE ICONS
(Cretan School)

**1.** The selection of icons was greatly assisted by Anastasia Drandaki, graduate of the Archaeology Department of the Philosophical School of the University of Athens.

**2.** M. Chatzidakis, «Aspects de la peinture religieuse dans les Balkans (1300-1550)», *Variorum Reprints*, London 1976, section II, pp. 196.

**3.** *Εἰκόνες Κρητικῆς Σχολῆς*, p. 10.

**4.** M. Constantoudake-Kitromelidou, «Οἱ Κρητικοὶ ζωγράφοι καὶ τὸ κοινό τους: ἡ ἀντιμετώπιση τῆς τέχνης τους στὴ Βενετοκρατία», *Κρητικὰ Χρονικὰ* per. 3, vol. 26 (1986), p. 225.

**5.** *Εἰκόνες Κρητικῆς Σχολῆς*, p. 6.

**6.** Ibid., p. 12.

**7.** M. Constantoudake-Kitromelidou, op. cit., p. 258.

**8.** M. Chatzidakis, *IEE*, vol. X, Athens 1974, p. 434.

**9.** Maria Vassilakes-Mavrakakes, «Ὁ ζωγράφος Ἄγγελος Ἀκοτάντος: τὸ ἔργο καὶ ἡ διαθήκη του (1436)», *Θησαυρίσματα* 18 (1981), pp. 290, 298. See also M. Manoussakas, «Ἡ διαθήκη τοῦ Ἀγγέλου Ἀκοτάντου (1436), ἀγνώστου Κρητικοῦ ζωγράφου», *ΔΧΑΕ* per. 4, 2 (1960-61), pp. 139-150.

**10.** Chatzidakis, *Ἕλληνες ζωγράφοι*, pp. 147-153, with bibliography.

**11.** The border of the icon, from the same wood, slightly raised, has a width of 2.4 cm. I believe that the two coloured bands of blue and coral which surround the icon, and the bold lines of the eyebrows of Christ and John the Baptist have been applied at a later date.

**12.** Above this, the signature is repeated with half-sized letters of a different black colour, perhaps due to Ioannis Kornaros, who added according to his habit, the word ΚΡΗ[ΤΟC].

**13.** Morphologically, Christ resembles the signed Christ of Angelos, in the Zakynthos Museum; see *Holy Image*, p. 124, fig. 43. The Virgin's portrait resembles the Virgin of the Deesis by Angelos in the Kanellopoulos Collection (Theano Chatzidakis, *L'art des icônes en Crète et dans les îles après Byzance*, Europalia, Greece, 1982, fig. 2).

**14.** Some rare mistakes, such as the flat, low chiton of John the Baptist with the superfluous slanting line of his hem, which extends behind the wooden throne of Christ, have not been commented on.

**15.** From a metochion of the Monastery.

**16.** M. Vassilakes-Mavrakakes, «Saint Phanourios: Cult and Iconography», *ΔΧΑΕ* per. 4, 1 (1980-81), pp. 223-238.

**17.** According to Vassilakes-Mavrakakes, seven icons of the Saint are known to have been painted by Angelos, op. cit., p. 293. To these known representations may be added the Saint of this Deesis icon.

**18.** The border, from the same wood, is repainted. The icon has been published also by Weitzmann, *Ikonen*, no. 22.

**19.** The signature 'hand of Angelos' is considered, in any case, a later addition, perhaps, by Kornaros. For Kornaros, see N. Tomadakis, «Ἰωάννης Κορνάρος, Κρὴς ζωγράφος (1745-1796)», *Κρητικὰ Χρονικὰ* Β΄ (1948), pp. 253-264.

**20.** D. I. Pallas, «Οἱ βενετοκρητικὲς μικρογραφίες Olschki 35398 τοῦ ἔτους 1415», *Πεπραγμένα Β΄ Διεθνοῦς Κρητολογικοῦ Συνεδρίου* Α΄, Athens 1967, pl. ΡΚΒ΄.

**21.** In facial type, Prochoros resembles the Kardiotissa of Angelos (*Holy Image*, p. 125, fig. 44) and the lower right apostle of the icon of 'Christ the Vine' by the same painter (*Εἰκόνες Κρητικῆς Σχολῆς*, pl. 10).

**22.** *Εἰκόνες Κρητικῆς Σχολῆς*, fig. 3 and pp. 18-19.

**23.** The surface of the icon is curved and the reverse has two supports.

**24.** Similarities may also be detected in the colours. In the drawing, the differences are secondary. The inscription on the Sinai icon also differs: *Holy of Holies*, taken, undoubtedly, from the hymnography of the feast (November 21). The inscription also occurs on an icon of Damaskinos with the same subject in Patmos, *Icons of Patmos*, p. 102. In the two-zoned icon of Sinai with the Nativity above and the Presentation in the Temple below the scene is depicted in the same manner. See Soteriou, *Εἰκόνες*, I, fig. 236. They date the icon (vol. II, p. 207) probably to the second half of the 15th century. The variant of the Presentation by Angelos was imitated by many painters. A similar representation is found in the sixth icon of the Dodekaorton of the iconostasis of the Sinai katholikon.

**25.** M. Chatzidakis, *IEE*, vol. X, p. 421.

**26.** M. Chatzidakis, «Les débuts de l'École Crétoise et la question de l'École dite Italogrecque, Études sur la peinture Postbyzantine», *Var. Repr.*, London 1976, section IV, pp. 178, 182.

**27.** M. Vassilakes-Mavrakakes, op. cit., p. 298.

**28.** *Εἰκόνες Πάτμου*, pl. 204b.

**29.** Ibid., p. 61. Concerning the colours of the face, the Archangel resembles the enthroned Virgin of the Benaki Museum (no. 3051), attributed to the atelier of Ritzos (*Εἰκόνες Κρητικῆς Σχολῆς*, p. 29). For the section from the waist up, there is considerable similarity to the icon of the half-length Archangel from the Spilia of Kissamos in Crete (*Βυζαντινὴ-Μεταβυζαντινὴ Τέχνη*, fig. 106 of p. 107). The technique of the icon, as M. Borboudakis has noted (pp. 107-108), relates it to the art of Andreas Ritzos.

**30.** *Εἰκόνες Πάτμου*, pl. 114 and pp. 101-102. Also in this icon, while the legs are rendered frontally, the body, the abdomen and the hip are depicted as if the right leg were at ease. The same, however, is the case with a military saint in the Peribleptos Church, Mystra (M. Chatzidakis, *Mystra* [1987], fig. 56). The same author (*Εἰκόνες Πάτμου*, pl. 205d) published the icon of the Archangel from Mount Sinai, which greatly resembles our icon. Is it the same or a different work?

**31.** The panel of the icon is carved in the centre with a rectangle (17.5×15 cm.), where the Virgin is depicted with the inscription: *The Hodegetria*.

**32.** Marisa Bianco Fiorin, «Un Inedita 'Madonna Hodigitria' di Andrea Rico da Candia», *Atti dei Civici Musei di Storia ed Arte di Trieste*, no. 8 (1973-75), pp. 5-9, fig. 2.

**33.** Christ, in his facial characteristics, resembles the Lord in the Deesis of Angelos fig. 77, and indication of the tie between the painters of the two icons. And from the other half-figures of the frame, the figures of Saints Nicholas and Anthony are close to the corresponding figures of the frame of the Ascension by A. Ritzos in Tokyo (for easy reference, see *Εἰκόνες Πάτμου*, pl. 201).

**34.** The frame is attached to the wooden board of the icon.

**35.** These headdresses are usual in the 16th century. See the wall paintings of the Monastery of Dilios on the island of Ioannina (Theopiste Liva-Xanthakes, *Οἱ τοιχογραφίες τῆς Μονῆς Ντίλιου*, Ioannina 1980, fig. 66, Dormition of Saint Nicholas), of the Stavronikita Monastery, Mount Athos (Chatzidakis, *Σταυρονικήτα*, figs. 11, 121. For icons of the beginning of the 16th century with the same feature, see also N. Zias, «Some Representations of Byzantine Cantors», *AAA* 1969, fig. 4). For the origin of headdresses from the Byzantine period, see the representation of the 14th *oikos* of the Akathistos Hymn in the wall painting of the first quarter of the 14th century in the church of Saint Nicholas Orphanos in Thessalonica (A. Xyngopoulos, *Οἱ τοιχογραφίες τοῦ Ἁγ. Νικολάου Ὀρφανοῦ Θεσσαλονίκης*, Athens 1964, figs. 101, 102). See also, Neil K. Moran, «Musikalische Gesten in der byzantinischen Malerei des späten Mittelaters», *Zograf* 14 (1983), pp. 52-58. In p. 59, abstr. in German.

**36.** J. Goar, *Euchologion* (2nd ed., Venice 1730), pp. 452-453.

**37.** As in the left edifice in the background in the icon of the Zoodochos Pigi at Sinai (*Εἰκόνες Πάτμου*, pl. 204b).

**38.** W. Hatch, *Greek and Syrian Miniatures in Jerusalem*, Cambridge, Mass. 1931, pl. XI and p. 68.

**39.** *Εἰκόνες Πάτμου*, pp. 55-56. Pseudo-cufic writing is often encountered, however, during the 16th century.

**40.** On the reverse side of the icon are two supports. The border is from the same wood, width 0.8 cm. Published by Chatzidakis, *Ἕλληνες ζωγράφοι*, p. 266, fig. 139. A large icon of the painter with the same subject is found in Zakynthos, see by the same author, *ΑΔ* 22 (1967), Β΄, p. 28.

**41.** M. Chatzidakis, op. cit., characterizes him as excellent.

**42.** Chatzidakis, *Ἕλληνες ζωγράφοι*, p. 265.

**43.** The Saint is more slender with more correct proportions than the same figure by Pavias (second half of the 15th century), who has a wide face (*Εἰκόνες Κρητικῆς Σχολῆς*, fig. 19). He is closer to Saint Anthony in half-length found on the border of the icon in the Benaki Museum, no. 3051 (Xyngopoulos, *Κατάλογος*, pl. 56D), and to the triptych no. 29537 of the same museum, dated around the year 1500.

**44.** Melchisedek is depicted totally naked and his body covered with long hairs in a Byzantine wall painting of 1367/8 (N. B. Drandakis, «Ὁ σταυροειδὴς ναὸς τοῦ Προδρόμου στὰ Χρύσαφα τῆς Λακεδαίμονος», *Λακωνικαὶ Σπουδαὶ Θ΄* [1988], fig. 15 and pp. 320-321).

**45.** The lower representations have a height of 6.3 cm.

**46.** *Holy Image*, p. 129, fig. 48, see also pp. 207-208. Ch. M. Koutelakes, *Ξυλόγλυπτα τέμπλα τῆς Δωδεκανήσου μέχρι τὸ 1700*, Athens-Ioannina 1986, p. 70, dates the Sanctuary doors to the end of the 15th century.

**47.** Ibid., pls. 10a, 10b, 10c and pp. 71, 73, 75.

**48.** For the urn (stamnos) see: D. Mouriki, «Αἱ βιβλικαὶ προεικονίσεις τῆς Παναγίας εἰς τὸν τροῦλλον τῆς Περιβλέπτου τοῦ Μυστρᾶ», *ΑΔ* 25 (1970), p. 218.

**49.** Chatzidakis, *Σταυρονικήτα*, fig. 30. See also Moses of the Metamorphosis church at Meteora. See also Chatzidakis, «Recherches», fig. 91.

**50.** Cufic letters are found in other works of the 16th century: on the mantle of Aaron on the border of an icon of Saint Anthony painted by the priest Demetrios fig. 88, in the depiction of Moses of Stavronikita and of the Metamorphosis of Meteora, in the angels of the Holy Liturgy of Stavronikita Monastery (Chatzidakis, *Σταυρονικήτα*, figs. 21-24), and elsewhere. The buildings in the background of the Annunciation of the Sanctuary doors resemble those in the icon of the Annunciation in Lavra, attributed to Theophanes (Chatzidakis, «Recherches», fig. 34).

**51.** I believe the figures of Moses and Aaron on the Sanctuary doors of the present iconostasis of the main church to be an imitation of these earlier works.

**52.** On the reverse side the icon has two supports. The frame of the icon is elaborate.

**53.** Chatzidakis, *Σταυρονικήτα*, fig. 167. See also figs. 162, 165. Worthy of attention is the decorative character of the folds of the breeches at the left knee of Saint Theodore Teron. For related examples see the saints of Theophanes in the same Monastery, op. cit., figs. 158, 165.

**54.** Ibid., fig. 167. See ibid., fig. 162 and the shield of Saint Victor.

**55.** On the reverse, the icon has two supports. The bold, black small lines which delineate the eyebrows and the outlines of the eyes and faces raise the suspicion that they may be later additions.

**56.** Earlier, in an icon of the 15th century in the Byzantine Museum in Athens, the entire subject 'In Thee Rejoiceth' is enclosed within a circle (K. Weitzmann, M. Chatzidakis, S. Radojčić, *Le grand livre des icônes* [Paris 1983], icons on pp. 118, 119). For the iconography of the 'In Thee Rejoiceth' see also: G. Galavaris, «Majestas Mariae in Late Greek and Russian Icons», in the vol. *Icons and East Christian Works of Art*, Michel van Rijn publication, p. 12.

**57.** Chatzidakis, *Σταυρονικήτα*, figs. 102, 134, 205.

**58.** On the reverse side of the icon are three supports.

**59.** *Εἰκόνες Πάτμου*, p. 68.

**60.** M. Chatzidakis, «Les débuts de l'École Crétoise...», *Variorum Reprints*, London 1976, p. 180.

**61.** The frame width is 7 cm., with splendid decoration of mother-of-pearl, and has in the lower section the inscription in capital letters: *Δι᾽ ἐξόδου καὶ συνδρομῆς ᾽Αν[α]στασίου Σιναΐτου μοναχοῦ τοῦ ἐκ Βουλγαρίας ἔτος ἀπὸ ᾽Αδὰμ + ΖCΚΓ΄ + ἔτος τὸ σ[ωτή]ριον + ΑΨΙΕ΄* (1715).

**62.** Below the Sanctuary doors, is the inscription: ΠΆΡΑCΧΕ ΛΎCΙΝ Χ(ΡΙΣΤ)Ε ΤΩΝ ΕΠΤΑΙΣΜΈΝΩΝ Τω ἘΖωΓΡΑΦΉCΑΝΤΙ ΤΉν ΔἘ ΕἰκωΝΑΝ, and below Symeon: ΧΕἸΡ ΔΑΜΑCΚΥΝΟΫ́ ΚΡΗ[ΤΟC] ͵ΑΦΟΑ΄. The letters, as in the others of the inscription Η ΫΠΑΠΑΝΤΗ ΤΟΥ ΧΡΙCΤΟΫ which are different from the type of letters on the scroll of the prophetess Anna, are considered a later addition, perhaps by Ioannis Kornaros. The type of inscription is not found on authentic works of Damaskinos. For the type of the inscription, see the recent unpublished dissertation by Maria Constantoudake-Kitromelidou, *Μιχαὴλ Δαμασκηνὸς (1530/35-1592/93), συμβολὴ στὴ μελέτη τῆς ζωγραφικῆς του*, vol. I, Athens 1988, pp. 138-144. For the icon of the Presentation at Sinai, see ibid., vol. II, p. 457.

**63.** Ibid., p. 457.

**64.** Compare this depiction of the Virgin to the Virgin of the Deesis from the wall painting of Stavronikita Monastery (1546). Chatzidakis, *Σταυρονικήτα*, fig. 2. Also the figures of Joseph, Anna and the Virgin can be compared to the corresponding figures of the icon at Lavra, Mount Athos. Chatzidakis, «Recherches», fig. 36.

**65.** Chatzidakis, *Icônes*, notes (p. 196) that the original date, after examination 'in situ', is 1578.

**66.** On a shelf of the north wall of the main church. For a colour photograph see also Weitzmann, *Ikonen*, fig. 20. The icon has been attributed by P. Vocotopoulos to Georgios Klontzas (P. Vocotopoulos, «῞Ενα ἄγνωστο τρίπτυχο τοῦ Γεωργίου Κλόντζα», *Πεπραγμένα τοῦ Ε΄ Διεθνοῦς Κρητολογικοῦ Συνεδρίου*, Β΄ [Heraklion, Crete 1986], p. 74 - if indeed this is the same icon).

**67.** Published by C. L. Kayser, Heidelberg 1840, pp. 129 and 133.

**68.** The executioner has a long moustache, but small beard (?) in the scene of the beheading of John the Baptist in the icon of Damaskinos, P. L. Vocotopoulos, «Icônes de Michel Damaskinos à Corfou», *Byzantion* 53 (1983), pl. VIII. 1.

**69.** An ostrich feather is used as an ornament for the equipment of the horse and even more on the headdress of the servant, in the Adoration of the Magi by Michael Damaskinos (*Βυζαντινὴ - Μεταβυζαντινὴ Τέχνη*, p. 135, fig. 138).

**70.** Xyngopoulos, *Κατάλογος*, pl. 11, no. 9 and pp. 17-18. The Sinai icon is more beautiful.

**71.** A similar effect is achieved by the chrysography of the himation of Christ in the wing of a triptych in the Benaki Museum (second half of the 15th century). *Εἰκόνες Κρητικῆς Σχολῆς*, fig. 37A and p. 44. See also fig. 36a and p. 43. Garments with many pleats are worn also by the figures painted by Klontzas in the Sinai icon with scenes from the monastic life. There, however, the folds are not so linear and sometimes form lighted triangles.

**72.** P. Vocotopoulos (see note 66), p. 74. In the same study (p. 64) the known signed icons of Klontzas are reckoned at 10, and the unsigned to be 11 or 12.

**73.** A. Paliouras, *Ὁ ζωγράφος Γεώργιος Κλόντζας (1540c-1608) καὶ αἱ μικρογραφίαι τοῦ κώδικος αὐτοῦ*, Athens 1977, p. 56.

**74.** For a brief, recent account of the features of the art of Klontzas, see Chatzidakis, *Icônes*, p. 74. See also Myrtale Acheimastou, «Εἰκὼν τῆς Δευτέρας Παρουσίας ἐκ τῆς Σύμης», *ΔΧΑΕ* per. 4, vol. 5 (1966-69), p. 225.

**75.** The icon has a wood-carved frame. At its apex appears the date 1758. The work has been published by Xyngopoulos, *Σχεδίασμα*, pl. 47.2. For other icons of Klontzas at Sinai, see also M. Constantoudake-Kitromelidou, «Τρίπτυχο τοῦ Γεωργίου Κλόντζα, ἄλλοτε σὲ ξένη ἰδιωτικὴ Συλλογή», *Πεπραγμένα τοῦ Ε΄ Διεθνοῦς Κρητολογικοῦ Συνεδρίου*, Β΄, Heraklion, Crete 1986, p. 237, note 109.

**76.** Ibid., p. 238, note 111 and p. 241, note 123, conjectures that the inscription and the date were not written by the painter.

**77.** According to Xyngopoulos, *Σχεδίασμα*, p. 175, the portico resembles those in works of the early Italian Renaissance and 'by the correct perspective of the buildings it belongs almost entirely to the art of the West'.

**78.** Lanterns similar to those hanging from the arch above of the table correspond to those found in the triptych published by P. Vocotopoulos, op. cit., pl. ΚΕ΄, fig. 7. It should be noted, however, that the ambo, upon which a young novice reads, was not depicted in correct perspective. The awkwardness of the painter in the handling of perspective has been referred to elsewhere. The headdresses worn by the reader on the ambo and by the figure who serves the food are Western. See, for example, an icon of Giotto, L. Coletti, *I primitivi* 1, Novara (1941), p. 87.

**79.** The icon, attached to the iconostasis, is surrounded by a frame, 1.5 cm. in width.

**80.** The same occurs in the Nativity and the Journey to Bethlehem in the triptych attributed to Klontzas. M. Constantoudake-Kitromelidou, op. cit., pl. ΜΒ΄.

**81.** Portrait types and further elements, such as the figure of the Virgin in the centre, support the attribution of the icon to Klontzas. The Tower of Babel, the Murder of Abel and the Crossing of the Red Sea are drawn in accordance with the miniatures of a codex which Klontzas illustrated in 1590-92. (A. Paliouras, op. cit., fig. 12.3 [lower right], fig. 69). In the small icon which depicts (lower right) the interrogation of Joseph by the council, the ciborium in the background is similar to that found in figs. 316 and 327 of the codex.

**82.** On an icon of the Greek Institute of Venice (Chatzidakis, *Icônes*, pl. 37, fig. 50) and on a wing of a triptych whose subject is nearer to the painting inside the rectangle of the Sinai icon. For the wing of this triptych see: P. Vocotopoulos, op. cit., pl. ΚΕ΄. As has been observed, the prolific Klontzas, even if he often returns to the same subjects, never repeats the exact composition (M. Constantoudake-Kitromelidou, op. cit., p. 241, note 127).

**83.** *Εἰκόνες Πάτμου*, p. 122.

**84.** On the reverse side of the icon are two supports. For the saints, see also P. Vocotopoulos, «Τὸ λάβαρο τοῦ Φραγκίσκου Μοροζίνη στὸ Μουσεῖο Correr τῆς Βενετίας», *Θησαυρίσματα* 18 (1981), pp. 272-273.

**85.** *Βυζαντινὴ - Μεταβυζαντινὴ Τέχνη*, p. 156, fig. 159. P. Vocotopoulos (op. cit., p. 157) dates the icon to the second quarter of the 17th century.

**86.** To these may be added the icon of the Tsakyroglou Collection, A. Karakatsane, *Εἰκόνες, Συλλογὴ Γεωργίου Τσακύρογλου*, Athens 1980, pp. 78-79, fig. 112 and the icon of Saint Sabbas (1659) of the Demetrios Oikonomopoulos collection, Chrysanthe Baltoyianne, *Εἰκόνες*, Athens 1985, pl. 64, fig. 76. For Tzanes see Chatzidakis, *Icônes*, pp. 128-131, N. B. Drandakis, *Ὁ Ἐμμανουὴλ Τζάνε Μπουνιαλῆς*, Athens 1962 and lately, by the same author an article with the same title in the periodical *Νέα Χριστιανικὴ Κρήτη* of the Metropolis of Rethymnon (in press).

**87.** The panel is attached to another thicker board and has a frame.

**88.** Xyngopoulos, *Σχεδίασμα*, p. 226, note 3. The nimbi must also have been overpainted.

**89.** This can be compared with John Climacus, icon of Tzanes (N. B. Drandakis, op. cit., 1962, pl. 17). See also the apostle of the Healing of the Blind (op. cit., pl. 34a).

**90.** Chatzidakis, *῞Ελληνες ζωγράφοι*, pp. 192-198; P. Vocotopoulos, «Τὸ λάβαρο τοῦ Φραγκίσκου Μοροζίνη στὸ Μουσεῖο Correr τῆς Βενετίας», op. cit., pp. 269-275; by the same, «Οἱ δεσποτικὲς εἰκόνες τοῦ Βίκτωρος στὴ Μονὴ Φιλοσόφου», *Πρακτικὰ Γ΄ Διεθνοῦς Συνεδρίου Πελοποννησιακῶν Σπουδῶν*, Athens 1987-88, pp. 241-251.

**91.** Located in the 'Gallery'. The carved wooden frame is gilded. In the middle of the crowning element is painted an unbearded figure.

**92.** Christ and the Virgin are reminiscent of the despotic icons by Victor in the Philosophos Monastery, P. Vocotopoulos, op. cit., pls. 7,9. For the Virgin see also Chatzidakis, *῞Ελληνες ζωγράφοι*, p. 201, fig. 63. On the reverse side of the central panel is written an annotation: *Το παρόν σφαλιστάρη αφιερωθην... εις την ἱεράν σύναξιν εις Τζουβανίαν της αιγύπτου και όποιος το αποξενώση να είναι ἡμερίς αυτού μετά του προδότου ἰούδα και να είναι ἀναθεματισμεν(ος) ὑπό παντων των αδελφών.*

**93.** Located in the 'Gallery'. And here anathemas have been written on the reverse side.

**94.** *Patmos, Treasures of the Monastery*, Ekdotike Athenon, Athens 1988, p. 178, fig. 50.

**95.** Chatzidakis, *῞Ελληνες ζωγράφοι*, p. 200, fig. 62.

**96.** The surface is curved. On the reverse side of the icon are two supports. A colour photograph has been published in *Ὁδηγὸς ῾Ιερᾶς Μονῆς Σινᾶ* (1985), fig. 132, where the icon is dated to the 17th century.

**97.** More accurate is the representation of the Monastery in an icon on the back of the archbishop's throne in the katholikon. In its inscription reference is made to the Archbishop of Sinai, Cyril, evidently, the Second, 1759-1789 (*Πανηγυρικὸς τόμος ἐπὶ τῇ 1400ῇ ἀμφιετηρίδι τῆς ῾Ιερᾶς Μονῆς τοῦ Σινᾶ*, Athens 1971, p. 519).

**98.** Ph. I. Piombinos, *῞Ελληνες ἁγιογράφοι μέχρι τὸ 1821*, 2nd ed., Athens 1984, p. 261.

**99.** G. Soteriou, «Εἰκόνα μὲ ἔθιμα τῆς Μονῆς Σινᾶ καὶ ἱστορικῶν σκηνῶν τῆς ἐρήμου», *ΔΧΑΕ* per. 4, vol. 2.

## ICONS FROM THE METOCHION OF THE SINAI MONASTERY IN HERAKLION, CRETE

**1.** Maria Kazanake-Lappa, «Εἰκονογραφικὲς παρατηρήσεις σὲ τρεῖς Κρητικὲς εἰκόνες μὲ τὴν παράσταση τῆς Δέησης», *Tenth Symposium of Byzantine and Post-Byzantine Art and Archaeology, Abstracts of the Proceedings*, Athens, May 18, 19, 20, 1990, p. 26.

**2.** Soteriou, *Εἰκόνες* I, p. 65, fig. 48.

**3.** D. Mouriki, *A Deesis Icon in the Art Museum*, Princeton University, 27/1 (1968), p. 16.

**4.** D. Mouriki, ibid., p. 19. This arrangement comes from Byzantine models and is often repeated in Post-Byzantine art. The figure of Christ can be compared with that of Christ Pantocrator in the Antivouniotissa Museum of Corfu. See P. Vocotopoulos, *Εἰκόνες τῆς Κέρκυρας*, ed. National Bank of Greece, Athens 1990, pp. 26-27, no. 12, fig. 18.

**5.** Soteriou, *Εἰκόνες* I, p. 165, fig. 178. In manuscripts, this condensed form is due to lack of space.

**6.** M. Borboudakis, «Βυζαντινὰ καὶ Μεταβυζαντινὰ μνημεῖα Κρήτης», *Κρητικὰ Χρονικὰ* 22 (1969), p. 527, pl. ΡΛΔ΄, 3. By the same author, *῾Ημερολόγιο Δήμου ῾Ηρακλείου*, 1985, no. 33, p. 137. By the same author, *Βυζαντινὴ - Μεταβυζαντινὴ Τέχνη*, Athens 1986, no. 142.

**7.** *Εἰκόνες Πάτμου*, pl. 201.

**8.** M. Borboudakis, op. cit., no. 141.

**9.** *Εἰκόνες Πάτμου*, no. 72, pp. 122-123, pl. 128.

**10.** Xyngopoulos, *Σχεδίασμα*, p. 214, pl. 55.2.

**11.** *Εἰκόνες Πάτμου*, p. 123. P. Vocotopoulos, *Εἰκόνες τῆς Κέρκυρας*, no. 127, p. 159, figs. 60, 298-300, 344 ΙΖ. This iconographic type predominates, with small variations, in details from the works of the later Cretan painters Emmanuel Lambardos, Victor, Silvestros Theocharis and Stephanos Tzangarolas.

**12.** *Εἰκόνες Πάτμου*, p. 12. P. Vocotopoulos, op. cit., p. 159.

**13.** M. Borboudakis, *῾Ημερολόγιο Δήμου ῾Ηρακλείου*, 1985, no. 14.

**14.** M. Vassilakes-Mavrakakes, «Saint Phanourios: Cult and Iconography», *ΔΧΑΕ* per. 4, vol. 1 (1980-81), pp. 223-238.

# CHURCH GOLD EMBROIDERIES


Th. Aliprantis, *Χρυσοκέντητα ἄμφια τῆς ῾Ι. Μονῆς Λειμῶνος Λέσβου*, Athens 1975.

A. Banck, *Βυζαντινὴ τέχνη στὶς ρωσικὲς συλλογές*, Leningrad - Moscow n.d. (Russian with english translation).

*Byzantinischer Kunstexport. Seine gesellschaftliche und künstlerische Bedeutung für die Länder Mittel-und Osteuropas*, ed. Heinrich Nickel, Halle-Wittenberg 1978.

E. Chatzidaki-Vei, *᾿Εκκλησιαστικὰ κεντήματα Μουσείου Μπενάκη*, Athens 1953.

A. Chatzimichali, «Τὰ χρυσοκλαβαρικὰ συρματέϊνα-συρμακέσικα κεντήματα», *Mélanges offerts à O. et M. Merlier*, vol. 2, Athens 1956, p. 447 ff.

V. Cottas, «Contribution à l' étude de quelques tissus liturgiques», *Atti del V Congr. Inter. Studi Bizantini II (Studi Bizantini e Neoellenici VI)*, Rome 1940, p. 87 ff.

N. Delialis, «῞Αμφια χρυσοκέντητα ἐκ τοῦ ἱεροῦ ναοῦ ῾Αγίου Νικολάου Κοζάνης», *Οἰκοδομή, ᾿Επετηρὶς ῾Ι. Μητροπόλεως Σερβίων καὶ Κοζάνης*, vol. Α΄, Kozani 1958, p. 332 ff.

I. Dimopoulos, *Τὸ ἐν Μόσχᾳ Συνοδικὸν Σκευοφυλάκιον*, Athens 1900, p. 56 ff.

F. Dölger, «Die zwei byzantinischen 'Fahnen' im Halberstädter Domschatz», *Geisteswelt des Mittelalters. Studien und Texte. Martin Grabmann zur Vollendung des 60. Lebensjahres von Freunden und Schülern gewidmet*, 1935, pp. 1351-1360.

N. B. Drandakis, «῾Ο ἐπιτάφιος τῆς Ζερμπίτσας (1539-1540)», *Τόμος εἰς μνήμην Κ. ῾Ι. ᾿Αμάντου*, Athens 1960, pp. 454-462.

—, «᾿Εκκλησιαστικὰ κεντήματα τῆς μονῆς ᾿Αρκαδίου», *Πεπραγμένα τοῦ Β΄ Διεθνοῦς Κρητολογικοῦ Συνεδρίου*, vol. Α΄, Athens 1967, p. 297 ff.

J. Ebersolt, *Les arts somptuaires de Byzance*, Paris 1923.

J. Flemming, *Byzantinische Schatzkunst*, Berlin 1979.

A. Frolow, «La Podéa, un tissu décoratif de l'église byzantine», *Byzantion* 13 (1938), p. 461 ff.

A. Grabar, *L' Iconoclasme byzantin. Dossier archéologique*, Paris 1957.

J. G. Herzog zu Sachsen, *Das Katharinenkloster am Sinai*, Leipzig-Berlin 1912.

G. Jacopi, «Cimeli del ricamo, della pittura e della toreutica nel Tesoro del Monastero di Patmo», *Clara Rhodos* VI-VII (1932, 1933, 1941), pp. 709-716.

P. Johnstone, *Byzantine Tradition in Church Embroidery*, London 1967.

—, «The Byzantine 'Pallio' in the Palazzo Bianco at Genoa», *Gazette des Beaux Arts*, March 1976, pp. 99-108.

C. Kallinikos, *῾Ο χριστιανικὸς ναὸς καὶ τὰ τελούμενα ἐν αὐτῷ*, 2nd ed., Athens 1958.

I. Kleomvrotos, Metropolitan of Mytilene, *Mytilena Sacra*, vol. Α΄, Athens 1970, pp. 69-107; vol. Β΄, Thessalonica 1974, pp. 34-43; vol. C΄, Thessalonica 1978, pp. 49-54 and 103-104.

C. Kourkoulas, *Τὰ ῾Ιερατικὰ ἄμφια καὶ ὁ συμβολισμὸς αὐτῶν ἐν τῇ ὀρθοδόξῳ ἑλληνικῇ ᾿Εκκλησίᾳ*, Athens 1960.

G. Millet, *Recherches sur l'iconographie de l'Évangile*, Paris 1916.

G. Millet-Hélène des Ylouses, *Broderies religieuses de style byzantin*. Plates, Paris 1939. Text, Paris 1947.

G. Millet, J. Pargoire, L. Petit, *Recueil des inscriptions chrétiennes de l' Athos*, Paris 1904.

M. A. Musicescu, *La broderie médiévale roumaine*, Bucharest 1969.

P. S. Nasturel, «L'épitaphios constantinopolitain du monastère roumain de Secoul (1608)», *Χαριστήριον εἰς ᾿Α. Κ. ᾿Ορλάνδον*, vol. 4, Athens 1967-68, p. 129 ff.

—, Un épitrachilion inédit de style byzantin: l'étole de Clément, métropolite de Philippes (1613), *Acta antiqua Academiae Scientarum Hungaricae* X, 1-3 (1962), pp. 203-210.

D. Pallas, «Μελετήματα λειτουργικὰ-ἀρχαιολογικά. Τὸ ὀράριον τοῦ διακόνου», *ΕΕΒΣ* 24 (1954), p. 158 ff.

—, «῾Ο ἐπιτάφιος τῆς Παραμυθιᾶς», *ΕΕΒΣ* 27 (1957), pp. 127-150.

—, «Passion und Bestattung Christi», *Miscellanea Byzantina Monacensia* 2, Munich 1965.

S. A. Papadopoulos, «᾿Επιγραφὲς ῾Ιερᾶς μονῆς ᾿Ιωάννου Θεολόγου Πάτμου», *Πατμιακὲς ἐπιγραφές*, Athens 1966.

—, «Νεοφύτου τοῦ ΣΤ΄ Πατριάρχου Κωνσταντινουπόλεως, ἔγγραφα καὶ ἀφιερώματα πρὸς τὴν ἱερὰν μονὴν ᾿Ιωάννου Θεολόγου Πάτμου», *Χαριστήριον εἰς ᾿Α. Κ. ᾿Ορλάνδον*, vol. 4, Athens 1967-68, p. 236 ff.

T. Papas, «Geschichte der Messgewänder», *Miscellanea Byzantina Monacensia* 3, Munich 1965.

—, Bishop of Hermoupolis, «Βιβλιογραφία λειτουργικῶν ἀμφίων τοῦ βυζαντινοῦ τύπου», *Θεολογία* 45 (1974), pp. 172-193; 48 (1976), pp. 313-329; 53 (1981), pp. 754-778.

—, «Κεντητὴ ῾Ωραία Πύλη τῆς ἐν Χάλκῃ ῾Ι. Μονῆς Παναγίας Καμαριωτίσσης», *Θεολογία* 50 (1979), pp. 22-30.

Ch. Patrinellis, A. Karakatsane, M. Theocharis, *Μονὴ Σταυρονικήτα, ῾Ιστορία, Εἰκόνες, Χρυσοκεντήματα*, ed. National Bank of Greece, Athens 1974, pp. 143-236.

E. E. Piltz, *Trois sakkoi byzantins*, Upsala 1976.

—, *Kamelaukion et mitra*, Upsala 1977.

Rabino, *Le Monastère*.

G. Soteriou, «Τὸ ὀράριον τοῦ διακόνου ἐν τῇ ᾿Ανατολικῇ ᾿Εκκλησίᾳ», *᾿Επιστημονικὴ ᾿Επετηρὶς Θεολογικῆς Σχολῆς Πανεπιστημίου ᾿Αθηνῶν*, vol. Α΄, 1926, p. 405 ff.

—, *Κειμήλια τοῦ Οἰκουμενικοῦ Πατριαρχείου*, Athens 1938.

—, «Τὰ λειτουργικὰ ἄμφια τῆς ὀρθοδόξου ἑλληνικῆς ἐκκλησίας», *Θεολογία* 20 (1949), pp. 1-14.

M. Soteriou, «Χρυσοκέντητον ἐπιγονάτιον τοῦ Βυζαντινοῦ Μουσείου ᾿Αθηνῶν», *Πρακτικὰ Χριστιανικῆς ᾿Αρχαιολογικῆς ῾Εταιρείας*, per. 3, 2 (1936), p. 108 ff.

H. D. Stojanović, *῾Η καλλιτεχνικὴ κεντητικὴ στὴν Σερβία ἀπὸ τὸν 14ο ὥς τὸν 19ο αἰῶνα*, Belgrade 1959 (in serbian language).

O. Tafrali, *Le trésor byzantin et roumain du monastère de Poutna*, Paris 1925.

—, *Le trésor byzantin et roumain du monastère de Poutna*, Paris 1925. Corrections by P. S. Nasturel, «Νέες πληροφορίες γιὰ μερικοὺς θησαυροὺς τῆς Μονῆς Πούτνα», *Romanoslavica* III-IV, Bucharest 1958-60 (in rumanian language).

M. Theocharis, «᾿Εκκλησιαστικὰ ἄμφια τῆς μονῆς Τατάρνης», *Θεολογία* 27 (1956), p. 123 ff.

—, «᾿Ανέκδοτα ἄμφια τῆς Μονῆς Φανερωμένης Σαλαμῖνος», *Θεολογία* 27 (1956).

—, «᾿Αφιερωτικαὶ ἐπιγραφαὶ ἐπὶ ἀμφίων τοῦ ῎Αθω», *Θεολογία* 28 (1957), σ. 452 κ. ἑξ.

—, «Un épitrachilion valaque aux Météores», *Revue des Études Roumaines*, Paris 1957.

—, «῾Η Μονὴ τῆς Ζάβορδας», newspaper *Καθημερινή*, of 6.12.1959.

—, «῾Η ἐνδυτὴ τοῦ ῾Αγίου Μάρκου», *ΕΕΒΣ* 29 (1959), p. 193 ff.

—, «῾Ο ἐπιτάφιος τῆς Συλλογῆς Mc Cormick», newspaper *Καθημερινή*, of 15.4.1960.

—, «῾Η Βυζαντινὴ εἰκὼν τοῦ ἐν Τεργέστῃ καθεδρικοῦ ναοῦ», *Πρακτικὰ ᾿Ακαδημίας ᾿Αθηνῶν* 37 (1962), p. 254 ff.

—, «Sur une broderie du Musée de Prague», *Byzantinoslavica* XXIV-1 (1963), pp. 106-110.

—, «῾Υπογραφαὶ κεντητῶν ἐπὶ ἀμφίων τοῦ ῎Αθω», *ΕΕΒΣ* 32 (1963), p. 496 ff.

—, «Οἱ ἐπιτάφιοι τῆς Μαριώρας», newspaper *Καθημερινή*, of 13.4.1963.

—, «Χριστόφορος Ζεφάρ», newspaper *Καθημερινή*, of 12.5.1963.

—, «Χρυσοκέντητα ἄμφια τῆς μονῆς Ταξιαρχῶν Αἰγιαλείας», *ΑΕ* 1960 (1965), Χρονικά, pp. 9-15.

—, «᾿Εκ τῶν μεταβυζαντινῶν ἐργαστηρίων τῆς Κωνσταντινουπόλεως», *ΕΕΒΣ* 45 (1966), p. 277 ff.

—, «P. Johnstone, Byzantine Tradition in Church Embroidery, London 1967», *Balkan Studies* 9 (1969), p. 535 ff. (book review).

—, «῾Ο ἐπιτάφιος τοῦ Παναγίου Τάφου», *Θεολογία* 41 (1970), pp. 690-704 and 753.

—, «I ricami bizantini», *Il Tesoro di San Marco*, opera diretta da H. Hahnloser, vol. II: *Il Tesoro e il Museo*, Φλωρεντία 1971, p. 91 ff.

—, «᾿Αντιμήνσια ἐκ τοῦ Σκευοφυλακίου τῆς Μονῆς τοῦ Σινᾶ», *Πανηγυρικὸς τόμος ἐπὶ τῇ 1400ῇ ἀμφιετηρίδι τῆς ῾Ιερᾶς Μονῆς τοῦ Σινᾶ*, Athens 1972, pp. ρλη΄-ρνβ΄.

—, «Περὶ νέας πραγματείας τῆς τεχνικῆς τῆς Μεταβυζαντινῆς Τέχνης», *Πρακτικὰ τῆς ᾿Ακαδημίας ᾿Αθηνῶν* 48 (1973), pp. 66-68.

—, «Le moine brodeur Arsénios et l'atelier des Météores au XVIème siècle», *Bulletin de Liaison du Centre Intern. d' Étude des Textiles Anciens*, no. 45,1 (1977).

—, «Les ateliers de Vienne et la broderie religieuse dans les pays orthodoxes», *Paper in the 16th International Congress of Byzantine Studies*, Vienna, Oct. 1982.

—, «Χρυσοκέντητα ἄμφια», *Οἱ Θησαυροὶ τῆς Μονῆς Πάτμου*, Ekd. Athenon 1988, pp. 185-221.

P. Trembelas, *Αἱ τρεῖς Λειτουργίαι κατὰ τοὺς ἐν ᾿Αθήναις κώδικας*, Athens 1935.

E. Turdeanu, «La broderie religieuse en Roumanie. Les épitaphioi moldaves au XVe et XVIe siècles», *Cercetari Literare* IV (1941), p. 164 ff.

—, «La broderie religieuse en Roumanie. Les étoles des XVe et XVIe siècles», *Buletinul Institutului Roman din Sofia*, I, 1, Bucharest 1941, p. 5ff.

V. Vatasianu, *L' arte bizantina in Romania. I ricami liturgici*, Rome 1945.


# CHURCH METALWORK


* I should like to convey my warm thanks to the Archbishop and Abbot of Sinai and to the fathers of the Monastery for their assistance during the course of my researches on Sinai. Warm thanks also to: Mme C. Arminjon, conservateur en chef at the Inventaire Général, Mme D. Gaborit-Chopin, conservateur en chef in the Département des Objets d'Art of the Louvre, and Mme G. François, assistant ingénieur to the CNRS in compiling the 'Corpus des émaux méridionaux', for their help during my research work in Paris; Mr P. Henwood, Archivist, who allowed me to consult his thesis; Mme D. Liscia, researcher at the University of Florence; L. Crociani, OSM; Professor C. Bouras, who placed at my disposal the full text, currently in press, of the late L. Bouras on the Byzantine candelabrum of Sinai, and Mrs M. Acheimastou-Potamianou, Director of the Byzantine Museum, Athens, for permitting me to study a cross in the Museum. In matters of inscriptions, I received valuable assistance from Mr G. Subotić, Director of the Institute of Art of Belgrade, Mr S. Kissas, Byzantinologist, Mr D. Nastase and Mr F. Marinescu, research workers at the National Research Foundation, Athens, and the priest-monk Ioustinos of the Simonos Petra Monastery (Mt. Athos). Finally, I would like to thank all colleagues and friends for their invaluable help in a variety of ways.


** Since it was not possible to conduct chemical analysis of the metals, the terms 'silver' and 'bronze' are used as conventions. This reservation also applies to the precious stones.

**1.** Amantos, *Σύντομος ἱστορία*, pp. 99-100.

**2.** Cf. inscriptions from 6th and 7th century items. M. Mundell-Mango, *Silver from Early Byzantium, The Kaper Koraon and Related Treasures*, Baltimore 1986, pp. 5-6.

**3.** Codex Sinaiticus, no. 2197A, p. 561.

**4.** Bečkerek was an important silverwork centre, particularly in the 16th century. See B. Radojković, *Srpsko Zlatarstvo XVI i XVII veka*, Novi Sad 1966, pp. 109-110.

**5.** D. Papastratou, *῾Ο Σιναΐτης Χατζηκυριάκης ἐκ Χώρας Βουρλᾶ. Γράμματα-Ξυλογραφίες 1688-1709*, Athens 1981, pp. 132-133.

**6.** Rabino, *Le Monastère*, p. 28.

**7.** Rabino, *Le Monastère*, p. 29. For the Greek spelling of 'πολυέλεος', see entry in P. Trembelas, *Μεγάλη ῾Ελληνικὴ ᾿Εγκυκλοπαιδεία*, vol. 20 (1932), pp. 486-487.

**8.** Cod. Sin. no. 2199, p. 250.

**9.** Cod. Sin. no. 2197A, p. 105.

**10.** Cod. Sin. no. 2199, p. 245.

**11.** Apart from the crosses in figs. 2 and 3-4, there are also some other works in copper alloy, complete or in fragments. See Weitzmann - Ševčenco, «Moses Cross», figs. 15, 16. A vessel in the shape of a bird with an animal-form handle is believed to date from the Fatimid period (10th - 12th century). See K. Weitzmann - F. Anderegg, «Mount Sinai's Holy Treasures», *National Geographic*, vol. 125, no. 1, Jan. 1964, p. 122. For the Middle Byzantine period, see also J. Galey, *Sinai and the Monastery of St. Catherine. Introductions by K. Weitzmann - G. Forsyth*, London 1979, p. 158. From the 14th-15th century, see two miniature icons, I. Kalavrezou-Maxeiner, *Byzantine Icons in Steatite*, Vienna 1985, nos. 160 and 167.

**12.** Rabino, *Le Monastère*, p. 33. Weitzmann - Ševčenko, «Moses Cross», pp. 385-398, figs. 1-18, K. Weitzmann - F. Anderegg, op. cit., p. 123 and A. Paliouras, *῾Ιερὰ Μονὴ Σινᾶ*, Athens 1985, fig. 82.

**13.** Weitzmann - Ševčenko, «Moses Cross», pp. 385 and 397, figs. 1, 9 and 10; M. Mundell-Mango, op. cit., p. 88, no. 7.

**14.** Weitzmann - Ševčenko, «Moses Cross», p. 386.

**15.** Ibid., pp. 387-389.

**16.** Ibid., p. 397. The objects of church treasures from the 6th and 7th centuries are attributed to Syrian workshops, see M. Mundell-Mango, op. cit., p. 15.

**17.** Weitzmann - Ševčenko, «Moses Cross», pp. 389-390, fig. 7. According to A. Grabar, it is not impossible that it functioned as a processional cross, in which case its position would have been in the Sanctuary, behind the altar, in the manner of the 10th-century cross at the Megiste Lavra Monastery on Mount Athos (A. Grabar, «La précieuse croix de la Lavra Saint-Athanase au Mont Athos», *CArch* XIX [1969], pp. 110-111, figs. 1-2). If this is so, its great weight would have necessitated its being carried by two people. For a similar example, see M. Mundell-Mango, op. cit., p. 194.

**18.** The identification of St. John is problematic; there is no supplementary inscription and the saints depicted — with the exception of St. Andrew who is holding a cross — are not differentiated. The Saint could be St. John the Evangelist, who is seen as a link between the Crucifixion and the Resurrection (Kartsonis, *Anastasis*, pp. 144-145). He could also be St. John Chrysostom, whose cult was particularly widespread in Constantinople during the Middle Byzantine period (see below for the question of origin) (Kartsonis, *Anastasis*, p. 100, note 17).

**19.** The silver gilt staurotheke decorated with enamel and niello in the Metropolitan Museum of New York (known as the Fieschi Morgan), the gold cross from Pliska in Bulgaria, the silver cross from Vicopisano in Italy and the triptych from Martvili in Georgia all belong to this category (for more detail, see Kartsonis, *Anastasis*, pp. 94-125, with relevant bibliography. See also the view of A. Tschilingirov, «Eine byzantinische Goldschmiedewerkstatt des 7. Jahrhunderts», *Metallkunst von der Spätantike bis zum ausgehenden Mittelalter*, A. Effenberger ed., Berlin 1982, pp. 76-89).

**20.** Kartsonis, *Anastasis*, pp. 119-120.

**21.** In the historiated reliquaries, and above all in the Fieschi-Morgan staurotheke (first quarter of the 9th century), we can recognize the early iconographic type of the Descent into Hell (Resurrection), in the shape which it probably took during the 8th century (Kartsonis, *Anastasis*, pp. 123-125 and 186-203), and the iconographic types of the Ascension and the Presentation in the Temple (Pliska and Vicopisano staurothekes), which also contain iconographic elements that appeared during the 9th century (Kartsonis, *Anastasis*, pp. 103-105). For the Ascension, see also N. Gioles, *Ἡ Ἀνάληψις τοῦ Χριστοῦ βάσει τῶν μνημείων τῆς α΄ χιλιετηρίδος*, Athens 1981, pp. 217 and 219.

**22.** Kartsonis, *Anastasis*, pp. 122-123, and L. Dontcheva-Petkova, «Une croix pectorale-reliquaire en or récemment trouvée à Pliska», *CArch* 25 (1976), pp. 65-66.

**23.** A group of enkolpia from southern Russia with decoration of this type is dated to around 1000 (A. Frolow, «Le médaillon byzantin de Charroux», *CArch* XVI (1966), pp. 46-48, figs. 4-6 and 10. Similar decoration is also encountered in a number of processional crosses of the Middle Byzantine period (L. Bouras, *Ὁ σταυρὸς τῆς Ἀδριανουπόλεως*, Athens 1979, pp. 11-12). From the point of view of this technique, the Sinai enkolpion resembles a cross in the Historical Museum of Moscow decorated with the Mother of God as Nikopoios ('Bringer of Victory') (L. Dontcheva-Petkova, «Croix d'or-reliquaire de Pliska», *Culture et art en Bulgarie Médiévale [VIIIe-XIVe siècle]. Bulletin de l'Institut d'Archéologie* 35 [1979], figs. 22 and 24).

**24.** Kartsonis, *Anastasis*, p. 103.

**25.** Only the figures of Christ and the Virgin are entirely in niello. The other figures are rendered in a mixed technique.

**26.** L. Bouras, «Δύο βυζαντινὰ μανουάλια ἀπὸ τὴ Μονὴ Μεταμορφώσεως τῶν Μετεώρων», *Βυζαντινά* 5 (1973), pp. 134-136.

**27.** L. Bouras, «Three Byzantine bronze Candelabra from the Grand Lavra Monastery in Mount Athos and Saint Catherine's Monastery in Sinai», *The 17th International Byzantine Congress 1986. Abstracts of Short Papers.* Washington D. C., Dumbarton Oaks, p. 42. The full-length version of this text is in press for the *ΔΧΑΕ*, vol. 15.

**28.** L. Bouras, «Byzantine Lighting Devices», *XVI Internationaler Byzantinistenkongress, Akten II/3, Jahrbuch der Österreichischen Byzantinistik* 32/3, Vienna 1982, figs. 1-2, and L. Bouras, «Three Byzantine bronze Candelabra», op. cit., see note 27.

**29.** Cf. the Iranian candelabrum of the 12th-early 13th century, J. Allan, «L' art du métal», *Trésors de l'Islam*, exhibition catalogue, Musée Rath, Geneva 1985, no. 261. Cf. the almond-shaped bosses on the base of the Sinai candelabrum with corresponding features on bronze mortars of the 11th-12th century; *The Arts of Islam*, exhibition catalogue, Hayward Gallery, London 1976, nos. 174 and 181. Compare also: Th. Ulbert, *Der Kreuzfahrerzeitlich Silberschatz aus Resafa-Sergiupolis (Resafa III)*, Mainz 1990, pp. 7-21.

**30.** These are the bowl from Beryozovo and the bowl from the Bazilevsky collection (V. P. Darkevich, *Byzantine Secular Art in the 12th and 13th centuries*, Moscow 1975, pp. 60-63, figs. 83-84, and pp. 78-84, figs. 104-114). V. P. Darkevich attributes a group of similar objects, including these bowls, to the art of the Imperial Court in the time of Manuel Comnenos and connects them with Byzantine feudal ideals (V. P. Darkevich, op. cit., pp. 249-259). This view is not accepted by A. Bank (A. Bank, *Prikladnoe iskusstvo vizantii IX-XII vv*, Moscow 1978, pp. 46-48, 51 and 62-63).

**31.** V. P. Darkevich, op. cit., figs. 193 and 290, fig. 298, figs. 303 and 304, fig. 313. Cf. also two ceramic plates of the 12th century, the mode of execution of whose decoration is a clear imitation of metalwork, *Βυζαντινὴ - Μεταβυζαντινὴ Τέχνη*, nos. 278 and 279.

**32.** A. Dumas, *Quinze jours au Sinaï*, Paris 1846 (2nd ed.), p. 87.

**33.** This information is contained in Rabino (*Le Monastère*, p. 21) and in K. Weitzmann (J. Galey, op. cit., see note 11, p. 158). Part of the plaque is visible in a partial photograph of the door to the katholikon (see A. Paliouras, op. cit., see note 12, fig. 75). Christ is standing on a half-moon with plant decoration on its extremities; His head has not survived. The corners are occupied by the full-length symbols of the Evangelists, with additional cast heads in the classical style. In the ground are scattered star-shaped decorative motifs in circles, and smaller engraved ones (23.2×11.3 cm.). For the enamel covers of books and the workshops which produced them, see M.-M. Gauthier, «Les reliures en émail de Limoges conservées en France», *Humanisme actif, Mélanges d'art et de littérature offerts à J. Cain*, Paris 1968, vol. I, pp. 271-287.

**34.** Ibid., pp. 276-277 and M. - M. Gauthier, «La croix émaillée de Bonneval au Musée de Cluny», *La Revue du Louvre et des Musées de France*, 4-1978, p. 281, fig. 27. The slightly hollowed-out panel into which the plaque is fitted may be the original, although most of the nails are not in place. The wooden frame on to which the panels are nailed is an addition; whether it is the original frame is unknown.

**35.** F. W. Stohlmann, «The Star Group of Champlevé Enamels and its Connections», *The Art Bulletin*, vol. XXXII-4, 1950, pp. 327-330, and M. -M. Gauthier, «La croix émaillée...», op. cit., pp. 272 and 280-281.

**36.** M. -M. Gauthier, «La croix émaillée...», op. cit., pp. 281-282. It is no coincidence that the miracle of St. Francis of Assisi receiving the gift of the Stigmata appears for the first time on two reliquaries of the same technique. See M. -M. Gauthier, op. cit., pp. 281-282, M. -M. Gauthier, *Les routes de la foi. Reliques et reliquaires de Jérusalem à Compostelle*, Freiburg 1983, pp. 138-140, no. 82, and *Musée de Cluny*, guide, p. 97, fig. 20.

**37.** From the stylistic point of view, there are greater resemblances with some of the scenes depicted on the reliquaries no. 9109 in the National Museum, Copenhagen, no. Ch. 1332 of the Hermitage Museum, Leningrad (F. W. Stohlman, op. cit., see note 35, figs. 1, 2-10), with plaques no. 1866. 60 in the Museum für Kunst und Gewerbe, Hamburg, and no. 14674 in the Musée de Cluny, Paris (F. W. Stohlman, op. cit., figs. 12 and 17), which also contains the so-called 'pax', no. 4522 (F. W. Stohlman, op. cit., fig. 13) and the Bonneval cross (M. -M. Gauthier, «La croix émaillée...», op. cit., fig. 6 and p. 281). In the Louvre, see the reliquary of St. Francis of Assisi (OA 4083), and in particular the shaft and the base (M. -M. Gauthier, *Les routes...*, op. cit., fig. 139).

**38.** M. -M. Gauthier, «La croix émaillée...», op. cit., p. 281. For the dissemination of the cult of St. Catherine in the West and among the Franks of Syria, see M. Labib, *Pèlerins et voyageurs au Mont Sinaï*, Cairo 1961, pp. 29 and 34-35, and Amantos, *Σύντομος ἱστορία*, pp. 35-36.

**39.** *Les Fastes du Gothique, le siècle de Charles V*, exhibition catalogue, Grand Palais, Paris 1981-1982, nos. 212, 215, 219, 221. See also no. 218, a reliquary with a piece of the saint's tomb. See also M. Campbell, *An Introduction to Medieval Enamels*, London 1983, fig. 47, and P. Henwood, «Administration et vie des collections d'orfèvrerie royales sous le règne de Charles VI (1380-1422)», *Bibliothèque de l' École des Chartes*, vol. CXXXVIII, 1980, p. 201.

**40.** Rabino, writing in 1938, states that this chaliche had only been discovered in the Monastery a few years before (Rabino, *Le Monastère*, p. 45, note 1, pl. XVIII). See also Galey, *Sinai...*, op. cit., p. 158.

**41.** P. Henwood, «Administration et vie...», op. cit., passim.

**42.** Ibid., pp. 182 and 207-212.

**43.** J. M. Fritz, *Goldschmiedekunst der Gotik in Mitteleuropa*, Munich 1982, pp. 146 and 148.

**44.** Rabino, *Le Monastère*, pp. 44-45.

**45.** The crowned lily replaces the ordinary lily which until that time had been the stamp of the goldsmiths of Paris in 1378, by order of Charles V. See P. Henwood, «Les orfèvres parisiens pendant le règne de Charles VI (1380-1422)», *Bulletin archéologique du Comité des Travaux Historiques et Scientifiques* 15 (1979), p. 89. The stamp with the letter A (?) inside the base —presumably that of the maker — and the coat of arms, possibly engraved at a later date, have not been identified. The coat of arms is erroneously numbered 86 by Rabino, instead of 89 (Rabino, *Le Monastère*, p. 68, fig. 11).

**46.** For the enamelling technique known as 'basse taille', see M. -M. Gauthier, *Émaux du Moyen Age Occidental*, Freiburg 1972, pp. 202-297, and D. Gaborit-Chopin, «Orfèvrerie et émaillerie», *Les Fastes du gothique...*, op. cit., pp. 220-224.

**47.** The lilies engraved in rhombuses and the stippled technique are features of the second half of the 14th century (cf. *Les Fastes du Gothique...*, op. cit., nos. 205, 211, 214 and 215). The manner of execution of the faces displays greater similarities with the figures on the enamelled plaque in the Louvre and with the representation of St. John the Baptist preaching (c. 1380-1400), see *Les Fastes du gothique...*, op. cit., no. 216. See also nos. 214 and 217, and cf. the enamelled miniature plaque with the Crucifixion on a chalice from a church in the community of La Mothe-Sainte-Heray (Niort). My thanks to Mme C. Arminjon for pointing this out. These miniature plaques appear to have been produced in advance. See similar cases in M. -M. Gauthier, *Émaux du Moyen Age...*, op. cit., p. 295.

**48.** Cod. Sin., no. 2215, p. 31r/59.

**49.** See A. Paliouras, op. cit., fig. 86.

**50.** One of the monograms can be read ΓΕΡΑΣΙΜΩ. Cf. the pieces of a painted cross in the Monastery which is similar, in the shape and the representation of the upper part, to the Sinai cross (K. Weitzmann, «Three painted Crosses at Sinai», *Studies in the Arts at Sinai*, Princeton 1982, pp. 409-414, figs. 1-3). Unfortunately, the main horizontal arm has not survived. The 'drops' at the extremities of the arms of the Sinai cross are also found in Italian crosses (see B. Montevecchi - S. Vasco Rocca, *Suppellettile ecclesiastica, 4. Dizionari terminologici*, Florence 1988, pp. 332-335).

**51.** G. Millet, *Recherches sur l'iconographie de l'Évangile aux XIVe, XVe, et XVIe siècles*, Paris 1960, pp. 413-415.

**52.** Cf. the metal crosses in L. Mortari, «Le croce nell'oreficeria del Lazio dal Medioevo al Rinascimento», *Rivista dell' Istituto Nationale d'Archeologia e storia dell' Arte*, S. III, II, 1979, figs. 143, 190, 223, and 250, and E. Steingräber, «Studien zur venezianischen Goldschmiedekunst des 15. Jahrhunderts», *Mitteilungen des Kunsthistorischen Instituts in Florenz*, II, 1962, figs. 1 and 3. For a similar example on a painted cross dating from c. 1500, see A. Papageorgiou, *Ikonen aus Zypern*, Geneva 1969, fig. on p. 73.

**53.** For the depiction of the Pelican, cf. E. Kirschbaum (ed.) *Lexikon der christlichen Ikonographie*, Rome, Freiburg, Basle, Vienna 1971, vol. III, pp. 390-392, entry on 'Pelikan'. The symbol is associated with the Resurrection of Christ and the Holy Eucharist, which in the Sinai cross is reinforced by the presence of the angels with the 'ripidia'. Cf. examples on metal crosses in L. Mortari, op. cit., figs. 133, 175 and 242 and E. Steingräber, op. cit., fig. 3.

**54.** E. Sandberg-Vavala, *La croce dipinta italiana e l'iconografia della Passione*, reissue of the 1929 edition, Rome 1980, fig. 105, and Belting, *Bild and Kult*, Munich 1990, figs. 229, 235, 238, 239, 242.

**55.** Ibid., fig. 249.

**56.** A. Papageorgiou, op. cit., see note 52, figs. on pp. 55 and 56. The Entry into Jerusalem has been executed according to the rare iconographic type, in which the movement is from right to left. In this connection, see P. Vocotopoulos, «Κρητικὲς ἐπιδράσεις στὴν κυπριακὴ ζωγραφικὴ τοῦ 16ου αἰώνα», *Πρακτικὰ τοῦ Β΄ Διεθνοῦς Κυπριολογικοῦ Συνεδρίου, Nicosia 1986, vol. II, Μεσαιωνικὸν τμῆμα*, pp. 587-590, figs. 1a and 2-4.

**57.** *Εἰκόνες Πάτμου*, no. 68, pls. 49 and 127.

**58.** For the enamelling techniques on gold or silver, relief or convex, known as 'ronde bosse', see M. -M. Gauthier, *Émaux du Moyen Age...*, op. cit., pp. 282-284, and D. Gaborit-Chopin, op. cit., see note 46, pp. 220-224.

**59.** Represented in the Monastery by a series of icons (Weitzmann, «Icon Painting»).

**60.** Weitzmann, «Icon Painting», pp. 57 and 59.

**61.** The Virgin in a short veil was established in Cypriot art in the well-known type of the 'Kykkos Virgin'. Soteriou, *Εἰκόνες*, I, fig. 188, and II, pp. 171-173; Belting, *Bild und Kult*, fig. 204; A. Papageorgiou, *Βυζαντινὲς εἰκόνες τῆς Κύπρου*, exhibition catalogue, Benaki Museum, Athens 1976, no. 27, and M. Frinta, «Relief Decoration in gilded pastiglia on the Cypriot Icons and its Propagation in the West», *Πρακτικὰ τοῦ Β΄ Διεθνοῦς Κυπριολογικοῦ Συνεδρίου, Nicosia 1986, vol. II, Μεσαιωνικὸν τμῆμα*, p. 542, pl. 7.

**62.** Compare the decoration on the knot of the cross with the quatrefoil on a Paris triptych in 'basse taille' enamel dating from the early 14th century, in the Boston Museum of Fine Arts, P. Brieger - P. Verdier, *L'art de la cour, France et Angleterre 1259-1328*, exhibition catalogue, Ottawa 1972, no. 61, fig. 83B.

**63.** The political and social conditions in Cyprus during the 15th century could have made possible the creation of forms of art such as the Sinai cross. See, in this respect, M. Garidis, *La peinture murale dans le monde orthodoxe après la chute de Byzance (1450-1600) et dans les pays sous domination étrangère*, Athens 1989, pp. 39-50.

**64.** M. Frinta, op. cit., see note 61, p. 541, fig. 5. See also A. Papageorgiou, «Κύπριοι ζωγράφοι φορητῶν εἰκόνων τοῦ 16ου αἰῶνα», *Report of the Department of Antiquities, Cyprus, 1975*, Nicosia 1975, pl. XXII, fig. 1.

**65.** For the name 'Syropoulos', see V. Laurent, *Les mémoires du Grand Ecclésiarque de l'Église de Constantinople Sylvestre Syropoulos sur le Concile de Florence (1438-1439)*, Rome 1971, pp. 3-4. See also Mouriki, «Thirteenth-century Icon Painting», pp. 59-60.

**66.** From the dependency in Crete; J. Braun, *Das christliche Altargerät in seinem Sein und in seiner Entwicklung*, reprint of the 1932 edition, Hildesheim - New York 1973, p. 128, and M. Collareta, *Calici italiani, Museo Nationale del Bargello*, Florence 1983, figs. 1-4b.

**67.** For similar examples, see J. Braun, op. cit., pl. C, fig. 11, and B. Montevecchi - S. Vasco Rocca, op. cit., see note 50, p. 137, no. 9.

**68.** B. Montevecchi - S. Vasco Rocca, op. cit., p. 104, no. 19.

**69.** Christ is depicted with His arms crossed at the wrists and not bent, while His head is leaning slightly to one side rather than drooping forward (*From Byzantium to El Greco. Greek*

*Frescoes and Icons*, exhibition catalogue, Royal Academy of Arts, London 1987, p. 188, no. 161 [N. Chatzidakis]). See a similar example on an Italian chalice in L. Mortari, op. cit., see note 52, fig. 140. The presence of the angels is also typical of Cretan icons. For the iconographic type of St. Catherine, see note 57 above.

**70.** The inscription on the base clearly states the place and time of its production: IN CRETE IN THE YEAR 1618. The hallmark with the Venetian lion is flanked by two others, one with the initial N and the other with the initials Z and B.

**71.** G. Ganzer, *Il tesoro del Duomo di Gemona*, exhibition catalogue, Udine 1985, nos. 8 and 9. See also O. Zastrow, «Un gruppo d'inedite pissidi nelle Civiche Raccolte d'Arte Applicata del Castello Sforzesco», *Rassegna di Studi e di Notizie*, vol. XIV (1987-88), pp. 476-478, fig. 20. A chalice without a hallmark in the Monastery sacristy is similarly decorated.

**72.** This is particularly noticeable in a plate belonging to the Monastery and depicting an enthroned Virgin and Child of the Cretan iconographic type, surrounded by a Renaissance design of intertwined leaves and fruits. Two of the hallmarks on the plate are identical to those on the reliquary, and the two pieces may even be the work of the same craftsman.

**73.** Evidence for relations with the Danubian provinces can be found as early as 1500, with a 'panagiarion' which may be from a workshop in Moldavia. See two similar 'panagiaria' in C. Nicolescu, *Argintăria laică și religioasa în Țările Române (sec. XIV-XIX)*, Bucharest 1968, nos. 215 and 216.

**74.** D. Mioc, *Documenta Romaniae Historica*, vol. IV, no. 89, pp. 114-115.

**75.** For the Great Dvornik Župan Koadă Chamberlain (10 January 1542 - 28 February 1548) to Radu Paisie, Prince of Wallachia, see N. Stoicescu, *Dicționar al Marilor Dregători din Țara Românească și Moldova sec. XIV-XVII*, Bucharest 1971. The inscription also refers to the Great Komis, 'comes stabuli' whose full name has not survived. During this period (10 September 1539-April 1545), the post was held by Badea Zălbău (N. Stoicescu, op. cit., p. 30). However, the remaining space would not have been sufficient for this name.

**76.** Vessels such as artophoria, reliquaries and kibotia in the shape of churches are symbols of the heavenly city of Jerusalem. The kibotion, which today is empty, is designed to be held by the deacon on his left shoulder, which is covered with a large kerchief, while he censes the church with his right arm. See in this respect, D. Pallas, «Μελετήματα λειτουργικὰ -ἀρχαιολογικά. 1. Τὸ ὀράριον τοῦ διακόνου», *ΕΕΒΣ* 24 (1954), pp. 161-165, fig. 4. This scene is depicted in wall paintings, embroideries and wood-carvings. G. Millet, *Broderies religieuses de style byzantin*, Paris 1947, vol. I, pls. CIV and CV.

**77.** Cf. the Gospel cover of figs. 11-12.

**78.** B. Radojković - D. Milovanović, *Masterpieces of Serbian Goldsmiths' Work. 13th-18th century*, exhibition catalogue, Victoria and Albert Museum, London 1981, p. 12.

**79.** For Dmitar from Lipova and references to the Sinai kibotion, see B. Radojković, op. cit., pp. 115-117, figs. 52, 53, and B. Radojković - D. Milovanović, op. cit., pp. 10 and 62-63, no. 105.

**80.** The kibotion from the Šišatovac Monastery has a Sanctuary of a different shape and is not so rich in iconic and aniconic decoration. The figures are more perfunctory, the Gothic elements are greater in number and clearer, the ground is rougher and without decorative motifs.

**81.** Cf. a kibotion dating from c. 1500 at the Bistrița Monastery (C. Nicolescu, *Arta metalelor prețioase în România*, Bucharest 1973, fig. 89) and the reliquary of St. Nephon (1515), Patriarch of Constantinople, in the Dionysiou Monastery, Mt. Athos (M. Beza, *Urme Românești in Răsăritul Ortodox*, Bucharest 1935, fig. on p. 52, and Y. Smyrnakis, *Τὸ Ἅγιον Ὄρος*, reprinted from the 1903 edition, Athens 1988, p. 509).

**82.** M. Beza (M. Beza, op. cit., p. 8) gives the date of foundation of this chapel by Alexander II, Prince of Wallachia (1568-1577) as 1576. This date, which is also given in reference to other benefactions to the Monastery by the same prince, is clearly taken from an earlier description of the Monastery (*Περιγραφὴ ἱερὰ τοῦ ἁγίου καὶ Θεοβαδίστου Ὄρους Σινᾶ*, Venice 1817, reissued Athens 1978, p. 135). However, the chapel must already have been standing by 1569, since in that year Roxandra Lăpușneanu dedicated a censer to it (see below). It must have been built in 1568-1569.

**83.** K. Papamichalopoulos, *Τὸ Μοναστήρι τοῦ Σινᾶ*, Athens 1932, p. 353, Rabino, *Le Monastère*, p. 46, M. Beza, op. cit., figs. on pp. 104, 105 and 107, and C. Nicolescu, *Arta metalelor...*, op. cit., fig. 66. It was customary to depict princes on wall paintings, manuscripts, embroideries and pieces of silverware. See, indicatively, C. Nicolescu, *Istoria Costumului de Curte în Țarile Române, sec. XIV-XVIII*, Bucharest 1970, pls. CVI, CXLIII, CIX and CXXVII. This last work, a gilt silver seal, depicts Alexander II Mircea and his son Mihnea.

**84.** Another cover was dedicated by Michael, Great Dvornik of Wallachia (September 1583 - March 1584), and his wife Maria.

**85.** For similar works, see C. Nicolescu, *Argintăria...*, op. cit., no. 332, and C. Nicolescu, *Arta metalelor...*, op. cit., figs. 65 and 68. This type was still being produced by workshops in Asia Minor in the 18th century (see Benaki Museum, nos. 485 and 577). Similarities with the concept of a background scattered with motifs can be found in embroideries from the same period, see P. Johnstone, *The Byzantine Tradition in Church Embroidery*, London 1967, figs. 64 and 65.

**86.** See in this respect M. Beza, op. cit., figs. on pp. 7 and 12, and N. Jorga, «Noi obiecte de artă găsite la Ierusalim, în Mănăstirea sf. Sava și la Muntele Sinai», *Buletinul comisiunii Monumentelor Istorice*, Annul. XXIV, Fasc. 70, Oct. - Dec. 1931, pp. 184-185. See also D. Papastratou, op. cit., pp. 43 and 135.

**87.** For Alexander Lăpușneanu (1552-1561 and 1564-1568) and his wife Roxandra, benefactors of quite a number of monasteries on Mt. Athos, see G. Cioran, *Σχέσεις τῶν Ρουμανικῶν χωρῶν μετὰ τοῦ Ἄθω καὶ δὴ τῶν Μονῶν Κουτλουμουσίου, Λαύρας, Δοχειαρίου καὶ Ἁγίου Παντελεήμονος ἢ τῶν Ρώσων*, Athens 1938, pp. 42, 229-233. See also P. Năsturel, «Le Mont Athos et les Roumains. Recherches sur leurs relations du milieu du XIVe siècle à 1654», *Orientalia Christiana Analecta* 227 (1986), pp. 153, 154, 195-196, 208, 211 and 221. The same prince also donated to the Sinai Monastery St. Paraskevi at Jassy and the Frumoasa Monastery (Jorga, *Byzance*, p. 163). See the portraits of Roxandra and her son Bogdan in the wall paintings of the Dionysiou Monastery, Mt. Athos (Jorga, *Byzance*, fig. on p. 136, r,v). The Lăpușneanu family is also depicted in the wall paintings of the Docheiariou Monastery (1568). See M. Garidis, op. cit. see note 63, pp. 165 and 354, fig. 171.

**88.** Chatzidakis, *Σταυρονικήτα*, figs. 67, 68.

**89.** J. Braun, op. cit., p. 622, figs. 533-534, 537-540, and J. Fritz, op. cit., figs. 607-611. In southeastern Europe this style was already known in the 15th century. See C. Nicolescu, *Arta metalelor...*, op. cit., figs. 33, 34.

**90.** M. Šakota believes that this censer served as a model for Serbian craftsmen of the 16th century (M. Šakota, *Riznica Manastira Banje kod Priboja*, Belgrade 1981, pp. 51-59, figs. 14, 15). Church-shaped censers in the Gothic style have also survived in the Sveta Trojica Monastery near Pljevlja and at the Monasteries of Studenica, Piva and Savina (B. Radojković, op. cit., figs. 79, 80, 85 and 86). The Sinai censer is simpler than these in terms of its base and body. Production of censers of this type continued until the 17th century (B. Radojkovic, op. cit., figs. 81-84 and 87).

**91.** J.G. Herzog zu Sachsen, *Das Katharinenkloster am Sinai*, Leipzig - Berlin 1912, p. 19, fig. 24.

**92.** No solution has yet been found to the problem of the origin of the examples of this type of kibotion preserved in the sacristies of southeastern Europe, such as those of the Banja Monastery near Priboj (1573), the Papraća Monastery (1586, B. Radojković, op. cit., fig. 88) and the Sucevița Monastery (1591, M. A. Musicescu - M. Berza, *Mănăstirea Sucevița*, Bucharest 1958, fig. 142). The prevailing opinion is that they are copies of an earlier Transylvanian model (M. Šacota, op. cit., pp. 46-51, fig. 11). The Sinai kibotion, with its clear Late Gothic features, is most similar to the Sucevița kibotion and to the censer of fig. 14, with which it must have formed a set given that both items were dedicated in the same year by highly-placed figures in the same region (Moldavia). Indeed, the possibility that they were made in the same workshop cannot be ruled out. The question remains of whether they were made by local or foreign craftsman on the basis of the earlier Transylvanian model. This type of article was still in production in the 17th century (B. Radojković, op. cit., fig. 90) and into the 18th century, though by then some of the characteristics had been degraded (Y. Ikonomaki-Papadopoulos, «Church Silver», *Patmos, Treasures of the Monastery*, Athens 1988, fig. 16.

**93.** Rabino, *Le Monastère*, p. 46. The inscription is to be read 'ΑΡΤΗ' and not 'αὐτῇ'. The liturgical inscriptions are from the Breviary for September and are taken from the services for the Exaltation of the Cross. Perhaps this cross came to Sinai through the Monastery's dependency in Parga.

**94.** B. Radojković, *Les objets sculptés d'art mineur en Serbie ancienne*, Belgrade 1977, p. 41.

**95.** See a similar kernel design in L. Marangou, *Μονὴ Παναγίας τῆς Χοζοβιώτισσας, Ἀμοργός*, Athens 1988, fig. 45, and M. Chatzidakis, «Βυζαντινὸ Μουσεῖο», *Τὰ Ἑλληνικὰ Μουσεῖα*, Athens 1974, fig. 36.

**96.** C. Koutelakis, *Ξυλόγλυπτα τέμπλα τῆς Δωδεκανήσου μέχρι τὸ 1700*, pp. 166-167.

**97.** The individual decorative features are encountered in works of the second half of the 16th century and the early 17th century. Cf. the domes on a censer (F. Çağman, «Ottoman Art», *The Anatolian Civilisations III, Seljuk -Ottoman*, exhibition catalogue, Topkapı, Istanbul 1983, no. E. 254). Cf.also the flower decoration of the frame with the cover of a gold Koran and the manner in which the ground, with its characteristic zig-zag lines, has been rendered (*Soliman le Magnifique*, exhibition catalogue, Grand Palais, Paris 1990, nos. 133 and 235).

**98.** From the Ioannina dependency. See Rabino, *Le Monastère*, p. 47 and Th. Mentzios, «Συμβολὴ εἰς τὴν ἱστορίαν τῶν ἐν Ἠπείρῳ Μονῶν τοῦ Σινᾶ», *Ἠπειρωτικὴ Ἑστία*, year V, June 1956, no. 50, pp. 535-538.

**99.** *Soliman le Magnifique*, op. cit., no. 4.

**100.** The delicacy of the arabesques on the niello is equivalent to the quality of a gold crest pin of the mid-16th century (*Soliman le Magnifique*, op. cit., no. 105).

**101.** Cf. the multi-lobed and rectangular plaques with flower decoration in relief and the stones with the similar ones on a helmet in the Topkapı Museum (*Soliman le Magnifique*, op. cit., no. 79). The stones, with their rectangular base and setting in the shape of flowers, are strongly reminiscent of Renaissance jewelry of the 16th century, a trend which was also to prevail in Constantinople. See Y. Hackenbroch - M. Sframeli, *I gioelli dell'Elettrice Palatina al Museo degli Argenti*, Florence 1988, no. 8.

**102.** The details which constitute evidence for the relationship between these two works include some of the decorative motifs, the ground filled with zig-zags and the clarity of the inscriptions in miniature. The fact that there are no similar works from Ioannina dating from the same period makes it impossible to link them to that centre as yet.

**103.** Rabino, *Le Monastère*, p. 45.

**104.** See in this respect M. Radojković, op. cit., pp. 121-123, figs. 60 and 134, 136.

**105.** C. Nicolescu, *Argintăria...*, op. cit., see note 73, nos. 102 and 103, and a chalice in the Kanellopoulos Museum, Athens, *Βυζαντινὴ - Μεταβυζαντινὴ Τέχνη*, no. 222 (A. Ballian). See also two chalices in the Panachrantou Monastery, Andros, one with an inscription in Cyrillic script and the date 1636, and the other in the Ayii Tessarakonta Lakedaimonos Monastery, dated 1628.

**106.** J.G. Herzog zu Sachsen, op. cit., pp. 18-19, fig. 25, and Rabino, *Le Monastère*, p. 47, where the inscription is wrongly attributed to the 'artoklasia' of 1678 (see below, fig. 24). On the bottom of the kibotion is a cylindrical handle to allow it to be carried. Some of the sides open by means of a system of metal rods.

**107.** Cod. Sin., no. 2215, p. 31r/59.

**108.** *Les Fastes du gothique...*, op. cit., nos. 179, 181, 186.

**109.** A. Boschkov, *Die bulgarische Volkskunst*, Recklinghausen 1972, pp. 192-193, no. 65. Cf. M. Ivanov, *Zlatarskite proizvedenija ot XVI-XIX v.v Museja na Bačkovskija manastir*, Sofia 1967, no. 27.

**110.** D. Drumev, *Zlatarsko Izkustvo*, Sofia 1976, p. 44. It is true that most of the known works — dated and with inscriptions — in enamel and filigree originate from centres which were active in the second half of the 17th century (e. g., Sofia, Tyrnovo, Voulgarochori). However, the lenghth of time for which these centres were active is not known to us. It should also be noted that publications on the subject have not exhausted the scope for the provision of evidence, in which they are often not helped by their illustrations.

**111.** K. Papamichalopoulos, op. cit., p. 353, and Rabino, *Le Monastère*, p. 46.

**112.** See Gospel covers in the Monastery of Our Lady 'Xenia' (Y. Ikonomaki-Papadopoulos, *Ἐκκλησιαστικὰ ἀργυρά*, Athens 1980, fig. 2), in the Museum of Greek Folk Art, Athens, no. 1633, whose origin can be traced to Adrianople and the Bačkovo Monastery (M. Ivanov, op. cit., see note 109, no. 32).

**113.** See M. Ivanov, op. cit., no. 33, D. Drumev, op. cit., fig. 31 and A. Boschkov, op. cit., pp. 178-179, no. 55. We know of another Gospel cover: that in the Byzantine Museum, Athens (no. Χ.Α.Ε. 5123/5ª), dated 1726. This appears to be the original, without filigree enamel but with degenerated late Gothic motifs which shows the length of time over which cast plaques of this type were used or re-used.

**114.** Cf. a Gospel cover with similar cast plaques of almost the same iconographic type but a different technique, see B. Filov, *Geschichte der bulgarischen Kunst unter der türkischen Herrschaft und in der neueren Zeit*, Berlin - Leipzig 1933, pl. 36b, and the other plaque from the same Gospel, D. Drumev, op. cit., fig. 82. See also, by way of example, plaques of differing technique in Y. Ikonomaki-Papadopoulos, *Ἐκκλησιαστικὰ ἀργυρά*, op. cit., figs. 1 and 3.

**115.** From the dependency in Athens. K. Papamichalopoulos, op. cit., p. 352, and Rabino, *Le Monastère*, p. 47.

**116.** For the bishopric of Lititza in the Metropolis of Philippoupolis, which was based in the town of the same name, see Gedeon, Bishop of Sardeis, «Ἐπισκοπικοὶ κατάλογοι Βορείου Θράκης», *Θρακικὰ* 8 (1937), pp. 146-149. In 1652 Lititza was raised to an archbishopric, and Theodosius, protosynkellos of Didymoteichon (1652-1681), who is mentioned in the inscription on the mitre, was appointed as its metropolitan.

**117.** Y. Ikonomaki-Papadopoulos, «Church Silver» *Patmos, Treasures of the Monastery*, p. 233.

**118.** For the ceremony of the 'artoklasia' and its significance, see I. Fountoulis, *ΘΗΕ*, Athens 1963, vol. 3, cols. 286-290, entry on 'ἀρτοκλασία'. See also G. Galavaris, *Bread and Liturgy. The Symbolism of Early Christian and Byzantine Bread Stamps*, Wisconsin 1970, p. 132. On Sinai, these loafs are stamped with a wooden stamp showing St. Catherine (G. Galavaris, op. cit., pp. 133-136, figs. 70-73).

**119.** K. Papamichalopoulos, op. cit., p. 353, and Rabino, *Le Monastère*, pp. 47-48.

**120.** For St. Metrophanes, see I. Konstantinidis, *ΘΗΕ*, Athens 1966, vol. 8, cols. 1132-1134, entry on 'Μητροφάνης'. Sabbas I Nemanya, Archbishop of the Serbs, died at Tyrnovo in Bulgaria and was initially interred there. See in this respect, A. Angelopoulos, *ΘΗΕ*, Athens 1967, vol. 10, cols. 1096-1099, entry on 'Σάββας'.

**121.** Cf. Gospel covers of 1577, 1581 and 1648, the work of craftsmen from Sofia (A. Boschkov, op. cit., see note 109, pp. 180-181, no. 57, pp. 184-185, nos. 59-60, and pp. 188-189, no. 62). The same concept in the execution of the depictions was used by the craftsmen of Ćiprovac (M. Ivanov, op. cit., p. 98, fig. 50).

**122.** Some of the features of this artoklasia can be seen in an artoklasia of 1622, the work of Neško Prolimleković (B. Radojković, *Srpsko Zlatarstvo*, op. cit., pp. 135-139, fig. 161).

**123.** The style of the filigree decoration displays similarities with the decoration on the censer of fig. 28. The stones are set in the same manner.

**124.** Ioakeim was at that time Abbot of the Stavronikita Monastery and was also a renowned manuscript-binder (C. Patrinellis, «Ἡ ἱστορία τῆς Μονῆς Σταυρονικήτα», *Μονὴ Σταυρονικήτα*, S. Papadopoulos [ed.], Athens 1974, pp. 34 and 37). This kibotion may have reached Sinai by purchase, a practice which was not unknown, as shown by inscriptions on the items themselves and by entries in the codices. See Rabino, *Le Monastère*, p. 44.

**125.** E. A. Jablonskaja, «Proizvedenija oružejnogo iskusstva Irana i Turcii XVI-XVII vekov», *Gosudarstvennaja Oružejnaja Palata*, Moscow 1988, figs. 141 and 142b.

**126.** In Russian silverware, this delicate flower decoration covers the ground, setting up a sharp contrast with the engraved motifs, which were influenced by Western Floral Baroque. See M. M. Postnikova-Losseva, N. G. Platonova, B. L. Ulianova, *Zolotoe i serbrjanoe delo XV-XX vekov*, Moscow 1983, p. 76, fig. 71, and p. 74, and M. V. Martynova, «Moskva-krupnejšij juvelirnyj centr XVII veka», *Gosudarstvennaja Oružejnaja Palata*, Moscow 1988, figs. 56-58.

**127.** The lost 'ripidia' of Serres Cathedral (early 16th century) and of the Monastery of St. John the Baptist, Serres (1594), also belong to this category. (A. Frolow, «Les émaux de l'époque post-byzantine et l'art du cloisonné», *CArch* II [1947], pp. 136-138, pl. XXI, fig. 2, and pl. XXII, figs. 1-2). The distance in time which separates these works and the kibotion and the fact that there are no intermediate links makes it impossible to connect them any closer. A Gospel cover from Bačkovo in the Byzantine Museum (no. B. M. 1399), although iconically decorated, is not stylistically related to the Sinai kibotion. Iconic decoration became common in the second half of the 17th century, though in the techniques of champlevé and painted enamel (M. Chatzidakis, *Βυζαντινὸ Μουσεῖο*, op. cit., fig. 31, and Y. Ikonomaki-Papadopoulos, «Church Silver», op. cit., fig. 25).

**128.** Jade was imported into Constantinople from the Far East and was believed to bring health and longevity. See S. Türkoğlu, «Höfische Goldschmiedekunst», *Türkische Kunst und Kultur aus osmanisher Zeit*, Recklinghausen 1985, vol. 2, pp. 303 and 309. This technique was also applied to rock crystal, jasper, porcelain, ivory and mother-of-pearl. See in this respect, E. Atil, *The Age of Sultan Süleyman the Magnificent*, exhibition catalogue, National Gallery of Art, Washington 1987, pp. 117-119, and, by way of example, figs. 60, 67, 68, 76, 78.

**129.** The stones inset in jade have been cut in a trapezoidal shape. The stones around the plaque are of colourless solid glass to which colour has been added with a reddish impasto at the base of the flower-shaped setting. Cf. a buckle with stones and enamel in the Benaki Museum, A. Delivorrias, *Ἑλληνικὰ παραδοσιακὰ κοσμήματα*, Athens 1980, fig. 56.

**130.** This style reached Constantinople from Western Europe. Cf. M. C. Di Natale, «I gioielli della Madonna di Trapani», *Ori e Argenti di Sicilia*, exhibition catalogue, Museo Regionale Pepoli, Trapani 1989, p. 66, fig. 7a, and p. 69, fig. 15.

**131.** S. J. Kovarskaja, I. D. Kostina, E. V. Šakurova, *Russian gold of the fourteenth to early twentieth centuries from the Moscow Kremlin Reserves*, Moscow 1987, figs. 46, 59 and 60-61.

**132.** For similar works, see A. Delivorrias, op. cit., p. 83, and M. Brouskari, «Λαϊκὰ κοσμήματα τοῦ Μουσείου Παύλου καὶ Ἀλεξάνδρας Κανελλοπούλου», *Ἐθνογραφικά* 7 (1989), p. 109, fig. 1, and p. 110, fig. 3, and S. Türkoğlu, op. cit., p. 308, no. 7/5.

**133.** This description refers to the lecterns of the Monastery (*Περιγραφὴ ἱερά...*, 1817, op. cit., p. 128). For the use of these materials in Islamic art, see M. Rogers, «Osmanische Holzarbeiten», *Türkische Kunst und Kultur aus osmanischer Zeit*, Recklinghausen 1985, vol. 2, pp. 320-324.

**134.** For Abbot Athanasios, see Amantos, *Σύντομος ἱστορία*, p. 61, and D. Papastratou, op. cit., passim.

**135.** K. Papamichalopoulos, op. cit., p. 353, and A. Paliouras, op. cit., fig. 87. Rabino erroneously attributes to this item the inscription on the kibotion of fig. 30 (Rabino, *Le Monastère*, p. 47). For 'the most holy Sophronius of Chios', with whose assistance the artoklasia was made, see D. Papastratou, op. cit., pp. 90 and 99.

**136.** F. Çağman, op. cit., nos. E.140 and E.254, and J. Raby, «Metalwork, Silver and Gold», *Tulips, Arabesques and Turbans*, Y. Petsopoulos (ed.), London 1982, figs. 17, 40, 41.

**137.** See in this respect, D. Papastratou, *Χάρτινες εἰκόνες. Ὀρθόδοξα θρησκευτικὰ χαρακτικά, 1665-1899*, Athens 1986, vol. II, pp. 338-341. The representation of the Monastery on the artoklasia has a battlemented wall characteristic of the woodcuts in the travels of P. Belon (1546, D. Papastratou, op. cit., fig. 1) and a caravan of camels, an iconographic element from an engraving by W. von Waltersweyl (1587). See M. Chatzidakis, «Δομήνικος Θεοτοκόπουλος καὶ ἡ κρητικὴ ζωγραφική», *Κρητικὰ Χρονικά* 4 (1950), pp. 404-407, fig. 6.

**138.** N. Jorga, *Documente privitoare la istoria Românilor vol. XIV al colecției «Hurmuzaki»*, Bucharest 1915, p. 303, no. CCCLXVI.

**139.** Y. Ikonomaki-Papadopoulos, «Church Silver», op. cit., pp. 227, fig. 21.

**140.** A work by a goldsmith of Stemnitsa dated 1676 is also mentioned at the Hozoviotissa Monastery, Amorgos (L. Marangou, op. cit., see note 95, p. 52).

**141.** K. Papamichalopoulos, op. cit., p. 353, Rabino, *Le Monastère*, p. 47, and K. Weitzmann - F. Anderegg, *Mount Sinai's...*, p. 122. The Skordilis family was one of the leading families of Crete; see E. Gerland, *Histoire de la Noblesse Crétoise au Moyen Age*, Paris 1907, pp. 66-67. Icons in the Monastery demonstrate that the relationship with Georgia went back at least as far as the Comnenos dynasty (Soteriou, *Εἰκόνες* II, p. 116).

**142.** There are similarities between the face of Christ and that of John the Baptist in the Telavi icon (late 16th century), and between the eyes of the Virgin and those of the Madonna and Child in the Alaverdi triptych (16th century). In this latter work there are also similarities in the folds of the robe (G. N. Tschubinashvili, *Georgian Repoussé Work VIIth to XVIIIth centuries*, Tiflis 1957, pls. 187 and 183-184).

**143.** The net of flowering shoots in the Sinai cover is closer to that of the Telavi icon (G. N. Tschubinashvili, op. cit., fig. 187) and also to the ground decoration in the Goris-Djvari cross, the dating of which, however, varies (1412-1604/5). See in this respect, G. N. Tschubinashvili, op. cit., fig. 185, Ch. Amiranashvili, *L'art des ciseleurs géorgiens*, Prague 1971, p. 158, fig. 104, and G. Abramishvili, «Jewellery and Metalwork in the Middle Ages», *Jewellery and Metalwork in the Museums of Georgia*, Leningrad 1986, figs. 209-213.

**144.** Ch. Amiranashvili, op. cit., pp. 154 and 158, and J. Raby, op. cit., p. 23.

**145.** For more detail on this issue, see C. Hernmarck, *The Art of the European Silversmith 1430-1830*, London 1976, vol. I, pp. 230-250, and vol. II, indicatively, figs. 591-596, 615-616 and 630-635.

**146.** B. Montevecchi - S. Vasco Rocca, op. cit., see note 50, p. 227.

**147.** For Mannerism, see C. Hernmarck, op. cit., vol. I, pp. 46-49, and J. F. Hayward, *Virtuoso Goldsmiths and the Triumph of Mannerism, 1540-1620*, London 1976, pp. 119-132.

**148.** The use of the fork began to spread in the early 17th century (J. F. Hayward, op. cit., p. 25).

**149.** H. Seling, *Die Kunst der Augsburger Goldschmiede*, Munich 1980, vol. I, pp. 33-37.

**150.** C. Hernmarck, op. cit., vol. I, p. 237.

**151.** The position of the decorative motifs indicates that the basin was intended to be set upright with the ewer in front of it, as in paintings. See J. F. Hayward, op. cit., p. 25, and C. Hernmarck, op. cit., vol. II, fig. 641. For similar decoration, see V. Brett, *The Sotheby's Directory Silver 1600-1940*, London 1986, p. 51, no. 3, p. 52, no. 9, and *Wenzel Jamnitzer und die Nürnberger Goldschmiedekunst 1500-1700*, exhibition catalogue, Germanisches Nationalmuseum, Nuremberg 1985, p. 243, no. 51 and p. 249, no. 63.

**152.** J. F. Hayward, op. cit., p. 24. See, for example, the engravings of B. Zan, in *Wenzel Jamnitzer...*, op. cit., p. 382, nos. 397-400.

**153.** For Tobias Kramer and the works which bear the stamp of his workshop, see H. Seling, op. cit., vol. III, p. 148, no. 1277, and vol. II, figs. 6, 33 and 84. We encounter the same decorative concept as that of the Sinai basin in two other works by the artist. See V. Brett, op. cit., p. 57, nos. 37 and 38.

**154.** The existence of an assay groove (Tremulierstich) implies that the object was submitted for testing to the goldsmiths' guild, in which case it would be stamped with the city hallmark. This was the case principally with ready-made items which the average craftsman would have for sale in his shop (J. F. Hayward, op. cit., pp. 19-20 and 39-40). The Augsburg city hallmark on the Sinai basin most closely resembles the hallmarks for the years 1620-1625. See in this respect, H. Seling, op. cit., vol. III, p. 19, and in particular no. 42.

**155.** Paisios Ayiapostolitis, Metropolitan of Rhodes, *Ἱστορία τοῦ ἁγίου Ὄρους Σηνᾶ καὶ τῶν περιχόρων αὐτοῦ. Ἔμμετρον σύγγραμμα συνταχθὲν μεταξὺ τῶν ἐτῶν 1577-1592 ἐκδιδόμενον νῦν τὸ πρῶτον μετὰ προλόγου ὑπὸ Α. Παπαδοπούλου Κεραμέως*, St. Petersburg 1891, p. 23, lines 582-584.

**156.** Amantos, *Σύντομος ἱστορία*, p. 51. Among them is the silver chest for the relics of St. Catherine (1688), Rabino, *Le Monastère*, pp. 25-26.

**157.** From the Athens dependency. K. Papamichalopoulos, op. cit., p. 352, and Rabino, *Le Monastère*, p. 47. This was Tsar Mikhail Feodorovich Romanov (1613-1645), with whom are associated quite a number of outstanding works and costly dedications to monasteries and churches.

**158.** Use of the mitre was introduced into Russia in 1589, after the establishment of the Russian Patriarchate. For the shape of the mitre, see P. Johnstone, op. cit., pp. 15-16, fig. 16. For the shape of the Russian mitre, see M. M. Postnikova-Losseva et al., op. cit., pp. 44-45.

**159.** The decoration of vestments with plaques in combination with pearls and precious and semi-precious stones, which were sewn on, began in the late 16th century. See, by way of example, T. Manushina - T. Nikolaeva, *Early Russian embroidery in the Zagorsk Museum Collection*, Moscow 1983, indicatively, p. 217, no. 37, p. 221, no. 38 and p. 248, no. 71. In 16th century examples, more than at any other time, the representations on the plaques were enhanced with niello. Similar plaques also formed part of the decoration of icon frames (T. Nikolayeva, *Collection of Early Russian Art in the Zagorsk Museum*, Leningrad 1968, nos. 123 and 124, and L. Pissarskaia, N. Platonova, B. Oulianova, *Les émaux russes XI-XIXe s.*, Moscow 1974, figs. 26-29.

**160.** Cf. a velvet mitre of 1604 with similar small niello icons and decoration of precious stones and pearls (T. Nikolayeva, op. cit., no. 120). Cf. also T. Nikolayeva, op. cit., no. 121, and L. Pissarskaia et al., op. cit., fig. 41.

**161.** From the dependency in Athens. The reverse of the triptych bears an engraved inscription indicating that it was also a reliquary. See the enkolpion of the Tsarina Irene (1589), M. Martynova, «Orfèvrerie Russe», *Trésors des Musées du Kremlin, 100 chefs-d'oeuvre*, exhibition catalogue, Paris 1979-1980, pp. 78-79, no. 22. This triptych protects the enkolpion and makes it easier to be carried. In dating the Sinai triptych, cf. the triptych of I. K. Griazev, senior state official, of the first third of the 17th century, which also has engraved angels on the inner side of its leaves (L. Pissarskaia et al., op. cit., fig. 31) and a reliquary cover of 1621 (M. Martynova, «Moskva...», op. cit., p. 75, fig. 42). The link at the top of the triptych shows that it was possible to use the whole object as an enkolpion. See in this respect, H. Newman, *An Illustrated Dictionary of Jewelry*, London 1981, fig. on p. 161.

**162.** K. Weitzmann - F. Anderegg, op. cit., see note 11, p. 122, and J. Galey, op. cit., p. 158. The iconographic type of St. Catherine is later (*Kunst der Ostkirche*, exhibition catalogue, Herzogenburg 1977, no. 53, fig. 15). For the manner of execution, see I. Kalavrezou-Maxeiner, op. cit., pp. 46-49.

**163.** For similar examples, see M. Martynova, «Orfèvrerie...», op. cit., p. 35, no. 3 and p. 83, no. 25.

**164.** See a detail from the helmet of Tsar Mikhail Feodorovich (1621), M. N. Larčenko, «Oružejnaja palata - veduščij centr proizvodsta vooruženija XVII veka», *Gosudarstvennaja Oružejnaja Palata*, Moscow 1988, p. 163, fig. 113.

**165.** See a 'brotherhood cup' with a cover (bratina) which belonged to the Tsarina Eudoxia, second wife of Tsar Mikhail (I. Nenarokomova - Y. Sizov, *Art Treasures from the Museums of the Moscow Kremlin*, Moscow 1980, no. 20). See also the riding saddle used by the same Tsar on official occasions (1637-1638), L. Pissarskaia et al., op. cit., fig. 40 and the icon frame surrounding the I. K. Griazev triptych (see above, note 161).

**166.** Apart from the works already referred to, the Kremlin workshops — under the supervision of German craftsmen — also produced Tsar Mikhail's symbols of office (1627-1628), L. Pissarskaia et al., op. cit., pp. 62-67, figs. 34-36. Later, in 1637-1638, the same craftsmen made the trappings used by the Tsar on official occasions, such as the saddle for his horse (L. Pissarskaia et al. op. cit., pp. 68-73, figs. 37-40).

**167.** See a cruciform clock with a base (1630-1640), *Gold- und Silberschätze aus der Sammlung Thyssen-Bornemisza*, exhibition catalogue, Haus der Kunst, Munich 1989, no. 31. See a combined clock and pectoral cross, F. X. Sturm and A. Winter-Jensen, *Montres genevoises du XVII siècle*, Geneva

1982, nos. 15 and 16.

**168.** From the Athens dependency. D. Landes, *L'Heure qu'il est. Les horloges, la mesure du temps et la formation du monde moderne*, Paris 1987, pp. 135-176, passim.

**169.** For the Saxon craftsmen of Transylvania, see J. Bielz, *L'art des orfèvres Saxons de Transylvanie*, Bucharest 1957, passim.

**170.** The case has a silver assay groove and an unidentified maker's mark with the initials T. M.

**171.** See similar decoration on a clock, F. X. Sturm and A. Winter-Jensen, op. cit., no. 12.

**172.** S. Mihalik, *L'émaillerie de l'ancienne Hongrie*, Budapest 1961, pp. 32-36, and J. Kolba - A. Nemeth, *Treasures of Hungary, Gold and Silver from the 9th to the 19th century*, Budapest 1986, p. 11. For the dating of the Sinai clock, cf. a cross with a rudimentary base in the Byzantine Museum, Athens, in floral baroque enamel and very well executed. Made in Kronstadt (Braşov) in 1668.

**173.** This trend had prevailed by the middle of the same century, initially in the workshops of Germany and particularly in Augsburg (C. Hernmarck, op. cit., vol. I, pp. 57-59). For Transylvania, see, by way of example, J. Kolba - A. Nemeth, op. cit., no. 34, and C. Nicolescu, *Argintăria...*, op. cit., nos. 162, 164 and 277.

**174.** For Abbot Ioasaph see Amantos, *Σύντομος ἱστορία*, pp. 53-56.

**175.** D. Landes, op. cit., pp. 155-156.

**176.** J. Bielz, op. cit., p. 35, and J. Kolba - A. Nemeth, op. cit., no. 67a.

**177.** See similar flower decoration on Gospel covers by George May II, in C. Nicolescu, *Argintăria...*, op. cit., nos. 357 and 358.

**178.** The mark of Stephan Weltzer II (1700-1734) consisted of the entwined letters S and W topped by a coronet. See C. Nicolescu, *Argintăria...*, op. cit., p. 29 and p. 52, no. 38. On the back of the buckle is the engraved silver standard.

**179.** C. Nicolescu, *Argintăria...*, op. cit., nos. 59, 286, 356.

**180.** For crosses of this type, see Y. Ikonomaki-Papadopoulos, «Τὰ ἐκκλησιαστικὰ ἀργυρὰ τῆς Νέας Καρβάλης», *Πρακτικὰ Β΄ τοπικοῦ συμποσίου «Ἡ Καβάλα καὶ ἡ περιοχή της»*, vol. II (offprint), Kavala 1988, p. 11, fig. 5, and Y. Ikonomaki-Papadopoulos, «Church Silver», op. cit., p. 236, fig. 31. The Sinai cross is very closely related to a cross in the Megiste Laura Monastery of Mt. Athos made by goldsmiths from Sinope (1758). There is fragmentary evidence to show that this town was a centre for metal-working (Y. Ikonomaki-Papadopoulos, «Church Silver», op. cit., p. 227).

**181.** From the Zakynthos dependency. For the panagiaria, see B. Radojković, *Les objets sculptés...*, op. cit., pp. 10-14. The Mother of God has the dominant position on the panagiarion, 'containing' Christ in the same way as the panagiarion contains the bread for the Eucharist. On this matter, see I. Kalavrezou-Maxeiner, op. cit., pp. 204-206, D. Mouriki, «Αἱ βιβλικαὶ προεικονίσεις τῆς Παναγίας εἰς τὸν τρούλλον τῆς Περιβλέπτου τοῦ Μυστρᾶ», *ΑΔ* 25 (1970), pp. 247-248.

**182.** This dual use seems to have begun as early as the 14th century. However, the liturgical nature of this type of item appears to have become less pronounced towards the end of that century (B. Radojković, *Les objets sculptés...*, op. cit., pp. 14-15, fig. 49b).

**183.** K. Papamichalopoulos, op. cit., p. 352, and Rabino, *Le Monastère*, p. 29. The Karaioannis family was among the best-known in Ioannina. See in this respect, Th. Mentzios, op. cit., pp. 539-540, and see also P. Aravantinos, *Χρονογραφία Ἠπείρου*, Athens 1856, vol. II, pp. 264-265 and note 4. For Anastasios Karaioannis, who is listed among the leading citizens, see P. Aravantinos, op. cit., pp. 266-267. Archimandrite Germanos also dedicated a second chandelier, which was made under his own supervision at Nizna (Rabino, *Le Monastère*, p. 29).

**184.** The models for this must have been corresponding Western European lighting devices of the 17th century (K. Hernmarck, op. cit., vol. I, pp. 217-218, vol. II, fig. 532). In the Sinai chandelier, the arms are in the shape of mythical beasts with birds' beaks and dragons' tails supporting a perforated lamp holder. The dragons are associated with Byzantine lighting devices, see L. Bouras, «Byzantine Lighting Devices», op. cit., p. 481, fig. 8.

**185.** Compare the Sinai chandelier with that which Neophytus VI, Patriarch of Constantinople, dedicated to the Monastery of St. John the Theologian on Patmos in 1736 and which probably came from a workshop in Constantinople (S. Papadopoulos, «Νεοφύτου ΣΤ΄ Πατριάρχου Κωνσταντινουπόλεως ἔγγραφα καὶ ἀφιερώματα πρὸς τὴν Ἱ. Μονὴν Ἰωάννου Θεολόγου Πάτμου», *Χαριστήριον εἰς Ἀναστάσιον Ὀρλάνδον*, vol. IV, pp. 240-242, pls. LXXXVII-LXXXVIII).

**186.** See in this respect, Th. Mentzios, op. cit., pp. 539-540. For Georgios Sougdouris, who taught at the Academy of Ioannina (1683-1709), see F. Michalopoulos, *Τὰ Γιάννενα κι' ἡ νεοελληνικὴ ἀναγέννηση (1648-1820)*, Athens 1930, pp. 35-37. Serbanis Sougdouris is mentioned with Anastasios Karaioannis in three contracts from the years 1741-1744 (P. Aravantinos, op. cit., p. 266).

**187.** P. Aravantinos, op. cit., p. 261, note 1.

# ILLUMINATED MANUSCRIPTS

## SELECT BIBLIOGRAPHY


V. N. Beneševič, *Catalogus codicum manuscriptorum graecorum qui in monasterio Sanctae Catharinae in Monte Sinai asservantur*, I and II, 1, St. Petersburg 1911, 1914, repr. Hildesheim 1965.

G. Galavaris, *The Illustrations of the Liturgical Homilies of Gregory Nazianzenus* (Studies in Manuscript Illumination, 6), Princeton, N. J. 1969.

—, *The Illustrations of the Prefaces in Byzantine Gospels* (Byzantina Vindobonensia, XI), Vienna 1979.

—, «Sinaitic Manuscripts in the Time of the Arabs», *ΔΧΑΕ* per. 4, 12, 1984 (1986), p. 117ff.

—, *Ἡ ζωγραφικὴ τῶν χειρογράφων στὸν δέκατον αἰώνα, Κωνσταντῖνος Ζ΄ ὁ Πορφυρογέννητος καὶ ἡ ἐποχή του*, Εὐρωπαϊκὸ Πολιτιστικὸ Κέντρο Δελφῶν, Β΄ Διεθνὴς Βυζαντινολογικὴ Συνάντηση, Delphi 1987, Athens 1989, p. 333 ff.

V. Gardthausen, *Catalogus codicum graecorum Sinaiticorum*, Oxford 1886.

D. Harlfinger, D. R. Reinsch, J. A. N. Sonderkamp and G. Prato, *Specimina Sinaitica. Die datierten griechischen Handschriften des Katharinenklosters auf dem Berge Sinai, 9. bis 12. Jahrhundert*, Berlin 1983.

J. R. Martin, *The Illustration of the Heavenly Ladder of John Climacus*, Studies in Manuscript Illumination, 5, Princeton, N. J. 1954.

I. Spatharakis, *Corpus of Dated Illuminated Greek manuscripts* (Byzantine Neerlandica, fasc. 8 I, Text, II, Plates), Leiden 1981.

K. Weitzmann, *Geistige Grundlagen und Wesen der Makedonischen Renaissance*, Cologne 1963; and English translation, *The Character and Intellectual Origins of the Macedonian Renaissance*, in *Studies in Classical and Byzantine Manuscript Illumination*, ed. H. L. Kessler, Chicago 1971, p. 176 ff.

—, *Illustrated Manuscripts at St. Catherine's Monastery on Mount Sinai*, Collegeville, Minn. 1973.

K. Weitzmann - G. Galavaris, *The Monastery of Saint Catherine at Mount Sinai. The Illuminated Greek Manuscripts. Vol 1: From the Ninth to the Twelfth Century*, Princeton, N. J. 1990.


# THE LIBRARY AND THE ARCHIVE

## THE ARABIC MANUSCRIPTS


A. S. Atiya, *The Arabic Manuscripts of mount Sinai. A hand list of the Arabic Documents and Scrolls microfilmed at the Library of the Monastery of St. Catherine Mount Sinai in 1954*, Baltimore 1955.

—, «The Arabic Treasures of the Convent of Mount Sinai», *The Egyptian Society of Historical Studies* 2 (1952), pp. 5-26.

—, «The Codex Arabicus of Mt. Sinai», *The Indian Archives* 7,1 1953, pp. 1-3.

K. W. Clark, «The Microfilming Projects at Mount Sinai and Jerusalem», *The Library of Congress Quarterly Journal of Current Acquisitions* 8 (1951), pp. 6-12.

—, *Checklist of manuscripts in St. Catherine's monastery Mount Sinai*, Washington 1952.

—, «Exploring the manuscripts of Sinai and Jerusalem», *The Biblical Archaeologist* XVI (1953), pp. 22-43.

Damianos, Archbishop of Sinai, «Εἰσήγησις ἐπὶ τῶν νεωστὶ εὑρεθέντων παλαιῶν χειρογράφων ἐν τῇ Ἱερᾷ Μονῇ Σινᾶ ἐν XVI Internationaler Byzantinisten Kongress, Wien 1981, Akten 11/4», *Jahrbuch der Österreichischen Byzantinistik* 32/4 (1982), pp. 105-116.

M. Dunlop Gibson, *A catalogue of the Arabic Manuscripts in the Convent of Saint-Catherina on Mount Sinai*, London 1894.

M. Kamil, *Catalogue of all manuscripts in the Monastery of St. Catharine on Mount Sinai*, Wiesbaden 1970.

Y. Meimaris, *Κατάλογος τῶν νέων ἀραβικῶν χειρογράφων τῆς Ἱερᾶς Μονῆς Ἁγίας Αἰκατερίνης τοῦ Ὄρους Σινᾶ*, Athens 1985.

—, *Katālūg al-Mahṭūṭāt al-arabiyyah al-muktasafah hadītan bi-Dayr Sānt Katarin al-mugaddas bi-Tūr Sīnā*, Athens 1985.

A. Saarisalo, «A Wagf-Document from Sinai», *Studia Orientalia*. Editit Societas Orientalis Fennica VI, Helsinki 1933.

A. Smith Lewis, *Studia Sinaitica, no XII. Forty-One Fascimiles of Dated Christian Arabic Manuscripts*, London 1907.


**1.** A. Smith Lewis, *Studia Sinaitica, no. XII Forty-one Fascimiles of Dated Christian Arabic Manuscripts*, London 1907, p. X.

**2.** Many scholars have worked on the Arabic manuscripts through the years. Here we shall mention only those who have compiled catalogues so that any reader who seeks further information has some guidance. The list starts with the head of the Theological College of the Holy Cross in Jerusalem, Theodoros Sarruf (1870); Margaret Dunlop Gibson's catalogue was published in 1894. In 1949-50 the Mission of the American Foundation of Mount Sinai Expedition of which Aziz Suryal Atiya, Professor at Alexandria University was a member, published an English catalogue in 1955. In 1951 his University colleague Murat Kamil published a catalogue in Arabic, translated into English in 1970. In 1968, during the Israeli occupation, the National Jewish and University Library of Jerusalem appointed B. Bayer to work on a summary catalogue. Finally, following the fire in the Monastery's Skevophylakion (1971) and the discovery of the new manuscripts (1975) by the Skevophylax father Sophronios, the Monastery relegated to the present author the study of the new Arabic manuscripts, a catalogue of which was published in 1985.

## THE SYRIAC MANUSCRIPTS

**1.** The Monastery's Collection of Syriac manuscripts, some 270 in number, was catalogued at the end of the 19th century by Mrs. Agnes Smith Lewis, a remarkable Scottish lady of great learning, who visited the Monastery several times in the 1890s (her twin sister, Mrs. Margaret Dunlop Gibson, made a catalogue of the Christian Arabic manuscripts).

**2.** The standard Syriac New Testament text, called the 'Peshitta' is a revision of this earlier version, dating from about A.D. 400.

**3.** A preliminary report published by Mother Philothea indicates a number of exciting new items, such as an illumination of King David, among some further folios of a beautifully calligraphed manuscript of the biblical book of Kings, dating from the 7th century at the latest.

## THE SLAVONIC MANUSCRIPTS

**1.** See I. C. Tarnanidis, *The Slavonic Manuscripts discovered in 1975 at St. Catherine's Monastery on Mount Sinai*, Thessalonica 1988, pp. 21-31 and 45-54.

## THE ARCHIVE


(Unknown), *Τὰ περὶ ἐκλογῆς καὶ χειροτονίας Ἀρχιεπισκόπου Σινᾶ ἐπίσημα ἔγγραφα*, Jerusalem 1860.

(Unknown), *Συνοπτικὴ δήλωσις τῶν κατὰ καιροὺς ἐκδιδομένων Πατριαρχικῶν καὶ Συνοδικῶν Σιγιλλίων περὶ τῆς Ἀρχιεπισκοπῆς τοῦ ὄρους Σινᾶ*, Constantinople 1867.

(P. Neoclis), *Τὸ κανονικὸν δίκαιον τοῦ πατριαρχικοῦ θρόνου τῶν Ἱεροσολύμων ἐπὶ τῆς Ἀρχιεπισκοπῆς Σινᾶ, ἐπιμαρτυρούμενον ὑπὸ ἐπισήμων ἐκκλησιαστικῶν ἐγγράφων*, Constantinople 1868.

C. Amantos, *Σιναϊτικὰ μνημεῖα ἀνέκδοτα* (documents), Appendix of periodical *Ἑλληνικά*, Thessalonica 1928.

A. S. Atiya, *The Arabic Manuscripts of Mount Sinai*, Baltimore 1955.

P. Gregoriadis, *Ἡ Ἱερὰ Μονὴ τοῦ Σινᾶ*, Jerusalem 1875.

P. Hidiroglou, *Κατάλογος ἐπισήμων ὀθωμανικῶν ἐγγράφων τῆς Ἱερᾶς Μονῆς τοῦ ὄρους Σινᾶ*, Nicosia 1980.

M. Kamil, *Catalogue of all Manuscripts in the Monastery of St. Catherine on Mount Sinai*, Wiesbaden 1970.

Sp. Kontoyiannis, *Τὸ Ἀρχεῖον τῆς Ἱερᾶς Μονῆς Σινᾶ*, Athens 1982.

K. Krumbacher, *Byzantinische Zeitschrift*, vol. 14, Leipzig 1905.

A. Papadopoulos-Kerameus, *Ἱεροσολυμιτικὴ Βιβλιοθήκη*, vol. III, pp. 231-232.


**1.** S. M. Stern, «A Fatimid Decree of 524/1130», *Bulletin of the School of Oriental and African Studies*, University of London 23, sec. 3 (1960), pp. 439-455.

# LIST OF ILLUSTRATIONS

51. Saint Nicholas with scenes from his life. Tempera on wood. Early 13th century.
52. Saint John the Baptist with scenes from his life. Tempera on wood. Early 13th century.
53. Saint Panteleimon with scenes from his life and martyrdom. Tempera on wood. Early 13th century.
54. Triptych with the Hodegetria Aristerokratousa and scenes from her life. Tempera on wood. Early 13th century.
55. Detail of fig. 54.
56. The Protomartyr Stephen. Tempera on canvas. Early 13th century.
57. Saint George. Tempera on canvas. Early 13th century.
58. The Crucifixion. Tempera on wood. First half of the 13th century, p. 184.
59. The Virgin Hodegetria Dexiokratousa. Tempera on wood. First half of the 13th century.
60. The Virgin Hodegetria Aristerokratousa. Tempera on canvas. Last quarter of the 13th century.
61. The Virgin Blachernitissa. Tempera on canvas. Last quarter of the 13th century.
62. The Virgin Hodegetria Dexiokratousa. Tempera on wood. Last quarter of the 13th century.
63. The Crucifixion. Front side of a two-sided icon. Tempera on wood. Last quarter of the 13th century.
64. The Anastasis. Reverse side of the icon in fig. 63.
65. Diptych. Saint Procopios and a variant of the Virgin Kykkotissa. Tempera on wood. Last quarter of the 13th century.
66. Saints Sergios and Bacchos. Reverse side of a two-sided icon. Tempera on wood. Last quarter of the 13th century.
67. The Crucifixion. Tempera on canvas. Last quarter of the 13th century.
68. The Nativity. Dodekaorton icon from an iconostasis. Tempera on wood. Third quarter of the 13th century.
69. The Baptism. Dodekaorton icon from an iconostasis. Tempera on wood. Third quarter of the 13th century.
70. The Forty Martyrs of Sebasteia. Tempera on wood. Late 13th – early 14th century.
71. The Crucifixion and the Nativity. Tempera on canvas. Late 13th – early 14th century.
72. Hexaptych with the Dodekaorton. Tempera on wood. Around the middle of the 14th century.
73. Saint Catherine. Catalan Retable of Martinus de Vilanova. Tempera on wood. 1387.
74. The Virgin Pelagonitissa. Tempera on wood. Early 15th century.
75. The Lamentation. Tempera on canvas. Early 15th century.
76. Great Deesis and saints. Tempera on wood. Second half of the 15th century.
77. Deesis. Work of the painter Angelos. Tempera. Around the middle of the 15th century.
78. Deesis with Saint Phanourios. Work of the painter Angelos. Tempera. Around the middle of the 15th century.
79. The Archangel Michael. Work attributed to the painter Andreas Ritzos. Tempera. Second half of the 15th century.
80. Saint John the Theologian dictates his Gospel to Prochoros. Work of the painter Angelos. Tempera. Around the middle of the 15th century.
81. The Presentation of the Virgin. Work attributed to the painter Angelos. Tempera. Around the middle of the 15th century.
82. The Virgin Hodegetria with half-length saints. Work attributed to the atelier of Andreas Ritzos. Tempera. Second half of the 15th century.
83. The Dormition of Saint Basil the Great. Tempera. Early 16th century.
84. Deesis with Saint Nicholas. Tempera on wood. 15th century.
85. Saint John the Baptist. Work attributed to the painter Michael Damaskinos. Tempera on wood. 16th century.
86. Symeon Theodochos with the infant Christ in his arms. Work attributed to the painter Michael Damaskinos. Tempera on wood. 16th century.
87. The Virgin of the Passion. Tempera. 1579.
88. Saint Anthony bordered with half-length saints. Work of the painter-priest Demetrios. Tempera. Late 15th - early 16th century.
89. The Presentation in the Temple. Tempera. Second half of the 16th century.
90. Sanctuary doors from the Chapel of Saint John the Baptist. Tempera. 16th century.
91. Saint Theodore Stratelates and Saint Theodore Teron. Tempera. Around the middle or the third quarter of the 16th century.
92. The Massacre of Saint Demetrios. Tempera. Late 16th century.
93. 'In Thee Rejoiceth'. Tempera. 16th century.

94. The Holy Ten Martyrs of Crete. Work of the painter Silvestros Theocharis. Tempera. First half of the 17th century.
95. Saint Phanourios. Work of the painter Ioannis Kolyvas. Tempera on wood. 1688.
96. Saint Catherine. Work of the painter and monk Jeremiah Palladas. Tempera on wood. 17th century.
97. Full-length Virgin and Child with Prophets. Work of the painter Emmanuel Tzanes Bounialis. Tempera. 1651 (?).
98. 'In Thee Rejoiceth'. Work of the painter Georgios Klontzas. Tempera. 1604 (?).
99. Icon with the representation of monastic life. Work of the painter Georgios Klontzas. Tempera. 1603 (?).
100. Sinai. Work of the painter Iacovos Moskos. Tempera. First quarter of the 18th century.
101. Triptych with Christ as High Priest in the middle panel. Work of the painter Victor. Tempera. 17th century.
102. Middle panel of a triptych with Christ as High Priest, Chrysostom and Basil. Work of the painter Victor (?). Tempera. 17th century.

# CHURCH GOLD EMBROIDERIES

1. Russian sticharion (epomis), with representations of the Blessed Virgin as the Burning Bush, the Monastery, Moses and St. Catherine. 18th century.
2. Aer - epitaphios, with a representation of the Lamentation at the Sepulchre. From a Smyrna workshop. 16th century.
3. Epitaphios. 1612/3.
4. Epitaphios of St. Catherine. Offering of the Protosynkellos of Sinai Azarias. From a Vienna workshop. 1805.
5. Podea, with a representation of St. Catherine. Offering of Ioannis Papapolyzos, benefactor of the Greek community in Vienna. From a Vienna workshop. 1763.
6. Epitaphios. Work of the embroideress Gregoria and offering of the Ecumenical Patriarch Constantios I. From a Constantinople workshop. 1842.
7. Pair of epimanikia. From a Sinope workshop. 17th century. The scenes on them are: above, the Flagellation of Christ and, below, 'Ecce Homo'.
8. Epigonation with a representation of Christ as Wonderful Counsellor. From a Cretan workshop. 1720.
9. Epigonation with representations of the Blessed Virgin as the Burning Bush, Moses, St. Catherine and a part of the Monastery. Offering of Cyril, Archbishop of Sinai. From a Constantinople workshop. 1746.
10. Cylindrical bishop's mitre (decorated with diamonds), with the symbols of the Four Evangelists in medallions; at the base, Christ and the Virgin and St. Catherine. Said to have belonged to Cyril, Archbishop of Sinai. Late 18th century.
11. Monastic soft cap, with representations of Christ as Great High Priest, St. Nikephoros and the Apostles Peter and Paul. Offering of Nikephoros Marthalis, Archbishop of Sinai. From a Cretan workshop. 1731.
12. Orarion of Nikephoros Marthalis, Archbishop of Sinai, with depictions of Moses and Aaron, the Virgin as the Burning Bush and St. Catherine, and, St. Laurence and St. Stephen. From a Cretan workshop. 1748.
13. Epitrachelion of the priest-monk Matthew, with scenes from the Christological cycle. From a Constantinople workshop. 15th century. Detail, p. 252.
14. Detail of the border of the epitrachelion in fig. 16.
15. Epitrachelion, with depictions of the Annunciation, St. George and St. Demetrius and Moses and Aaron. Work of Christopher Zephar and offering of Anastasios Moralis, benefactor of the Greek community in Vienna. 1752.
16. Epitrachelion, with embroidered inscription of the 'Hosanna'. Offering of Ananias, Archbishop of Sinai. 1671.
17. Lavaron, with a representation of the Transfiguration. The donor Hilarion of Sinai seems to be the embroiderer. 1673.
18. Pyle of St. Catherine, with scenes from her life and martyrdom. Offering of Nikolaos Dimitriou. From a Vienna workshop. 1770.
19. Mandyas, with representations of the Four Evangelists. Offering of Constantios, former Archbishop of Constantinople and Sinai. Early 19th century.
20 - 23. Pomata and poloi from the mandyas in fig. 19.
24. Sakkos 'of Cyril of Crete', with a representation on the front of Christ as the Vine. 17th century.
25. The reverse side of the sakkos 'of Cyril of Crete', with a representation of the Jesse Tree. 17th century.

# CHURCH METALWORK

1. Enamelled panel, showing Christ in Glory. Limoges technique. Central Italy (?). c.1225-1235.
2. Bronze cross, with engraved scenes from the delivery of the Tablets with the Commandments to Moses, verse from 'Exodus' and dedicatory inscription. 6th century.
3-4. Bronze enkolpion-reliquary, with scenes from the Christological cycle worked in inlaid silver and niello. 10th century.
5. Bronze candelabrum, with engraved decoration of an character and medallions showing saints. 11th-12th century.
6-7. Silver gilt processional cross, with relief and enamel decoration worked in 'basse taille' and 'ronde bosse' techniques. Work of Alexios Siropoulos. Cyprus (?). Second half of the 15th century (?).
8. Silver gilt chalice, with translucent enamels worked in the 'basse taille' technique. Gift of King Charles VI of France. Parisian workshop. 1411.
9. Chalice, with Late Gothic and Renaissance features and relief figures from Cretan iconographic types. Silver with gilding. 16th century.
10. Silver gilt, church-shaped casket, with relief figures, Ottoman-type interlacing and Late Gothic ornaments. Offering of officials of the court of Wallachia. 1542-1545.
11. Gospel cover, with a depiction of the donor, Alexander II Mircea, Prince of Wallachia, and his family. Wallachian workshop. 1568-1577.
12. The reverse side of the Gospel cover in fig. 11.
13. Reliquary with open-work, engraved, figurative and aniconic decoration and features of Venetian silverwork. Stamped work of a Cretan workshop. 1619.
14. Silver gilt censer with Late Gothic features. Offering of Roxandra, widow of Alexander Lăpuşneanu, Voevod of Moldavia, to the Chapel of St. John the Baptist. 1569.
15. Silver gilt church-shaped casket, with Late Gothic features. Offering of Georgios, Bishop of Radauţi in Moldavia. 1569.
16. Silver gilt Gospel cover, with the Crucifixion and Descent into Hell in relief and engraved floral interlacing of an Eastern type. Gift of the priest-monk Ioakeim of Crete, surnamed Skordilis. From a workshop in eastern Georgia. 1604.
17. Silver and gold leaf buckle, decorated with plant motifs by the jewelled technique. Opaque, translucent and painted enamels. From a Constantinople workshop. Second half of the 17th century.
18. Enkolpion of silver, gold leaf and jade with encrusted gold, precious stones and enamels. From a Constantinople workshop. 17th century.
19. Enkolpion of silver and jewelled gold leaf, opaque and translucent enamels. From a Constantinople workshop. Second half of the 17th century.
20. Silver gilt mitre, with figures in relief and aniconic decoration of an Ottoman character. Niello, turquoises, pearls, stones. Collective gift of the Christians of the city of Ioannina. 1636.
21. Silver gilt triptych, with engraved decoration. Contains a chalcedony enkolpion with a representation of St. Catherine, set in gold and enamels. From a Kremlin workshop. Second quarter of the 17th century.
22. Enkolpion, with a small painted icon in a silver gilt frame, decorated with filigree enamels, turquoises, pearls and glass paste stones. 1663.
23. Silver gilt casket in the shape of a church, with enamelled figures and floral decoration in niello. Originally donated to the Stavronikita Monastery on Mt. Athos. From a Constantinople workshop (?). 1672.
24. Artoklasia of silver with gilding, figurative engraved and relief decoration, filigree enamels, turquoises and glass paste stones. Collective offering. From a Sofia workshop. 1678.
25. Silver gilt chalice, with open-work, aniconic decoration in the Ottoman style, enamelled rosettes and niello. 1633.
26. Silver gilt cross, with floral decoration and interlacing of Ottoman type, flanking dragons and small icons. Arta. 1626.
27. Combined clock and cross, with mounting covered with painted enamels. Property of the Abbot Ioasaph. From a Transylvania workshop. A little before 1660.
28. Censer in the shape of a church, with cast, enamelled panels, filigree enamels and glass paste stones. 17th century.
29. Detail of fig. 27. The clock, the work of Michael Rener, in its case. From a Braşov workshop.
30. Silver gilt church-shaped casket, with engraved figures. Enamelled and cast, open-work decoration of oriental character. Offering of the priest-monk Anastasios of Crete. Work of Daniel and Poullos. 1635.

31. Silver gilt mitre, with small engraved icons framed with pearls. Gift of the Tsar Mikhail Fedorovitch. From a Moscow workshop. 1642.

32. Silver gilt mitre, with engraved figures. Floral, open-work decoration, enriched with filigree enamels. Offering of the Protosynkellos of Sinai Nikephoros of Crete. Work of Anastasios. Voulgarochori. 1678.

33. Artoklasia, with a model of the Monastery of St. Catherine, Moses receiving the Commandments and the tomb of the Saint. Silver with gilding, niello, enamels and coral. Collective offering. Work of Eustathios from Trikkala. 1679.

34. Benediction cross, with gilt mounting enriched with filigree decoration against an enamelled background, pearls and glass paste stones. Offering of the priest-monk Makarios of Crete.

35. Cross for the blessing of holy water, with silver gilt frame, decorated with champlevé enamels, pearls and coral and glass paste stones. Work of Georgios Moukios of Stemnitsa in the Peloponnese. 1683.

36-37. Pastoral staffs. Constantinople, 17th century. 36. Ivory inlaid gold and decoration of mother of pearl shell, turtle shell and ebony. 37. Silver pastoral staff, decorated with filigree enamels and jade, inlaid gold, turquoises and precious stones.

38. Pastoral staff of the Abbot Athanasios, with ivory finial, with inlaid gold and precious stones, shaft of copper, covered with champlevé and painted enamels. From a Constantinople workshop. 1714.

39. Silver basin with gilding, with engraved and relief decoration in the Mannerist style. From the workshop of Tobias Kramer. Augsburg. c. 1620.

40. Silver gilt buckle, with relief figures of Peace and War and decoration in the Floral Baroque style. Work of Stephan Weltzer II. Brașov. 1716.

41. Cross for the blessing of water, with frame of gilt silver, enriched with decoration in filigree, granules, enamels, pearls, coral and glass paste stones. Work of Georgios Mousis. 1779.

42. Wooden panagiarion, with Jesse Tree in low, open-work relief, set in silver gilt, filigree, granules, enamels, coral, pearls and glass paste stones. Second half of the 18th century.

43. Silver chandelier with gilding, two lines of branches and floral decoration in low relief. Offering of the Archimandrite of Sinai Germanos. Work of the brothers Serbanos and Eustathios Sougdouris. Ioannina. 1752.

## ILLUMINATED MANUSCRIPTS

1. Homilies of Gregory Nazianzenus (cod. 339). Gregory is about to write his Sermons, parchment. 1136-1155.
2. The Heavenly Ladder (cod. 423). 11th century.
3-6. Lectionary (cod. 204). Christ, the Virgin Mary, Hosios Peter of Monobata and the Evangelist Mark. c.1000.
7. Lectionary (cod. 208). Deesis. 12th century.
8. Homilies of St. John Chrysostom on the Gospel of Matthew (cod. 364). The Emperor Constantine IX Monomachos between the Empress Zoe and her sister Theodora. 1042-1050.
9. Cod. 364. The Evangelist Matthew offers his Gospel to St. John Chrysostom.
10. Homilies of Gregory Nazianzenus (cod. 339). Nativity.

11. Cod. 339. The Baptism of Christ.
12. Cod. 339. The Descent into Hell.
13. Cod. 339. The Martyrdom of the Seven Maccabees.
14. Cod. 339. In the title miniature St. Gregory is addressing St. Mamas. The other illustrations represent the Incredulity of Thomas, the rite of the consecration of a church and St. Gregory teaching at a domed church.
15. Cod. 339. In the title miniature St. Gregory and Julian the Tax Collector are represented as authors. In the margin an ordinary taxation scene in Byzantium. Julian, seated at a table, demands the taxes from the debtors.
16. Cod. 339. St. Gregory participates in the Vision of the Prophet Habakkuk. In the title miniature the young Christ-Emmanuel is seated on an arc of heaven. In the margin Christ is shown as Angel surrounded by Archangels carrying sceptres.
17-22. Cod. 339. Initials (O, E, Δ and M) illustrated with charming birds and fascinating animals, real and fantastic, in imaginative compositions.
23. The Book of Job (cod. 3). The banquet of Job's sons and daughters. 11th century.
24. Cod. 3. Job's herds grazing in idyllic pastures.
25. Cod. 3. In a palatial setting Job and his wife are conversing with one another.
26. Cod. 3. Devastated by a series of disasters and smitten by the Devil, Job sits naked on a heap of dung and receives food from his wife who is, however, afraid to approach him.
27. Cod. 3. Sophar, the king of Minaeans, escorted by a vanguard, rides to meet Job, in order to offer him support in his misfortunes.
28. The Christian Topography by Cosmas Indicopleustes (cod. 1186). Map of the world and paradise with personifications of the winds over the waters of the ocean. Beginning of the 11th century.
29. Cod. 1186. The Vision of Moses and the Receiving of the Law.
30. Cod. 1186. The motion of the stars with angels standing in a zodiac-like circle.
31. Cod. 1186. The earth is shown as a mountain swimming in the primeval ocean.
32. Cod. 1186. Gazelle, exotic birds and palm trees.
33. Psalter and New Testament (cod. 2123), of the year 1242. The Emperor John VIII Palaeologue, a later miniature, was added to the codex in the 16th century.
34. Cod. 2123. The Emperor Michael VIII Palaeologue, a later miniature, was added to the codex in the 16th century.
35. Sticherarion (cod. 1234). The Annunciation. 1469.
36. Four Gospels (cod. 198). The Evangelist John and a donor-monk. 13th century.

## THE LIBRARY AND THE ARCHIVE

1. Acts of the Apostles (cod. 275). The Apostle Paul between the Apostles Timothy and Silouanos. Parchment. Minuscule script. 11th century.
2. Psalter (cod. 74). Heading, illuminated initial letter. Bombazine. Minuscule script, by the hand of Jeremiah the Sinaite of Crete. 1619/20.
3. The 'Theodosian Lectionary' (cod. 204). Subheading ('gate'), double initial letter. Parchment. Majuscule biblica script. 10th-11th century.

4. Scroll and roller (New Finds, no. E6). The Liturgy of St. Basil. Illuminated initial letter. Minuscule script. 12th century.
5. Readings from the Book of Genesis (cod. 7). Heading and initial letter. Parchment. Majuscule 'ogivale diritta' script. Donated by the monk Constantios Lependrenos. 10th-11th century.
6. The 'Uspenskij Psalter' (New Finds, no. MΓ33). Parchment. Majuscule 'ogivale inclinata' script. 862/3.
7. Holy Bible - The Apostolic Fathers. 'Codex Sinaiticus' (New Finds, no. MΓ1). Majuscule biblica script. Middle of the 4th century.
8. Papyrus fragment: Old Testament (Chronicles). 7th century.
9. Papyrus fragment. Part of a verse from the hymn of the Three Children and verses from the New Testament including the Gospel according to Luke. 6th or 7th century.
10. Parchment codex, Arabic (New Finds no. 52). The Apostle Paul's Epistle to the Romans. 9th-10th century (?).
11. Paper codex, Arabic (Old Collection, no. 343). St. John Climacus. 1612.
12. Lectionary. Parchment codex, Arabic (New Finds, no.14). Full-page depiction of St. John the Evangelist. 9th century.
13. Paper codex, Arabic (Old Collection, no. 343). The Heavenly Ladder. 1612.
14. Syriac manuscript (no. 16). Apology of the philosopher Aristeides to the Emperor Hadrian. 8th century.
15. Syriac manuscript (New Finds, no. M24, part of Syr. 28). Miniature illumination with a portrait of King David at the beginning of the Syriac translation of the 'Book of Kings' (III). 7th century.
16. The first page of a Slavonic Sinaitic Euchologion in 'glagolitic' script. Beginning of the 11th century.
17. Syriac manuscript (no. 111). Paracletic Canon (Hymn of Intercession) to the Theotokos. Anthology written on Mt. Melan (near Antioch) in 1242.
18. Turkish document, no. 4, paper. 'Achtiname' for the Sinaitic metochion at Chania. 1858.
19. Turkish document, no. 137, paper. Decree of Ibrahim Pasha of Egypt. 27th April, 1668.
20. Paper document. 'Apantachousa'. Circular written in Turkish with Greek characters.
21. Slavonic chrysobull of the Tsar of Russia, Theodorovich Michail, no. 4-89, parchment. 1630.
22. Lead seal from a bull of a Greek document no. 4-28 (sigillion of the Ecumenical Patriarch Parthenios). Obverse with a depiction of the Virgin with Christ. 1643.
23. Seal depicted in fig. 22. Reverse. Bears the inscription: 'Parthenios, by the Grace of God, Archbishop of Constantinople, New Rome and Ecumenical Patriarch'.
24. Rumanian document of the Voevod of Hungro-Wallachia John Constantine Basharaba. Parchment. Bears the seal in sealing wax within a metal covering. 1689.
25. French document, no. 241, paper. Decree assuring the Monastery's rights and privileges with the personal signature of Napoleon Bonaparte. 1798.
26. A page from the 'Mega Etymologicon'. The edition of 1499 produced by Nikolaos Vlastos and Zacharias Kalliergis. (Qto.).
27. An example of a rare printed scroll. 'The Liturgy of St. John Chrysostom'. Venice 1549.
28. 'Works of St. John Chrysostom'. Frontispiece of the edition by Henri Savile, printed at Eton, England, in 1613 (Qto.).

# INDEX

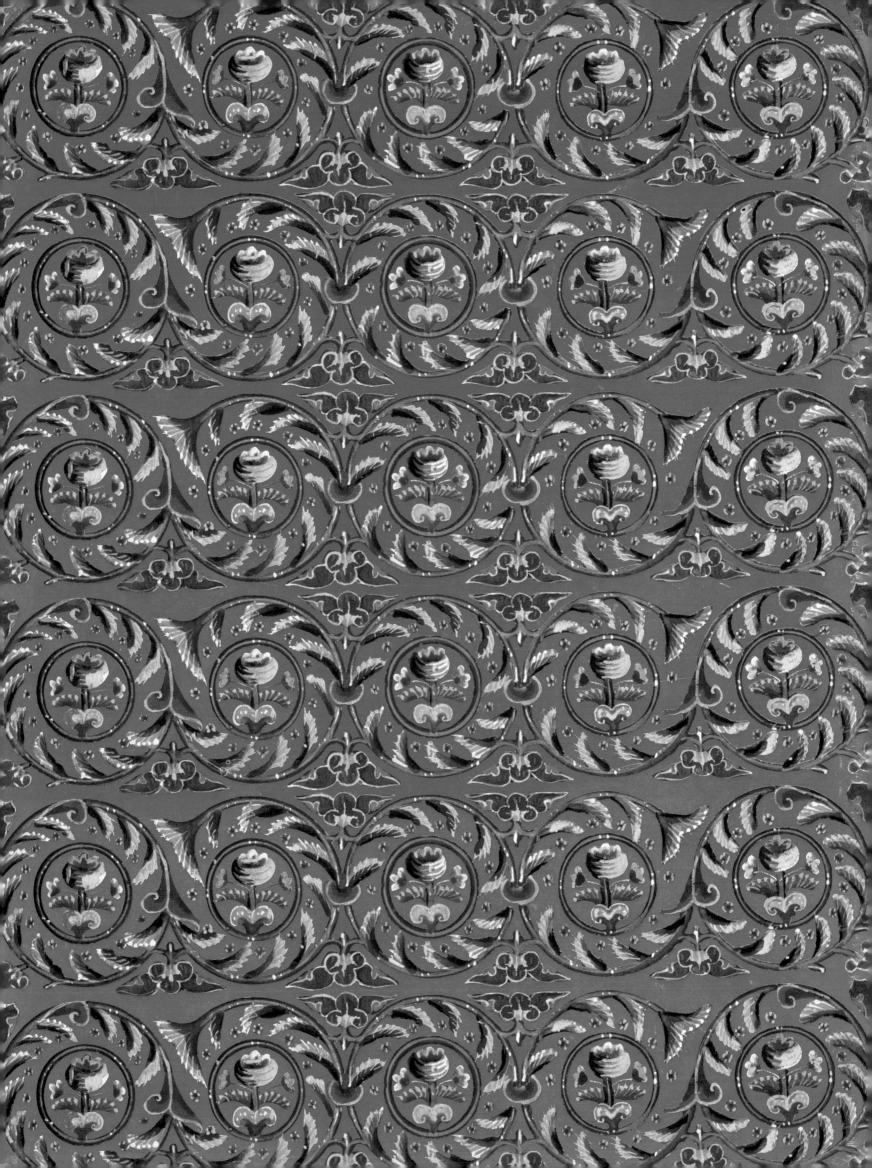